The **Rough Guide** to

Yellowstone and Grand Teton

written and researched by

Stephen Timblin

with additional contributions from

Charles Hodgkins

www.roughguides.com

Contents

Colour section 1

Introduction 6
Where to go 8
When to go 10
Things not to miss 12

Basics 17

Getting there............................ 19
Getting around......................... 24
Health and personal safety 28
Travelling with children............. 31
Travel essentials 32

The Parks 41

1 Northern Yellowstone.......... 43
2 Southern Yellowstone 63
3 Grand Teton 85
4 Day hikes 109
5 Backcountry hiking and
   camping............................ 144
6 Summer activities 158
7 Winter activities 170

Listings 179

8 Accommodation................. 181
9 Eating and drinking........... 189
10 Park programmes and
   tours 195

Out of the Parks 199

11 Jackson and around 203
12 West Yellowstone and
   Big Sky 215
13 Gardiner and the Paradise
   Valley 228
14 Cooke City and around 234
15 Cody and around 238

Contexts 249

History 251
Geology, flora and fauna........ 263
Books 271

Small print & Index 275

Hydrothermal Yellowstone colour section following p.112

The wolves of Yellowstone colour section following p.176

◄◄ Oxbow Bend, Snake River ◄ Bugling bull elk, Yellowstone

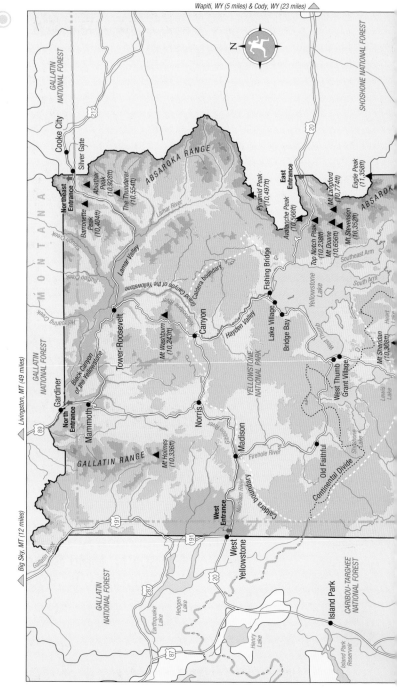

Wapiti, WY (5 miles) & Cody, WY (23 miles)

N

SHOSHONE NATIONAL FOREST

GALLATIN NATIONAL FOREST

Cooke City

Silver Gate

212

ABSAROKA RANGE

Northeast Entrance

Abiathar Peak (10,928ft)

Barronette Peak (10,404ft)

The Thunderer (10,554ft)

Lamar River

Pyramid Peak (10,497ft)

East Entrance

20

Avalanche Peak (10,566ft)

Eagle Peak (11,358ft)

Mt Langford (10,774ft)

ABSAROKA

Top Notch Peak (10,238ft)

Mt Doane (10,656ft)

Mt Stevenson (10,352ft)

M O N T A N A

Lamar Valley

Grand Canyon of the Yellowstone

Caldera boundary

Fishing Bridge

Southeast Arm

Yellowstone Lake

South Arm

Buffalo Creek

Hellroaring Creek

South Creek

Slough Creek

Tower-Roosevelt

Yellowstone River

Mt Washburn (10,243ft)

Canyon

Hayden Valley

Lake Village

Bridge Bay

West Thumb

GALLATIN NATIONAL FOREST

Gardiner

North Entrance

89

Mammoth

Back Canyon of the Yellowstone

Norris

Gibbon River

Madison

Mt Holmes (10,336ft)

GALLATIN RANGE

YELLOWSTONE NATIONAL PARK

Firehole River

West Thumb

Grant Village

Mt Sheridan (10,308ft)

Heart Lake

Livingston, MT (49 miles)

Big Sky, MT (12 miles)

Madison River

Old Faithful

Continental Divide

Lewis Lake

Shoshone Lake

Caldera boundary

West Entrance

West Yellowstone

191

191

20

287

Gallatin River

Hebgen Lake

Earthquake Lake

Henry Lake

87

Island Park

CARIBOU-TARGHEE NATIONAL FOREST

Island Park Reservoir

GALLATIN NATIONAL FOREST

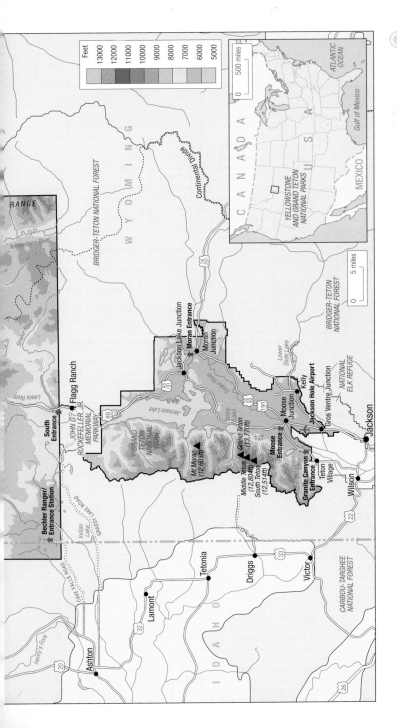

Feet
13000
12000
11000
10000
9000
8000
7000
6000
5000

0   500 miles

ATLANTIC OCEAN

C A N A D A

U S

MEXICO

Gulf of Mexico

YELLOWSTONE AND GRAND TETON NATIONAL PARKS

0   5 miles

RANGE

Yellowstone River

Snake River

Lewis River

BRIDGER-TETON NATIONAL FOREST

W Y O M I N G

Continental Divide

Jackson Lake Junction

Moran Entrance

Moran Junction

Lower Slide Lake

BRIDGER-TETON NATIONAL FOREST

Flagg Ranch

South Entrance

JOHN D. ROCKEFELLER, JR. MEMORIAL PARKWAY

Bechler Ranger/ Entrance Station

Indian Lake

GRASSY LAKE ROAD

CANE FALLS ROAD

Jackson Lake

GRAND TETON NATIONAL PARK

Mt Moran (12,605ft)

Grand Teton (13,770ft)

Middle Teton (12,804ft)

South Teton (12,514ft)

Jenny Lake

Snake River

Moose Junction

Moose Entrance

Granite Canyon Entrance

Teton Village

Kelly

Jackson Hole Airport

Gros Ventre Junction

NATIONAL ELK REFUGE

Jackson

Wilson

I D A H O

Ashton

Lamont

Tetonia

Driggs

Victor

CARIBOU-TARGHEE NATIONAL FOREST

Henry's Fork

Introduction to

Yellowstone and Grand Teton

Famously labelled "America's best idea", Yellowstone became the world's first national park in 1872. From its inception, it took six decades for the storied park to celebrate its three millionth visitor; these days, well over three million sightseers and outdoor enthusiasts arrive every year from across the globe. But even given the perennial crowds, Yellowstone's original nickname – Wonderland – remains an apt one: within the boundaries of the lower 48's second-largest national park (only Death Valley is bigger) sits one unique sight after another, a Mother Nature's theme park of magnificent mountain scenery, remarkably diverse wildlife and hydrothermal phenomena on a mind-bending scale.

Carved out of a block of Edenic wilderness in northwest Wyoming, Montana and Idaho, the 2.2 million-acre park takes in the glorious colours of the **Grand Canyon of the Yellowstone**, frigid **Yellowstone Lake** and rainbow-hued hot springs, along with roaring waterfalls, belching mudpots and, of course, the singular spectacles of geysers such as **Old Faithful**. All this would be more than enough to justify its status as the country's signature national park, but Yellowstone is further blessed with an astonishing array of wildlife. More than sixty species of mammals call the park home, including huge populations of easily spotted **bison** and **elk** along with more reclusive scatterings of **wolves**, **bighorn sheep** and **grizzlies**. More than three hundred species of birds swoop through the area, while a variety of trout – including the celebrated **cutthroat** – swim within Yellowstone's seemingly countless streams and lakes.

Just down the road – and one of North America's most spectacular national parks in its own right – is the outdoor paradise of **Grand Teton**, where the serrated peaks of the **Teton Range** are a visual pageant unto themselves, rising abruptly without foothills to tower 7000ft above the valley floor. A string of gem-like lakes brushes the base of the peaks, while beyond them lies the broad, sagebrush-covered valley known as **Jackson Hole**, broken by the winding **Snake River**. Wildlife is also prevalent in Grand Teton, including healthy populations of gangly **moose** and speedy **pronghorn**.

The ever-growing **popularity** of the two parks is the area's Achilles heel, both from the perspective of visitor enjoyment and the pressure put on the environment by so much human traffic. Expanding communities, including huge vacation "cabins" for the super-rich, have been gobbling up virgin landscape for years, and if you visit the parks during the height of summer, be prepared for hordes of tourists. But if you let yourself get frustrated by it all, you'll be missing something very special. Chance **encounters** – be it a rare geyser eruption, a wolf or grizzly sighting, or that perfect Teton sunset – are the most memorable part of any visit, and these require an easy pace with plenty of scope for patient lingering. Speeding through the parks and checking off sight after sight in quick succession could mean missing something wonderful right under your nose, and unless you have two or more weeks and look forward to covering long distances by car, forget about trying to see everything. Getting out of the car and *into* the parks is what really matters, so budget plenty of time for **hikes** – including at least one overnighter, if possible – and lazy picnics, along with other **outdoor activities** ranging from fishing and rafting to cycling and wildlife watching.

Where to go

Given Yellowstone's immense size and the fact that it's accessible from all directions during peak visiting season, it doesn't boast a true centre. Instead, the park has a number of "village" hubs of varying sizes located near the busiest junctions along its 154-mile-long **Grand Loop Road**. Shaped like a giant figure eight, the Grand Loop was designed to pass most of the park's main attractions, and while the entire road could conceivably be travelled in one very long day – speed limits and frequent, wildlife-caused traffic jams keep traffic moving slowly – it deserves at minimum three or four days, not including time for hikes and other diversions.

To keep things manageable, we've grouped the Grand Loop's top half, along with the highways branching off to the North and Northeast Entrances, into Northern Yellowstone (Chapter 1). The two main villages here are **Mammoth Hot Springs** and **Canyon Village**; the former is home to an old army fort and bizarre travertine terraces, while the latter is set near the magnificent **Grand Canyon of the Yellowstone**. Other must-see sights in the park's northern half include wildlife-rich **Lamar Valley** and the alien landscape of superheated **Norris Geyser Basin**.

Southern Yellowstone (Chapter 2) takes in the longer, lower half of the Grand Loop, as well as the highways to the West, South and East Entrances. Here bison graze contentedly by the steaming geysers of **Upper**, **Midway** and **Lower Geyser Basins**, while patches of bright yellow monkey flowers and frequent rainbows add colour to the already bright palettes swirling by the edges of numerous hot springs. The village at **Old Faithful** is the biggest in the park, with a mix of gorgeous historic buildings, sparkling new visitor facilities and forgettable trinket shops vying for your attention. To the east, **West Thumb**

◄ National Museum of Wildlife Art, Jackson

Geyser Basin sits on the shores of **Yellowstone Lake**, the park's largest, most tempestuous natural feature. Along its northern shores, **Bridge Bay**, **Lake Village** and **Fishing Bridge** host most of the lakeside activity, including a marina and historic hotel. To the south and east of Yellowstone Lake lies untrammelled wilderness laced with some of the park's best hiking trails, while north towards Canyon Village is **Hayden Valley**, a paradise for bison and a great place to end the day watching the sunset glow on the **Yellowstone River**.

▲ Walkers in lodgepole pine forest, Yellowstone

Due south, the long menu of outdoor activities at extraordinary **Grand Teton National Park** (Chapter 3) may have you budgeting extra time for your stay. After gawking at the brash **Teton Range** from any number of fine roadside vistas – including **Snake River Overlook**, **Oxbow Bend** and towering **Signal Mountain Summit Road** – your next decision is whether you start hiking, paddling or biking. The foot trail to **Hidden Falls** and **Inspiration Point**, reached via ferry across idyllic **Jenny Lake**, is a superb first jaunt, while the relaxed rafting trips along the winding **Snake River** and lazy bike rides through **Antelope Flats** and along **Teton Park Road** are equally sure to leave lasting impressions.

As for the parks' outlying towns, choosing which to visit can be a matter of location as much as preference. Commercialized **West Yellowstone** (Chapter 12), low-key **Gardiner** (Chapter 13) and tiny but lively **Cooke City** (Chapter 14) all border Yellowstone just inside Montana's borders, and make convenient stopovers for meals and overnight stays. West Yellowstone is the gateway to **Big Sky** and **Gallatin Valley**, home to an enormous ski resort and top-tier whitewater rafting, respectively, while smaller Gardiner hosts Yellowstone's Heritage and Research Center. Beyond Yellowstone's East Entrance and through lovely **Wapiti Valley**, Buffalo Bill Historical Center in **Cody** (Chapter 15) is an essential stop for anyone interested in Western history. Finally, five miles south of Grand Teton sits buzzing **Jackson** (Chapter 11), the region's most sophisticated gateway. At one time a laidback ranching town, it now offers a cosmopolitan blend of galleries, restaurants and high-end hotels, along with one of the country's top ski resorts in nearby **Teton Village**.

When to go

Traditionally running between Memorial Day in late May and Labor Day in early September, the **summer** high season sees a steady stream of vacationing families lined up at the entrance gates of both Yellowstone and Grand Teton. Campgrounds quickly fill up, while visitor centres and boardwalks are clogged with a maddening mix of camera-crazed tour groups and excited (or just bored) kids. Weather, however, is typically best in summer, with improved trail conditions and wildflower blooms at their most vivid. Even during the busiest late June to mid August timeframe, hikers will find ample solitude and plenty of free backcountry sites, while those willing to be out at dawn will have a couple of hours of peaceful wildlife spotting ahead of them.

If the thought of sharing Old Faithful with a thousand strangers is still too much to bear, consider visiting during one of the **shoulder seasons**. Weather is far more temperamental and area amenities are often shuttered, but the more relaxed pace can compensate for these inconveniences. **Spring** is a transitional time, with snow gradually receding to leave behind muddy bogs and roaring waterfalls. Some roads and many trails remain closed until mid May, with the weeks around late May and early June offering fine opportunities for relatively quiet early summer travel. **Autumn** is the best time to miss the huge crowds yet still experience all, or most, of what the parks have to offer. With many schools starting back up in mid August nowadays, the week before Labor

▶ Bison standing by Old Faithful

Day is a golden time to visit, while the rest of September and early October sees great fishing and hiking conditions, along with active wildlife spotting as creatures enter a feeding frenzy in preparation for **winter**. While this final season is truly a magical and secluded time, road closures, perilously cold temperatures and greatly limited services add complications that must be considered when planning a visit.

While the area's **climate** varies a good deal by both **season** and **altitude**, it can snow at any time throughout

the year, making a waterproof jacket, fleece, hat and gloves essential wardrobe companions. Throughout **summer**, expect warm sunny days punctuated by short, yet possibly fierce, mid-afternoon thunderstorms leaving brilliant rainbows in their wake; evening temperatures flirt with freezing, keeping campers rolled up tightly in their sleeping bags. Additional gear and caution is required through late **spring** and **autumn**, when periods of mild, near-perfect hiking conditions are balanced with freezing rain and sudden snowstorms. **Winter** temperatures are guaranteed to be frigid, and whether observing wolves from afar in early morning or tackling the slopes at one of the area's superb ski resorts, you'll want to keep bundled up in multiple layers of warm clothing.

Average temperatures and rainfall

	Jan	Feb	Mar	Apr	May	Jun	Jul	Aug	Sep	Oct	Nov	Dec
Old Faithful, Yellowstone												
High (°F/°C)	23/-5	28/-2	35/2	42/6	51/11	61/16	70/21	70/21	60/16	48/9	33/1	25/-4
Low (°F/°C)	-3/-19	0/-18	4/-16	16/-9	25/-4	34/1	37/3	36/2	29/-2	21/-6	9/-13	1/-17
Rainfall (in)	2	1.5	1.8	1.5	2.1	2.1	1.7	1.7	1.6	1.3	1.7	1.7
Gardiner, MT												
High (°F/°C)	33/1	40/4	46/8	57/14	67/19	77/25	85/29	84/29	74/23	60/16	41/5	32/0
Low (°F/°C)	14/-10	18/-8	25/-4	31/-1	38/3	47/8	53/12	52/11	43/6	34/1	23/-5	14/-10
Rainfall (in)	.4	.3	.6	.6	1.6	1.4	1.2	.8	.9	.7	.7	.5
Jackson, WY												
High (°F/°C)	24/-4	31/1	40/4	49/9	59/15	70/21	80/27	79/26	71/22	55/13	37/3	26/-3
Low (°F/°C)	0/-18	3/-16	12/-11	20/-7	30/-1	37/3	41/5	39/4	33/1	24/-4	13/-11	1/-17
Rainfall (in)	2.5	2	1.7	1.4	1.9	1.9	1.3	1.3	1.4	1.2	2.2	2.4

15

things not to miss

It's impossible to see everything in and around Yellowstone and Grand Teton in one visit – and we don't suggest you try. What follows is a selective look at certain highlights in and around the parks, including top spots for hiking, cycling, fly-fishing, skiing and simply taking in the extraordinary landscapes. The highlights are arranged in five colour-coded categories to help you find the very best things to do, see and experience. All highlights have a page reference, where you can learn more.

01 Lamar Valley Page **52** • Apart from its breathtaking beauty, this wide valley is also the pre-eminent place in the Rockies for spotting bison, elk, pronghorn and predators such as wolves and grizzly bears.

02 **Winter in the parks** Page **170** • Visiting Grand Teton and particularly Yellowstone in the snowy season isn't easy – many roads close completely and temperatures plummet – but the solitude, silence, hoar-maned wildlife and frosty scenery make it well worth the effort.

04 **Cycling in Grand Teton** Page **165** • Whether riding unpaved Mormon Row or along the dedicated path between Moose and Jenny Lake, there's no greater biking backdrop than the jagged Tetons.

03 **Old Faithful Inn** Page **183** • A "log cabin" of epic proportions, the revered *Old Faithful Inn*'s soaring lobby and inviting outside deck have enthralled visitors for well over a century.

05 Hiking in Laurance S. Rockefeller Preserve Page **89** • The newest trail network in the parks is ideal for quiet ambles through forests, along lakeshores and over rushing streams.

06 Jackson Hole Mountain Resort Page **212** • The complete package for expert skiers, with hair-rising chutes, ultra-steep bowls, formidable backcountry routes and even the occasional foraging moose.

07 West Thumb Geyser Basin Page **75** • A dramatically set geyser basin where sapphire-coloured hot springs and gurgling mudpots bubble away next to immense Yellowstone Lake.

08 Snake River Brewing Page **209** • Award-winning beers, good pub grub and a vibrant atmosphere make this microbrewery and restaurant, ever popular with locals, a smart first choice for a night out in Jackson.

10 Wolf-watching with the Yellowstone Association Institute Page **196** & *The wolves of Yellowstone* **colour section** • Increase your chances of spotting these captivating predators by taking a field trip with this nonprofit organization.

09 Artist Point Page **58** • Despite often being thronged with visitors, this stunning viewpoint over the Grand Canyon of the Yellowstone and thundering Lower Falls never disappoints.

11 Buffalo Bill Historical Center Page **241** • Cody's marquee attraction and one of the most engaging museums in – and on – the West, with five distinct collections that range well beyond Buffalo Bill ephemera.

13 Sunset on Lunch Tree Hill Page 105 •

Overlooking moose-rich Willow Flats, this historic spot is a peaceful place to watch the sun dip behind the shark-toothed Tetons.

14 Fly-fishing in Yellowstone

Page 159 • From the steaming Firehole River in early summer to Slough Creek in autumn, Yellowstone's two-hundred-plus trout-filled streams are fabled fishing grounds that draw anglers from around the world.

12 Old Faithful Page 72 •

Yellowstone's essential sight, as much to witness its dependable 105–185ft eruptions as to answer questions from curious friends back home.

15 Menor's Ferry Historic District Page 91 •

A restored homestead cabin and replica ferry in the heart of Grand Teton offers insight into the lives of Jackson Hole's earliest white settlers.

Basics

Basics

Getting there 19

Getting around 24

Health and personal safety 28

Travelling with children... 31

Travel essentials... 32

Getting there

When flying to the Yellowstone region, the first order of business is choosing where to land. Several smaller airports serve the region, with most requiring a connection via a larger international airport (typically Denver or Salt Lake City), meaning cheap tickets can be hard to find. Given the lack of nearby depots, trains aren't much of an option; buses, meanwhile, call in at the larger gateway communities, but not in the parks themselves. In order to experience Yellowstone and Grand Teton fully, most people will, therefore, want to seriously consider hiring a car. For those who live within 500 miles of the parks or have a considerable amount of extra time, driving their own vehicle may be a reasonable alternative.

Flights from the US and Canada

If you're willing to tack on a half-day's drive, the airport at **Salt Lake City**, Utah (SLC; ☎801/575-2400, ⒲www.slcairport.com) has excellent links to the rest of the US and Canada, with direct flights arriving daily from many major towns and cities. Barring a fare war, round-trip prices to Salt Lake City start at around US$300 from New York, US$200 from Los Angeles and around Can$500 from Vancouver and Calgary (the only two Canadian cities with direct flights).

To land close by the parks – or in the case of Jackson Hole's airport, *within* one of them – you'll have to pay more, though prices tend to fluctuate wildly based on availability and season. **Jackson Hole Airport** (JAC; ☎307/733-7682, ⒲www.jacksonholeairport.com) fields direct flights from Chicago (summer only), Denver, Los Angeles and Salt Lake City, while Bozeman, Montana's **Gallatin Field Airport** (BZN; ☎406/388-8321, ⒲www.bozemanairport.com) has direct flights from Denver, Minneapolis, Phoenix, Salt Lake City, San Francisco and Seattle. Cody's **Yellowstone Regional Airport** (YRA; ☎307/587-5096, ⒲www.flyyra.com) has direct flights from Denver and Salt Lake City, while tiny Yellowstone Airport in West Yellowstone (WYS; ☎406/646-7631, ⒲www.yellowstoneairport.org) hosts flights from Salt Lake City in summer only. For more information on these airports, see chapters 11, 12 and 15.

Flights from the UK and Ireland

If you're coming from **London** or one of Britain's many regional airports, flying to within driving distance of Yellowstone requires at least one stopover. One of the quickest routes is from London to Jackson Hole via Denver – the flight to Denver takes around ten hours, while the leg onwards to Jackson adds another 90min, not including stopover. For **two-stop flights**, travellers can choose between a wide array of options on American, British Airways, Continental, Delta, United and others, with connections through Chicago, Detroit, Salt Lake City or Washington DC. A basic round-trip economy-class ticket to Jackson or Bozeman from London will cost around £750 in high season and about £100–150 less during other times; flying into Salt Lake City and driving north only shaves around £25 off the ticket price, so unless you fancy five hours behind the wheel after a transcontinental flight, it's best to fly directly to Jackson Hole.

Choices for those who don't live around London are less efficient, as itineraries will involve taking a flight from a regional airport such as **Manchester**, **Glasgow** or **Dublin**, then a connecting flight (or flights) to the Yellowstone region from a US airport (usually Chicago or New York). Another option is to use a European carrier that will fly you to a hub such as Paris, Amsterdam or Frankfurt for a connecting flight to the US, then a shorter hop on to the Yellowstone region. While these trips can become eighteen- to twenty-hour odysseys, it could be worth it for the right fare.

Flights from Australia, New Zealand and South Africa

Unsurprisingly, there are no direct flights from **Australia** and **New Zealand** to anywhere near Yellowstone, so you'll invariably have to touch down on the US West Coast before taking a connection to Salt Lake City (or two connections to one of the closer airports in Wyoming or Montana). The good news is that many flights to San Francisco or Los Angeles are nonstop, with total travel time from Sydney and Auckland to Salt Lake City taking anywhere from fourteen to twenty hours, depending on stopovers. In the unlikely event you travel from Australia through Asia (not an option from New Zealand), you'll usually have to spend a night – or at least most of a day – in the airline's home city.

Travelling from Australia's East Coast cities, **fares** to Salt Lake City cost around Aus$2200–2300, while from Perth they may be Aus$400 more. Daily flights run from Sydney to Salt Lake City via San Francisco or Los Angeles on United and Delta; adding a connection onwards to Jackson or Bozeman can add another Aus$250. Itineraries from Australia to the US West Coast via Asia have become exorbitantly priced in recent years – fares over Aus$4000 are now the norm – so unless you've got money to burn, you'll want to avoid Asia entirely.

From **New Zealand**, the most affordable flights to the US West Coast depart from **Auckland** and touch down in San Francisco before continuing on to Salt Lake City (NZ$2000–2100); itineraries routed through Los Angeles can cost up to NZ$450 more. Trips beginning in Christchurch and Wellington cost the same for those beginning in Auckland, with cooperated Air New Zealand/ United flights dominating the current market.

Six steps to a better kind of travel

At Rough Guides we are passionately committed to travel. We feel strongly that only through travelling do we truly come to understand the world we live in and the people we share it with – plus tourism has brought a great deal of **benefit** to developing economies around the world over the last few decades. But the extraordinary growth in tourism has also damaged some places irreparably, and of course **climate change** is exacerbated by most forms of transport, especially flying. This means that now more than ever it's important to **travel thoughtfully** and **responsibly**, with respect for the cultures you're visiting – not only to derive the most benefit from your trip but also to preserve the best bits of the planet for everyone to enjoy. At Rough Guides we feel there are six main areas in which you can make a difference:

• Consider what you're contributing to the **local economy**, and how much the services you use do the same, whether it's through employing local workers and guides or sourcing locally grown produce and local services.

• Consider the **environment** on holiday as well as at home. Water is scarce in many developing destinations, and the biodiversity of local flora and fauna can be adversely affected by tourism. Try to patronize businesses that take account of this.

• Travel with a purpose, not just to tick off experiences. Consider **spending longer** in a place, and getting to know it and its people.

• Give thought to how often you **fly**. Try to avoid short hops by air and more harmful night flights.

• Consider **alternatives to flying**, travelling instead by bus, train, boat and even by bike or on foot where possible.

• Make your trips **"climate neutral"** via a reputable carbon offset scheme. All Rough Guide flights are offset, and every year we donate money to a variety of charities devoted to combating the effects of climate change.

If you'll be initiating your trip from **South Africa**, you can expect your itinerary to be routed through Europe (Paris is the most common transfer point, with London, Amsterdam, Munich and Frankfurt other options) and take anywhere from 26 to 32 hours before you finally touch down in Salt Lake City. Fares typically cost ZAR12,500–13,500, and the best deals are generally found on KLM, Lufthansa, Air France and American.

Trains

For the first half of the twentieth century, travelling to Yellowstone by **train** on the Union Pacific was the most popular mode of arrival. By 1960, however, regular services to West Yellowstone's depot were suspended due to the dominance of car travel, and nowadays travelling by train is mainly an option for those who refuse to fly or drive a long distance. US passenger carrier Amtrak (☎1-800/872-7245; ⊛www.amtrak.com) does not have a single route that runs through Wyoming or southern Montana, meaning the closest that train passengers can get to the parks is around 300 miles, from where they'll need to rent a car and drive the remaining distance.

The most northerly Amtrak route, the **Empire Builder**, connects Seattle to Chicago (46hr). This is a good option if you're planning to also visit northern Montana's Glacier National Park, as the train makes several stops in the park's area. To the south, the **California Zephyr**, which runs from Chicago to San Francisco (52hr), calls in at Salt Lake City. Note that long-distance Amtrak **fares** are rarely less expensive than flying.

Buses

Bus travel is the most tedious and time-consuming way to get to the Yellowstone region; what's worse is that for all the discomfort, it won't really save you much money. The sole long-distance operator in the region, **Greyhound** (☎1-800/231-2222, ⊛www.greyhound.com), stops at Jackson,

21

West Yellowstone and, further afield, Bozeman, so you'll still need to rent a car or book a shuttle or tour service to see the parks themselves.

The main reason to consider using Greyhound is if you're planning to visit a number of other places en route to Yellowstone. The company's **Discovery Pass** (ⓦwww.discoverypass.com) is good for unlimited travel around the US and Canada within a set time: 7 days of travel costs US$239; 15 days, US$339; 30 days, US$439; and 60 days, US$539. Domestic passes are only valid from the date of purchase, so it's useless for Americans to buy them in advance; visitors from overseas, however, can buy passes before leaving home, then have them validated at the start of their trip.

By car

From Alabama to Alberta, cars cruising through Yellowstone and Grand Teton sport licence plates from across the US and Canada, proof positive that the region is one of North America's prime **road-trip** destinations. Driving your own car offers the greatest freedom and flexibility; if you don't have one or are visiting from abroad, a long list of rental agencies do business in the region's towns and airports (see opposite for listings).

One crucial thing to bear in mind when driving in and around the parks, especially in winter, is that roads can often become hazardous. See p.25 for tips on driving in inclement conditions.

Approaching the parks

Yellowstone occupies the far northwest corner of Wyoming, overlapping very slightly into Montana and Idaho. Two of the park's **five main entrances** are in Wyoming: Hwy-14/16/20 through the park's **East Entrance**, and Hwy-89/191/189 via the **South Entrance**, both of which are shut throughout winter. The driving distance from Cody to the East Entrance is 52 miles, while the route to the South Entrance from Jackson is an unforgettable 57-mile drive through **Grand Teton** and the slim **John D. Rockefeller, Jr. Memorial Parkway**.

The park's other three entrances are all in Montana. Busiest in summer (but closed to cars in winter) is the **West Entrance**, bordering the gateway town of **West Yellowstone**, about 90 miles south of Bozeman and 110 miles northeast of Idaho Falls, Idaho. Nearly as popular, the year-round **North Entrance** at **Gardiner** is Yellowstone's historic original portal, located 50 miles south of Livingston and 80 miles from Bozeman. The sleepy **Northeast Entrance** is a few miles west of tiny **Cooke City**, located 80 miles northwest of Cody and about 125 miles from Billings, Montana; although open year-round, it's effectively only accessible in summer since Hwy-212 east beyond Cooke City remains closed for over half the year. Yellowstone's sixth entrance – by far the most isolated and least used – is at the **Bechler Ranger Station** in the park's southwest corner, the final stop on a winding, dead-end road that leads about 20 miles east from **Ashton**, Idaho.

Grand Teton, located entirely in Wyoming, has entry points from the north, south and east. Speedy Hwy-191 is the main artery, shooting north from **Jackson** and spanning the vertical length of the park to Yellowstone's South Entrance. From **Teton Village** northwest of Jackson, the

Miles to Yellowstone (West Yellowstone Entrance)

(Estimated driving time in parentheses.)

Atlanta 2000 miles (33 hours)	**Miami** 2650 miles (44 hours)
Boston 2450 miles (40 hours)	**Minneapolis** 1050 miles (17 hours)
Chicago 1450 miles (24 hours)	**New York** 2250 miles (37 hours)
Denver 650 miles (11 hours)	**San Francisco** 950 miles (16 hours)
Detroit 1750 miles (29 hours)	**Salt Lake City** 325 miles (5 hours)
Houston 1700 miles (29 hours)	**Seattle** 750 miles (12 hours)
Los Angeles 1000 miles (16 hours)	**Washington, DC** 2150 miles (36 hours)

slower Moose-Wilson Road passes through another southern entrance, **Granite Canyon Entrance Station** (closed in winter), en route to park headquarters in Moose. Hwy-26/287 enters the park from the east at **Moran Entrance Station**, located 55 miles from Dubois, Wyoming.

Airlines, agents and operators

Airlines

Air Canada ⓦ www.aircanada.com.
Air France ⓦ www.airfrance.com.
Air New Zealand ⓦ www.airnewzealand.com.
Alaska Airlines ⓦ www.alaskaair.com.
American Airlines ⓦ www.aa.com.
British Airways ⓦ www.ba.com.
Continental Airlines ⓦ www.continental.com.
Delta ⓦ www.delta.com.
Frontier Airlines ⓦ www.frontierairlines.com.
JetBlue ⓦ www.jetblue.com.
KLM ⓦ www.klm.com.
Lufthansa ⓦ www.lufthansa.com.
SkyWest Airlines ⓦ www.skywest.com.
Southwest Airlines ⓦ www.southwest.com.
United Airlines ⓦ www.united.com.
US Airways ⓦ www.usairways.com.
Virgin Atlantic ⓦ www.virgin-atlantic.com.

Agents and operators

Backroads US ☏ 1-800/462-2848 or 510/527-1555, ⓦ www.backroads.com. Cycling, hiking and multi-sport tours designed for the young at heart (including families), with a strong emphasis placed on going at your own pace. Yellowstone and Grand Teton options range from a week in the region's best hotels to several nights of camping out.
Cosmos UK ☏ 0844/573 0662, ⓦ www.cosmostourama.co.uk; US ☏ 1-800/276-1241, ⓦ www.cosmos.com. Escorted vacation packages with an independent focus. The 13-day National Parks & Canyon Country package (from $1550) begins in Denver and ends in Las Vegas, spending three nights in and around Yellowstone along the way.
Exodus UK ☏ 0845/287 7563, ⓦ www.exodus.co.uk; US ☏ 510/654-1879 or 1-800/843-4272. Adventure tour operators taking small groups on specialist programmes in countries around the world. Beginning and ending in Salt Lake City, the 14-day Yellowstone Wildlife Trek (from £2300) spends a full week in Yellowstone and Grand Teton before continuing north to Glacier National Park.

Explore UK ☏ 0845/013 1537, ⓦ www.explore.co.uk; US ☏ 1-800/715-1746; Canada ☏ 1-888/216-3401, ⓦ www.exploreworldwide.com; Australia ☏ 1300/414 151, ⓦ www.exploreworldwide.com.au. Offers a wide range of small-group tours, treks, expeditions and safaris on all continents. On the 15-day Yellowstone and Western Trails tour (from $2900), you can expect to spend all but two nights camping.
North South Travel UK ☏ 01245/608 291, ⓦ www.northsouthtravel.co.uk. Friendly, competitive travel agency offering discounted fares worldwide. Profits are used to support projects in the developing world, especially the promotion of sustainable tourism.
Priceline ⓦ www.priceline.com. Particularly useful for finding discount accommodation at major chain hotels; also offers airfare discounts for travellers with flexible travel dates.
STA Travel UK ☏ 0871/2300 040, US ☏ 1-800/781-4040, Australia ☏ 134 782, New Zealand ☏ 0800/474 400, South Africa ☏ 0861/781 781; ⓦ www.statravel.co.uk. Worldwide specialists in independent travel; also offers student IDs, travel insurance, car rental, rail passes and more. Good discounts for students and under-26s.
Trailfinders UK ☏ 0845/058 5858, Ireland ☏ 01/677 7888, Australia ☏ 1300/780 212; ⓦ www.trailfinders.com. One of the best-informed and most efficient agents for independent travellers.
Travel CUTS Canada ☏ 1-866/246-9762, US ☏ 1-800/592-2887; ⓦ www.travelcuts.com. North American youth and student travel firm.
Travelers Advantage ☏ 1-800/835-8747, ⓦ www.travelersadvantage.com. Geared toward frequent travellers, this discount travel club features cash-back deals and discounted car rentals. Membership required: $1 for one-month trial, $20/month thereafter.
TrekAmerica UK ☏ 0844/576 1400, ⓦ www.trekamerica.co.uk; US ☏ 1-800/873-5872, ⓦ www.trekamerica.com. With a full complement of tours through the US and Canada, this long-standing tour company gears its offerings towards adventure-seeking twenty- and thirty-somethings. The 14-day Mountain Trail package (from $1500) sweeps a long arc from Seattle through Yellowstone and Grand Teton en route to Los Angeles, spending four days in the parks along the way; if you're keen on seeing much of the same terrain at a slower pace, the 21-day Rocky Mountain High tour (from $2100) also winds its way through the parks.
USIT Ireland ☏ 01/602 1906, Northern Ireland ☏ 028/9032 7111, ⓦ www.usit.ie. Ireland's main student and youth travel specialists.

Getting around

Whether it be a car, RV, motorcycle or – for the heartiest of visitors – bicycle, you'll need your own transportation to fully explore the Yellowstone region. Public transportation options are basically non-existent, with only Jackson having anything resembling a fully realized bus network. Though bus plans for both Yellowstone and Grand Teton have been suggested for decades, there has been little funding for such programmes, and given both visitor apathy and the overall size of the parks, a major public transportation network remains a pipe dream. Park tours by bus, however, are readily available and vary greatly by subject and length; see Chapter 10, "Park programmes and tours", for further details on the best options.

Driving

Driving is by far the best – and in many cases, the only – way to get around the parks. Along with the ease of keeping your own flexible schedule, travelling by car allows you to best explore the region's wide-open landscapes, backcountry roads and scenic vistas. Indeed, for many visitors, cruising with the windows down by the Tetons or curving alongside Yellowstone Lake will be a highlight of the trip.

Road conditions are for the most part good, other than in winter when most roads in Yellowstone close for the season, along with Teton Park Road within Grand Teton; see Chapter 7 for in-depth details on winter closures. Upon entering Yellowstone or Grand Teton, along with a newspaper (see p.38) and map you'll be given a sheet detailing any current **road closures** or delays – typically due to construction, but sometimes caused by rockslides, flooding or other natural activity. It's a good idea to check conditions ahead of time, either through the parks' websites or by calling area road hotlines (see box below) as alerting yourself to major closures can help you plan detours in advance.

Road condition hotlines

Grand Teton ☎307/739-3682.
Yellowstone ☎307/344-2117.
Idaho ☎1-888/432-7623.
Montana ☎1-800/226-7623.
Wyoming ☎1-888/996-7623.

Unpredictable price swings notwithstanding, gas will likely cost anywhere between $2.50 and $3 a gallon (3.8 litres), with service stations easy to find both within the parks and in the gateway communities. Note that you're best off never letting your supply dip below a quarter of a tank, as areas with 30-mile gaps (or longer) between stations do exist.

Rules of the road

Driving conditions in the parks are good in summer, with the most dangerous distractions being attention-grabbing scenery and wildlife wandering onto roads. While the major roads within **Yellowstone** are paved and as wide as a minor highway, driving within the park does require a fair amount of patience. Due in large part to the park's abundant wildlife, the maximum **speed limit** within Yellowstone is 45mph, something worth keeping in mind when planning your route. Over one hundred large mammals – deer, moose, bear, elk and bison – are killed each year by drivers, so always obey the speed limit and remain alert for crossing creatures. If the thought of killing an animal and causing potentially heavy damage to your vehicle aren't reasons enough, be aware that park police do not hesitate in giving out expensive **tickets** to those caught speeding.

Aside from the usual army of slothful RVs poking along, slowdowns on park roads tend to result from so-called **bison jams** caused by the ton-weight creatures crisscrossing roads; **backups** stemming from

Winter driving

If you're unaccustomed to driving in icy conditions, it's best to be very conservative and, if possible, simply avoid driving during snowstorms. Basic equipment for winter driving in the Yellowstone region includes snow tyres and/or chains, an ice-scraper for clearing your windshield and a shovel for clearing away built-up snow. It also pays to have warm clothes, blankets and extra food and water on hand in case you do get stuck along the way, along with a cell phone (provided you can get a signal).

If your car is equipped with snow tyres – definitely double-check this when booking a rental car for a winter trip in the area – you'll be in good shape for general highway and town driving in winter. Highways and other major roads are regularly cleared throughout winter, as are town and city streets, though you should not rely on less significant roads being cleared every day. At times you may see emergency road signs indicating drivers are required to carry chains in certain areas.

Even if you take every imaginable precaution, you may find yourself on a stretch of road covered in an unbroken sheet of ice. Snow tyres won't help you much here, and if you have no alternative but to keep driving, you'll need to be extremely careful. The best reaction to skidding on ice depends on whether your vehicle is equipped with anti-lock brakes (ABS): if it's not, firmly pump the brakes until you regain control of the vehicle; if it is equipped with ABS, your vehicle should automatically pump its brakes after you press the brake pedal, which in turn should keep the wheels from locking up.

gawkers pulling over to gaze at moose, elk and other roadside animals are just as routine. Given all this potential for delay, you're best off giving yourself as much extra time as possible to reach your destination.

Unlike Yellowstone, maximum speed limits vary within **Grand Teton**. Though not at all unusual, animals cross the park's roads less frequently, and the major artery, north/south **Hwy-191** (also Highways 26/89/287 in spots), is treated for the most part like a typical US highway, with speed limits of 55mph. From the northern edge of John D. Rockefeller, Jr. Memorial Parkway down to the southern boundary of the park, Hwy-191 is about 55 miles long, and it's possible to make the journey in under an hour and a half in good conditions; note that the 25-mile stretch between Moran Entrance Station and the park's southern boundary does not require drivers to pay an entrance fee, giving road-trippers a free head-on vista of the Tetons to the west. Speed limits on the rest of Grand Teton's roads range from 10 to 45mph and, as in Yellowstone, are attentively enforced by park police.

Outside the parks, the maximum speed limits on interstates in Wyoming, Montana and Idaho is 75mph. On state highways, the maximum is typically 65mph, with lower

signposted limits – usually 35–45mph – in built-up areas, and 20mph near schools when children are present. If a **police** officer pulls you over, don't get out of the car, and certainly don't reach into the glove compartment until you're given the OK to do so; simply sit still with your hands on the wheel, be polite and don't attempt to make jokes.

Apart from the obvious fact that Americans drive on the right, various rules of the road may be unfamiliar to **foreign drivers**: US law requires that any alcohol be carried unopened in the trunk of the car; it's illegal to make a U-turn on an interstate or any place where a single or double unbroken line runs along the middle of the road; it's also illegal to park on a highway, and for passengers to ride without fastened seat belts. At junctions, you're permitted to turn right on a red light if no traffic is approaching from the left; it's also important to recognize **four-way stops**, at which all traffic must come to a complete stop before proceeding in order of arrival.

It can't be stressed too strongly that **driving under the influence (DUI)** is a very serious offence in the US. If a police officer smells alcohol on your breath, he or she is entitled to administer a breath, saliva or urine test. If you fail, you'll assuredly be locked up with other inebriates in the "drunk tank" of the nearest stockade until you sober up. Your case will later be heard by a judge, who at the very least can fine you up to several thousand dollars and, in extreme (or repeat) cases, imprison you for thirty or more days.

Renting a car

After reclaiming luggage, the first order of business for most visitors upon touching down in the region will be **renting a car**. Each of the airports – in Jackson, Bozeman, Cody and, further afield, Salt Lake City – hosts at least a couple of the rental agencies listed below. Renters are supposed to have held a licence for at least one year (though this is rarely checked); those under 25 years of age will pay a higher insurance premium. A credit card is essential, as rental companies invariably do not accept cash deposits.

4WD vehicles are readily available, but you'll pay extra for them – and also end up paying more at the gas pump. All major roads within the parks are accessible in a regular car, meaning a 4WD is only necessary in good weather if you plan to drive lots of backcountry roads; still, a 4WD is an undeniably good choice for winter driving. Note also that **ski/bike racks** can often be requested as well.

It's worth booking in advance online to get a good deal on rentals of a week or more; otherwise, phone the major firms' toll-free numbers and ask for their best rate – most will try to beat the offers of their competitors, so it never hurts to haggle a bit. Also, be sure to have printed confirmation of your booking to present when collecting your vehicle; otherwise, you run the risk of driving off in the least desirable (or most expensive) car available at your time of arrival.

One oddity about car rental rates is that **cheaper deals** are almost always available if you rent for one week or more. In fact, rental companies' strict adherence to weekly discounted rates can lead to the bizarre situation where it's cheaper to rent a car for fourteen days than for ten.

Important details to check are whether your rate includes free unlimited mileage (nearly all do nowadays) and what the insurance cost will be. When looking at some of the cheaper rental firms, keep in mind that there can be a big difference in the quality of cars from company to company; industry leaders such as Hertz and Avis tend to have newer, lower-mileage cars often fitted with air conditioning and decent stereo systems featuring line-in connections for MP3 players – no small consideration when embarking on a long drive. Virtually all US rental cars have automatic transmissions.

When you rent a car, read the small print carefully for details on the **Collision Damage Waiver (CDW)** – sometimes called a Liability Damage Waiver (LDW) or a Physical Damage Waiver (PDW). This is a form of insurance that usually isn't included in the rental charge, but is well worth considering; American drivers are likely already covered by their own vehicle insurance (it's a good idea to check before you leave home), but foreign visitors should definitely give weight to accepting this option since it specifically covers the car you're driving – in any case, your rental agreement insures you for damage sustained to other vehicles. At around $15 a day, CDW does add considerably to the daily rental fee, but without it you're liable for every scratch to the car – even those that aren't your fault. Some credit card companies offer automatic CDW coverage to anyone using their card; again, check before leaving home.

If you **break down** in a rented vehicle, you can normally call an emergency assistance number provided by the rental agency on your agreement. If you're not carrying your own, you might consider renting a **mobile phone** from the car rental agency (or from outlets at major airports); you often only have to pay a nominal amount until you actually use it. At the very least, having a phone at your disposal can be reassuring – and a potential lifesaver should something go terribly wrong.

Car rental agencies

Alamo Ⓦ www.alamo.com.
Avis Ⓦ www.avis.com.
Budget Ⓦ www.budget.com.
Dollar Ⓦ www.dollar.com.
Enterprise Ⓦ www.enterprise.com.
Hertz Ⓦ www.hertz.com.
National Ⓦ www.nationalcar.com.
Thrifty Ⓦ www.thrifty.com.

Renting an RV

Recreation vehicles – aka **RVs**, motorhomes or camper vans – can be rented starting at around $1000–1250 a week in off-season, and $1600 a week in summer. The idea of travelling with your own accommodation may sound liberating, but it's far from cheap. On top of the rental fees, you'll need to take into account the **cost of gas** (some RVs get twelve miles to the gallon – or less) and any drop-off charges, in case you plan to undertake a one-way trip. Also, keep in mind that although you're travelling with a roof overhead, you'll still need to pay to "camp out" in the parks, with RV sites averaging over $30 per night. Outside the parks, it's rarely legal to simply stop and spend the night by the roadside – on the contrary, you're expected to stay in designated RV parks that are nearly as expensive as those in national park campgrounds, or – once hook-ups are factored in – even a basic motel room.

The Recreation Vehicle Rental Association (☎703/591-7130, ⓦwww.rvra.org) has a directory of rental firms in the US and Canada. Near Yellowstone, Cruise America (☎1-800/671-8042, ⓦwww.cruiseamerica.com) has rentals available in Belgrade, Montana, just west of Bozeman; in Bozeman itself, try C and T Motorhome Rentals (☎406/587-8610 or 1-800/481-8610, ⓦwww.ctrvrentals.com).

Cycling

As roads within Yellowstone are fairly narrow, and since drivers tend to be distracted by scenery and wildlife, **cycling** within the park is certainly not the safest way to get yourself around. Cycling through Grand Teton is somewhat better given the flatter roads and longer straights, but even here many roads have narrow to non-existent shoulders and plenty of heavy vehicle traffic – including RVs with their dangerously wide mirrors – with which cyclists must contend.

That said, scores of visitors each year cycle through both parks, often on longer trips through the Rockies – or even cross-country. It's important to choose your routes carefully to ensure you don't take on an entirely unrealistic itinerary through extreme mountainous terrain; you're likewise best off planning your trip early or, better yet, later in the season, when there's less traffic rumbling along park roads.

Both parks do their best to make conditions fair for bicycle travellers, with downloadable **brochures** available on their websites. A limited number of first-come, first-served hiking/biking campsites are available at most Yellowstone **campgrounds**, but given the distances between them, you may want to book ahead; otherwise, you run the risk of arriving late in the afternoon to a fully booked campground.

For **long-distance cycling**, you'll need a helmet, bright clothing, maps, spare tyres, tools, panniers and, certainly not least, a quality multi-speed bike. Don't immediately splurge on a mountain bike unless you're planning a lot of off-road use; in fact, good road conditions and trail restrictions in both parks make a touring bike the smartest choice for a visit to Yellowstone and Grand Teton. Keep in mind that cycling on interstates is both illegal and very dangerous.

For information on tour operators, bike rentals in the region and shorter, non-travel-based bike routes, see Chapter 6, "Summer Activities".

Health and personal safety

Staying safe while visiting Yellowstone and Grand Teton is mainly a case of exercising common sense. For reasons unknown to park rangers, some visitors tend to assume that once in a national park, the rules of the wild are suspended and they've entered a realm where all sharp edges have been dulled. This, of course, is hardly the case. While there indeed are guardrails, warning signs and similar safety precautions at some of the parks' more heavily trafficked areas, for the most part there is nobody watching over you. Emergency call boxes are not dotted throughout the backcountry, the native animals are not trained to be human-friendly and rangers are not babysitters employed specifically to monitor a visitor's every move.

If you're prepared for the worst, the worst by and large won't happen. Should you have a serious accident in the region, however, emergency services will generally get to you quickly (remote locations notwithstanding). For emergencies or ambulance, dial ☎911. If you're well enough to drive or able to have someone to drive you, there are clinics and hospitals located throughout the region – those within the parks and gateway towns are listed below.

Fortunately, most visitors will leave with only sore legs or perhaps mild sunburn. As with any other outdoor location, use **sunscreen** and wear a hat when warranted (which, incidentally, is often), and work your way up towards the toughest hikes instead of trying to tackle a 3000ft ascent over 5 miles on the first day of your visit. It's also worth carrying insect repellent for **mosquitoes**, which can become amazingly annoying in summer and turn even the most mild-mannered visitor into a raving lunatic within minutes. Other insects to watch for include **ticks**, which can pass on Colorado Tick Fever and Rocky Mountain Spotted Fever. Both have similar symptoms: headaches and muscle aches, nausea, vomiting, skin rash and abdominal pain – if any occur within two weeks, contact a doctor. Ticks generally attach themselves to

Medical clinics and hospitals

Yellowstone
Lake ☎307/242-7241. Open late May to mid Sept daily 8.30am–8.30pm; closed rest of year.

Mammoth ☎307/344-7965. Open year-round Mon–Thurs 8.30am–5pm, Fri 8.30am–1pm.

Old Faithful ☎307/545-7325. Open mid May to early Oct daily 8.30am–5pm; closed rest of year.

Grand Teton
Jackson Lake Lodge ☎307/543-2514. Open late May to late Sept daily 10am–6pm.

Cody
West Park Hospital 707 Sheridan Ave ☎307/527-7501. 24hr emergency care.

Jackson
St John's Medical Center 625 E Broadway ☎307/733-3636. 24hr emergency care.

West Yellowstone
Yellowstone Family Medical Clinic 11 S Electric St ☎406/646-0200. Open Mon–Fri 8am–3pm.

bare legs and hairy body areas as you walk through brush, forest or grassland; if you find one burrowing into your skin, grab it by the head with a pair of tweezers and counteract its resistance by firmly pulling it out.

Lastly, foreign visitors should bear in mind that many medications available over the counter at home require a **prescription** in the US – most codeine-based painkillers, for example – and that local brand names can be confusing; ask for advice at any **pharmacy** listed in the gateway town chapters.

Animals

When it comes to interacting with **animals** in the parks, tales of incredible foolishness and feats of wanton ignorance abound. From families lining up for a bison-side group portrait to hikers feeding baby bears, there's no limit to the amount of common-sense rules willing to be broken by visitors a little too entranced by Rocky Mountain wildlife. As hundreds of park signs note, animals here – from the smallest squirrel to the biggest bear – are not tame and should be viewed with caution. The basic rule of thumb is: If an animal reacts to your presence, you are too close, and it's your responsibility to back away – not the animal's.

Actual **dangerous encounters** with animals are rare and not too difficult to avoid; basic precautions include never surrounding an animal or blocking its line of travel, avoiding sudden movements in their presence and not approaching them. This last point is one that visitors with cameras pressed up to their faces seem to forget – some photography enthusiasts have learned the hard way that a camera makes a pitiful shield against a charging bison. Specifically, you must stay at least 100 yards away from bears and at least 25 yards away from all other animals, including elk, bison, coyote, moose and wolves. Come winter, you should double these distances, as conserving energy during the coldest season is a major key to survival for these animals; spooking them can have drastic consequences.

Finally, basic as it may sound to most park visitors, **feeding** any wild animal is strictly forbidden. As is often said, "A fed bear is a dead bear", and this commonly applies to all creatures, large or small. Feeding animals – including birds – causes them to become overly reliant on and comfortable around humans, leading to aggressive or dependent behaviour, again with drastic consequences.

Water safety: lakes, rivers and thermal features

Water quality is excellent throughout the Rockies and it's quite safe to drink from taps. However, while mountain streams and lakes may look clean and inviting, all stream and lake water should be boiled, purified, filtered or chemically treated before you **drink** it to avoid the risk of giardia contamination or a similar bacterial disorder; see Chapter 4, "Day hikes", for further details.

Aside from car accidents, **drowning** is the most common cause of accidental death within the parks. Given the region's altitude and long winters, rivers and lakes are numbingly cold; water temperatures in Yellowstone Lake, one of the more extreme examples, average a frigid 45°F (7°C), giving capsized paddlers about 20 minutes of survival time. Along with icy temperatures, rivers, especially in spring and early summer, run swift and strong and can quickly overpower even the most skilled swimmers. Only swim in designated areas (listed on p.169), and always remain alert when near water, especially when travelling with children. On certain backcountry trails, you may also need to **ford rivers** and streams to continue onward; again, see Chapter 4, "Day Hikes", for tips.

Yellowstone's unique **thermal features** can likewise be fatally dangerous; *always* stay on designated trails and boardwalks when in a thermal area. These paths not only keep the delicate formations from being destroyed, but can keep you from breaking through any thin crusts and suffering a severe scalding (or worse). Never travel through thermal areas after dark, and keep in mind that it's illegal to bathe in waters completely of thermal

For in-depth details on **bear encounters**, see the box on pp.110–111.

origin. Visitors with children in tow should take a few moments to explain the dangers of hot springs, geysers and mudpots, as the bright colours and peculiar formations of these hydrothermal features can be particularly mesmerizing to youngsters.

Weather

It's commonly said in Wyoming that if you don't like the **weather**, all you need to do is either wait five minutes or travel five miles. Daily temperature swings of fifty degrees or more aren't uncommon, and thunderstorms and blizzards can swing through with surprising rapidity any month of the year. With this in mind, hikers should always pack warm, waterproof layers regardless of the temperature or duration of the hike. For detailed suggestions on what to pack for longer trips, see Chapter 5, "Backcountry hikes".

The most dangerous and possibly deadly threat from being caught unprepared in freezing weather is **hypothermia**, a condition brought on when your body loses more heat than it can produce. Telltale signs of its onset include slowed or slurred speech, uncontrollable shivering and intense drowsiness, and anyone displaying these symptoms should seek medical attention immediately. If in the backcountry, you can fight the onset of hypothermia by getting the victim into a warm, windless shelter – be it a tent, cabin or, in an extreme emergency, thick stand of trees or hastily dug snow cave – right away. After removing all wet clothing, the victim then needs to be warmed: skin-to-skin is often the sole solution, meaning two naked bodies snuggled tightly in a single sleeping bag. Warm – but not too hot – beverages can help increase body temperature, but under no condition should alcohol be used. since it actually lowers body temperature.

Another threat in winter is **frostbite**, which is characterized by a loss of feeling and, visually, a lack of colour in body parts directly exposed to freezing temperatures. Though not as dangerous as hypothermia, anyone displaying frostbite-like symptoms should also seek medical attention straight away. If this is not an option, avoid undue pressure on affected areas – for example, avoid walking, if at all possible, on frostbitten feet, and do not rub frostbitten body parts – and immerse them in comfortably warm water until proper care arrives or is found.

Lightning, a result of the region's unpredictable weather, also presents a potentially significant danger. Should you be caught in a thunderstorm, avoid exposed ground and move as quickly and safely as possible to a forested area. Should lightning approach rapidly, seek out clumps of shrubs or trees of uniform height, and position yourself in a crouch atop insulated material such as a sleeping pad or even just an article of clothing. If in a group, do not huddle together; rather, spread out at least twenty feet apart until the danger passes.

Altitude sickness

Finally, be aware of the possibility of **altitude sickness** within the Yellowstone region, especially if you've travelled to the area directly from sea level. The condition's symptoms – which include lightheadedness, weakness, headache, nausea and breathlessness – are brought on by the body's struggle to process less oxygen at a higher altitude. Although there isn't actually less oxygen in the atmosphere up in the mountains, the barometric pressure is lower at lofted altitudes, so your body absorbs less oxygen from the air. Altitude sickness can be exacerbated by pushing it too hard on your first day; fatigue, poor nutrition and, unsurprisingly, a fierce hangover can also make it worse.

At the not exactly Himalayan heights attained in Yellowstone and even Grand Teton, altitude sickness is unlikely to bring on serious problems such as hydrocephalus (water on the brain). However, it's not unlikely for those who live at far lower altitudes to feel some of the above symptoms on a mountain hike; if this occurs, descend as quickly and safely as you can to a considerably lower altitude, if possible. Once you've done that, be sure to drink plenty of fluids (excepting alcohol), eat well and, above all, rest. If you follow these steps, the problem should sort itself out within 24 hours.

Travelling with children

Families looking to wean their kids off a steady diet of television, video games and the internet would be hard-pressed to find a better place to do so than the Yellowstone region. The parks go out of their way to cater to youngsters with programmes that all but the most hardened PlayStation junkies should enjoy, while certain gateway towns similarly lay out loads of family-friendly options. That said, parents should remember that both parks have their wilder elements and, unlike at a theme park or zoo, things have not been child-proofed. Kids must be clearly instructed on how to act around animals, be versed in safety precautions in thermal areas and always be kept close by when near water or heights.

For starters, many of the region's adult-oriented activities are perfectly suited for kids. Most of Yellowstone and Grand Teton's fireside **ranger programmes** are child-friendly and supply a free night's entertainment for the family; check park newspapers or the bulletin boards at visitor centres and campgrounds for current schedules. Similarly, the "shootouts" performed in Jackson and Cody nightly in summer are designed with families in mind, as are other events such as rodeos, parades and the popular, Old West-themed outdoor dining extravaganzas known as cowboy cookouts.

Many **outdoor activities** – from relaxed river-rafting trips and trail rides to skiing and snowboarding in winter – present fun opportunities for kids, often with the added bonus of reduced child rates. Depending on age, fitness and enthusiasm, many of the hikes listed in Chapter 4, "Day Hikes", can be taken by families as well.

As for kid-specific learning, a good place to start is the book section at most any park visitor centre. Most boast a wide selection of **children's titles**, ranging from simple picture and colouring books to native histories and activity guides based around wildflowers, rocks, animal tracks and more. Park **websites** (Ⓦwww.nps.gov /yell, www.nps.gov/grte) also have "For kids" sections, with plenty of pages to print out and use later during park exploration. Best is "Windows Into Wonderland" (see "Useful websites", see p.39), which offers a large selection of so-called electronic field trips covering Yellowstone's wildlife, natural history and more.

Kids can also join Yellowstone's **Junior Ranger Program** ($3), open to children between 5 to 12 years old. Sign up at any park visitor centre to receive a twelve-page guide filled with all manner of activities. Once a child completes enough of the outlined goals – which include attending a ranger-led programme and taking a short hike – they're suitably rewarded with a patch and even a brief "swearing-in" ceremony as a Junior Ranger. Grand Teton operates a similar programme ($1) at its Craig Thomas (Moose) and Colter Bay visitor centres, through which kids 8–12 can earn a "Young Naturalist" patch.

A final and more rewarding – albeit costlier – option for kids is to attend an **educational programme**, either with the family or alone on a camp-like break. One top option is the four-day Yellowstone for Families tour offered by the Yellowstone Association Institute (see p.196), which includes wildlife tracking, short hikes, photography and even painting; the package includes four nights lodging at *Mammoth Hot Springs Hotel*, daily breakfast and lunch, and in-park transport, all for about $1500 for a family of four. Down the road near Grand Teton National Park, **Teton Science Schools** (Ⓣ307/733-1313, Ⓦwww.tetonscience.org; see p.197) has a selection of summer programmes for six-year-olds and up, including teen courses on fly-fishing, backpacking, natural history and field ecology that span five days to four weeks.

Travel essentials

Costs

One unavoidable expense when visiting the parks is the **entrance fee**, priced at $25 per vehicle or $12 per person on foot, bicycle or skis; both are valid for seven days. See the "Park passes" section on p.36 for details on other types of passes.

Accommodation is likely to be your biggest single expense. Few hotel or motel rooms in the region cost under $60, and hostel accommodation is very limited. It's more usual to pay $60–100 for anything halfway decent in town, while rates for rooms in the parks and at the area's ski resorts can climb much higher. Camping, of course, is the cheapest way to go, with backcountry sites in both parks requiring only a free permit. Campsites at designated car-friendly campgrounds within the parks cost $12–20 per night, while those dotting nearby national forests range from free to $15 a night.

As far as **activities** go, hiking is the cheapest choice, costing nothing as long as you've got the proper gear. Fishing requires a state or park licence (see p.159), while rafting and horseback trips average $45–60 for two-hour to half-day trips. Come winter, all-day lift tickets at the area's premier resorts cost $81–91 (about half that at the lesser ski

hills), although snowshoeing and cross-country skiing are both good bargains, with one-day rentals generally priced in the $15–20 range. Those interested in snow-mobiling can expect to pay well over $100 for a half-day of fun, while guided trips into Yellowstone – currently the only way into the park on a snowmobile – start at around $200.

Electricity

110V AC. Most plugs are two-pronged and rather insubstantial. Some travel plug adapters don't fit American sockets, and British-made equipment won't work unless it has a voltage switching provision.

Entry requirements

Although US entry regulations have continually tightened up since 9/11, citizens of 36 countries – including the UK, Ireland, most Western European nations, Australia and New Zealand – visiting for a period of less than ninety days can still enter on the **Visa Waiver Program**; South African citizens remain ineligible for the Visa Waiver Program at the time of writing. The requisite visa waiver form (I-94W) is provided by airlines during check-in or on the plane before you complete and present it to an immigration official on arrival.

However, even with an I-94W form, each traveller must undergo the **US-VISIT** process at immigration, where both index fingers are scanned and a headshot is taken for file. Also, all passports accompanying an I-94W must now be a **machine-readable e-Passport**, and any issued after October 2006 must include a digital chip containing biometric data (most countries now automatically issue these, but check to be sure); anyone with an older passport will require some sort of visa for even a short stay in America. **Canadian** citizens must now provide documentation, although an enhanced secure driver licence is still an acceptable alternative to a passport – check ⓦwww.dhs.gov for updates on this.

Average daily budgets

These sample figures are based on one person travelling in a group of at least two with shared lodging and include meals ($45), accommodation ($60) and gas ($10), but not potential expenses such as tours and bicycle rental.

US$115
Can$115
£73
€86
Aus$116
NZ$150
ZAR786

Prospective visitors to the US from nations not indicated above require a valid passport and a non-immigrant visitor's visa for a maximum ninety-day stay. How you obtain your visa depends on your country and status on application – contact your nearest US embassy or consulate with queries. Regardless of nationality, visas are not issued to convicted criminals or anyone who owns up to being a drug dealer, fascist or even communist.

Finally, most travellers do not require inoculations to enter the US, though you may need **certificates of vaccination** if you're coming from cholera- or typhoid-infected areas in Asia or Africa – check with your doctor before you begin your trip.

Insurance

Although not compulsory, international travellers should have some form of **insurance**. Medical costs in the US, even for minor treatments, are shockingly high, so check to verify your coverage before beginning your trip.

Internet

Public computers with **internet** access are nearly non-existent in both parks. However,

Rough Guides travel insurance

Rough Guides has teamed up with WorldNomads.com to offer great **travel insurance** deals. Policies are available to residents of over 150 countries, with cover for a wide range of **adventure sports**, 24hr emergency assistance, high levels of medical and evacuation cover and a stream of **travel safety information**. Roughguides.com users can take advantage of their policies online 24/7, from anywhere in the world – even if you're already travelling. And since plans often change when you're on the road, you can extend your policy and even claim online. Roughguides.com users who buy travel insurance with WorldNomads.com can also leave a positive footprint and donate to a community development project. For more information go to ⓦ**www .roughguides.com/shop**.

should you bring along a laptop on your trip, the upper lobby inside Grand Teton's *Jackson Lake Lodge* (see p.187) has free wireless access, as does the lounge bar next to the *Mammoth Dining Room* in Yellowstone (see p.191). Online access in the gateway towns is much more prevalent, where local libraries and casual cafés (particularly in Jackson) can be invaluable resources; check the Listings section within each gateway town chapter.

Living in and around Yellowstone

Provided you don't mind being handed potentially uninspiring tasks, getting **work** in and around Yellowstone is relatively easy for US citizens and those with valid work visas, and both the summer and, to a lesser extent, winter seasons see long lists of positions become available. Besides students, visitors from other countries hoping for an extended legal stay in the United States should apply for a special work visa at the closest American Embassy before setting off. Different types of visas are issued, depending on your skills and planned length of stay, but unless you've got close relatives (parents or children over 21) or a prospective employer to sponsor you, your chances for a prolonged stay at best.

Now that the US government has introduced fines as high as $10,000 for companies caught employing anyone without a **social security number** (which effectively proves you're part of the legal workforce), **undocumented work** is not nearly as easy to find as it once was. Even in traditionally casual establishments such as restaurants and bars, things have fairly tightened up, and if you do find work, it's likely to be less visible and more poorly paid – think dishwasher instead of server. Making up a social security number, or borrowing one from somebody else, is of course completely illegal.

Those with the necessary work visa or social security number, however, will have no problem finding casual, seasonal work – provided you apply early. Ski resorts and area businesses start hiring in early November, while companies and establishments hiring summer staff usually fill all vacancies by early June. Most of the available positions focus on menial or customer service work in shops, hotels or restaurants, although if you have special skills relevant to the service industry or a sport, you may be able to land a position in your field. Don't expect plush accommodation or to make much more than minimum wage doing casual work – but at least you'll have plenty of scope for summer hiking, or perhaps a free ski pass.

Foreign students have a slightly better chance of a prolonged stay in the Yellowstone region, especially those who can arrange a semester or year abroad through their home university. Otherwise, you can apply directly to a university near Yellowstone, such as Montana State in Bozeman; if you're admitted – and if you can afford the painfully expensive fees charged to overseas students – it can be a great way to get to know the country, as the US grants more or less unlimited visas to those enrolled in full-time education. Another possibility for students is to explore the **Exchange Visitor Program** offered by the US government, for which participants are awarded a J-1 visa that entitles them to accept paid summer employment and apply for a social security number. The most prevalent jobs within the programme are **summer camp** counsellor and au pair positions, and while neither are lucrative nor everyone's idea of a good time, such work could provide a path to an extended US stay.

Local job sources

The following online resources may prove helpful in finding work in and around Yellowstone in advance.

Coolworks ⓦwww.coolworks.com. Places mainly younger workers in seasonal service industry positions within national parks, as well as at ski resorts and ranches, and with tour companies.

Craigslist ⓦwww.craigslist.org. Both Montana and Wyoming have their own dedicated sections on this all-in-one wonder site, good for not just daily job listings but also finding a place to live, buying/selling gear and a whole lot more.

Delaware North Companies ⓦwww .yellowstonegeneralstores.com. The concessionaire in charge of over a dozen general stores within Yellowstone offers many kitchen and retail positions annually.

Grand Teton Lodge Company ⓦwww.gtlc.com. Operating all lodging and dining facilities at *Jackson Lake Lodge*, *Jenny Lake Lodge* and Colter Bay Village, this respectable company hires more than a thousand employees each summer – check its website for loads of job postings.

Montana Workforce Division ⓦjobs.mt.gov. Official job site for the state of Montana; registration is required for most in-depth searches.

Wyoming Works ⓦwww.wyomingatwork.com. Official job site for the state of Wyoming; as with Montana's online job repository, registration is mandatory for the best results.

Xanterra ⓦwww.yellowstonejobs.com. Dedicated website for Yellowstone's largest (and sole lodging) concessionaire, with hundreds of positions ranging from housekeeper and restaurant server to snowcoach mechanic; the first place to look if you want to live and work within the park.

Yellowstone Park Service Stations ⓦwww .ypss.com. Yellowstone's smallest concessionaire, in charge of several gas stations and automotive repair shops; available positions include retail, accounting/clerical and auto tech.

Study and work programmes

If you're a non-US citizen and considering visiting the Yellowstone region to work, study or volunteer, several international organizations can help you find a job, school or assignment.

AFS Intercultural Programs ⓣ1-800/AFS-INFO, Canada ⓣ1-800/361-7248, UK ⓣ0113/242 6136, Australia ⓣ1300/131 736, NZ ⓣ0800/600 300, South Africa ⓣ11/447 2673; ⓦwww.afs.org. Intercultural exchange organization with programmes in over fifty countries including the US. Best for high school students looking to live abroad.

American Institute for Foreign Study US ⓣ1-866/906-2437, UK ⓣ020/7581 7300, Australia ⓣ02/8235 7000, ⓦwww.aifs.com. Language study and cultural immersion, as well as au pair and Camp America programmes.

BUNAC US ⓣ1-800/462 8622, UK ⓣ020/7251 3472, Australia ⓣ03/9329 3866, South Africa ⓣ021/418 3794; ⓦwww.bunac.org. Organizes working and volunteering holidays in a range of US destinations for students.

Camp America US ⓣ1-866/222-2074, Canada ⓣ902/422 1455, UK ⓣ020/7581 7373, Northern Ireland ⓣ028/9067 1929, Australia ⓣ02/8235 7000, New Zealand ⓣ09/416 5337; ⓦwww .campamerica.co.uk. Well-known company that places young people as counsellors or support staff in US summer camps.

Council on International Educational Exchange (CIEE) US ☎1-207/553-4000, ⓦwww .ciee.org. Leading NGO offering study programmes and volunteer projects around the world.
Earthwatch Institute US & Canada ☎1-800/776-0188, UK ☎01865/318 838, Australia ☎03/9682 6828; ⓦwww.earthwatch.org. Scientific expedition project that spans over fifty countries with environmental and archeological ventures worldwide, including Jackson Hole.

Mail

Post offices, located in a number of park villages and area towns, are usually open Monday to Friday from 9am to 5pm; some are open Saturday from 9am to noon or 1pm.
Letters weighing up to an ounce and sent within the US cost 44¢, while standard-size postcards cost 28¢; for most areas outside the US, airmail postcards and letters weighing up to an ounce cost 98¢. Airmail between the US and UK/Ireland may take a week, and up to two weeks for Australia, New Zealand and South Africa. Note that domestic letters not carrying a **zip code** are liable to get lost or at least seriously delayed; post offices – even abroad – should have directories for major US cities, while ⓦwww.usps.com has a handy zip code finder.Letters can be sent c/o **General Delivery** (what's known elsewhere as **poste restante**) to the larger post offices in the region – namely, Jackson and Cody – but must include the zip code and will only be held for thirty days before being returned to sender; make sure there's a return address on the envelope. To send a package out of the US, you'll need a green **customs declaration form**, available at any post office.

Maps

Along with the twenty-plus detailed maps within this guide, the excellent official maps handed out at park entrance stations should fulfil your needs while exploring by car. Hikers, however, will want **topographic maps** of any areas through which they plan to tramp – see Chapter 4, "Day hikes", for recommendations on the best such items for both parks.

Money

Constant upheaval in global money markets causes the relative value of the **US dollar** against other currencies to vary considerably.

At the time of writing, US$1 buys £0.60–0.70, €0.70–0.80, Can$1–1.05, Aus$1–1.20, NZ$1.30–1.50 and ZAR7–8.

ATMs are fairly easy to find throughout the region. In the parks, try any of the general stores, while banks, supermarkets and most convenience stores are the best places to check in the gateway towns. Seeing as you'll pay a small transaction fee for each withdrawal (usually $1–2), it makes sense to pull out a larger amount and budget accordingly. Banks in Jackson, Cody and West Yellowstone should be able to **exchange foreign travellers' cheques**, but it's unlikely you'll be able to exchange actual currency for US dollars.

Credit cards are accepted almost universally throughout the region, and are often necessary to rent gear or reserve a tour or guide. MasterCard, Visa and American Express are most prevalent, while other cards may not be accepted (or even recognized) in the US.

Wiring money

Having money **wired** from home using one of the companies listed below is neither convenient nor cheap, and should be considered a last resort.

Money-wiring companies

American Express US ☎1-888/227-4669, ⓦwww.americanexpress.com; UK ☎0870/600 1060, ⓦwww.americanexpress.co.uk.
MoneyGram US ☎1-800/666-3947; Ireland ☎0800/6663 9472; UK ☎0800/8971 8971; ⓦwww.moneygram.com.
Western Union US ☎1-800/325-6000; Australia ☎1800/649 565; New Zealand ☎09/270 0050; UK ☎0800/833 833; Ireland ☎1800/395 395; ⓦwww.westernunion.com.

Opening hours and public holidays

Both Yellowstone and Grand Teton are **open** 24 hours a day throughout the year. Come winter, however, most of Yellowstone's **entrance** stations and roads close, as does Teton Park Road within Grand Teton. See Chapter 7, "Winter Activities", for details on winter closures.

Business hours for specific visitor attractions, stores and services are included in the relevant accounts throughout the guide.

US national holidays

January 1 New Year's Day
January 3rd Monday Dr Martin Luther King, Jr's Birthday
February 3rd Monday Presidents' Day
May Last Monday Memorial Day
July 4 Independence Day
September 1st Monday Labor Day
October 2nd Monday Columbus Day
November 11 Veterans Day
November 4th Thursday Thanksgiving
December 25 Christmas

Visitor centres and **ranger stations** are typically open daily from 9am to 5pm, with extended hours (often 8am–7pm) during the height of summer. **Shops and services** are generally open Monday to Saturday from 9am to 5pm (sometimes opening earlier and closing later); many stores are also open on Sundays, and it's worth noting that Jackson and Cody have 24hr supermarkets.

On the national **public holidays** listed above, banks and offices are liable to be closed all day, with shops reducing their hours or closing altogether. The traditional summer season for tourism in the US runs from **Memorial Day** to **Labor Day** (see above for approximate dates). Attractions and businesses throughout the Yellowstone region – from visitor centres to restaurants – follow this timetable, with many closing or drastically reducing their hours outside these times. Unsurprisingly, the summer season is the busiest time in the parks, though with schools starting as early as mid August in many places, the last few weeks of summer aren't as busy as they once were.

Park passes

The most basic **entrance pass** to Yellowstone and Grand Teton costs $25 per vehicle, and is valid for seven days in both parks; rates drop to $20 for motorcyclists and snowmobilers, and $12 for bikers, hikers and skiers. Be sure to keep your receipt, as you'll need to show it each time you re-enter one of the parks.

If you plan to return to the parks over several weeks or longer, the $50 **Park Annual Pass** allows entry to Yellowstone and Grand Teton for a whole year; in the event you'll be touring a number of national parks around the US, meanwhile, your best investment is the $80 (and terribly unwieldy) **America the Beautiful National Parks and Federal Recreational Lands Annual Pass**, good for vehicle admission to most federally managed recreation sites across the country. US citizens or permanent residents 62 and older need only pay $10 for the **Senior** version of the pass, which provides lifetime access to all national parks; a free Access version does the same for all US citizens and permanent residents who are blind or permanently disabled.

Pets

While visiting Yellowstone and Grand Teton, visitors are best off leaving pets at home, as there's a long list of strict rules that must be followed when bringing them into the parks. For starters, pets are not allowed in the backcountry, nor on most trails and boardwalks, and they must be leashed at all times when out of the car; in addition, pets may not be left in cars alone for any long period of time. There are no kennels within the parks, so if you must bring a pet on your trip, check Yellowstone's website (Ⓦ www.nps.gov.yell) for a list of several reputable kennels in the region.

Phones

There are very few **area codes** in the Yellowstone region; Wyoming (Ⓣ 307), Montana (Ⓣ 406) and Idaho (Ⓣ 208) each have just one code. It's always necessary to include the area code (preceded by 1) when dialling beyond the local area, even though you may be in the same area code. For example, although Ⓣ 307 is the code for all of Wyoming, a call from Cody to Jackson is considered a long-distance call, so the prefix Ⓣ 1-307 must be dialled first.

Any number with Ⓣ 800, Ⓣ 866, Ⓣ 877 or Ⓣ 888 in place of the area code is **toll-free**; most major hotels, government agencies and car rental firms make these available, and we've listed them throughout the guide.

In virtually all cases, you're best off buying a **pre-paid phonecard** – universally available at convenience stores, gas stations and supermarkets – that allows for calls around the world. Often sold in increments of $5, $10 and $20, these are reasonably good value and can be used from both private and public phones.

Note that without a pre-paid phonecard, making calls from **hotel rooms** is always more expensive than from a pay phone; however, some hotels offer free local calls from rooms, so ask when you check in. Even with the ubiquity of mobile phones, **public telephones** can still be found in many locations – outside visitor centres, on street corners, and in hotels, bars and restaurants. These take 5¢, 10¢ and 25¢ coins, and the cost of a local call from a public phone is usually 50¢; when necessary, a voice comes on the line telling you to pay more. **Long-distance calls** are generally pricier – you'll need plenty of change – though much less expensive if made between 6pm and 8am; the cheapest rates are after 11pm and at weekends.

Mobile phones

For the most part, US visitors contracted with a major provider should find that their **mobile phones** work within certain areas of both parks, albeit much more widely in Grand Teton than Yellowstone; in Jackson, Cody and West Yellowstone, coverage is more consistently dependable. If visiting from **overseas** and you want to use your mobile phone, you'll need to check with your service provider as to whether this is possible, in addition to what it will cost; unless you have a tri-band phone, it's unlikely that a mobile bought for use in your home country will work in the US. Visit ⓦ www.telecomsadvice.org.uk for further information on using your mobile abroad.

Senior travellers

Yellowstone and Grand Teton cater well to **senior travellers**. As well as the obvious advantages of being free to travel for longer periods during the quieter, less expensive seasons of the year, these visitors are eligible for a tremendous variety of discounts.

Foremost among these deals is the **America the Beautiful National Parks and Federal Recreational Lands Senior Pass**, a $10 card that entitles any US citizen or permanent resident 62 and over to free admission for life to all federally managed recreation and historic areas – a list that includes nearly four hundred national parks, monuments, historic sites, seashores and the like; it also extends free park admission to up to three accompanying passengers in the cardholder's vehicle. Available at all Yellowstone and Grand Teton entrance stations, the pass

Useful telephone numbers

Emergencies ☎911 For fire, police or ambulance.
Operator ☎0.
Local directory information ☎411.
Long-distance directory information ☎1 + area code/555-1212.
Yellowstone information ☎307/344-7381.
Grand Teton information ☎307/739-3300.
International calls to the Yellowstone region:
Dial your country's international access code + 1 for the US + area code + phone number.

International calls from Yellowstone:
Dial ☎011 + country code + phone number. (Country codes: Australia ☎61, Ireland ☎353, New Zealand ☎64, South Africa ☎27, United Kingdom ☎44. For all other codes, dial ☎0 for the operator or check the front of the local White Pages.)

also offers a fifty percent reduction on camping, swimming and boat launch fees, so senior US travellers have little reason not to make this $10 investment.

Touring Yellowstone and Grand Teton is a breeze, provided you have your own transportation. A large percentage of sights within the parks can be seen either from the roads or via short paved walks, and disabled parking spots abound.

Before heading to the Yellowstone region, however, it's worth doing a bit of homework on **health** matters. The **high altitude** of the northern Rockies in general – and its mountain passes specifically – can aggravate certain conditions, and anyone with heart problems should tread carefully over 10,000ft, something to keep in mind if driving the Beartooth Highway east of Yellowstone, which crests nearly 11,000ft. Respiratory conditions can also be aggravated, so visitors with emphysema should avoid higher altitudes completely. Consult with your doctor about any other personal health concerns prior to hitting the road.

Time

The Yellowstone region is in the Mountain Time Zone, one hour ahead of the US West Coast (Pacific Time Zone), two hours behind the US East Coast (Atlantic Time Zone) and seven hours behind Greenwich Mean Time (GMT). Daylight Savings Time in the US, which advances clocks one hour early in the year before rolling them back one hour toward year's end, is observed between the second Sunday in March and the first Sunday in November.

Tipping

Unless service has been woefully substandard, you shouldn't walk out of a bar or restaurant without leaving a **tip** of at least fifteen percent; the same amount should be added to taxi fares. A hotel porter should receive roughly $1 for each bag carried. When paying by credit card, you're expected to add the tip to the bill before filling in the total amount and signing. Tour leaders, ski instructors, fishing guides and those in similar positions should also be tipped for a job well done.

Tourist information

Upon arriving at either park, you'll be handed a short stack of printed material that includes a handy park **map**, the seasonal park **newspaper** and any updates on road detours or construction delays. A helpful read overall, park newspapers are particularly useful for current schedules of ranger lectures and walking tours, along with up-to-date details on vital services such as lodging, campgrounds and restaurants.

Offering a wealth of information and typically located near major areas of interest are park **visitor centres**. Yellowstone is home to nine such venues in a range of sizes, including a brand-new building at Old Faithful and a seasonal desk inside the West Yellowstone Visitor Center just outside the park's West Entrance. To the south, five visitor centres are available in and adjacent to Grand Teton, including two relatively recent (and unmissable) centres at Moose and the Laurance S. Rockefeller Preserve. Basic contact information for each location is listed below; see individual chapters for opening/closing dates and hours of operation, along with accounts of the exhibits and amenities within each.

Visitor centre contact information

Yellowstone

Albright Visitor Center (Mammoth) ☎307/344-2263; see p.46.
Canyon Visitor Education Center ☎307/344-2550; see p.56.
Fishing Bridge Visitor Center ☎307/344-2450; see p.80.
Grant Visitor Center ☎307/344-2650; see p.76.
Madison Information Station ☎307/344-2821; see p.66.
Norris Geyser Basin Museum and Information Station ☎307/344-2812; see p.60.
Old Faithful Visitor Education Center ☎307/344-2750; see p.72.
West Thumb Information Center No phone; see p.76.
West Yellowstone Visitor Center ☎406/646-4403; see p.217.

Grand Teton

Colter Bay Visitor Center ☎307/739-3594; see p.106.

Craig Thomas Discovery and Visitor Center (Moose) T307/739-3399; see p.90.
Flagg Ranch Information Station T307/543-2327; see p.108.
Jenny Lake Visitor Center T307/739-3343; see p.102.
Laurance S. Rockefeller Preserve Visitor Center T307/739-3654; see p.90.

Outside the parks

The parks' five primary **gateway towns** all have visitor centres of varying usefulness, with the two largest and best located in Jackson and West Yellowstone; details for each of these are listed in the respective town chapters. Beside and beyond the gateway towns, both parks are completely encircled by national forests, which are nearly as scenic as the parks in many spots – and far less regulated. To the north and west of Yellowstone is **Gallatin National Forest**, a 1.8-million-acre tract established in 1899; its district offices in Gardiner (T406/848-7375) and Hebgen Lake (T406/823-6961) near West Yellowstone are the most useful stopovers for park visitors. To the east of Yellowstone is even larger **Shoshone National Forest**, the country's first national forest (originally set aside as part of Yellowstone Timberland Reserve in 1891) and stretching from the Montana border south to Lander, Wyoming. Headquarters for the 2.4-million-acre area are in Cody (T307/527-6241), though you'll also pass the informative **Wapiti Ranger Station** (T307/578-1200) when driving along the Buffalo Bill Cody Scenic Byway east of Yellowstone.

To the west of Yellowstone's southern reaches – as well as most of Grand Teton – is **Caribou-Targhee National Forest**, which comprises more than three million acres of land dotting eastern Idaho and just into western Wyoming; its two closest field offices are in Driggs (T208/354-2312) and Ashton (T208/652-7442), both in Idaho. Finally, flanking Grand Teton from the southwest all the way around to the northeast is the largest of all these public land holdings, 3.4-million-acre **Bridger-Teton National Forest**. Teton and Gros Ventre Wilderness areas are both included in Bridger-Teton's vast acreage, and are

managed by the Forest's Jackson office (T307/739-5400), located near the town's fine visitor centre.

Useful websites

While there are only a few places to access the internet within the parks themselves, the following sites may prove helpful when planning your trip from home or during a stay in one of the gateway communities.

General information

National Park Service W www.nps.gov/yell, www.nps.gov/grte. Packed with innumerable handy details – including PDFs of most newspapers and bulletins handed out at park visitor centres – the official sites for Yellowstone and Grand Teton should be the first online stop for anyone looking for all-purpose information.
Windows Into Wonderland W www.windowsinto wonderland.org. Created by the National Park Service, this wonderful kids' site is cleverly designed around novel "electronic field trips" that allow young users to learn about everything from Yellowstone's long history to the modern plight of the region's pronghorn.
Wolves in and around Yellowstone W www .nps.gov/yell/naturescience, www.niwa.us, www.wolftracker.com, www.wolf.org. From official government reports to naturalist blogs, the Web is filled with several sites about Yellowstone's alternately beloved and despised wolves; this small sampling includes sites offering updates on current issues and pack formations, with links to other sites.
Yellowstone Volcano Observatory (YVO) W volcanoes.usgs.gov/yvo. The official site for the YVO – a research and education partnership between Yellowstone National Park, the US Geological Survey and University of Utah – monitors geologic activity in the park and offers up-to-the-minute updates. Also features links to recent stories on volcanic or earthquake activity in the region.

Government websites

Australian Department of Foreign Affairs W www.dfat.gov.au.
British Foreign & Commonwealth Office W www.fco.gov.uk.
Canadian Department of Foreign Affairs W www.international.gc.ca.
Irish Department of Foreign Affairs W www .foreignaffairs.gov.ie.
New Zealand Ministry of Foreign Affairs W www.mfat.govt.nz.

South African Department of Foreign Affairs
Ⓦ www.dfa.gov.za.
US State Department Ⓦ www.state.gov.

Outdoor activities

Climbing Ⓦ www.tetonclimbing.blogspot.com.
Climbing and backcountry information for the Tetons;
only updated in summer.
Cross-country skiing and snowshoeing
Ⓦ www.yellowstone.net/skiing.htm. Suggestions
for day trips around Mammoth, Tower and Old
Faithful.
Fishing Ⓦ www.yellowstoneflyfishing.com,
www.greater-yellowstone.com/fishing.html. Maps,
charts, videos and more.
Hiking Ⓦ www.yellowstone.net/hiking.htm,
www.grand.teton.national-park.com/hike.htm. Lists
of popular hikes, trail descriptions and information on
backcountry camping.
Swimming and soaking Ⓦ www.swimmingholes
.org/we.html. Site devoted to hot springs all over the
western US, with a section dedicated to the
Yellowstone region. Includes helpful information on
how to reach the elusive Mr Bubbles hot spring in
Yellowstone's Cascade Corner – one of the few such
soaking-friendly features in the park.

Park support organizations

Grand Teton Association Ⓦ www
.grandtetonpark.org. Since 1937, this organization
has dedicated itself to supporting interpretive and
educational activities in its namesake park, from
operating several visitor centre bookstores to
presenting historical festivals in and around the park.
Its website stocks an excellent selection of books
related to the park and its outlying region.
Grand Teton National Park Foundation Ⓦ www
.gtnpf.org. A nonprofit organization devoted to raising
private funds for projects that preserve and protect
the national park; its most recent large-scale project
was the new Craig Thomas Discovery and Visitor
Center at Moose.
Greater Yellowstone Coalition Ⓦ www
.greateryellowstone.org. Working to keep the Greater
Yellowstone ecosystem intact and healthy by limiting
development in critical grizzly and bison habitat, this
conservation group's greatest legacy is perhaps its
role in halting the New World Mine just northeast of
Yellowstone in the mid 1990s.
Yellowstone Association Ⓦ www.yellowstone
association.org. Yellowstone's major nonprofit
educational partner – see p.196 for a detailed
description of its year-round offerings.

The Yellowstone Park Foundation Ⓦ www.ypf
.org. Founded in 1996, this fundraising group has
become a major force by spearheading Yellowstone
projects ranging from trail improvements and
improved visitor facilities to wildlife studies.

Travellers with disabilities

Travellers with **disabilities** are likely to find
Yellowstone and Grand Teton – as with the
US in general – to be much more in tune
with their needs than most other countries.
Both parks have done an admirable job
updating their facilities and continue to do
so whenever funding permits. Visitors in
wheelchairs will find that most toilets in
picnic areas and campgrounds are accessible, as are several self-guided boardwalk
trails; Yellowstone even features an accessible fishing area on the Madison River and
an accessible backcountry campsite at Ice
Lake. Both parks have accessibility information available at their entrance stations
and visitor centres, as well as on their
respective websites.

Citizens or permanent residents of the US
who provide documentation certifying
permanent disabilities can obtain the
**America the Beautiful National Parks and
Federal Recreational Lands Access Pass**,
a free lifetime entrance pass to both parks,
as well as all other federally operated parks,
monuments, historic sites, recreation areas
and wildlife refuges that charge entrance
fees. The pass must be picked up in person,
and also provides a fifty percent discount on
fees charged for camping, boat launching
and parking, and similar charges.

Major **car rental** firms can provide vehicles
with hand controls; note that these are usually
only available on more expensive models,
and you'll need to reserve well in advance.

Contacts and resources

Yellowstone Park Accessibility Coordinator, Box
168, Yellowstone National Park, WY 82190-0168
☏ 307/344-2017, TDD ☏ 307/344-2386, Ⓦ www
.nps.gov/yell.
Grand Teton TDD (Telecommunications Device for
the Deaf) ☏ 307/739-3400, Ⓦ www.nps.gov/grte.

The Parks

The Parks

1 Northern Yellowstone 43

2 Southern Yellowstone 63

3 Grand Teton 85

4 Day Hikes 109

5 Backcountry hiking and camping 144

6 Summer activities 158

7 Winter activities 170

Northern Yellowstone

A long with the entrance roads from Gardiner to the north and Cooke City to the northeast, **northern Yellowstone** covers the upper half of the park's figure-eight Grand Loop Road; the section of the park covered by the road's southern section is detailed in Chapter 2. If Old Faithful is the star attraction within the park's southern half, then the **Grand Canyon of the Yellowstone** leads the pack of must-see sights within the northern half – even if the region's geysers and hot springs dried up long ago, the canyon would have still earned Yellowstone its national park status. Carved by the Yellowstone River, which makes a dramatic entrance by way of two impossibly picturesque waterfalls, the canyon's steep honey-coloured walls are dappled in rusted oranges and reds. The panorama from **Artist Point**, at the canyon's south end, is the park's most photographed scene for very good reason, and it pays to arrive early to beat the crowds and get the best light conditions.

North of the Canyon area, the Yellowstone River flows past the hulking mass of **Mount Washburn** and near **Tower Fall** into the Northern Range, home to some of the country's largest elk and bison populations. Prosaically referred to as "North America's Serengeti" for its abundant wildlife, nearby **Lamar Valley** is also home to predators such as grizzlies, wolves and mountain lions, and many repeat visitors spend much of their time parked roadside here hoping for a sighting.

The two final highlights of the north loop are major hydrothermal sites. The first, **Mammoth Hot Springs**, stays open to car traffic year-round and is an essential stop for both its fascinating travertine terraces and **Fort Yellowstone**, home to the US army from 1886–1918 and now the park headquarters. To the south is **Norris Geyser Basin**, boasting the world's tallest spouter, **Steamboat Geyser**, along with scores of eerily sizzling pools and steaming vents.

Sights and orientation

The following tour of northern Yellowstone begins at **Mammoth Hot Springs**, the most accessible village within the park; **Gardiner**, Montana is only five miles away. The nearly fifty-mile highway heading east from Mammoth through the wildlife-rich Northern Range to tiny Cooke City is the sole portion of the Grand Loop Road open through the winter months. Just past rustic **Roosevelt Lodge**, the highway splits off from the Grand Loop and leads through famed **Lamar Valley**, a pre-eminent area for spotting the likes of bison, elk, pronghorn and wolves from the roadside.

South from Roosevelt and back on the Grand Loop, the highway passes narrow **Tower Fall** before climbing past **Mount Washburn** and over **Dunraven Pass** in a thrilling series of hairpins bordered by steep drops. Much of the roadway here runs parallel to (but not within sight of) the epic **Grand Canyon of the Yellowstone**, the multicoloured walls of which can be seen from dramatic side roads edging the

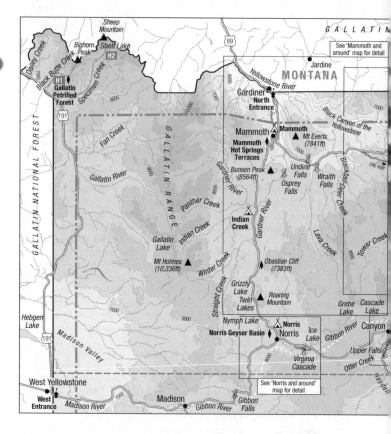

north and south rims. After gawking at powerful **Upper and Lower Falls**, visitors can repair to nearby Canyon Village to eat, sleep or drop in on Yellowstone's finest visitor centre. From here, the road west leads to **Norris Geyser Basin**, then north past striking Obsidian Cliff and brilliant Golden Gate Canyon back to Mammoth; the area south of Canyon Village, including Hayden Valley, is covered in Chapter 2.

Mammoth Hot Springs and around

Long the entry point for explorers, **Mammoth Hot Springs** has always been park headquarters. Regional visitors were coming to bathe in the springs' allegedly therapeutic waters since the early 1870s, and within a decade the railroad was ferrying in tourists by stagecoach from a string of steadily approaching terminals to the north, eventually ending at Gardiner's 1903 train station. By 1883, when the hastily erected *National Hotel* opened its doors, Mammoth was in full bloom, home to all manner of buildings from stables to the homes of park administrators and the first of Yellowstone's souvenir stands. With the park in desperate need of law and order, the army took over in 1886, setting up camp by the hot spring

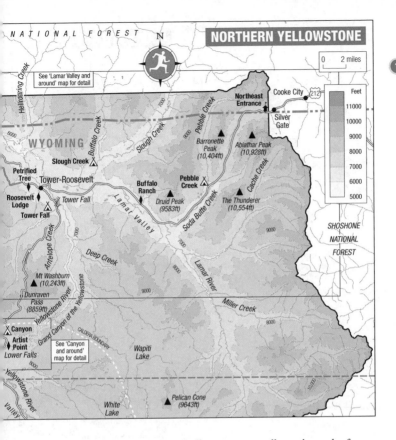

terraces and eventually building **Fort Yellowstone**, a small town's worth of stone structures incorporated within Mammoth village and remaining in full use today.

Lower in altitude and thus typically warmer than Yellowstone's other visitor hubs, Mammoth remains open to cars year-round. Buzzing with a mix of tourist and administrative activity, the area demands at least a full afternoon's attention. At Mammoth's northern end are the rows of buildings built by the army, including what is now the **Albright Visitor Center**, the best place to begin a visit to this area of the park. To the west are the visitor amenities, centred around the rather plain **Mammoth Hot Springs Hotel**, built mostly in 1937 on the site of the demolished *National Hotel*.

Mammoth's elk

Particularly around dawn and dusk, it can seem as if there are more elk in Mammoth than people. Drawn year-round to the area's irrigated grasses, the grazers are a common fixture, to the point that residents must fence in all their trees and flowers to keep them from being nibbled away. Regardless of how comfortable the elk seem, they are *not* tame: cows with calves are particularly irritable in spring, while bulls get more aggressive during the autumn rut. Keep at least a **25-yard distance at all times** – including your car, as bulls have charged and even attacked vehicles on occasion.

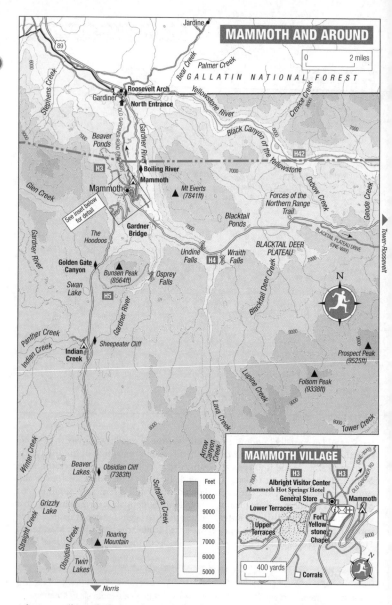

A longer walk south leads to the most popular attraction, unique **travertine terraces** of barnacle-like deposits cascading down vapour-shrouded hillsides.

Albright Visitor Center and Fort Yellowstone

The first thing many visitors do when touring Mammoth, and often Yellowstone on the whole, is pay a visit to the **Albright Visitor Center** (late May to early

Sept daily 8am–7pm, rest of year 9am–5pm; ☎307/344-2263). Housed in what used to be the army's bachelor officers' quarters, the 1909 stone structure marks the northwestern edge of **Fort Yellowstone** and acts as official park headquarters. Along with an information desk and a Yellowstone Association-stocked bookstore, **exhibits** inside focus on the park's natural and human history, from the earliest expeditions and the army's 32 years in control through the Park Service decades since.

Of most interest are the glass cases displaying items from the two expeditions that literally put Yellowstone on the map – the Washburn Expedition of 1870 (see p.253) and the Hayden Survey of 1871–72 (see p.254) – including a knife and tobacco pouch used by gutsy Captain Gustavus Doane and five pistols belonging to Nathaniel Pitt Langford; both were key members of the Washburn Expedition, with Langford becoming Yellowstone's first-ever Superintendent within a year of their return. Skip the bland twenty-minute films in the nearby theatre and instead head further back to the rooms lined with works by artist **Thomas Moran** and photographer **William Jackson**, each brought along on the Hayden Survey to provide visual evidence to a public that, at the time, was sceptical at best of the park's purported geothermal wonders. Until being moved to the temperature-controlled confines of Yellowstone's Heritage and Research Center in Gardiner (see p.231) in 2005, many of Moran's original field sketches, along with other historical artefacts, were stored in the building's leaky basement, causing a mad ranger rush to evacuate them during storms. The sole Moran original on display now is an 1892 painting entitled "Lower Falls of the Yellowstone". Jackson's black-and-white photos of the park's geysers and expedition members are worth a similarly long look, as is his massive box camera on display. Further displays upstairs hold bits and pieces from the fur-trapping era and local Sheepeater tribe, including numerous taxidermy exhibits; quotes from Washburn Expedition member **Truman Everts** (see box, p.50) pepper displays throughout.

Just around the corner from the centre are the **Mammoth Clinic** and **Post Office** (Mon–Fri 8.30am–5pm), the latter built in 1936 in a style known as French Renaissance Moderne. Painted white with light blue trim, it's one of Yellowstone's most elegant buildings, guarded by a pair of stone grizzlies and, on occasion, flesh-and-blood elk grazing on the front lawns.

Fort Yellowstone

For fifteen years from its creation in 1872, a succession of five civilian superintendents was put in charge of Yellowstone. Hamstrung by minuscule budgets, these administrations were overwhelmed by a maddening combination of poachers, petty thieves, greedy businesses and souvenir-stealing tourists willing to chip Yellowstone away one pocketful at a time. A tightfisted Congress had little choice but to call in the **army**, and on August 13, 1886, **Captain Moses Harris** from Fort Custer in the Montana Territories marched in with fifty men and assumed the title of Park Superintendent. Harris was the first of a dozen officers to successfully lead the park, with the army staying on until 1918 when the newly formed National Park Service could take over. (For a more detailed story, see the "History" section in Contexts, p.258.)

As the main hub of activity within Yellowstone, Harris immediately set about erecting temporary **Camp Sheridan** by the base of the terraces to the south. Realizing that it wasn't going anywhere soon, the army began lobbying Congress for more funds, and by 1891 the first series of buildings within permanent **Fort Yellowstone** were erected; two more major waves of construction occurred in 1897 and 1909. Most of these buildings remain standing and now function as offices and residences for park employees, and are best seen on a **walking tour** beginning from the Albright Visitor Center. Pick up the useful *Fort Yellowstone Tour Guide* (50¢), including a map outlining a thirty-minute self-guided tour, or check inside the visitor centre for details on free, hour-long, summer evening tours led by park rangers.

The most appealing of the nearly two dozen buildings spread along Fort Yellowstone's two main streets include the sandstone **Field Officer's Quarters**, a suitably impressive home built in 1909 for the post commander and still the residence of the current Park Superintendent, and the simple yet elegant **chapel** at the fort's southeastern end – built in 1913, it was the army's final structure and was constructed using native stone now attractively flecked with orange lichen. The chapel's interior can only be seen during one of three weekly services (April–Nov: interdenominational services Sun 8.30 & 10am; Catholic Mass Sat 7pm). A short walk from the chapel is one of the fort's more dejected-looking buildings, the **Guard House**, built in 1909 and still the park jail to this day. To complete the tour as a temporary inmate might, walk west, past the old barracks and stables that now house park offices and equipment, to the 1903 **US Engineer's Office**, located across from the visitor centre. Designed by the same architectural firm behind New York City's Grand Central Station, the striking green-roofed structure is known locally as both the "Pagoda" for its triangular roof, and the "Temple of Truth", as it has long housed the park's courthouse.

Mammoth Hot Springs Terraces

Building the boardwalks weaving through **Mammoth Hot Springs Terraces** – a short walk south of Fort Yellowstone – is one of the most thankless jobs in Yellowstone. There's no telling when one of the carefully crafted wooden paths can become obsolete, as the colourful springs and terraces are capable of drying up at any time, evinced by dormant terraces seen throughout this area. Be prepared to spend much of your time on boardwalks skirting somewhat underwhelming thermal activity, and don't be surprised if that colourful terrace you remember from a previous visit is now parched and crumbling away.

That's not to say Mammoth's terraces have all dried out. The overall activity has remained consistent for centuries, and you're guaranteed a weird and wild

---

Mammoth mementos

A park brochure claims that, at Mammoth, "rock forms before your eyes". Certainly that's overstating the case, but only slightly. It's estimated that as much as a dozen tonnes of travertine are deposited in the area each week, with some terraces growing a foot taller in just a year's time. Taking advantage of this natural feat, Yellowstone entrepreneurs in the late 1880s used the springs for a one-of-a-kind **curio business**. Started by one-time Assistant Superintendent (and later hotelier) **George Henderson** and perfected afterwards by Mammoth storeowner **Ole Anderson**, racks were placed under flowing water at the most active terraces. Before touring the park, visitors would drop off trinkets such as pine cones and tin toys to be placed on these racks. It only took a few days for the item to become completely covered in travertine, so when these same visitors returned, they were the proud owner of a "**coated specimen**". Before being eventually banned, Anderson began coating a wide range of items – vases, statues, decorative horseshoes – and selling so many that his store became known as the Specimen House. These items are rare antiques today, as the era's bumpy wagon and train rides tended to jar the travertine loose; nonetheless, Yellowstone's Heritage and Research Center has a few of Anderson's creations in its collection.

selection of chalky-white terraces tinted a splendid array of greens, yellows, browns and oranges by various heat-loving micro-organisms known as thermophiles. These sculpted terraces are composed of **travertine**, a form of limestone that, having been dissolved and carried to the surface by boiling water, is deposited as tier upon tier of steaming stone. The springs may lack the drama of the more explosive geysers, but there's nothing else in the park that quite resembles this alien arrangement; groups of **elk** often provide a curious photo opportunity as they bask amid them for warmth. It takes around ninety minutes to stroll the two sections of boardwalk that traverse the Upper and Lower Terraces, with an additional thirty minutes needed to loop Upper Terrace Drive by car. Free ninety-minute ranger **tours** of the terraces depart from Palette Spring throughout summer – inquire at the Albright Visitor Center's information desk for exact times.

Lower Terraces

The spider's web of boardwalks spilling across and up the steep hillside of the **Lower Terraces** lead past Mammoth's most famed travertine sights. Towards the flatter, northern end of the terraces looms **Liberty Cap**, the 45ft cone of a dormant hot spring thought to be 2500 years old, so named by the Hayden Survey in 1871 for the peaked hats worn by colonial resistors during the Revolutionary War. At nearby **Palette Spring**, water cascades down the scalloped edges of colourful steps ranging from three inches to three feet in height; another dormant hot spring cone, **Devil's Thumb**, sits here as well. The hillside beyond is covered with large expanses of travertine terraces, some of which have been dormant for well over a decade. Even when dry, however, the likes of **Cleopatra Terrace** and **Minerva Terrace** – the latter aptly named after the Roman goddess of sculptors – are remarkable, coloured a near-blinding snowy white and composed of thousands of tiny terraces facing all directions. The uphill hike north to Beaver Ponds (see **H3**, p.116) also begins beside the Lower Terraces.

Upper Terraces

A long row of wooden steps climb from the Lower Terraces to the **Upper Terraces**, but as many of the sights are strung along a paved 1.5-mile drive, it's worth being lazy this one time and driving to Upper Terrace Drive. The first stop on the narrow one-way loop is also the finest, with boardwalks leading to a series of viewpoints looking over the Lower Terraces and down to Fort Yellowstone. The most intriguing of the ever-changing hydrothermal features is steamy **Canary Spring**, which bubbles up on the edge of an expanse of white limestone dotted with small terraces. The picturesque spring earned its name in the late 1800s due to a preponderance of yellow bacteria, still present today along with brilliant blue and orange tones. Beyond here, many of the named features along the road such as **New Highland Terrace** and **White Elephant Back Terrace** have been dormant for years, leaving little more than crumbling limestone in their wake. A dramatic exception is **Orange Spring Mound**, a giant brain-shaped blob of travertine with steaming water leaking down all of its sides; bracketed by gnarled dead trees and half-coated with bright orange bacteria, it's perhaps Mammoth's most strangely photogenic feature.

North to Gardiner

Montana's friendly town of **Gardiner** hugs the park border only five miles north of Mammoth, and the main connecting highway dips down nearly 1000ft through a dusty, desert-like canyon formed by the **Gardner River** (see p.228 for an explanation of the different spellings). From Fort Yellowstone, the road north twists down past *Mammoth Campground* and an incongruous, suburban-like tract of employee homes before curving alongside **Mount Everts** (7842ft), named after wayward explorer Truman Everts (see box below) and layered in fossils washed up from an ancient inland sea. At the two-mile mark, the road crosses into Montana at the **45th Parallel**, indicating that you're halfway between the Equator and North Pole; considering that temperature extremes here can range between -20 and 100°F, you'll probably feel far closer to one or the other, depending on the season.

Also at the border is the parking area for the **Boiling River** section of the Gardner, a popular **swimming hole** located along a dirt path a half-mile upstream (back toward Mammoth), where thermal waters spill down travertine terraces to create ideal soaking conditions. The river is closed in spring and early summer when swollen by snowmelt, but reopens in late June and remains open until winter; note that bathing suits are required, and if visiting in September or October, be sure to not get caught amid the area's massive herds of elk in rut that often mingle riverside. To find the best **soaking pools** rimmed by stones, walk to the very end of the trail where it makes a swooping left turn back toward the river.

From the Boiling River parking area, it's three more miles to the North Entrance Station and the **Roosevelt Arch** (see p.230) just beyond. On the way, keep an eye out for bighorn sheep clinging to the steep, rocky walls on both sides of the highway.

Lost in Yellowstone

The second organized party to explore Yellowstone was the nineteen-man **Washburn Expedition**, which spent a month trudging through the wilderness in the late summer of 1870. There were no battles with natives or bloody grizzly attacks to spice up their tales, and other than severe malnutrition toward the tour's end, the harshest fate to befall the group fell on **Truman C. Everts**. Everts, at 54 the party's oldest explorer, was between jobs at the time the expedition left from Helena, Montana, and joined for the adventure; he ended up with plenty more than he bargained for, however, after accidentally splitting off from the party south of Yellowstone Lake. His fellow explorers sent out search parties, but dense forest and a sudden snowstorm made tracking impossible, and they were forced to continue on without their comrade after several days, leaving behind caches of precious supplies in their wake. The hopelessly near-sighted Everts never did find the trail, and instead camped by Heart Lake, living on little more than roots while hoping to be found. The disoriented explorer eventually struck north, and for a total of 37 days, wandered lost in Yellowstone, misplacing one important item after another – including a lens he used to start fires – while slowly wasting away. Though most of Helena's citizens believed Everts to be dead, members of the Washburn Expedition offered a $600 reward for finding him upon their return. Two brave locals immediately set off in search and, some days later, found the shoeless, dirt-encrusted Everts in the park's northern reaches, five miles east of what is now known as **Mount Everts**; in a near-tragic turn, the men nearly shot him at first, mistaking him for a bear. Frostbitten and emaciated, the barely alive Everts was carried back to Montana and slowly nursed back to health. The dramatic experience must not have left much lasting harm, as Everts fathered a son two decades later at the ripe age of 75. A thoroughly cantankerous man, Everts also refused his saviours their just reward – he brazenly claimed he would have made it back safely without their help – while also complaining bitterly until his death at 85 that the far more grand Mount Sheridan, above his camp at Heart Lake, should have been named after him.

East to Tower-Roosevelt

The 47-mile road east from Mammoth to the Tower-Roosevelt Junction, and beyond to the Northeast Entrance, is the only highway in Yellowstone open through the winter. It's only eighteen miles from Mammoth to the junction fronting *Roosevelt Lodge*, but a number of diversions mean you can easily spend several hours along this initial section in any season. Keep your camera at the ready, as the road passes through Yellowstone's **Northern Range**, 200,000 acres of open country that hosts some of the park's largest populations of wolves, coyotes, grizzly and black bears, bison and mule deer. With upwards of 10,000 elk living hereabouts as well, this is also the finest stretch in the park for witnessing bull elks bugling and challenging each other for mates during the autumn rut.

After crossing the 200ft-tall **Gardner Bridge** just over a mile east of Mammoth, the road leads past two turn-offs, each with waterfall views. First is **Undine Falls**, where a roadside platform looks over to the falls off Lava Creek, plunging 60ft over three tiers. Several unmarked paths lead down to different vistas (as well as a smaller plunge downstream), but **only go with an expert guide**; several visitors have fallen to their deaths in the area. Far less risky is the short trail out to **Wraith Falls** (see █ **H4** █, p.117), leading south from the highway a mile further on. Continuing east, the highway passes by marshy **Blacktail Ponds**, where bison occasionally get stuck in the quicksand-like mud and soon become easy prey for grizzlies and local scavengers. Also along this stretch of road is the **Forces of the Northern Range Trail**, a half-mile boardwalk featuring exhibits that touch briefly on glaciation and wildflowers; while here, look for the fascinating casts of wolf tracks, as well as the board describing Huckleberry Ridge Tuff, the first of three supervolcano eruptions to have occurred in the region over the last two million years.

Blacktail Plateau Drive and the Petrified Tree

Halfway between Mammoth and Roosevelt, the one-way eastbound **Blacktail Plateau Drive** cuts off the main highway for a slow seven-mile ramble across wildlife-rich Blacktail Deer Plateau. When accessible – the road is open only to cross-country skiers in winter, and closes whenever the mud becomes too much in summer – it's well worth the scenic detour, passing through peaceful, rolling sagebrush hills offering panoramic views before rejoining the highway just before the narrow half-mile turn-off leading to the **Petrified Tree**. Fenced in to protect it from the fate of the two other trunks that also stood here before they were chipped away by souvenir hunters, this tall and jagged trunk was once a redwood tree that became coated in volcanic ash some fifty million years ago. Additional petrified trunks can be seen in neighbouring Gallatin Petrified Forest (see █**H1**█, p.115).

Tower-Roosevelt and Lamar Valley

Open year-round, the Northeast Entrance Road winds eastward from the **Tower-Roosevelt Junction** through **Lamar Valley**, the scene of daily life-and-death struggles between predators (grizzlies, wolves, mountain lions) and prey (elk, bison, pronghorn, mule deer). This valley is where two of the country's most storied wildlife experiments began, namely the restoration of both bison (see box, p.54) and the grey wolf (see *The wolves of Yellowstone* colour section). It's also where the park's first gamekeeper, **Harry Yount**, was stationed in 1880 to help stop the illegal slaughter of animals; Yount lasted only one frigid winter, but he's considered the forefather of the modern-day park ranger. Back at the highway junction, **Roosevelt Lodge** holds a tiny, rustic cluster of amenities and a bustling horse corral, while two miles south a short paved trail leads to a raised viewing platform for **Tower Fall**, although the best view is from the bottom, reachable on foot. South again looms the largest landmark in the area, **Mount Washburn**, whose lookout tower can be accessed by a much more demanding half-day hike or bicycle ride.

Lamar Valley

We stopped at this place and for my own part I almost wished I could spend the remainder of my days in a place like this where happiness and contentment seemed to reign in wild romantic splendor surrounded by majestic battlements which seemed to support the heavens and shut out all hostile intruders.

Osborne Russell, 1835

As one of the area's earliest explorers, Osborne Russell may have had a different name for **Lamar Valley** – he called it Secluded Valley – but his descriptions ring true to this day. The wide-open valley is a genuine highlight of Yellowstone, with wildlife-watchers gathering come sunrise and sunset at the many roadside viewpoints between Slough Creek and Pebble Creek with folding chairs and binoculars, patiently waiting for a bear to lumber out of the forest or a wolf pack to gallop into view in hot pursuit of an ill-fated elk.

With few specific sights in Lamar Valley per se, it's the overall scenic beauty along this thirty miles of highway leading to the Northeast Entrance that makes for such an essential tour. After crossing high above the **Yellowstone River**, the road from *Roosevelt Lodge* leads five miles east past a handful of trailheads (including **H6**, p.118) and across the **Lamar River** to the turn-off for *Slough Creek Campground* (see **H7**, p.118). Look for the mailbox tucked beside the restroom at the intersection here; it's used by the isolated *Silver Tip Ranch*, tucked into Absaroka-Beartooth Wilderness beyond the park's northern border fifteen miles away and accessible only by horse. For the next ten miles, the road then dips and curves along and away from the Lamar River as it slices through narrow **Lamar Canyon** and, further upstream, spills across the grassy valley floor in huge lazy bends. Cottonwood trees line the riverbanks, around which groups of elk and pronghorn weave among herds of bison.

Halfway through Lamar Valley, the road passes the park's premier education facility, the Yellowstone Association's Buffalo Ranch (see p.54), before meeting the rushing intersection of the Lamar River and **Soda Butte Creek**. This is a good spot to watch hyperactive American dippers diving in and out of the water for bugs, as well as bighorn sheep clinging to the steep crags of Druid Peak (9584ft) on the road's opposite side. As the Lamar River cuts south, the road switches to the banks of Soda Butte Creek, passing the Soda Butte Trailhead (see **H8**, p.119) on the way out of Lamar Valley and on to *Pebble Creek Campground*. En route to the campground, you'll pass a huge **travertine mound** created by a now-dormant hot spring that gives Soda Butte Creek its name. The final ten miles to the Northeast Entrance, half of which run through Montana, are most notable for dramatic head-on views of the fortress-like masses of **Barronette** and **Abiathar Peaks**, as well as late-summer fishing in Soda Butte Creek. For details on the tiny towns of Silver Gate and Cooke City beyond the Northeast Entrance, see Chapter 14.

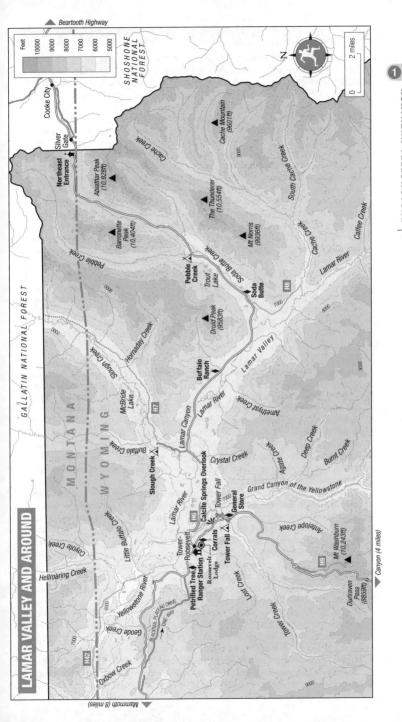

LAMAR VALLEY AND AROUND

Beartooth Highway

SHOSHONE NATIONAL FOREST

GALLATIN NATIONAL FOREST

MONTANA

WYOMING

Cooke City

Silver Gate

Northeast Entrance

Abiathar Peak (10,928ft)

Barronette Peak (10,404ft)

Pebble Creek

Cache Mountain (9601ft)

The Thunderer (10,554ft)

Mt Norris (9936ft)

South Cache Creek

Cache Creek

Calfee Creek

Lamar River

Cache Creek

Pebble Creek

Trout Lake

Soda Butte

Soda Butte Creek

Druid Peak (9583ft)

Buffalo Ranch

H8

Lamar Valley

Lamar River

Amethyst Creek

Deep Creek

Burnt Creek

McBride Lake

Slough Creek

Homaday Creek

Buffalo Creek

Slough Creek

Lamar Canyon

H7

Crystal Creek

Agate Creek

Grand Canyon of the Yellowstone

Little Buffalo Creek

Coyote Creek

Hellroaring Creek

Lamar River

Calcite Springs Overlook

H5

Tower Fall

General Store

Antelope Creek

Tower-Roosevelt

Petrified Tree

Ranger Station

Roosevelt Lodge

Corrals

Tower Fall

Mt Washburn (10,243ft)

H9

Dunraven Pass (8859m)

Lost Creek

Tower Creek

BLACKTAIL PLATEAU DRIVE ONE-WAY

Geode Creek

Yellowstone River

Oxbow Creek

H2

Mammoth (8 miles)

Canyon (4 miles)

Feet
10000
9000
8000
7000
6000
5000

N

0   2 miles

53

1

Bison in Yellowstone

Considering the massive herd usually seen grazing within Lamar Valley, it's hard to fathom that **bison** were once nearly completely hunted out of the entire Yellowstone region. While the park can proudly claim to be the sole area of the United States where bison have continually lived in the wild since primitive times, their total destruction was only a few poachers' bullets away.

By 1901, Yellowstone's total bison population had dipped to as few as two dozen. To protect the remaining creatures – and, it must be said, for the enjoyment of tourists – a pen was built in Mammoth in the early 1900s. In addition to the native population, ranched-raised bison were imported and placed inside, and within five years the herd of nearly sixty bison had outgrown its enclosure. The solution was to move them to the newly built **Buffalo Ranch** in Lamar Valley in 1907, and gamekeepers at the ranch managed to raise bison numbers to more than a thousand by the 1930s, treating them like domestic cattle and feeding them hay throughout the winter months. A portion of this "tame" herd was even used in filming the 1933 Western, *The Thundering Herd*. By the early 1950s, management practices evolved to more natural approaches, and operations at the ranch were suspended. Bison were set free to roam as they pleased, though the park still employed drastic **culling** measures due to mistaken assumptions on over-grazing; as a result, the 1960s saw bison numbers plummet to fewer than three hundred. Culling was banned in 1968, after which the current practice of letting nature balance out the population was employed. With abundant terrain to graze upon, Yellowstone's bison population has thrived, and now around 3900 bison roam the park in **two main herds**: the Northern Herd in and around Lamar Valley's high plateaus; and the Central Herd, a catch-all term for bison living everywhere else in the park, although most in this latter group roam through Hayden, Firehole and Pelican Valleys.

Bison and brucellosis

Were bison able to recognize the borders between Yellowstone and the surrounding ranchlands, their rousing success story would perhaps be complete. Without fences holding them back, however, bison tend to roam, particularly during fierce winters when frozen grazing grounds force them to search elsewhere for food. Sadly, around half of Yellowstone's bison population tests positive for **brucellosis** (a disease that causes cattle to abort their young), a fact that has spawned one of the region's most heated debates over the past few decades. In the 1980s, cattle ranchers in Montana managed to get their stock certified as brucellosis-free; while it's difficult for bison to infect cattle – transmission is thought to occur only when cattle eat the afterbirth of bison – it's not impossible, and Montana's powerful livestock industry has fought hard to keep bison off its lands.

The original solution was a **bison hunt** on Montana land around Yellowstone, instituted in the late 1980s. In truth, it wasn't much of a "hunt", considering the ease with which one can feasibly walk directly up to a bison and fire at point-blank range; noisy public outcry led to the hunt's discontinuance within five years, although the Montana legislature did approve bison hunting on Forest Service, Bureau of Land Management and tribal (specifically, Flathead and Nez Percé) lands, all near or bordering Yellowstone, in 2005. One current solution involves "hazing" bison that wander outside park boundaries back into Yellowstone with gunshots, snowmobiles and even helicopters. Bison that don't return are rounded up into holding pens and then shipped off to **slaughter** if they test brucellosis-positive, an inelegant solution at best. Several new plans are afoot, including a brucellosis-reducing vaccination programme proposed by Yellowstone wildlife managers and still awaiting a verdict, yet the issue is sure to remain a contentious one as long as bison and cattle continue to cross paths. Also throwing a tricky curve into the controversy is the fact that some **elk** in the region also test positive for brucellosis; however, as elk hunting plays a vital role in the local economy, these animals are neither slaughtered nor similarly targeted. For more information on this complex topic from the conservationist point of view, visit Ⓦ www.buffalofieldcampaign.org.

Tower Fall and around

Named after one of Yellowstone's most famous visitors and earliest boosters, **Roosevelt Lodge** opened in 1920, one year after Theodore Roosevelt's death. Save for a gas station and small ranger station, there's little reason to stop here unless you're hungry for bbq ribs and chicken, considering a horseback or wagon ride, or spending the night. The **corral** here is the park's best, with a range of rides heading northeast for lovely Northern Range vistas. A short drive south leads to **Calcite Springs Overlook**, from where you have a clear, if vertigo-inducing view of pale, spookily steaming slopes alongside the Yellowstone River far below. Osprey are commonly seen swooping about or nesting in the gorge, known properly as the Narrows, while bighorn sheep graze around the rim above the volcanic basalt columns that compose the canyon wall opposite.

Over the next half-mile, several viewpoints afford more vistas into the downstream end of the Grand Canyon of the Yellowstone before reaching the parking area for **Tower Fall**. An upper platform about 150 yards past the General Store overlooks the impressive 132ft falls, formed as Tower Creek rushes through a rocky chute before plunging in a long, uninterrupted stream between a crown of volcanic stone pinnacles. The view from the bottom is even more dramatic, making the steep half-mile walk down definitely worth the effort. Known alternately as Little Falls and Lower Falls by early trappers and prospectors, the cascade has long been a busy meeting place – the **Bannock Trail**, historically used by hunting parties from Shoshone, Nez Percé and other native tribes, weaves directly past. Following this same trail, the Washburn Expedition camped here and named the waterfall in 1870, but it was the sketches and subsequent paintings made by Thomas Moran the following year that fully etched it into the country's conscience.

South to Canyon: Mount Washburn and Dunraven Pass

The highway between Tower Fall and Canyon to the south combines the park's most hair-raising curves with its finest panoramic roadside views. The seventeen-mile stretch, topping out at **Dunraven Pass** (8859ft) due west of **Mount Washburn** (10,243ft), is a curvy thrill-ride for motorcycles and sports cars, even with the imposed 25mph speed limit. Those in RVs still have a white-knuckle ride ahead of them, and nervous drivers may want to skip the route entirely. Six miles uphill from Tower Fall, rough **Chittenden Road** leads a mile to a car park from which hikers and bikers can head up Mount Washburn (see **H9**, p.120); the final destination, a three-storey fire tower upon the peak, is clearly visible from the road.

From this point to Dunraven Pass four miles away, gale winds are common, and tall piles of ploughed snow crowd the roadside until June. Heading southbound, the views become increasingly more dramatic – keep a lookout for **bighorn sheep** by the roadside – culminating in a jaw-dropping vista just beyond the pass. Overlooking an untrammelled stretch of wilderness that knows no roads and very few trails, the panorama takes in the Absaroka Mountains and Mirror Plateau – a huge backcountry expanse home to rarely seen waterfalls and abundant wildlife – with the pale patches of both the Grand Canyon of the Yellowstone and Washburn Hot Springs breaking up the sea of deep green in the foreground. From here, it's four miles downhill to Canyon, passing **Cascade Lake Picnic Area** – starting point for a wildflower-rich hike to Cascade Lake and Observation Peak beyond (see **H10**, p.121) – along the way.

Canyon and around

For more than twenty miles, the **Yellowstone River** roars and tumbles between the sheer golden cliffs of the **Grand Canyon of the Yellowstone**, the width of which varies between 1500 and 4000 feet, and its depth between 800 and 1200 feet. Almost the entire length of the canyon runs somewhat parallel to the road between **Canyon Village** and Tower-Roosevelt on the north loop, but you're too far from it while driving to enjoy any decent views. The finest viewpoints are clustered around the busy junction at Canyon Village; the most visited is **Artist Point**, and the moment you glimpse **Lower Falls**, juxtaposed with sheer canyon walls fired with streaks of orange and red, the origins of the vista's name will become instantly clear. Hayden Survey painter Thomas Moran was the first to capture the falls on canvas in 1871, and artists still flock to draw what may be the most reproduced painting subject in North America.

The road south of Canyon through picturesque Hayden Valley and past malodorous Mud Volcano is covered in Chapter 2, "Southern Yellowstone".

Canyon Village

Long a popular stopping point for visitors, **Canyon Village** has a storied architectural history. Two rickety hotels had already been built here when the celebrated *Canyon Hotel* began construction in 1910. Designed by Robert Reamer, the man behind *Old Faithful Inn* (see p.183), the 430-room inn billed itself "a miracle in hotel building" due to its sheer size and speedy construction, and featured a lounge large enough to host a full orchestra. While successful for decades, the costs of running such a huge enterprise eventually overtook any profits, and the run-down building was sold for $25 to a wrecking crew in 1959, although it burned down under mysterious circumstances the following year before the crew could do its job.

Nowadays most of the village's buildings are far less inspired, a testament to the National Park Service's "Mission 66" programme, a decade-long initiative to update facilities that ended with the agency's fiftieth anniversary in 1966. Dominating the scene is **Canyon Lodge** which park brochures brag is longer than a football ground. With a raft of exposed diagonal support beams propping up its low-slung profile, it's likewise about as charming as a football ground, though considering that several thousand guests dine here daily in high season, the size is warranted. Along with a gift shop, the lodge houses a decent restaurant and lounge, a small deli and a workaday cafeteria. Across the car park is one of Yellowstone's largest general stores (including an inviting diner and coffee/ice-cream bar), as well as a sporting goods store. Further away in the opposite direction, huge *Canyon Campground* is fronted by a handy laundry and shower facility.

There is hope for the aesthetic revival of Canyon Village, however, with the 2006 opening of the innovative **Canyon Visitor Education Center** (May–Sept daily 8am–8pm; Oct daily 9am–5pm; ☎307/344-2550), an event that marked Yellowstone's first major visitor centre development in more than three decades. Taking inspiration from the burned-down *Canyon Hotel*, the building's designers used stone quarried from nearby Gardiner along with a cedar-shingle roof, all to winning effect. Inside, the two-storey space manages to strike visitors as both intimate and grand, while the focus of the centre's sparkling exhibits aims squarely at the park's volcanic history. The most engaging display is a truly enormous relief model of Yellowstone that uses illuminating lights to demonstrate the park's most significant geothermal and seismic events over the eons; after you've given it the once-over up close, walk upstairs to the balcony for a terrific overhead view. Other exhibits worth a stop include a large rotating globe pinpointing volcanic hot spots

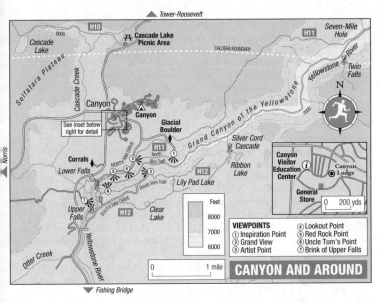

VIEWPOINTS
① Inspiration Point ④ Lookout Point
② Grand View   ⑤ Red Rock Point
③ Artist Point   ⑥ Uncle Tom's Point
                ⑦ Brink of Upper Falls

CANYON AND AROUND

▼ Fishing Bridge

around the world, and the requisite taxidermy displays upstairs – look for the adult and young bison, in particular. There's also a theatre regularly showing the short, informative film *Land to Life*, as well as an information desk and large bookstore on-site.

Grand Canyon of the Yellowstone

Here the very ground is changed, as if belonging to some other world. The walls of the cañon from top to bottom burn in a perfect glory of color, confounding and dazzling when the sun is shining...All the earth hereabouts seems to be paint.

John Muir, 1885

From Canyon Village, two roads trace the north and south rims of the **Grand Canyon of the Yellowstone**, accessing over a half-dozen marked viewpoints. Several of the viewing platforms stick to the rim, from where you can best appreciate naturalist John Muir's sentiments. To fully appreciate the Grand Canyon's two waterfalls – stubby **Upper Falls** travels 109ft, while **Lower Falls** tumbles an impressive 308ft – you'll want to head down into the canyon on a series of steep paths and staircases. Indeed, if you only have the time to explore one area of Yellowstone on foot, consider doing so here. Canyon is renowned for its superb **network of trails**, and while only one path leads to the canyon floor (the demanding Seven-Mile Hole Trail; see H11, p.121), several others weave around the rim and beyond, offering breathtaking views that change dramatically as the sun moves across the sky. While it's possible to view both falls along the North and South Rim Trails alike, a bend in the river prevents seeing both simultaneously unless flying in a plane.

The North Rim

The 2.5-mile **North Rim Drive**, which runs one-way southbound from Canyon Village, provides vehicle access to several viewpoints on the canyon's north side, and while you can simply park and take in the views from atop the rim, it's worth your time and effort to take at least one downhill hike to get even with the falls themselves. The easternmost overlook, **Inspiration Point**, is at the end of a mile-long spur road; a series of steps lead to a small, gusty platform best for views of the canyon walls, streaked with hourglass-shaped landslides every few hundred yards. En route to Inspiration Point, stop to ponder the immense power of glaciers at **Glacial Boulder** – the enormous chunk of granite, estimated to weigh 500 tonnes, was brought and deposited here by a passing glacier from the Beartooth Mountains forty miles away. A trailhead by the boulder leads to a view of Yellowstone's tallest waterfall, narrow **Silver Cord Cascade** (see **H11**, p.121), approximately one mile further on.

Grand View is next on the main drive, and while's there's no view of the falls, it's worth stopping for another angle of the multicoloured canyon and to watch for **osprey**, which build nests atop precarious pinnacles within the canyon itself. **Lookout Point**, beyond the next bend, offers the first unblocked view of Lower Falls, while a trail leading from **Red Rock Point** switchbacks down an uneven path and wooden steps to an even better view, where you can watch the powerful falls splash. The emerald-green stripe to the side of the falls indicates deeper water, marking a notch in the lip of the brink. The last and most impressive viewpoint is also the toughest to reach, located down a steep ten-minute walk offering a view of the Upper Falls a short way down. After completing the last of ten switchbacks, take your time to enjoy the **Brink of Lower Falls**, from where you can see up close the awesome power of the 2.2 million gallons of water which froth over every minute, all while watching the thunderous falls make short work (geologically speaking) of the rock walls below.

South of North Rim Drive, another road leads to the **Brink of Upper Falls**, from where you can walk a short distance for a closer look at the swirling pool created by Upper Falls. If you're part of a convoy, this is a good spot to park one car before walking the paved three-mile **North Rim Trail** back to Inspiration Point and your second vehicle.

The South Rim

The shorter South Rim Drive has only two vistas of note, but both are extremely popular and therefore best visited early or late in the day. The first, **Uncle Tom's Trail**, descends steeply into the canyon to a gently vibrating, spray-covered platform right in the face of Lower Falls, itself closed in by rust-red and golden-coloured canyon walls; all able-bodied souls should make the heart-racing trip down the path's 328 metal steps to soak up what is undoubtedly one of the most memorable views in the park. Close to a mile downstream, **Artist Point** trades in the intimacy of Uncle Tom's small viewing platform for panoramic grandeur; it seems that virtually everyone who has visited Yellowstone has stopped here for a long look. The upper and lower decks afford majestic views both towards Lower Falls and downstream into the canyon, and provided the crowds aren't too much to bear, it's worth sticking around for one of the fifteen-minute ranger talks given up to ten times daily. If you have time to spare, consider heading further downstream into the backcountry to Point Sublime and beyond (see **H12**, p.122).

West to Norris

Forming the waist of the Grand Loop's figure-eight, the twelve-mile road between Canyon in the east to Norris in the west begins by climbing up **Solfatara Plateau**, a reasonably flat expanse dotted with several of Yellowstone's most accessible backcountry lakes, including Cascade, Grebe, Wolf and Ice Lakes. Atop the plateau, wonderful views look west to the rounded masses of the Madison Range, after which the road plunges downhill for a couple miles en route to the **Virginia Cascade** turn-off. The 2.5-mile one-way (routed eastbound) side road hugs the steep northern rim of Gibbon River Canyon while passing the 60ft sparkling waterfall as it slips over the rim of the Yellowstone Caldera, above which the Gibbon River narrows to a calm creek as it exits Virginia Meadows. Back on the Grand Loop, just before reaching Norris Junction, a **picnic area** makes for a peaceful spot for a nap, or to try your luck at fishing the Gibbon.

Norris and around

Yellowstone's **Norris** region is named after buckskin-wearing **Philetus W. Norris**, the park's second Superintendent from 1877–1882 (for more on his story, see p.256). Along with Madison Junction fifteen miles to the southwest, Norris Junction is the only major intersection in the park without a restaurant, general store or indoor accommodation. Unlike Madison, however, there's still plenty to see, particularly for dedicated geyser-gazers. Massive **Norris Geyser Basin** is Yellowstone's oldest, hottest and most dynamic hydrothermal area, and it takes several hours to explore its two large loops.

North of the geyser basin and guarding the entrance to heavily wooded *Norris Campground* is the **Museum of the National Park Ranger** (daily: late May to Sept 9am–5pm; free), housed in a large log cabin originally built as an army outpost in 1908. Honouring rangers from across the park system, exhibits and posters inside focus on their varied responsibilities, from law enforcement to firefighting to search-and-rescue. Another room inside re-creates the conditions for men first stationed here, soldiers who suffered mightily in winter when only one or two men were posted to patrol the frigid area on snowshoes. More memorable than the

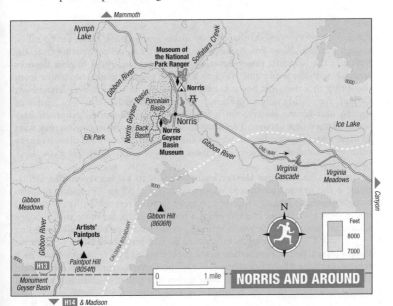

small museum's exhibits, however, is the cabin itself, fronted by a wide porch featuring burlwood columns.

Southwest of the geyser basin sits **Gibbon Meadows**, a photogenic expanse where elk frequently graze. A short road off the highway here leads east to **Artists' Paintpots**, where a mile-long loop climbs uphill through burned forest and past an amazing collection of gurgling mudpots and dirty-pink, puddle-sized pools, everything in sight seemingly awaiting the dip of a giant paintbrush. The road further southwest to Madison Junction, including Gibbon Falls, is covered in Chapter 2, "Southern Yellowstone".

Norris Geyser Basin

Norris Geyser Basin is divided into two main sections, **Back Basin** and **Porcelain Basin**, and both are in dramatic contrast with the lovely settings of most of the park's other geyser basins. Partly because the basin sits at the intersection of three faults, ground temperatures can become incredibly hot – geologists have measured temperatures over 450°F within the ground here – and boardwalks have had to be moved several times due to intense ground heat. Because of this, it nearly goes without saying that it's particularly important to stick to marked trails in this area at all times.

At the intersection of the two loops sits the **Norris Geyser Basin Museum** (daily: late May to Sept 9am–6pm; free), two rooms separated by an open walkway. Built in 1929, the squat log-and-boulder structure houses basic panels detailing hydrothermal geology, including an explanation of the natural plumbing beneath nearby Steamboat Geyser. A ranger staffs the outdoor **information desk** between the two rooms, and also leads at least one walk, talk and campfire programme daily. There's no posted schedule for geyser eruptions as there are at Old Faithful because Norris Geyser Basin's activity is too unpredictable to forecast. Closer to the parking area in a stand-alone hut is one of the Yellowstone Association's **bookstores**.

Back Basin

Patched with forest, an odd-shaped loop snakes around **Back Basin** for 1.5 miles, though a cutoff allows you to halve the trip if you so desire. Starting from the museum, the loop first passes **Emerald Spring**, where yellow sulphur deposits combine with the pool's blue water to form the glorious green colour that lends the spring its name. Just beyond, two viewing platforms look over **Steamboat Geyser**, the world's tallest (on the rare occasions it decides to blow). Capable of forcing near-boiling water 380ft into the air, major Steamboat eruptions have occurred anywhere between a few days to several decades apart, so you may want to think twice about sitting to wait for the next one. In the meantime, its angry main vent tantalizes onlookers with lesser bursts of ten to forty feet a couple of times a day.

Further south, **Echinus Geyser**, surrounded by rocky, sea urchin-like formations, is the largest known acid water geyser; every 35 to 75 minutes it spews crowd-pleasing, vinegary eruptions of forty to sixty feet while the eponymous spring next to it sizzles like butter on a hot pan. There are more than a dozen additional named features worth seeking out alongside the boardwalk: sparkling lemon-lime **Cistern Spring**, which drains to feed Steamboat Geyer's eruptions; **Pearl Geyser**, one of the prettiest in the park, rimmed by a circle of pinkish rock reminiscent of mother-of-pearl; and, **Porkchop Geyser**, a spring that exploded in 1989, blowing open its vent from mere inches to a span now seven feet wide and tossing rocks more than two hundred feet away in the process.

Porcelain Basin

A tour of fascinating **Porcelain Basin** begins from a viewpoint on the museum's north side. From here, you can look across a psychedelic swirl of light blue pools, orange streaks of microscopic thermophiles and patches of deep green lodgepole, all seen through a veil of wispy white steam pouring from **Black Growler Steam Vent** on the hillside below. A half-mile loop leads downhill past **Ledge Geyser**, capable of eruptions over 125ft high, to the photogenic runoff from the pools of **Whirligig Geyser** and **Pinwheel Geyser**; the hotter water of Whirligig hosts a long mat of heat-loving orange bacteria, while a streak of green algae streams out of cooler Pinwheel. If short on time, skip the longer western portion of the loop, where the most interesting site is **Crackling Lake**, a large pond that sounds like a massive bowl of Rice Krispies.

North to Mammoth

The first four of the 21 miles north from Norris to Mammoth climbs and dips through forest untouched by the fires of 1988, the canopy creeping up to the road's edge. Just past Twin Lakes, **Roaring Mountain** is a barren hillside pockmarked with scores of steaming fumaroles. Much more powerful when named in the late 1800s, steam still pours off the face of the mountain, its one-time roar now more of a hiss that's audible only when there's a break in traffic. Geologists have found that heat-seeking microbes known as *sulfolobus acidocaldarius* live on the surface of the mountain, feeding on the gases rising from below.

A five-minute drive further north, the road passes another storied mountain (see box below), **Obsidian Cliff**. Created by a lava flow some 180,000 years ago, this ribbed cliff rising upwards of 200ft was of vital importance to native tribes, who came to mine its plentiful black volcanic glass for use as projectile points and other tools; prehistoric artefacts made from this obsidian have been found as far away as Michigan to the east and Mexico to the south. Nowadays, travel on or near the cliff is forbidden, and punishment for taking obsidian is harsh.

From here, the highway north traces Obsidian Creek through a narrow, then past a marshy zone that's one of the better areas in Yellowstone to spot a **moose**. The creek then runs into the Gardner River near isolated *Indian Creek Campground*,

---

Jim Bridger's tall tales

Spending the warmer months of the year trapping in small groups and winters bivouacked in lonely forts, the mountain men of the fur-trapping era turned to storytelling for entertainment. One of the best was **Jim Bridger**, a talented scout, trapper and guide from Virginia who roamed the northern Rockies for decades throughout the mid 1800s. Renowned for his exaggeration-laced yarns, several of Bridger's tales were set in Yellowstone, not surprising given both the mind-boggling reality of the park's landscape and the fact he was one of the first white men to explore the region. In one such story, he told of sitting down among a forest of petrified trees – a plausible tale, until he reached the part about the petrified birds that landed nearby singing their petrified songs. Another of his most outlandish tales was set at **Obsidian Cliff**. As the story goes, Bridger was out hunting one day when he spied a large bull elk. After firing a perfect shot, the elk failed to fall – and continued grazing as if nothing happened. Bridger crept closer and closer, repeating his shots until he ended up face to face with a wall of glass. He then realized that he'd been shooting not at an elk, but at the image of one reflected through Obsidian Cliff. Not only that, but the cliff's glass face had acted like a telescopic lens and the bull elk was, in fact, grazing peacefully miles away.

beyond which a turn-off leads to **Sheepeater Picnic Area** – best appreciated for its close-up view of the same type of 500,000-year-old basalt columns seen above the Yellowstone River near Tower. More of these columns dot Sheepeater Canyon downstream, as seen on the hike to Osprey Falls (see **H5**, p.117) that begins from the Bunsen Peak Trailhead, a couple of miles north of here across from bucolic Swan Lake Flat. Past the trailhead, the road cuts through dramatic **Golden Gate Canyon** on a hanging road originally built for stagecoaches in the late 1800s; the current concrete bridge dates to the 1970s. Predominantly volcanic ash and pumice, the canyon's yellow rock represents the finest exposure of the earth-shattering Huckleberry Ridge Tuff, which erupted during Yellowstone's first volcanic cycle two million years ago. Past the canyon, the road spirals downhill, passing by the **Hoodoos** – bizarre rock formations suitable for low-key rock climbing – and a staging area for winter snowcoaches before passing Upper Terrace Drive and dropping into Mammoth.

Southern Yellowstone

The first explorers to report on Yellowstone's marquee attraction, **Old Faithful**, were the members of the Washburn Expedition, who on September 18, 1870 tramped into Upper Geyser Basin with spirits sagging. Not only had they recently lost fellow adventurer Truman C. Everts (see box, p.54), but they were also running perilously low on food. In just two wondrous days spent marvelling at the area's steaming sights, their mood had risen to new heights and they had named several of the park's big-name geysers, including Giant and Giantess, Beehive and Grotto, and even Old Faithful (named by Henry Dana Washburn himself). Paved paths, boardwalks and interpretive signs now figure prominently in the geyser basins that dominate **southern Yellowstone**, and the scenes remain just as awe-inspiring today as they did when Washburn and company first visited.

Encompassing the lower half of Yellowstone's Grand Loop Road along with the roadways leading to the West, South and East Entrances, southern Yellowstone's long list of attractions are led by steady Old Faithful and enormous **Yellowstone Lake** to the east. The region's most important feature, however, can't really be enjoyed from a finite viewpoint; in fact, its existence was uncovered as relatively recently as the late 1960s by geologist Bob Christiansen. With high-altitude NASA photos in hand, Christiansen was amazed to learn that the ancient volcanic crater he was searching for was far larger than he ever imagined, spreading out over half of the park's territory. Created by three earth-shattering "supervolcano" eruptions between two million and 640,000 years ago, this massive basin is now known as the **Yellowstone Caldera**.

Gurgling beneath the caldera is one of the world's most active volcanic hot spots, a massive chamber of magma bubbling perilously close to the surface beneath a thin crust of earth. This molten rock is the furnace stoking the park's hydro-thermal wonders, making the caldera's 1300-plus square miles, outlined clearly on park maps, home to the largest concentration of geysers, hot springs, mudpots and fumaroles in the world. The majority of these are dotted within easily accessed clusters, including **Upper**, **Middle**, **Lower** and **West Thumb Geyser Basins**; other hydrothermal areas, such as **Shoshone Geyser Basin**, are tucked away deep in the backcountry. The northern half of Yellowstone Lake is also within the caldera boundaries, and its murky bottom is home to a myriad of superheated vents, underwater springs and bizarre, spire-shaped geological formations.

Outside the caldera's boundary in southern Yellowstone lies mainly untram-melled wilderness. Some of the region's best hikes are accessed via the East and South Entrance roads, most notably a stiff climb up Avalanche Peak or a trip out to Heart Lake, respectively. Beyond these roadways are the extremely isolated southeast and southwest regions of the park, including **Bechler Ranger Station** at the end of a long dirt road in Cascade Corner in the southwest, and **Thorofare**

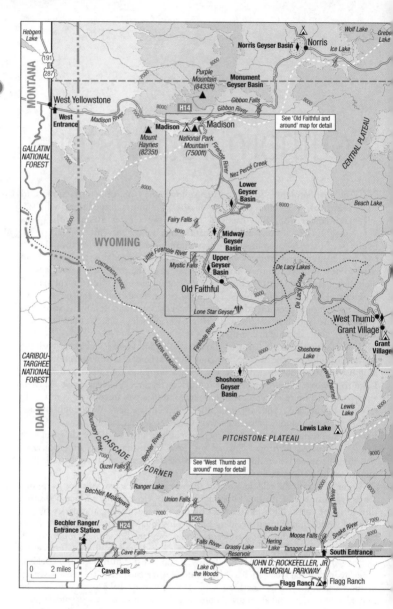

Ranger Station in the park's deep southeast, an area recognized as the most remote in the lower 48 United States.

Sights and orientation

The following tour of southern Yellowstone begins at **Madison Junction**, fifteen miles east of the park's busiest entry point, the **West Entrance Station**. South of

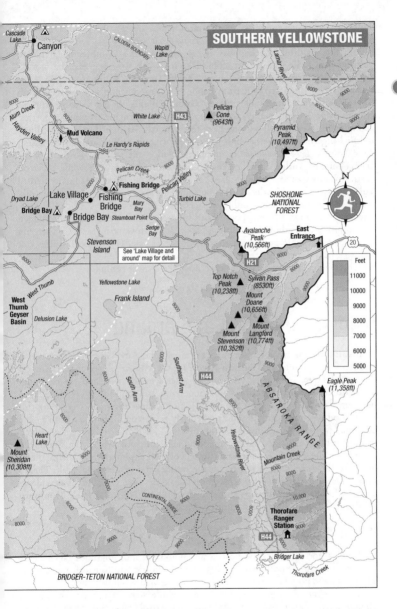

Madison, the Grand Loop follows the Firehole River upstream, weaving for fifteen unbelievable miles through the heart of Yellowstone's geyser country. Northern-most **Lower Geyser Basin** hosts the bubbling mud of Fountain Paint Pot and the towering eruptions of Great Fountain Geyser, while **Midway Geyser Basin** showcases Grand Prismatic Spring, rung with fluorescent orange and yellow bacteria. **Upper Geyser Basin** to the south is the largest of the park's hydrothermal centres and boasts several of the world's most famous geysers and pools, along with the extraordinary, recently restored *Old Faithful Inn* (see p.183).

From Old Faithful, the highway twists east over the Continental Divide to **Yellowstone Lake**, the largest alpine lake in North America, and the world's second-largest freshwater lake above 7000ft (behind South America's Lake Titicaca). The views across it from beside the gorgeous pools of **West Thumb Geyser Basin** are remarkable; nearby **Grant Village**, the park's southernmost visitor village, is useful mainly as a spot to fill up on information, gas and groceries. Lining the shores of Yellowstone Lake to the north, **Bridge Bay**, **Lake Village** and **Fishing Bridge** together host most of the lakeside visitor activity, including the expansive *Lake Yellowstone Hotel* and the park's sole marina. To the east lies lovely **Pelican Valley** and the **Absaroka Mountains** beyond, while the road north towards Canyon Village follows the Yellowstone River past noxious **Mud Volcano** as well as **Hayden Valley**, an immense dale frequented by bison, elk, bears, wolves and, as such, wildlife spotters.

Separated from the Grand Loop Road by more than twenty miles of rugged backcountry, **Cascade Corner** in the park's far southwestern reaches is the only other road-accessible portion of southern Yellowstone. Overlooked by the vast majority of visitors, this remote corner is a waterfall-filled heaven for hikers, horseback riders and anglers looking to leave the crowds behind.

Madison Junction and around

Madison Junction sits at the confluence of the Firehole and Gibbon Rivers, which meet to form the mighty **Madison River**. It's the least developed intersection on the Grand Loop, with only *Madison Campground* to the west and the charming **Madison Information Station** (June–Sept daily 9am–6pm; ☏307/344-2821) to the south. As headquarters for the park's Junior Ranger Program (see p.196), this 1929 wood-and-stone structure is a particularly good stop for families, with a table of animal pelts and skulls inside for kids to handle; half-hour talks are also offered throughout the day. A plaque commemorates the spot where the Washburn Expedition allegedly camped towards the end of their explorations in 1870 and first discussed the novel idea of protecting the wonderland as a national park. There's little evidence backing the claim that this is indeed the same spot, but it's an undeniably idyllic place regardless, with the rocky hulk of **National Park Mountain** (7549ft) towering behind the start of the Madison River.

West Entrance Road

Madison's information station hosts a tiny bookstore, but for food, gas or other supplies, the closest option is bustling **West Yellowstone** fourteen miles west. The pretty and popular drive curves alongside the Madison River almost the entire way, with over a dozen viewpoints accessing the water – a boon for anglers, photographers and picnickers. From Madison, the road first cuts through **Madison Canyon** and past several picturesque mountains – including the Three Brothers, Mount Jackson (8276ft) and Mount Haynes (8231ft) – that loom over both sides of the river. After crossing **Seven-Mile Bridge**, the landscape opens up considerably, with the Madison River flowing in a wide ribbon across a marshy meadow often dotted with elk and, in spring and autumn, bison; charred tree trunks also pepper the scene, stark reminders of 1988's wildfires. Two miles before passing through the West Entrance Station and into West Yellowstone (see Chapter 12, p.215), the highway crosses into Montana.

North to Norris

There are no major sights along the fourteen miles of road between Madison and Norris to the north, but it's worth budgeting extra time for a short hike and slower driving for roadside photo-ops along the **Gibbon River**. From Madison, the highway immediately passes the trailhead for **Purple Mountain** (see H14, p.124) and then **Terrace Springs**, where a roadside boardwalk leads around a trio of steamy pools. The **Tuff Cliff Picnic Area** a mile beyond is more interesting, located beneath a rocky escarpment of light, honeycombed rocks created by a series of spectacular volcanic ash flows. Just over four miles from Madison is the most popular stopover, **Gibbon Falls**, which tumbles 85ft over the rim of the Yellowstone Caldera. Park fifty yards downstream for the best photo perspective, where you'll be able to frame the horsetail-like falls in their entirety, along with the web of logs smashed together at the cascade's base. Upstream, the highway parallels the Gibbon more closely, eventually passing the trailhead for bizarre **Monument Geyser Basin** (see H13, p.123).

Just beyond, the road cuts through elk-rich Gibbon Meadows and past Artists' Paintpots en route to Norris Geyser Basin, all of which are covered in Chapter 1, "Northern Yellowstone".

South to Lower Geyser Basin

South of Madison, the road towards Old Faithful follows the **Firehole River** upstream. Just over a mile from the junction, **Firehole Canyon Drive** leads one-way (southbound) alongside the river for a couple of very scenic miles through the eponymous canyon. The spur road's first section runs along the canyon floor, where steep rhyolite cliffs block out the sky like pockmarked skyscrapers. Rising alongside the volcanic rock, the side road then works its way to a head-on view of **Firehole Falls**, a squat, 40ft wall of crashing water. If cars are parked alongside the road a short ways beyond the falls, it means the **Firehole Swimming Area** is available for a dip in the river. This is one of two spots in the park where swimming in thermally heated river water is openly permitted, with the soaking-friendly Boiling River north of Mammoth (see p.50) being the other. This popular swimming spot is accessed via a set of wooden steps across from the pit toilets, and it's a huge relief on a hot summer day; there's no lifeguard on duty and bathing suits are required, and it's also a punishable offence to access the water here when it's officially closed (typically between mid Sept and mid June). Just beyond this point, Firehole Canyon Drive rejoins the Grand Loop Road at **Firehole Cascades**, a narrow and rocky channel where the Firehole's waters violently pinball back and forth. From here, it's a short way south to Fountain Flat Drive, the northern edge of Lower Geyser Basin.

Old Faithful and around

The heart of Yellowstone's geyser country stretches fifteen miles along the steaming Firehole River, divided between **Lower**, **Midway** and **Upper Geyser Basins**; the last of these is the largest, home to famed **Old Faithful** as well as the area's numerous amenities. Each of the basins, however, boasts unique charms, and

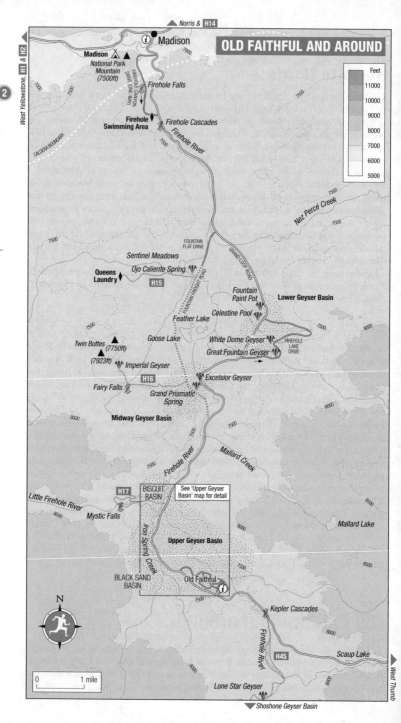

OLD FAITHFUL AND AROUND

▲ Norris & H14

ⓘ Madison

Madison

National Park Mountain (7500ft)

FIREHOLE CANYON DRIVE (ONE-WAY)

Firehole Falls

West Yellowstone, H1 & H2

CALDERA BOUNDARY

Firehole Cascades

Firehole Swimming Area

Firehole River

Nez Percé Creek

FOUNTAIN FLAT DRIVE

Sentinel Meadows

Ojo Caliente Spring

Queens Laundry

H15

FOUNTAIN FREIGHT ROAD

GRAND LOOP ROAD

Fountain Paint Pot

Lower Geyser Basin

Celestine Pool

Feather Lake

White Dome Geyser

FIREHOLE LAKE DRIVE

Goose Lake

Great Fountain Geyser

Twin Buttes (7750ft)

(7923ft)

Imperial Geyser

H16

Excelsior Geyser

Fairy Falls

Grand Prismatic Spring

Midway Geyser Basin

Firehole River

Mallard Creek

Little Firehole River

H17

BISCUIT BASIN

See 'Upper Geyser Basin' map for detail

Mystic Falls

Iron Spring Creek

Upper Geyser Basin

Mallard Lake

BLACK SAND BASIN

Old Faithful ⓘ

N

Kepler Cascades

Firehole River

H45

Scaup Lake

West Thumb ▶

Lone Star Geyser

▼ Shoshone Geyser Basin

Feet	
	11000
	10000
	9000
	8000
	7000
	6000
	5000

0   1 mile

it takes at minimum a full day to properly explore them. It's easy to get overwhelmed by the seemingly endless collection of gushing geysers and burbling hot springs, so it pays to break up a tour over several days if possible, sprinkling in hikes, a bike ride or fishing trip, or visits to nearby portions of the park not as focused on thermal features, such as the Grand Canyon of the Yellowstone (see p.57). Whether you're here for a few hours or a full week, your first point of order should be the sparkling-new **Old Faithful Visitor Education Center**, where the eruption times of six of the park's top predictable geysers are posted. Upper Basin's **Grand Geyser** and **Riverside Geyser** are both worth planning a day around, as is the eruption of **Great Fountain Geyser** in Lower Basin.

Lower Geyser Basin

The first major sight along the southbound drive from Firehole Cascades, **Lower Geyser Basin** features a trio of diversions. Northernmost is **Fountain Flat Drive**, a mile-long road leading southwest along the Firehole River. Used mainly by fly-fishermen, the road doesn't pass any thermal features of note, but dead ends at a trailhead from which hikers can tramp west to peaceful Sentinel Meadows and the ruined bathhouse by Queens Laundry (see H15, p.125); a bike trail leads south from here five miles along flat **Fountain Freight Road** to Fairy Falls Trailhead. South of this side road, Grand Loop Road crosses narrow Nez Percé Creek and through Fountain Flats, a smooth green expanse dotted with grazing bison throughout early summer, and capped with rising steam from the numerous geysers and springs to the south.

Some of this steam rises from the essential **Fountain Paint Pot Trail**. Accessible year-round (in winter via snowcoach and snowmobile), this fairly short boardwalk loop offers a grab bag of every type of hydrothermal feature found in the park. **Fountain Paint Pot** itself is aptly named, a great gurgling mixture of clay minerals and silica particles that just needs a good stir to blend the streaks of orange and red into its dominant heavy cream colour. There are two stunning, deep-blue pools named **Silex** and **Celestine**, the latter the site of a gruesome incident in 1981 (see box below), as well as a couple of hissing fumaroles and a small cluster of geysers that erupt frequently, if not spectacularly; an exception is **Fountain Geyser**, which erupts between ten and fifty feet approximately every eight hours. Entirely dependent on its seasonal supply of water, enigmatic **Red Spouter** is a hot spring during springtime months, a mudpot in summer and a fumarole vent come autumn; it's also been known to erupt like a geyser, giving it the attributes of all four hydrothermal features.

Across from the Fountain Paint Pot Trail is the exit for one-way (northbound) **Firehole Lake Drive**, curving three miles past a series of angry, sizzling pools and

---

Celestine tragedy

As detailed by park historian Lee H. Whittlesey in *Death in Yellowstone* (see "Books" section of Contexts, p.272), the **Celestine Pool** along the Fountain Paint Pot Trail was the site of a tragic incident on July 20, 1981. Two visitors, David Kirwan and Ronald Ratliff, were touring the boardwalk when Ratliff's dog escaped from their truck and dived into the pool. Both men ran to the spring, and Kirwan – ignoring the pleas from several other bystanders not to go in – stepped in before diving head-first into the deeper water in an effort to save his friend's dog. It only took a moment for the scalding water, later measured at just over 200°F, to burn Kirwan completely; he died the next day in a Salt Lake City hospital. After being pulled out of the pool by Ratliff (who sustained second-degree burns to his own feet doing so), Kirwan reportedly mumbled: "That was a stupid thing I did."

pond-sized hot springs. Highlights of the detour are glorious **Great Fountain Geyser**, sitting in the middle of a remarkable terraced platform of sinter on which pools of water reflect the sky above, and **White Dome Geyser**, a 15ft-tall gesyer cone rung with pink and orange thermophiles. Estimated **eruption times** (9–12 hours apart) are posted at Old Faithful's visitor centre, so if possible, plan your visit to coincide with one of Great Fountain Geyser's dramatic hour-long bursts, which average 100ft but can occasionally double that height.

Midway Geyser Basin

Just down the road and four miles north of Old Faithful, **Midway Geyser Basin** is the smallest of the area's geyser basins, home to only two noteworthy thermal features; both, however, are among the largest and most electrifying in the park. On the opposite side of a bridge across the Firehole, **Excelsior Geyser** – now mostly a huge, bubbling crater – disgorges thousands of gallons of superheated water into the river below each minute. One of the park's more eccentric geysers, Excelsior erupted regularly until the late 1880s before going inexplicably quiet for a full century, at which point it blew its stack continuously for two days in 1985. Based on the impressive photograph on display at the site, you wouldn't want to be standing on the boardwalk the next time it goes off.

Nearby, the park's largest hot spring, **Grand Prismatic Spring**, is named for its amazing spectrum of rich colours, from royal blue to fiery orange. The ground views of the 370ft-wide spring are certainly not as dramatic as the overhead shots invariably seen on postcards and posters, but they're still worth the walk for flashes of bright colour through the steam, and a close-up look at the acres of bright bacterial mats surrounding it.

Just south of Midway Geyser Basin is **Fairy Falls Trailhead**, the starting point of a popular hike to the eponymous falls and Imperial Geyser beyond (see `H16`, p.125); a popular bike route also begins here.

Hydrothermal stunts, cooking and vandalism

Over the years, Yellowstone's hydrothermal features have been put to numerous uses beyond selling postcards and calendars. Some of these long-gone practices were quickly banned – such as the **soaping** of geysers, which caused them to erupt quickly but also damaged their plumbing – while others were officially condoned for a period. The early tradition of "specimen-coating" in Mammoth was one such example (see box, p.48), while a separate enterprise was launched by Henry Brothers, who built a business (**Brothers Bathhouse and Plunge** by *Old Faithful Inn*) using thermal water from Solitary Geyser to fill a large swimming pool and a half-dozen smaller tubs. A much smaller operation, **Chinese Spring**, directly north of Old Faithful, was originally named Chinaman Springs after the Asian attendant who used it to clean visitor laundry. Similarly, **Handkerchief Pool** in Black Sand Basin was used as a crowd-pleasing washing machine; rangers would instruct bystanders to drop a handkerchief inside, and wait as the hot water swirled it downwards and returned it minutes later. Of course, not every item made its way back up, and one ranger reported finding dozens of handkerchiefs – as well as coins, a horseshoe and even a sparkplug – upon trying to unplug the vent in 1929.

Perhaps most famous of all was **Fishing Cone** in West Thumb Geyser Basin, into whose boiling waters anglers dipped fresh-caught trout for decades, cooking a meal on the spot. For the most part, visitors are more respectful these days, though vandalism – such as tossing rocks, sticks, coins and the like into geysers – still occurs in spite of posted signs warning against such activities.

Upper Geyser Basin

It's not a stretch to say that an overwhelming percentage of Yellowstone visitors view an **Old Faithful** eruption at some point during their visit, an assertion reinforced by the many facilities and service buildings surrounding the geyser in a vast half-circle. As if by some cosmic plan, the world-famous spouter sits alone at the southern tip of **Upper Geyser Basin** in a spot that guarantees full attention. To the north, thermal features dot both sides of the Firehole River for two awe-inspiring miles, ending at **Biscuit Basin** on the opposite side of the road. Alongside Iron Spring Creek and one half-mile west of Old Faithful, **Black Sand Basin** completes Upper Geyser Basin's colossal collection of geysers and pools.

Along with its raft of established buildings – three large lodges, two general stores and a backcountry ranger station – the village at Old Faithful now includes

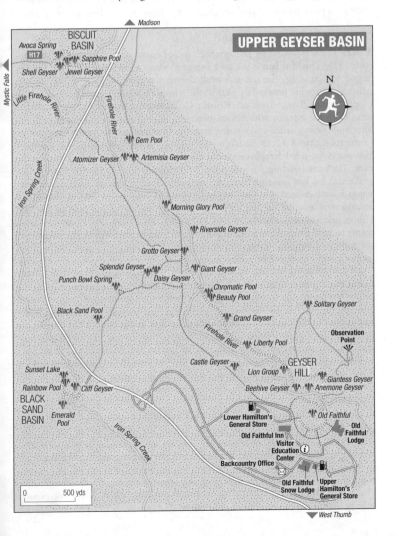

▲ Madison

UPPER GEYSER BASIN

BISCUIT BASIN

Avoca Spring
H17

Sapphire Pool

Shell Geyser   Jewel Geyser

Little Firehole River

Mystic Falls

Firehole River

Iron Spring Creek

N

Gem Pool

Atomizer Geyser   Artemisia Geyser

Morning Glory Pool

Riverside Geyser

Grotto Geyser

Splendid Geyser   Giant Geyser
Punch Bowl Spring   Daisy Geyser

Chromatic Pool
Beauty Pool

Black Sand Pool

Solitary Geyser

Grand Geyser

Firehole River   Liberty Pool

Observation Point

Castle Geyser

GEYSER HILL

Lion Group

Sunset Lake

Rainbow Pool   Cliff Geyser

Giantess Geyser

Beehive Geyser   Anemone Geyser

BLACK SAND BASIN   Emerald Pool

Iron Spring Creek

Old Faithful

Lower Hamilton's General Store

Old Faithful Inn

Visitor Education Center (i)

Backcountry Office

Old Faithful Snow Lodge

Old Faithful Lodge

Upper Hamilton's General Store

0   500 yds

▼ West Thumb

the shimmering **Old Faithful Visitor Education Center** (daily: summer 8am–8pm, winter 9am–5pm, closed Nov–Dec and March–April; ☏307/344-2750). Upon its 2010 opening, many agreed that its main allure lies not in its interactive exhibits covering all the expected park topics (hydrothermal features, geology, lakes, volcanic activity), but rather the grand building itself, where, in the lobby, impossibly tall picture windows perfectly frame the brand-name geyser outside. The centre was largely constructed using recycled materials, with a shallow foundation designed to prevent damage to the hydrothermal system percolating just beneath the earth hereabouts. Along with the theatre, information desk and suitably well-stocked Yellowstone Association bookstore, one of the most popular stops inside is the "Young Scientist" exhibit geared toward children. **Estimated eruption times** for Old Faithful, as well as Castle, Grand, Daisy, Riverside and Great Fountain Geysers are posted here daily, while a host of ranger-led programmes, including guided geyser walks, are scheduled regularly.

Old Faithful Inn and around

A suitable counterpoint to Yellowstone's most famous natural attraction, shingle-coated **Old Faithful Inn** is the park's most glorious structure. Likely the world's largest log building, the inn was built during the bitter winter of 1903–04 to satisfy the growing demand of well-heeled visitors wanting to spend more time in Upper Geyser Basin. Architect **Robert C. Reamer**, a mere 29 years old at the time, filled the interior with beams, banisters, railings and other decorative flourishes built from gnarled and twisted branches in an attempt to reflect the chaos of nature itself. Amid this forest-like web, the seven-storey **lobby** was built around a 500-ton, four-sided **fireplace** pieced together with rhyolite mined within the park. The main building, known as the "Old House", features a series of steep roof peaks and has lost none of its charm over the decades, though additions of two wings have increased the inn's original 140-room capacity to 329. A recent $20 million refit lessened the impact of a century-plus of wear and tear on the Old House, and although many of the building's updates – from steel beam reinforcements to new electrical and plumbing systems – aren't apparent to the naked eye, the return of original features such as the sunken sitting area around the main fireplace will be noticed by return visitors.

Old Faithful Inn is but one of several historic buildings in this area. The **Lower Hamilton's Store**, which actually predates *Old Faithful Inn* by seven years, is the oldest structure still in use in Upper Geyser Basin, featuring a one-of-a-kind knotty-pine porch from which you can watch geysers erupt in the distance. On the east side of Old Faithful sits **Old Faithful Lodge**, designed in 1923 by another famed national park architect, Gilbert Stanley Underwood. The low log-and-stone lodge remains a rustic space, somewhat lost in the shadows of *Old Faithful Inn* and the modern *Old Faithful Snow Lodge* nearby, though it does feature both a porch and a wall of windows facing out onto the great geyser.

Old Faithful

For well over a century, dependable **Old Faithful** has been the most popular geyser in the park, erupting more frequently than any of its higher or larger rivals. As a result, a half-moon of concentric benches now surround it at a respectful distance on the side away from the Firehole River; these grandstands quickly fill with hundreds of visitors in the minutes leading up to an eruption, and empty even quicker once the show ends. For any sense of calm – football crowd-like chants of "OLD-FAITH-*FUL*!" from anticipatory onlookers aren't uncommon here in high season – you'll want to arrive around sunrise; better yet, try to plan a night-time visit under a bright full moon, or hike up to nearby Observation Point above Geyser Hill (see below).

While the legend that Old Faithful once blew off every hour, on the hour, never held true, the geyser's eruptions did, in fact, once average close to sixty minutes apart. Due to earthquakes rattling its underground plumbing over the years, the geyser now performs for expectant crowds every 92 minutes on average, with a minimum gap of just under an hour and a maximum of three hours. Approximate **eruption schedules** are displayed in the visitor centre and in the *Old Faithful Inn*'s lobby, and are also available on a recorded information line at T307/344-2751. The first sign of **activity** is a soft hissing as water splashes repeatedly over the rim; after several minutes, a narrow column of water shoots to a height of 105–185ft, with the geyser ultimately spurting out as much as 8500 gallons of heated water.

Geyser Hill

A short walk across the Firehole River from Old Faithful, **Geyser Hill** contains close to a dozen named hydrothermal features in a tight loop. The stubby **Beehive Geyser** doesn't look like much when inactive, but its tight cone, combined with powerful plumbing, forces a narrow spray as high as 200ft during its five-minute eruptions that occur, on average, twice daily. The nearby **Lion Group** is more active, with four geysers atop a large mound that "roar" when erupting.

Also on Geyser Hill is a mile-long trail leading up to **Observation Point**, from which you can watch Old Faithful and other nearby geysers shoot off while sitting high above the action. If you take the steep uphill walk (a 160ft climb), be sure to complete the trail by passing scenic **Solitary Geyser** to the northwest; formerly a hot spring, Solitary began erupting after it was tapped in 1915 to fill the pools within Brothers Bathhouse and Plunge (see box, p.70) near *Old Faithful Inn*. Even

---

Kipling's Upper Geyser Basin tour

Decades before becoming the first English language writer to win the Nobel Prize for Literature, British writer **Rudyard Kipling** toured the world as a travel writer, publishing his tales in various newspapers (collected in his *From Sea to Sea: Letters of Travel*). After visiting Burma, China and Japan, Kipling travelled to the United States, where in 1889 he embarked on a stagecoach tour of Yellowstone National Park. While his acerbic account spends much of its time teasing the park's visitors and soldiers, he also writes eloquently about the "howling wilderness…full of all imaginable freaks of fiery nature". A bubbling pool is likened to a "goblin splashing in his tub", while the eruption of Old Faithful is "a plume of spun glass, iridescent and superb, against the sky". One of his most entertaining accounts within the "miraculous valley" of Upper Geyser Basin takes place at **Riverside Geyser**, a description that continues to ring true well over a century later:

"I think they call it Riverside Geyser. Its spout was torn and rugged like the mouth of a gun when a shell has burst there. It grumbled madly for a moment or two and then was still. I crept over the steaming lime – it was the burning marl on which Satan lay – and looked fearfully down its mouth. You should never look a gift geyser in the mouth. I beheld a horrible slippery, slimy funnel with water rising and falling ten feet at a time. Then the water rose to lip level with a rush and an infernal bubbling troubled this Devil's Bethesda before the sullen heave of the crest of wave lapped over the edge and made me run. Mark the nature of the human soul! I had begun with awe, not to say terror. I stepped back from the flanks of Riverside Geyser saying: 'Pooh! Is that all it can do?' Yet for aught I knew the whole thing might have blown up at a minute's notice; she, he, or it being an arrangement of uncertain temper."

though both the pipeline and pools are long gone, the geyser continues to erupt 5–10ft every few minutes.

Castle Geyser north to Gem Pool

Old Faithful is certainly the most famous geyser in Upper Geyser Basin, but it's hardly the most spectacular. A few miles of boardwalk and paved path – much of the latter bike-accessible – weave northwest from Old Faithful past dozens of other geysers, several of which spew higher or have a more attractive setting than their better-known sibling. Though its steamy blasts only reach 75ft, **Castle Geyser** is a must-see for its massive sinter cone, thought to be thousands of years old. The tallest predictable spouter in the park is **Grand Geyser**, located off the boardwalk on the opposite (east) side of the Firehole River. This colossus blows, on average, twice daily for twelve to twenty minutes in a series of powerful bursts climbing to 200ft; don't be deterred by crowds – the show is worth waiting for.

Further north, **Giant Geyser** may erupt only a dozen times per year, but its hour-long spurts reach as high as 250ft. Less powerful but more picturesque, **Riverside Geyser** (see box, p.73) is one of the park's most photogenic geysers: perched on the banks of the Firehole, it blows for twenty minutes every six hours, spraying a 75ft tower of rainbow-streaked water over the river. Few leave the area without taking a snapshot of nearby **Grotto Geyser** as well, featuring a twisted cone that resembles a hobbit hole carved from alabaster. Uphill from here to the southwest, **Daisy Geyser** is one of the most predictable geysers in the park, shooting a jet of water 70ft high at a conspicuous angle every three hours.

In this area as well are a number of hot springs, with **Morning Glory Pool** the most attractive – be sure to make the 1.5-mile walk or bike ride from Old Faithful to eyeball the pool's distinctive yellow-orange outer rings and mesmerizing blue depths. Perfectly named after the funnel-shaped flower, Morning Glory has lost some of its lustre over the years thanks to vandals tossing vent-blocking objects, including seemingly innocuous stones and branches, into the pool. No bikes are allowed past Morning Glory, but consider hoofing north another half-mile to stare into the sparkling blue depths of **Artemisia Geyser** and **Gem Pool**.

Biscuit and Black Sand Basins

Biscuit Basin, three miles up the Grand Loop Road from Old Faithful and also accessible via the footpath leading past Artemisia Geyser and Gem Pool, is named for the biscuit-shaped rocks that used to ring **Sapphire Pool** until a 1959 earthquake disintegrated them. The pool is still true blue, moving from bright yellow on its edges to a deep turquoise centre. Beyond Sapphire, an easy boardwalk loop leads past several lesser hydrothermal features to the trailhead for Mystic Falls (see H17, p.126). To the south, **Black Sand Basin**, where a plateau of volcanic black sand is split by gurgling Iron Spring Creek, also possesses its own distinct charms. Attractions include several lovely hot pools, including deep-green **Emerald Pool** and gorgeous **Sunset Lake**, whose central geyser constantly sends waves lapping onto its vermilion shores. Nearby, creekside **Cliff Geyser** looks like the ideal six-person hot tub – until it spurts out boiling water 30ft into the air. Note that it's possible to walk or cycle along paved paths from the Old Faithful area to Biscuit Basin and Black Sand Basin.

Eastward to West Thumb

The highway east from Old Faithful to the West Thumb junction climbs, swoops and dips as relentlessly as a seventeen-mile-long roller-coaster track. A couple of miles from Old Faithful, a viewing platform juts over the Firehole River for a head-on view of **Kepler Cascades**, a 125ft streak of whitewater tumbling down three separate steps. Nearby Lone Star Trailhead is the entry point for a flat trail along the Firehole River to nearby **Lone Star Geyser** and beyond (see **H45**, p.152); it's a popular route with both runners and bikers in summer, and cross-country skiers come winter. After climbing steeply east to Continental Divide-straddling Craig Pass (8262ft), the highway passes the **DeLacy Creek Trailhead**, starting point for a popular trail that's the shortest path to **Shoshone Lake**, three miles due south.

West Thumb, Grant Village and around

It takes a creative mind to picture it on current maps, but early explorers drew **Yellowstone Lake** in the shape of a left hand, hanging downwards with its wrist at its north end as if ready to pinch **Heart Lake** to the south. Thanks to this bit of anthropomorphic cartography, the lake's westernmost extension became known as **West Thumb**. Connected by a narrow neck, the "thumb" is actually a caldera within a caldera, created by a powerful volcanic explosion 160,000 years ago that eventually filled with water. These underground forces are most certainly visible today at **West Thumb Geyser Basin**, easily the largest collection of hydrothermal features on Yellowstone Lake. South of the geyser basin is humdrum **Grant Village**, the park's southernmost base and worth a stop for its visitor centre.

West Thumb Geyser Basin

Although it lacks the explosiveness of the geysers in the Old Faithful area, **West Thumb Geyser Basin** boasts an astonishing setting, perched right on the edge of

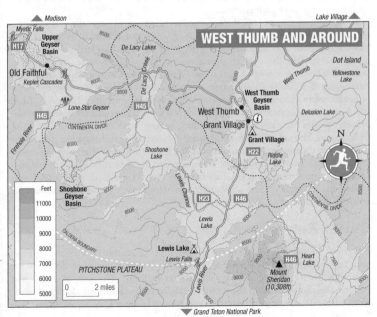

75

Yellowstone Lake with the Absaroka Mountains clearly visible far across the eastern shores. A string of hot pools empty right into the tranquil waters and fizz away into nothing, and it's easy to see why early tourists made use of the so-called **Fishing Cone** hot spring on the lake's edge by cooking fresh-caught fish in its boiling waters (fishing by the now-dormant cone, typically covered by lakewater until midsummer, was banned after a fisherman was burnt by an eruption in the 1920s). A half-mile of boardwalk loops around the geyser basin, starting near a log hut built in 1925 as a backcountry ranger station that's now an information station and bookstore in summer (daily: May–Sept 9am–5pm).

From here, the path leads past a string of pools and springs and around the lake's edge. One of these, the eye-catching **Abyss Pool**, does indeed look bottomless; it's been measured at 53ft deep – one of the park's deepest – and has been known to erupt as high as 100ft. The boardwalk curves right up to the edge of **Black Pool**, letting you peer down into its formerly dark 40ft depths that now sparkle green, indicating a lower water temperature than that of bright blue pools. Elsewhere in the basin, a set of mudpots bubble away contentedly while fumaroles blow steady plumes of steam into the air. While there have been no regular geyser eruptions here in recent years, West Thumb's stunning lake vista and collection of other-worldly colours make it an unmissable sight in the park – try visiting in early morning for a breathtaking sunrise over the water.

Grant Village

In part to protect encroaching thermal features, the marina, cafeteria and cabins once located at the West Thumb junction were torn down in the early 1980s, with the action subsequently moving to **Grant Village**. The unsightly development is named after Ulysses S. Grant, the eighteenth president of the United States who signed the bill creating Yellowstone National Park in 1872. The former Civil War hero also has a picturesque peak by Frost Lake on the park's eastern border named after him, a far more fitting tribute.

While handy for its general store, backcountry office and post office, there's little aesthetic order to Grant Village's hodgepodge collection of buildings. The restaurants and indoor accommodation are some of the least inspired in the park – though to be fair, the sites at gigantic *Grant Village Campground* are pleasantly wooded. The main reason to visit is the **Grant Visitor Center** (daily: May–Sept 8am–7pm; ☎307/344-2650), where the park's 1988 wildfires (see box opposite) are extensively chronicled. A dated, but nonetheless compelling 25-minute film, *Ten Years After Fire*, runs throughout the day, while exhibits educate visitors on the critical role fire plays in forest regeneration; be sure to ask for a free copy of "The Yellowstone Fires of 1988" park newspaper insert at the information desk. Also look for the display dedicated to the amazing **lodgepole pine**, Yellowstone's most common tree. Though not true of all lodgepoles, many of the female trees of this species sprout serotinous cones that open to spread their seeds only after being blasted by the heat of fire, a major reason why these trees are so common in recently burned areas.

South Entrance Road

There are no major sights along the twenty miles of road between Grant Village and Yellowstone's **South Entrance**, but there's certainly plenty to do as several trailheads branch both east and west off the highway. The first of these, just beyond the sign indicating the Continental Divide, is **Riddle Lake Trailhead**, from where it's an easy stroll out to its eponymous lake (see H22, p.129). Just two

The fires of 1988

The now infamous **summer of 1988** began like most others in Yellowstone. Following an unusually dry winter, precipitation increased in spring, and while lightning started a handful of forest fires, there was little reason to be concerned and most burned themselves out as expected. June, however, brought near-drought conditions, and the moisture content of trees and grasses dipped to dangerously low levels. The hope that July would bring moisture never came to pass, and by the middle of that month, it was obvious the park's natural fire programme would need to be suspended.

By late July, firefighters were called in to battle the many fires burning throughout the park. It was an impossible battle, however, as high winds combined with low humidity and the already dry wood to cause a summer-long firestorm of epic proportions. All in all, **51 separate fires** – nine caused by humans, the rest by lightning – raged, some burning as high as 200ft and leaping across chasms as wide as the Grand Canyon of the Yellowstone. Every one of the park's visitor complexes, including Old Faithful and Grant Village, had to be evacuated at one point or another (Grant was evacuated twice), as did the park gateway towns of Silver Gate and Cooke City in Montana. All in all, some 25,000 people were employed in battling the blazes at a cost of $120 million, and miraculously, no firefighters inside the park lost their lives. Thanks to both a bit of luck and the heroic efforts of firefighters, historic buildings such as *Old Faithful Inn* were saved. Snowfall beginning on September 11 finally tamed the blazes, but not before 36 percent of Yellowstone – just under 800,000 acres – had burned, with even more razed in the surrounding national forests.

The sight of the country's flagship national park in flames was broadcast as a **public relations disaster**. Park authorities correctly insisted the wildfires were a natural part of the forest's ecological cycle, clearing out two-hundred-year-old trees to make way for new growth, but a long list of dire predictions were nonetheless made. Some argued the mass of downed and dead trees would lead to another major fire, or claimed visitor numbers would drop precipitously and never climb back; however, beginning in 1989 (when Yellowstone enjoyed its highest visitor numbers of any year that decade), park visitation increased beyond 1987 levels, a trend that continued into the 1990s and beyond.

There's no doubt that Yellowstone's ecosystem has changed, including a major decline in its moose population and the fact that slow-growth trees like whitebark pine and Engelmann spruce will require decades to return. But nearly 25 years later, it's abundantly clear the park is still alive and well, thanks in part to this dramatic and necessary burst of new growth.

---

miles further south, the highway passes **Shoshone/Dogshead** (see H23, p.129) and **Heart Lake Trailhead**s (see H46, p.153), with **Mount Sheridan** (10,308ft) towering over Heart Lake to the east; combining a small backcountry geyser basin, an appealingly isolated lake and memorably panoramic views, the latter is one of the finest hikes in Yellowstone. From here, the highway hugs the eastern shore of **Lewis Lake** for two miles, giving roadside fishermen a chance to cast for a variety of trout. The lake's southern end is home to wooded *Lewis Lake Campground*, as well as a boat dock offering paddlers a chance to explore backcountry Shoshone Lake via the Lewis Channel.

South of the campground turn-off, the road begins tracing a parallel route to the **Lewis River** by **Lewis Falls**, where tour buses often stop to let visitors arriving from the south snap photos of the rather underwhelming 30ft cascade. The road progressively climbs further above the sparkling blue band of water, with viewpoints looking across steep **Lewis Canyon**. It's a dramatic scene, as most of the area is still heavily scarred with fire damage from 1988; look for the interpretive sign explaining how 80mph winds enabled the crowning, frighteningly hot

Huck Fire to hop the adjacent, one-third-of-a-mile-wide canyon. A mile from the South Entrance Station, the road crosses Crawfish Creek. A parking area to the northeast accesses a short path to lovely **Moose Falls**, a 30ft plunge bracketed on both sides by moss-covered rocks dotted with wildflowers. At the park boundary, the highway draws near to the **Snake River** and enters the John D. Rockefeller, Jr. Memorial Parkway, covered in detail in Chapter 3, "Grand Teton".

Lake Village and around

It takes only a moment's glance to realize a simple fact about **Yellowstone Lake** (7733ft) – it's massive. According to famed mountain man and storyteller Jim Bridger (see box, p.61), the lake was so big that just before going to sleep, he could yell "wake up!" and doze blissfully while the echo crossed the water, eventually returning to rouse him from his slumber hours later. The lake's actual figures need no such exaggeration: it boasts a **surface area** of 132 square miles, with a shoreline that's 141 miles in length. Completely natural – the Yellowstone River flowing in from the south and out to the north is the longest undammed

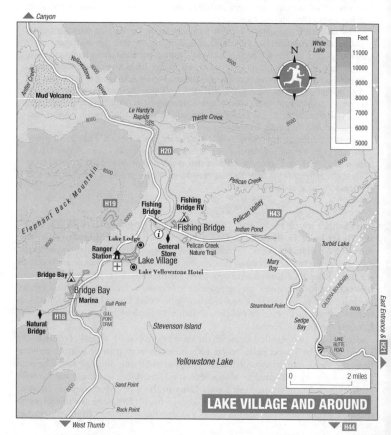

river in the continental US – its average depth is around 140ft, and its deepest known underwater canyon stretches a whopping 430ft downward. In fact, it used to be even bigger, at one point reaching 200ft higher and covering ground as far north as Hayden Valley.

Despite its size and central location, there's actually not a great deal of activity on the water itself. Yellowstone Lake doesn't suffer fools gladly, nor does it take all that kindly to even the most knowledgeable rowers and sailors. It only takes a few minutes for the wind to churn the calm surface into six-foot waves, and by late August the **surface temperature** peaks at a still-uncomfortable 65°F (18°C). Typically frozen for nearly half the year (late Dec to late May), average water temperatures are closer to 45°F (7°C), which means you've got a paltry survival time of only 15–20 minutes if forced to swim. Plenty of fishermen do head out to try their luck with cutthroat trout and the invasive lake trout (see box, p.81), and canoeists and kayakers hit the water to camp overnight at one of forty backcountry sites lining the shore. Keep in mind, however, that it's highly recommended for first-timers to attempt these activities with a knowledgeable guide.

Still, there's plenty to do around the lake, from hiking and biking to wildlife watching, or simply gazing across it towards the Absaroka Mountains that gouge the horizon beyond its eastern shore. The area's most bustling hub is **Lake Village**, home to the swanky **Lake Yellowstone Hotel**, as well as the more rustic **Lake Lodge**. To the south, **Bridge Bay** is where you'll find the lake's sole marina, while north is **Fishing Bridge**, at one time an exceedingly busy junction but now more relaxed after the Park Service moved many facilities from here to protect bear habitat. The highway north from Fishing Bridge passes by both **Mud Volcano** and picture-perfect Hayden Valley en route to Canyon Village, while the road east climbs up and over the Absarokas to the **East Entrance** and, beyond that, Cody.

Bridge Bay

Between West Thumb and **Bridge Bay** twenty miles to the north, the highway sticks to the shores of Yellowstone Lake most of the way, passing through charred remnants of 2009's Arnica Fire en route, near the northern shore of West Thumb. Around a half-dozen designated picnic areas line the road, but there are few sights in particular to look out for other than **Gull Point Drive**, just before Bridge Bay itself. This two-mile side road hugs the lake even more closely with a straight-on view of **Stevenson Island**, just over a mile offshore and named after James Stevenson, second in command on the 1871–72 Hayden Survey and possibly one of the first men to climb Grand Teton (see the box on p.102 for more on this controversial claim). Across from the northern entrance to Gull Point Drive is the trailhead for **Natural Bridge**, an impressive span of rock nearby (see `H18`, p.126). Bridge Bay itself is a sheltered gem that's a jumping-off point for backcountry water taxis (see `H44` for one such trip description, p.151); there's also a small store where bait is sold and a ranger station, along with the park's largest campground. Motorized and non-motorized boats can be rented, and fishing trips and pleasure cruises are charted as well; see Chapter 6, "Summer activities", for full details.

Lake Village

Located between Bridge Bay to the south and Fishing Bridge to the north, **Lake Village** is centred around the sprawling **Lake Yellowstone Hotel**. With a section dating back to 1889, the buttercup-yellow inn is the oldest standing building in Yellowstone. Built by the Yellowstone Park Association – a front for the Northern

Pacific Railroad – the original eighty-room hotel was much more basic. Guests would often arrive via steamship across the lake from West Thumb, one of the main reasons the front of the hotel faces the lake and away from the road leading in. When architect Robert Reamer began *Old Faithful Inn* in 1903, he was also asked to expand *Lake Yellowstone Hotel*, and today's grandiose, Southern mansion-style structure is mostly his creation. Reamer's tall Ionic columns and fifteen false balconies created a structure a world apart from the outsized log cabin at Old Faithful, a testament to the architect's wide-ranging aesthetic. Thanks to an extensive renovation throughout the 1980s, the old hotel has aged gracefully, and it remains one of the finest places to stay in the park. Even if not staying here (the hotel's dining room is one of Yellowstone's finest), the building is worth a quick tour or, better yet, an evening drink in the airy Sun Room overlooking the lake.

Also fronting the grassy expanse on the lakeside of the hotel are the **Lake Clinic** (see p.28), a small general store and the **Lake Ranger Station**, built in 1923 during the early years of the Park Service era. Designed in part by then-Superintendent Horace Albright, the log cabin features an octagonal community room built around a stone fireplace where rangers could exchange stories after a day in the field. Further away but within walking distance, **Lake Lodge** was built two years earlier to accommodate the new influx of car-driving visitors. A much larger, yet still cosy log building, it's a comfortable stopping point for its roaring fireplaces and comfortable couches that make for particularly welcome respite on chilly, damp days.

Just north of Lake Village en route to Fishing Bridge a mile north, the road passes by the trailhead for **Elephant Back Mountain** (see **H19**, p.127), up which a moderately stiff hike rewards visitors with good views over the village and vast lake beyond.

Fishing Bridge

The Yellowstone River flows north out of Yellowstone Lake at **Fishing Bridge**, and the outlet is a major spawning ground for the native **cutthroat** who swim here in great numbers starting in early June to lay eggs upon the river's gravel bed. For decades, the actual Fishing Bridge spanning the neck of the river was a popular casting spot dating back to its original construction in 1902, with anglers lined up pole-to-pole along its length. Fishing has been banned from the existing bridge (erected in 1937) since the early 1970s to protect the native trout, but you can still linger on it to observe the fish swimming below – or to watch for their predators, including grizzlies and bald eagles. Adjacent to the bridge on the east side is the starting point for an enjoyable hike along the Yellowstone River to watch trout jump at **LeHardy's Rapids** (see **H20**, p.127) during their annual spawn.

The tiny cluster of amenities east of the bridge consists of a gas station, *Fishing Bridge RV* campground and the most pleasantly atmospheric **General Store** in the park, complete with a diner and coffee/ice-cream counter tucked away at the back. Opposite here is the historic **Fishing Bridge Visitor Center** (daily: May–Sept 8am–7pm; ℡307/344-2450), known for its ornithology exhibits and distinctive architecture. Built in 1931 and designed by Herbert Maier, who created similar structures at Norris and Madison, the arresting native rock and log building looks like the lakeside vacation home of Snow White's seven dwarves. Inside, display cases holding decades-old stuffed models of sandhill cranes, osprey and a particularly ferocious bald eagle fit in perfectly with the charmingly antiquated mood of the building; you'll also find a helpful information desk and bookstore. Behind the visitor centre is an invitingly long stretch of sandy **beach**, and as the water here is some of the shallowest and warmest in Yellowstone Lake, it's an ideal spot to picnic and soak in the sun on warm summer days.

Paradise recovered...for now

A haven for fly-fishermen, Yellowstone's **fisheries** were nearly paradise lost decades ago, and they remain a fragile ecosystem today. By the 1960s, nearly a century of rampant overfishing and poor management practices forced park officials into the unpopular move of banning the sport from some of the most popular areas, including Fishing Bridge. Regulations became increasingly strict through the ensuing decades, leading to a **complete ban** in 2001 on keeping native sport fish caught anywhere within Yellowstone. These rules have certainly helped the local **cutthroat**, Arctic grayling and mountain whitefish populations, but today's biggest problems plaguing the region's rivers and lakes stem from **invasive and non-native species**, a much tougher foe to conquer.

Although stocking no longer occurs within the park, managers had previously run major stocking programmes from the park's inception until the 1950s. **Brook, brown** and **rainbow trout** were all introduced into the park's rivers, while Shoshone and Lewis Lakes were filled with **lake trout**. It's uncertain just how lake trout got into Yellowstone Lake from Lewis Lake in the mid 1980s – some believe it was the work of a single self-interested individual – but soon after the first one was reeled up, it was clear that the lake's cutthroat population was in mortal danger. A single adult lake trout can eat at least 40 cutthroat a year, and this is more than just bad news for anglers. The loss of cutthroat would be devastating to the local bear and eagle population, just two of forty-plus mammals and birds that rely on cutthroat as a mainstay of their diet. Lake trout are now *piscis non grata* in Yellowstone, and officials are doing all they can to reduce, if not eliminate the invader: gill nets have been used to catch hundreds of lake trout at a time, and there's no creel-limit on lake trout while fishing Yellowstone Lake. In fact, park policy dictates that all lake trout caught in Yellowstone Lake and its tributaries must be killed on the spot.

The fight to protect local cutthroat – split into Yellowstone, Westslope and Snake River subspecies – is also being waged in local rivers, where non-native trout have been overpowering them in recent years. Attempts to place the fish on the endangered species list have gone unsupported by the US Fish and Wildlife Service, but both park officials and dedicated nonprofit organizations have pressed on with heroic plans. In one such example, a strategy to restore Westslope cutthroat to Specimen Creek in Yellowstone's northwest corner was approved in 2006, the year after a previously unknown group of genetically pure Westslope was miraculously found in an isolated stream; these fish have greatly boosted cutthroat restoration efforts. At the time of writing, park biologists are optimistic at the prospect of an imminent native trout conservation plan and an influx of funding to redouble lake trout removal. For more information, visit ⓦ www.greateryellowstone.org.

North to Canyon

The highway north from Fishing Bridge traces the Yellowstone River, which runs flat and wide for the most part as it flows towards the chaos of Upper and Lower Falls at Canyon, fifteen miles away (see Chapter 1, "Northern Yellowstone"). Along the way, a pair of key sights – one intriguingly garish, the other truly magnificent – beckon: pallid **Mud Volcano** and bucolic **Hayden Valley**, respectively. Several picnic areas and road-adjacent access to the short riverside boardwalk at **LeHardy's Rapids** precede Mud Volcano by a few miles.

Mud Volcano

It's likely you'll already have visited a geyser basin or two before arriving at **Mud Volcano** several miles north of Fishing Bridge, and if you thought the outpouring of sulphurous gases elsewhere in the park was an intense olfactory experience, you're in for a real treat here. Thanks to a higher level of acidity, this collection of mudpots and cauldrons makes up the moodiest (some would say ugliest) of the park's thermal regions, where a one-mile boardwalk winds through gurgling pools of sickly grey and yellow mud, past trees that have been steamed to death, and out to the bleak and barren shores of **Sour Lake**, itself the perfect set for a horror movie. Joining a free ranger-led tour (daily: late May to early Sept, 4pm) gives you the chance to get off the boardwalk and into the backcountry for two hours, where the **Gumper**, which blew into existence in the 1970s, bubbles with big grey globs of odious mud.

Across the road from Mud Volcano is the isolated pool known as **Sulphur Cauldron**. It won't surprise you to learn that this sickly yellow, arrowhead-shaped bubbling pit is thought to be the most acidic in the entire park, with a pH level nearly equivalent to that of battery acid.

Note that groups of bison often congregate in the Mud Volcano and Hayden Valley areas, causing jams that may delay traffic for some minutes.

Hayden Valley

After the terrors of Mud Volcano, the sight of **Hayden Valley** due north is literally a breath of fresh air. Indeed, there may not be a more sudden change in the landscape anywhere else in Yellowstone, from stinking mudpots to a vast, blue-sky valley that's one of the richest habitats for bear, bison and elk anywhere in the US. The Yellowstone River winds its way north across the wide-open plain of the valley floor, a patchwork of dusty green grasses, silvery grey sagebrush and the crystalline blue waters of Trout, Elk Antler and Alum Creeks. Only Lamar Valley to the north is more popular with **wildlife spotters**, and during the sunrise and even more spectacular sunset hours, roadside viewpoints here fill with expectant onlookers. It's not unusual to look over hundreds of bison and elk grazing peacefully, while numerous waterfowl and even beaver can be spotted swimming in the rivers and creeks below; the greatest crowd-pleasers, grizzly bears and wolves, have been known to openly roam through the valley as well.

East Entrance Road

The highway east from Fishing Bridge bends around the northeast shores of Yellowstone Lake before winding up and over Sylvan Pass on the way to the **East Entrance**, 27 miles away. Even if you're not heading to Cody, at the very least head a mile east of Fishing Bridge to view one of the finest sights along the entire stretch, **Pelican Valley**. Shifting from wet marshlands in May and early June to a meadow of dusty yellow grasses dotted with grazing bison by late August, the valley is of vital importance to area wildlife, including grizzly bears who have historically flocked here in spring to hunt spawning trout. Whirling disease and invasive lake trout (see box, p.81) have wreaked havoc on the native cutthroat in **Pelican Creek** in recent years, however, and fishing is now banned throughout the entire valley. To further protect wildlife, overnight camping is forbidden as well, though there are still a few fine hikes routed through here. When bison are present, visitors often park at the bridge over Pelican Creek to photograph the tranquil scene, while just west of here, the half-mile **Pelican Creek Nature Trail** is worth a stroll to the lakeshore. Past the bridge, a side road across from **Indian Pond** leads to popular **Pelican Valley Trailhead** (see **H43**, p.150); Indian Pond itself was formed by a hydrothermal blowout that created a crater in which water eventually pooled.

Beyond here the highway rounds pretty **Mary Bay** – a particularly fruitful spot for grizzly-spotting in spring and early summer – and past numerous thermal features puffing away near the lake's edge, including **Steamboat Springs**. Plenty of lakeside viewpoints line the curvy road, giving drivers a chance to enjoy the views safely. After cutting away from the lake, the highway leads through a mile of heavily burned forest to **Lake Butte Road**, a favourite spot for photographers and hopeless romantics at sunset; heading uphill for a mile, the side road leads north off the highway to a superb **vista** over the lake from which the jagged Tetons can be seen, with the rounded hump of Mount Sheridan in the foreground.

Avalanche Peak and Sylvan Pass

Along with travellers heading to Cody via surreal Wapiti Valley (detailed in Chapter 15), peak-bagging hikers should continue east towards the park boundary. For seven twisting miles after its junction with Lake Butte Road, the highway climbs up the **Absaroka Range** to narrow Sylvan Lake, where the serrated pinnacle of Top Notch Peak (10,245ft) looms in the background. Just beyond, opposite tiny Eleanor Lake, is the trailhead for **Avalanche Peak** (10,566ft; see **H21**, p.128), one of the best peak hikes in Yellowstone. After cresting **Sylvan Pass** (8530ft), the roadside views become even more stunning, the north side dominated by immense cliffs while a heavily forested canyon formed by **Middle Creek** lines the south side. Descending some 1500ft from the pass, the road eventually passes through the isolated East Entrance Station at Middle Creek itself, together leading to meet the North Fork of the Shoshone River a few miles east.

Cascade Corner

Named for its wealth of **waterfalls** – most of which spill off the **Bechler** (Beckler) and **Falls Rivers** – Yellowstone's remote **Cascade Corner** is rustic, rugged and quite scenic, with very little in the way of amenities or roadside sights; the few thousand visitors who come here each summer to hike, ride horses and fish are rewarded with plenty of peace and solitude. Known alternately as the **Bechler Area**, this southwest corner of the park is unconnected by road to any other portion of the park, and is reachable only by foot trails from the north, via dirt-track Cave Falls Road from Ashton, Idaho, to the west, or even bumpier Grassy Lake Road from Flagg Ranch to the east (see p.107). The only permanent sign of occupation is around the **Bechler Ranger Station**, a cluster of small buildings that includes the Bechler River Soldier Station, erected by the army in 1911 as an outpost to curtail poaching in the area.

From the west, the drive in ends at **Cave Falls**, which drops only 20ft but is the park's widest at 250ft across. The rest of the fifty-plus waterfalls must be seen either on foot or horseback, including **Union Falls**, a 250ft plunge widely considered Yellowstone's prettiest waterfall (see **H25**, p.131). Equally memorable is **Bechler Meadows**, a vast ocean of grass with the rear of the Tetons visible to the south (see **H24**, p.130). While only these two hikes have been profiled in the guide, there are dozens of other options, including an unforgettable three-night trip launching from Old Faithful in the north and covering thirty miles, mainly along the Bechler River Trail, to the Bechler Ranger Station.

Practicalities

Due to heavy snowpack, plenty of rain and marshy meadows, travel within Cascade Corner is not recommended until at least mid July. Even if you don't mind the knee-deep mud, most of the rivers will be too swift and deep to ford any earlier, limiting your hiking or horseback-riding options immensely. While the many waterfalls are at their strongest earlier in the summer, the best time to visit is between mid August and mid September, when trails are dry (or at least drier) and the ferociousness of biting insects has subsided to reasonable levels.

The park doesn't operate any drive-in camping facilities in Cascade Corner, though Caribou-Targhee National Forest's *Cave Falls Campground* just outside the Yellowstone boundary rarely fills. A quick drive from Cave Falls along its eponymous road, the campground has 23 well-spaced sites, most spread along the Falls River, for only $10 a night. There are also numerous **backcountry sites** strung along area trails, and permits can be organized at Bechler Ranger Station, where you should check in even if you're day-hiking. Also note that you'll have to bring along all your food and drink, as the closest shop is an hour's drive west in tiny Ashton.

3

Grand Teton

T he majesty of the peaks within **GRAND TETON NATIONAL PARK**
has always left wide-eyed onlookers searching for ways to best describe
them. Native tribes had numerous names for the jagged spires, from the
Three Brothers to the evocative Hoary Headed Fathers, given the purplish
peaks' propensity for being dusted in silvery-white snow. The Shoshone knew
them as the *Teewinot* ("many pinnacles"), while early white explorers called the
range the Pilot Knobs, sky-high lighthouses used to navigate the surrounding
wilderness. The designation that stuck, *Les Trois Tétons* (literally "The Three
Breasts"), was bestowed in the 1830s by overly imaginative French-Canadian
fur-trappers as they approached the mountains from the west.

The mountains themselves are so much the dominant feature of Grand Teton's
485 square miles that it's worth identifying the major summits before describing
much else. While the forty-mile-long Teton Range comprises twelve main
peaks over 12,000ft, there are seven clearly dominant points from south to
north: **Nez Percé** (11,901ft); **South Teton** (12,514ft); **Middle Teton** (12,804ft);
Grand Teton (13,770ft), naturally the tallest of the bunch; **Teewinot Mountain**
(12,325ft); **Mount Owen** (12,928ft), and, looming apart from the rest, the
hulking mass of **Mount Moran** (12,605ft). The mountains are an obvious
magnet for both hardy hikers and skilled climbers, and are also the subject of
countless portraits – the Tetons are reputedly listed third behind Mount
Fujiyama and the Matterhorn as the most photographed mountains on earth.

The string of peaks, however, occupies only the western third of the park, which
was created in 1929 and expanded two decades later. Attracting a comparable share
of attention from its 3.8 million annual visitors are the lakes and rivers east of the
Teton Range, along the floor of Jackson Hole. The ribbon of picturesque glacial
lakes, including gem-like **Jenny Lake**, hugging the range's base are largely the
scene of idyllic gazing and the occasional chilly swim, while larger **Jackson Lake**
– essentially a reservoir created by Jackson Lake Dam – buzzes with sailboats,
rowboating fishermen and motorboats towing waterskiers throughout summer.
And the somewhat tamed **Snake River**, known by early explorers as the Mad
River for its ferocious pre-dam runoff, draws fly-fishermen and gentle raft rides
known as "float trips" down its grand southern flow.

As the flat valley floor of Jackson Hole hosted settler homesteads for decades
before being turned into a national park – even today, chunks of privately owned
lands remain within Grand Teton's boundaries – there are also several **historical
attractions** worth visiting, from the photogenic remains of ranch buildings to a
restored ferry crossing manned by docents in period dress. It's also worth noting
that **wildlife**, while not as bountiful as in Yellowstone to the north, is still
plentiful here; indeed, you're more likely to spot a moose chomping willows
around Jackson Lake or the Gros Ventre River than anywhere in Yellowstone.

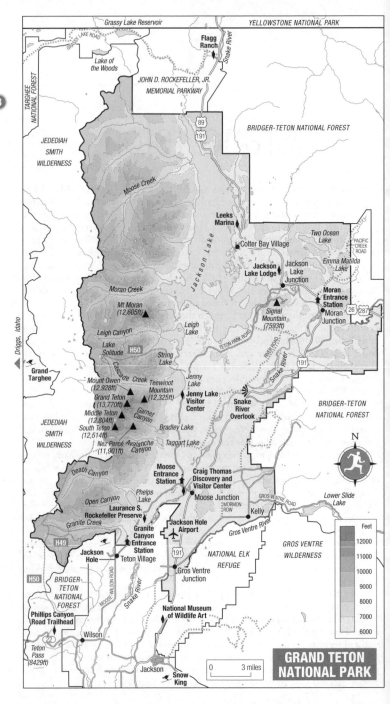

Park orientation

Save for the shuttles from *Jackson Lake Lodge* and Colter Bay to Jackson, there's no useful public transport within the park, and you'll ideally want a car (or bike) to get around. No road crosses the Tetons inside the park boundary, but those that run along their eastern flank were designed with an eye to the mountains, affording stunning views at every turn. It's possible to drive the length of the park and back in a day, but to take in a quick look at the best sights along with a hike or two, budget at least two or three days for exploration, if not more.

Grand Teton splits easily into **three main divisions**: a southern third, encompassing Moose Junction, the Laurance S. Rockefeller Preserve and the Gros Ventre River area, along with the two approaches from Jackson; the park's central section, aligned along Teton Park Road and its speedier counterpart, Hwy-191, across the Snake River to the east; and its northern region, home to the busy visitor hubs of *Jackson Lake Lodge* and Colter Bay Village. In the latter third's section of the chapter, we've also included **John D. Rockefeller, Jr. Memorial Parkway**, a bridge of land connecting the park to Yellowstone, and named after Grand Teton's patron saint.

Southern Grand Teton

Two roads head north into Grand Teton from Jackson: narrow **Moose–Wilson Road**, which is routed by Teton Village to the **Granite Canyon Entrance** and **Laurance S. Rockefeller Preserve**, and the much more frequently used – and faster – **Hwy-191**. Both lead to **Moose Junction**, home to park headquarters along with a cluster of appealing historic attractions and amenities. Whichever route you choose, try to loop back down to Jackson on the other road when you leave the park to see what you missed on the way in. Similarly, time permitting, take a couple of hours at least to explore the park's rustic southeastern corner, crisscrossed as it is by a series of dusty, bike-friendly roads accessing the hamlet of **Kelly** and the **Gros Ventre Slide** (see p.93) – both reachable year-round – along with the beautiful barns lining **Mormon Row**.

Hwy-191 north to Moose

Many visitors first lay eyes on the Tetons from this stretch of highway, both because the regional airport is located here and day-trippers from Jackson can drive

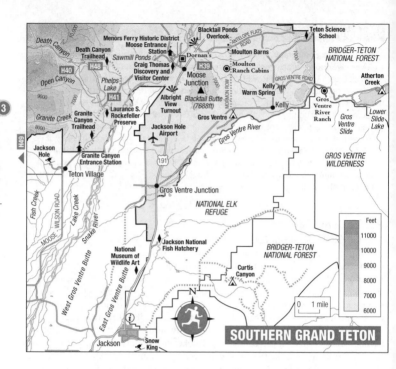

less than thirty miles north to Moran Junction without having to pay an entrance fee. A few miles past the National Museum of Wildlife Art and just past the turn-off for the Jackson National Fish Hatchery – each detailed in Chapter 11 – the highway enters Grand Teton National Park, a moment commemorated with a roadside viewpoint. Although this is only the first of many such dramatic vistas to come, a huge chunk of visitors understandably stop for a photo with the iconic national park sign in the foreground and the Tetons falling away into the horizon.

Soon after, the highway speeds over the **Gros Ventre River** and its eponymous road junction to the entryway for **Jackson Hole Airport**, some five miles from the park entrance. Open since the 1930s, it's the only commercial airport located within a US national park, and despite the noise created by low-flying aircraft buzzing over the valley, one would be hard-pressed to find more spectacularly set landing strips anywhere in the country. Continuing north, between the airport and Moose Junction three miles away is **Albright View Turnout**. Named after Horace Albright, former head of both Yellowstone and the National Park Service and a major catalyst in the creation of Grand Teton National Park (see box opposite) the stunning view here focuses on Albright Peak (10,552ft), a straightforward climb in summer that becomes an expert-only backcountry skiing descent in winter.

Granite Canyon Entrance Station north to Moose

Just under 1.5 miles north of Teton Village, Moose-Wilson Road enters Grand Teton National Park at the **Granite Canyon Entrance Station**, open year-round save for a couple of weeks during November and December for maintenance. After winding though attractive stands of aspen and brush for a half-mile, a three-mile portion of the road becomes unpaved and rather bumpy as it approaches **Granite Canyon Trailhead**, an entry point for hikes through Granite and Open Canyons.

Roughly one mile further on, Moose-Wilson Road returns to tarmac before, four miles south of Moose, reaching the turn-off for the immaculate **Laurance S. Rockefeller Preserve**, a 3100-acre parcel of land based around the Rockefeller

A brief history of Grand Teton National Park

Ranching and farming in **Jackson Hole** – originally known as Jackson's Hole after trapper Davey Jackson – date back to the 1880s, when homesteaders and cattle first began colonizing the valley. That the mostly smaller homesteads managed to eke out a living on the brutally tough lands here for a few decades is a testament to the perseverance and hard-working nature of the settlers; still, a major drought beginning in 1918, along with calf and crop prices plummeting at the end of World War I, led many farms and ranches to the brink of bankruptcy. Into this scene stepped Yellowstone Superintendent **Horace M. Albright**, who had long wanted to extend Yellowstone south to cover the **Tetons** (as did several of his predecessors dating back to Army Superintendent S.B.M. Young in the late 1890s). In 1923, Albright joined local ranchers and business owners inside **Maude Noble's cabin** by the Snake River for a historic meeting to discuss protecting the valley. Albright endorsed the idea of protecting the valley as part of Yellowstone, with the ranchers being compensated for the loss of their land by the government. Sceptical of any form of federal control, many of the attendees agreed with the overall idea, realizing it was their best hope out of a tough situation – but refused on the principle of US government involvement. Sensing the end was near, these ranchers began circulating a petition to consider selling their land to other interests in order to turn the valley into a privately run, but still protected recreation area.

During the same period, Albright introduced the National Park idea to **John D. Rockefeller, Jr**. while taking the wealthy philanthropist on a twelve-day tour of the region in 1926 (see p.105 for more on their historic stop at **Lunch Tree Hill**). Buoyed by the inspiring mountain scenery and dismayed by the hodgepodge of commercial interests invading the valley, Rockefeller quickly latched onto the plan, creating the **Snake River Land Company** the following year to begin purchasing ranches throughout the valley with the eventual hope of donating the land to the government for parkland. Ever the businessman, however, Rockefeller tried to keep his association with the company silent, knowing that if word of the actual buyer got out, ranchers would double or triple the selling prices of their land; commercial aspirations were likewise not entirely absent from the process, as the condition remained that the Rockefeller-owned **Grand Teton Lodge Company** would retain the right to operate lodges and other tourist amenities within the park.

Minor stumbles along the way notwithstanding, things went according to plan, and **Grand Teton National Park** was officially created in 1929. The earliest incarnation of the park – pieced together from parts of the already federally controlled Teton National Forest, created in 1897, along with Rockefeller's acquisitions – was much smaller than it is today, containing only the Teton Range itself along with the string of smaller glacial lakes at its base (and not Jackson Lake). Local opposition was minimal, as little useable ranching and timberland was included. However, when word got out the following year that Rockefeller was the man behind the Snake River Land Company, locals felt betrayed and tempers flared. Angered by the apparent conspiracy and ever distrustful of East Coast interests, residents refused to accept any land donated by Rockefeller; this forced the hand of **President Franklin Roosevelt**, who created **Jackson Hole National Monument** in 1943, a neighbouring parcel to Grand Teton that included nearly 35,000 acres of land donated to the National Park Service by Rockefeller, along with Jackson Lake and additional acreage from Teton National Forest. By 1950, local anger and distrust had subsided enough to finally combine the National Park and Monument, cementing Grand Teton's present-day boundaries.

family's former JY Ranch, which once ringed the southern edge of nearby Phelps Lake. Laurance, son of John D. Rockefeller, Jr., transferred his family's retreat to the National Park Service in two segments prior to his 2004 death, relinquishing his family's sole, decades-held right to motorboat on Phelps Lake in the process; considering the estimated value of the land ($160 million), the gift is believed to be one of the most generous in Park Service history. With the Rockefeller clan's financial backing, the ensuing few years saw the Park Service endeavour to return the land to its **natural state** by removing all ranch structures, roads and utilities, and today the Preserve is the portrait of beauty and tranquillity, as well as a model of sustainable design. Carve out two-thirds of a day to fully immerse yourself in its slow-paced charms, including its one-of-a-kind visitor centre and exceptional network of easy to moderately demanding hiking trails (see **H40**, p.142 and **H41**, p.143).

Begin by arriving no later than mid morning, as the Preserve's **small parking area** contains room for only about fifty cars, a purposeful decision designed to reduce mass visitor impact; if full, you'll have to wait until a space becomes available. From the gravel car park, it's a short walk to the invitingly airy **visitor centre** (daily: late May to early Sept 8am–6pm, rest of Sept 9am–6pm; ☎307/739-3654), itself a major departure from every other visitor centre you'll visit in Grand Teton and Yellowstone. Rather than the usual array of text-heavy placards and taxidermy displays, the sparsely arranged centre features **experiential exhibits** focusing on the sights and sounds of nature. Of special note is the **Soundscape Room**, where visitors are enveloped in a sonic collage of thunderstorms, birds, insects and streams – stand on the circular plate of thick glass in the middle of the room to best experience its plethora of gently panned sounds. Elsewhere in and around the centre, you'll find a comfortable reading room (complete with fireplace), a docent-staffed information desk and several chairs near the entrance ripe for relaxing in.

A little over one mile further on, Moose-Wilson Road soon meets the turn-off for warmly named **Death Canyon Trailhead**, reached via a rocky 1.5-mile road best suited to 4WD vehicles, or at least those with high clearance. Several first-rate hikes head out from here (including **H48**, p.154), one of which is the one-mile uphill tramp along the **Valley Trail** to **Phelps Lake Overlook**, where you can raise your water bottle and toast the philanthropic spirit of the Rockefellers as you soak in views of the turquoise-green waters of the park's fourth-largest lake.

Beyond the turnoff for Death Canyon Trailhead, Moose-Wilson Road weaves its way north to Moose, passing by **Sawmill Ponds** and some prime **moose** habitat en route.

Moose

The heart of visitor activity in Grand Teton's southern region is **Moose**, a dusty spread of buildings and side roads divided by the **Moose Entrance Station**, where you'll need to pay the $25 entrance fee (or prove you've already done so) to head north on Teton Park Road. A short way before the toll booth is a **post office** (Mon–Fri 9am–1pm and 1.30–5pm, Sat 10–11.30am) from which you can send postcards sporting a Moose postmark, while just past the park boundary is the small historic zone known as **Menors Ferry Historic District**, which portrays the lives of early Jackson Hole homesteaders.

Moose also boasts the **Craig Thomas Discovery and Visitor Center** (daily: summer 8am–7pm, winter 9am–5pm; ☎307/739-3399), which saw its curtain rise to great fanfare in 2007. Acting as both park headquarters and flagship information hub, the impressive complex – named for the late, conservation-minded US senator from Wyoming – requires a short walk from the parking area, all the better to appreciate how its exterior design shields the mountains from view until you enter the main building itself, at which point you're assailed by a regal Tetons vista through **massive picture windows** that take their cue from those in the upper lobby of *Jackson Lake Lodge*. As you roam the centre's exhibits and sizeable bookstore, be sure to periodically look down at your feet, where metal floorbeams identify and point directly toward specific peaks, one by one, and "video rivers" float by on floor-embedded monitors. Backcountry permits are also available at the well-staffed information desk, as is general park intelligence; the building's 154-seat auditorium, hampered by construction delays, is due to open in 2011.

Menors Ferry Historic District

Just past the Moose Entrance Station is the turn for **Menors Ferry Historic District**, where a collection of buildings provides a fine peek into early Jackson Hole settlement history. As one of the few spots in the valley where the Snake River consistently sticks to a single, narrow channel, the banks here make for an ideal spot for a bridge or ferry. Learning of this soon after arriving in 1894, **William D. Menor** squatted on 150 acres off the west bank of the river to begin his homestead, which of course included a **ferry crossing**. Menor's business was a quick success and played a key role in transporting both settlers and vacationers en route to local dude ranches. By 1918, Menor grew tired of the business and sold it to his neighbour Maude Noble, who promptly doubled the crossing's rates; locals were surely overjoyed when a steel bridge was built south of the crossing in 1927, ending the ferry's monopoly and prompting Noble to sell her land to the Snake River Land Company within two years.

Following the interpretive loop clockwise from the car park, the first building of note is Menor's original **homestead cabin**, open for viewing and frequently attended by a docent in period dress (daily: mid May to late Sept 9am–4.30pm). The whitewashed cabin was built in three obvious sections, and as rickety an affair as it seems, the place was a veritable mansion for an unmarried homesteader, including such creature comforts as a wooden floor and glass windows. A few steps away from the cabin is the spot where Menor launched his ferry, a clever contraption consisting of two pontoons with a plank platform laid on top. Attached to a system of cables and steered with a pilot wheel, the current of the river itself would propel the ferry across the water – not always an accident-free undertaking, as at least one recorded case exists where a tree trunk drifting downstream slammed into the ferry hard enough to snap the cables, beaching the vessel (and a hopping mad Menor) on a gravel bank downstream. When budgets allow, the Park Service runs a **replica ferry** across the river, an experience worth lining up for.

Past the landing, a **transportation shed** houses a random collection of wagons dating back to the late 1800s, but the **Maude Noble Cabin** beyond is of more interest. Moved here from nearby Cottonwood Creek after Noble purchased Menor's homestead and interest in the ferry, the structure was the site of a watershed 1923 meeting between local residents and Yellowstone Superintendent Horace Albright that helped jumpstart the notion of protecting the Tetons and Jackson Hole from development (see the box on p.89 for more details).

On the opposite side of the car park is the **Chapel of Transfiguration** (Episcopal services each Sunday: late May to late Sept, 8am and 10am). Built in 1925, its interior is simple, with a few pews cut from local aspen and a large picture window framing a heavenly view of the Tetons; among other chapels in the region, only the equally small Soldier's Chapel facing Lone Mountain in Big Sky (see p.223) comes close to having such a dramatic altar view.

Dornan's

Across the riverbanks from the rest of Moose, **Dornan's** (℡307/733-2415, ⓦwww.dornans.com) is effectively a park concessionaire. The private in-holding has been owned by the same family since Evelyn Dornan established a small fifteen-acre homestead here in 1922. Nowadays, amenities strung along the short drive include a small grocery store and deli; a fly shop and float trip operator, a bicycle rental shop and an outdoor goods store, in addition to year-round cabins, a gas station and a few dining options. Among the latter grouping, the best bet is *The Pizza Pasta Company* and its attached Wine Shoppe, from which you can buy a bottle, bring it to the popular upper deck of the relaxed restaurant and watch the sun set over the Tetons as the Snake River's golden shimmer turns ink-black.

East of Moose

Save for **Mormon Row**, the area east of Moose is an under-visited corner of Grand Teton, overlaid by a series of flat roads popular with cyclists on account of both light traffic and terrific wildlife-spotting opportunities. Two notable geological formations stand out in this area, the closest being **Blacktail Butte** (7688ft), which sprouts up from the sagebrush plains just east of Hwy-191. Visible for miles in all directions, the large, broad-shouldered hump is popular with both climbers and hikers (see **H39**, p.141). Along the park boundary further east are the foothills of the **Gros Ventre Range** (pronounced "grow-VAWN"), framing the eastern side of Jackson Hole and home to Sheep Mountain, where the staggering **Gros Ventre Slide** occurred in 1925. Sheep Mountain is also known locally as **Sleeping Indian**, as from the valley floor it appears to form the shape of a native chief, complete with headdress, laying flat on his back. Some claim the name of the range itself (meaning "big belly" in French) comes from this giant imaginary chief's stomach, but the more plausible explanation comes from another bout of miscommunication between French-Canadian fur trappers and natives. In an attempt to explain to the trappers that the natives living in these mountains were always hungry, members of the Plains tribes to the east rubbed their hands over their bellies. The trappers – quite possibly the same creative group who came up with the fantastical handle *Les Trois Tetons* – mistook this to mean the mountain-dwellers had large bellies, and thus the name Gros Ventre was born.

Gros Ventre Junction and Kelly

When entering Grand Teton from the south on Hwy-191, the first worthwhile side-trip begins at **Gros Ventre Junction**. Heading northeast from this intersection, Gros Ventre Road follows the sparkling **Gros Ventre River**, dotted with stands of cottonwood trees, to *Gros Ventre Campground* about five miles away. Keep a lookout for cyclists – this is a particularly popular stretch with local tour groups – and wildlife; in fact, this is one of the finest areas in Grand Teton for animal watching, with the sagebrush flats to the northwest a favourite gathering spot for the park's **bison** herd. On the road's opposite side, short paths access the river, lined with ideal spots for setting up a tripod to photograph **bald eagles** that perch waterside high upon cottonwood branches. Make plenty of noise if you approach the water, as **moose** are commonly found near the edge.

A few miles beyond the campground entrance is **Kelly**, a tiny village dating back to the 1890s that was once one of Teton County's largest communities, narrowly losing out on the county seat to Jackson by only a few votes in the early 1920s; later that decade, the town was inundated in a flood of biblical proportions and barely survived (see box, p.94). Other than a small grocery store and the picnic table outside the post office, there's little here to detain visitors. Several miles north of town and tucked into an attractive wooded valley is **Teton Science School**, hosting day-long wildlife tours, seminars, and short and long courses – see p.197 for details.

Mormon Row

A short drive east of Moose is the area's most popular attraction, **Mormon Row**. This stretch of historic barns can be reached from the south along a dirt road (look for a poorly signed turn just east of *Gros Ventre Campground*), or more easily via **Antelope Flats Road**, which connects to Hwy-191 north of Moose Junction. Clustered around the intersection of these two side roads are a series of old wooden structures in various states of disrepair, including two proud buildings – known as the **Moulton Barns** – that might be the most photographed barns on the planet, framed by the shark-toothed Tetons in the background and surrounded by grazing bison and blooming wildflowers throughout summer. Now maintained by the Park Service, the structures were built by homesteaders in the early 1900s, most of whom were Mormons escaping drought conditions in modern-day Utah. All the homesteads that weren't already sold by the 1920s were scooped up by the Snake River Land Company, save for an acre in-holding still owned by descendants of the barn-building Moultons and now home to the excellent *Moulton Ranch Cabins* (see p.187 for details). Even if you're not staying the night, stop by the front gate, where the friendly proprietors have posted a **map** detailing the original settlers and their plots from 1918, including the phonetically spelled "Grovont" homestead.

Past Mormon Row, Antelope Flats Road continues east across gently sloping terrain – a migratory path of the region's **pronghorn** – to an intersection with **Shadow Mountain Road**; a southward turn leads towards Kelly and the Gros Ventre Slide, while to the north the winding road turns to gravel and snakes in and out of Bridger-Teton National Forest, affording stupendous views of the Tetons before eventually emerging out by *Triangle X Ranch* near the historic Cunningham Cabin along Hwy-191.

Gros Ventre Slide and around

A few miles north of Kelly sits the **Gros Ventre Road** junction amid working cattle fields. Heading east and out of Grand Teton, the meandering road leads up to the area's most intriguing sight, the Gros Ventre Slide, just under five miles away. Less than a half-mile from the turn-off, the road passes **Kelly Warm Spring**. The small, spring-fed pond is a popular spot with local citizens (and bison) for a quick dip in its warm, squishy-bottomed pool; no more than three feet deep, it's most fun for kids, who can splash while trying to catch the tiny minnows swimming about. Less than 1.5 miles onwards, the road passes by a popular sight for Western movie buffs: a **cabin** used in the filming of *Shane*. While an entire town set was built west of here on Antelope Flats, this dilapidated frame is one of the few remaining structures left from the Oscar-winning 1953 film.

After passing the cabin, the road leaves the national park to enter **Bridger-Teton National Forest**. As if on cue, the landscape begins to change as the road again veers near the Gros Ventre River and climbs steadily past progressively redder bluffs. Tiny viewpoints every few hundred yards hold vistas into the dramatic river valley below – much of it home to *Gros Ventre River Ranch*, a working dude ranch with space for forty guests (see p.185) – before reaching the **Gros Ventre Slide Geological Area**. The view here looks straight across the river valley to the wide scar caused by an earth-shaking landslide in 1925 (see box, p.94). Dramatic as the reddish gash may be, the true power of the massive slide is best appreciated on the half-mile loop starting below the parking area. Ramshackle signs along the **interpretive trail** point out local flora, but it's the head-on view of the slide and flood area, where the remains of bleached tree trunks and large boulders are scattered about like tossed playing cards, that demands attention. At the loop's far end is a fine view of **Lower Slide Lake** to the east, created by the slide itself.

Landslides and torrents

On June 23, 1925, a rancher living at the foot of **Sheep Mountain** heard a noise he couldn't identify. It had been a very wet spring, and water had seeped into the layers of rock above his ranch. What he experienced over the next two minutes was the **Gros Ventre Slide**, one of the largest landslides ever witnessed. A nearly mile-long slump of the mountain – estimated to be fifty million cubic yards of rock, sandstone and shale – broke free, tumbling into the valley below and sliding as far as 300ft up the opposite slope. Witnesses likened it to a massive tidal wave rushing down the mountain; within minutes, the debris blocked the Gros Ventre River and **Lower Slide Lake** began to form behind a huge natural dam. Engineers debated the strength of the 200ft-high earthen dam and determined it would hold, which it did until May 18, 1927, when it gave way and the lake spilled out, virtually washing away the town of **Kelly** – only the church and a handful of other buildings survived the torrent – and killing six people. The deadly wall of cascading water was a mile wide in some places, and it drenched towns along the Snake River basin for days, leaving deposits of mud upwards of three feet high in Jackson, over ten miles away.

Beyond the slide area, the landscape continues to meld into the red and orange bluffs that local **bighorn sheep** call home. Towards the centre of Lower Slide Lake, by the lakeside is serviceable *Atherton Creek Campground* (mid May to late Sept; 23 sites; $12). Beyond here, the road worsens considerably, leading five miles to another pair of National Forest **campgrounds** (*Red Hills*, *Crystal Creek*). Drive slowly, as this stretch is used by local mountain bikers looking for a bumpy road ride; trailheads along the way lead up Horsetail, Redmond and Miners Creeks, all good for isolated treks into Bridger-Teton. Beyond the campgrounds, the road continues to meander for another ten miles or so before finally petering out, passing **Upper Slide Lake** along the way.

Central Grand Teton

The heart of Grand Teton stretches from Moose Junction north to Jackson Lake Junction, spanning all the major peaks in the Teton Range along with most of the park's glacial lakes, including **Jenny Lake** and the southern end of **Jackson Lake**. Two major roads bisect the area, forming an epic 45-mile loop dotted with viewpoints and side roads boasting the park's best vistas, along with numerous trailheads and points of historic interest. The more celebrated of the two is **Teton Park Road**, which hugs the base of the peaks and accesses both popular **Signal Mountain Summit Road**, with panoramic views 800ft above the valley floor, and **Jenny Lake Scenic Loop**, a one-way route affording memorable views of the mountains that tower over the lake's west shore. Further from the peaks to the east and on the opposite side of the Snake River, the views from speedier **Hwy-191** are more panoramic and best timed to be seen around dawn or dusk.

Hwy-191: Moose to Jackson Lake Junction

Directly north of Moose Junction, a car park at **Blacktail Butte** accesses a set of rough steps leading up to some popular climbing routes. Just beyond the Antelope Flats Road turn-off leading to Mormon Row, the highway passes **Blacktail Ponds**

Overlook; from the overlook, a steep, rocky slope leads down to the ponds themselves. Once prime beaver habitat, these ponds today are visited by fishermen who cut across the marshy meadow to cast lines from the banks of the Snake River (permitted Aug–Oct only).

A couple of miles ahead is **Glacier View Turnout**, where a head-on view of the Grand Teton is fronted by the cottonwood- and Engelmann spruce-lined path of the Snake River, with several hundred yards of sagebrush flats in the foreground. It's a neat encapsulation of the park's varied landscapes that's capped off by **Teton Glacier** itself, the largest of a dozen still-active glaciers flowing down shaded mountain pockets within the park; note the glacial debris piled up beneath it, looking like scoops of rock dumped by the most enormous bulldozer one could ever imagine. The park's current glaciers are not remnants of the last major ice age, known as the Pinedale Period; rather, they were formed approximately 1000 years ago and have been shrinking since the so-called Little Ice Age ended around 1850.

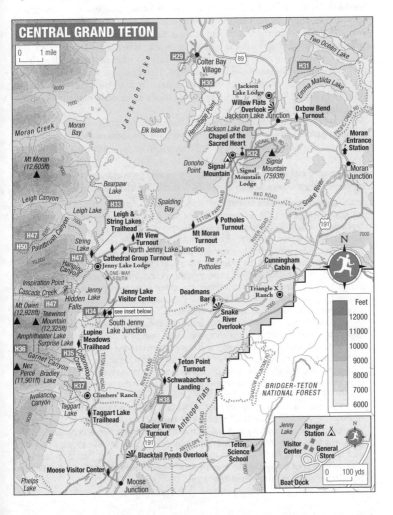

Global warming is certainly accelerating the process, and most climatologists now predict that Teton Glacier will be a memory within fifty years.

The next turn-off from the highway accesses **Schwabacher's Landing**, located one mile down a gravel road and of most interest to boaters. The area around the landing, however, also makes for a lovely picnic spot, where you can spot trout facing upstream, snagging bites of their own lunch as you eat yours. Afterwards, consider taking a meandering stroll along the banks of the Snake (see H39, p.141) – head north for the finest photo opportunities. Back on Hwy-191 and about another mile past Schwabacher Road is **Teton Point Turnout**, where another view of the Tetons melts hearts as signs interpret the region's unique geology.

Snake River Overlook to Cunningham Cabin

Continuing northward on Hwy-191, you soon arrive at the first of two celebrated scenic viewpoints between here and Jackson Lake Junction: **Snake River Overlook**, three miles north of Teton Point Turnout across the grey-green expanse of Antelope Flats. This spot is particularly popular with photographers at dawn and dusk, when the Tetons are at their most angular, looking like broken shards of glass cutting into the sky. The Snake River bends widely in the foreground, and from this vantage point it's easy to note the steep, 200ft-high banks marking the course of the larger ancient river that once flowed through the valley. To try to get two bends of the river in your shot (as Ansel Adams did in his iconic 1942 photo *The Tetons – Snake River*), take a short walk past the northern end of the turnout and look back.

After Snake River Overlook, Hwy-191 immediately spills downhill, cutting through a patch of thick forest to the turn-off for **Deadmans Bar**. After a very steep entry, this side road turns to gravel, leading in under a mile to a popular raft

---

Murder at Deadmans Bar

While the area around **Deadmans Bar** is perfectly peaceful today, it was the sight of a bloody incident in 1886. In the summer of that year, only two years after settlers first began arriving in Jackson Hole, four Germans, including a man named **John Tonnar**, set up a claim on the Snake River hereabouts to take up placer mining. They hoped to extract gold from the riverbed, as the gravel here was reputed to be rich with the valuable mineral. The precious metal was indeed present, but separating it out quickly and profitably proved to be a near-impossible task. Perhaps this complication is what led to arguments within the group – or perhaps, as Tonnar later claimed, it was the fact that the other miners ganged up on him, roughing him up in an attempt to scare him off and keep his share of the gold after the hard work of digging was completed. Whatever the cause of disagreement, Tonnar murdered his three companions – one by gunshot, the other two by axe-bludgeoning – then weighed the bodies down with rocks and hurled them into the river.

The crime may have gone unnoticed had Tonnar done a better job disposing of the bodies, but soon afterward, a group of vacationers floating down the Snake made the gruesome discovery of the dead men floating just below the surface. A posse was quickly formed to track Tonnar down, which they did with surprising ease – perhaps still in a state of shock, he had not travelled far and was found working on the ranch of local homesteader Emile Wolff cutting late summer hay. Sent to jail in Evanston, two hundred miles south, he was put on trial the following spring and pleaded not guilty. His story of abuse at the hands of the other miners must have struck a chord with the jury, as he was – much to the surprise of the judge and local populace – actually found **not guilty**. Directly after the trial, Tonnar smartly boarded the first train out of town and was never heard from again.

Gunfight at the Cunningham Cabin

As with nearby Deadmans Bar, the **Cunningham homestead** played a major role in one of Jackson Hole's earliest violent dramas. Contrary to the myths promoted by several Hollywood Westerns filmed in Jackson Hole decades later, the homesteading period here was a generally peaceful time, with gun battles nearly nonexistent and poachers, not villainous bandits, assuming the role of major scoundrels. In the fall of 1892, however, Cunningham was approached at his first ranch on Flat Creek, closer to Jackson, by two men looking to buy hay for a group of horses they had in tow. Along with selling them hay, Cunningham agreed to let the men winter in his cabin twenty miles to the north. Throughout the snowy months, rumours that the two men were **horse thieves** swirled about, and when a posse of riders from nearby Driggs, Idaho, arrived in April 1893 looking for the culprits behind a recent equine theft, they were pointed in the direction of Cunningham's cabin. In total, 16 armed men – including several residents of Jackson who joined the posse in town – rode to the homestead in the middle of the night and announced their presence at dawn. A gunfight quickly ensued, and when the smoke cleared both of the alleged rustlers had been killed. The posse had originally set out to arrest the men, not kill them, and without a trial or even concrete evidence that the two men were the actual thieves to begin with, the incident of vigilantism was quickly hushed over, even today remaining one of the region's darkest, most secretive chapters.

launch along the Snake that's named after one of Jackson Hole's most grisly tales (see box opposite). While the story makes for great campfire fodder, there's little to see here today, so continue further north along Hwy-191 as it squiggles past **Hedrick Pond** to *Triangle X Ranch*, offering week-long stays and guided fishing/float trips throughout summer, and snowmobiling in winter (see p.174 for details).

North of the ranch on the other side of the highway is the historic **Cunningham homestead**, known as the Bar Flying U Ranch when established by J. Pierce Cunningham in the late 1880s. Cunningham, who arrived in Jackson Hole in 1885, already had a ranch closer to Jackson, but he decided to stake out a new homestead for himself here since its soil – filled with sediments left behind by an ancient glacial lake – was better than most in the valley. Though the scene of a macabre shoot-out in its early days (see box above), the homestead evolved into one of the region's most successful, eventually expanding to over five hundred acres. Cunningham likewise became one of the valley's leading citizens, but by the mid 1920s even he was feeling the combined pinch of drought and plummeting agricultural prices, leading him, like most others, to sell his holdings to the Snake River Land Company in 1928.

Once home to several buildings, including a comfortable ranch house, all that stands today is a long and low-slung **cabin**. The first building Cunningham built to "prove up" his homestead claim, this "dog-trot"-style, sagging structure – actually two small cabins connected by an open breezeway – is maintained in its original condition, with its horizontal logs chinked with dirt mortar, its roof sporting a thick layer of earth and its west-facing "windows" (read: square openings in the walls) boasting million-dollar views of the Tetons above a dirt-packed floor. Afterwards, walk the half-mile loop around the property, littered with homestead reminders such as postholes, building foundations and irrigation ditches and gates. The overall spread provides an evocative backwards glance into the rough existence of homesteaders in the late 1800s and early 1900s, who had to figure out how to scratch out a living raising cattle and crops such as hay, alfalfa and oats in a valley averaging a slim sixty frost-free days a year; indeed, a popular saying among settlers in Cunningham's times went, "If summer falls on a weekend, let's have a picnic."

Moran Junction to Oxbow Bend

Six miles north of Cunningham Cabin, **Moran Junction** is the end of the line for visitors taking a free tour of Grand Teton via Hwy-191. If driving north towards this junction around dawn or dusk, pull over for a moment to listen for a random howl; the park's eastern corner around **Uhl Hill** (7443ft) has become a favourite hunting ground for **wolves**. From Moran Junction, you can continue north within the park, passing through the **Moran Entrance Station**, or leave Grand Teton by heading east on Hwy-26/287 over Togwotee Pass (9658ft) towards Dubois, Wyoming, 55 miles away. The road crosses over the **Buffalo Fork** of the Snake River and past scenic **Buffalo Valley Road** to Bridger-Teton National Forest's *Hatchet Campground* (mid May to late Sept; 9 sites; $10) eight miles away. Just beyond is Bridger-Teton's Buffalo Ranger District office, where information on the area's many outdoor activities, including superb trout fishing on the Buffalo Fork, is available.

From the Moran Entrance Station, it's five miles west to Jackson Lake Junction. About one-third of the way there, **Pacific Creek Road** splits off to the north, accessing trails leading around **Two Ocean Lake** and **Emma**

A Teton geological primer

The Rockies on the whole, including the nearby Snake River and Gros Ventre Ranges, are composed of mountains formed between forty and eighty million years ago. The **Teton Range**, however, is the baby of the system, dating back as far as nine million years, when two massive blocks along the **Teton Fault** began pushing against one another. Movement along the fault, running roughly along the same lines as Teton Park Road, started to release the intense stress caused by the stretching and thinning of the earth's crust. As the blocks along the fault grinded against one another, the mass to the west rose as the block on the east sank. The most commonly used example to illustrate the action is a trap door, with one side lifting to create the Tetons, the other falling to form **Jackson Hole**. Standing on the flat valley floor, it's easy to think that the block forming the Tetons did all the work; however, geologists estimate that the Jackson Hole block has actually fallen four times as far as the Teton block has risen.

This dramatic faulting and lifting, however, is only part of the story. As soon as the mountains and valley floor began forming, **erosion** kicked in with its sculptural work. Wind and rain each played significant roles, but glaciers created the most spectacular effects. The three most recent glacial advances are known as the **Buffalo Period**, the oldest at around 200,000 years; the **Bull Lake Period**, covering the region close to 140,000 years ago; and the **Pinedale Period**, at its peak only 25,000 years ago. Created by years of continual snowfall followed by minor or no snowmelt, glaciers up to several thousand feet thick formed during these periods. Gravity and their own massive size forced them into movement, and as these seas of ice flowed downhill and through Jackson Hole, they carved away at rocks, transporting incredible amounts of debris with them along the way. Evidence of their handiwork can be found virtually everywhere throughout the park, including spectacular **U-shaped canyons** such as Cascade and Death Canyons. At the base of these canyons, deposits of glacial debris known as **moraines** formed natural dams, leading to the creation of the **piedmont lakes** – Jenny, Phelps, Taggart, Bradley, String and Leigh – at the range's base; **cirque lakes**, such as Lake Solitude high above Paintbrush Canyon, and **kettle lakes**, like the Potholes west of the Snake River, were created by glaciers as well. Even the flat valley floor owes its current existence to glaciers, which scraped its plains nearly pancake-flat. The dozen glaciers that remain within the park today are not leftovers from these major periods, but instead formed several thousand years ago during a minor ice age; today, they're all disappearing at a steady pace.

Matilda Lake (see **H31**, p.135). It's certainly not an essential detour, and the road can be rough and slow-going, but there's a desirable **picnic area** at Two Ocean Lake despite being one of the few spots in the park not dominated by a view of the Tetons.

Back on the highway heading westbound, a few miles beyond Pacific Creek Road is the second of the two especially notable viewpoints along Hwy-191, **Oxbow Bend Turnout**. A loop in the Snake River that's cut off from the main channel, the big bend hosts plenty of **wildlife** in and around its calm waters, from river otters and moose to osprey, great blue herons and pelicans; visitors line the banks accordingly throughout the day in search of the perfect photo. Panoramically speaking, the massive bulk of **Mount Moran** (12,605ft) is the star of the show here, and on particularly clear days, Skillet Glacier on the mountain's front face appears clearly in the river's mirrored reflection.

Teton Park Road

Informally known as the Inner Loop Road, **Teton Park Road** stretches twenty miles from Jackson Lake Junction down to Moose. A more leisurely route than the "outer loop" of Hwy-191, the road unveils one spectacular view after another as it curves around Jackson Lake to hug the Tetons by their base. Top highlights include **Signal Mountain Road**, a five-mile drive up to Jackson Hole's most dramatic viewpoint, and beautiful **Jenny Lake**. Named for the Shoshone wife of famed Jackson Hole trapper and guide "Beaver Dick" Leigh – Jenny and their children all died tragically of smallpox in 1876 – the lake is dramatically set at the mouth of Cascade Canyon and reflects the peaks that tower 7000ft over its surface; in fact, there's more vertical distance from the lake's surface to the summit of Grand Teton than from lake level to sea level.

Jackson Lake Dam and around

From Jackson Lake Junction, Teton Park Road cuts south along the edge of Willow Flats before crossing **Jackson Lake Dam**, the lake to the right and the controlled flow of the Snake River to the left. Car parks on both sides of the dam allow for a closer look at the 60ft-high concrete structure, originally built in the early 1900s and thoroughly retrofitted in the 1980s (see box, p.100). Pretty as Jackson Lake looks from atop the dam in early summer, it's easy to forget that the visible body of water is in truth a reservoir, dammed to impound the Snake River and irrigate farms in Idaho's Snake River Valley. This reality comes into focus by late summer, when the drained lake shrinks and leaves behind wide, muddy banks. Sitting forty feet beneath the water's surface when the reservoir is full, the original Jackson Lake was nearly 10,000 acres smaller than today's version.

On the lake side of the road a short way from the dam is the **Chapel of the Sacred Heart**, a popular summer wedding spot. Built in 1937, the log cabin hosts Catholic services between June and September (Sat 5.30pm, Sun 5pm; ☎307/733-2516). Inside is a lovely piece of purple-and-gold stained glass with the sacred heart at its centre, while behind the chapel is a serene lakeside **picnic area** featuring a terrific view of Mount Moran across the water.

Signal Mountain Lodge and Road

Up next on the southbound tour along Teton Park Road is **Signal Mountain Lodge**, once an exclusive fishing resort and now a privately operated cluster of amenities. While the lakeside setting is splendid, some of the fading facilities themselves are a time warp back to the 1970s; along with motel rooms, cabins and

The damming of Jackson Lake

"Let me pause to lay my ineffectual but heartfelt curse upon the commercial vandals who desecrated the outlet of Jackson's Lake with an ugly dam to irrigate some desert land away off in Idaho...There is more beauty in Jackson's Hole than even such a beastly thing could kill; but it has destroyed the august serenity of the lake's outlet forever; and it has defaced and degraded the shores of the lake where once the pines grew green and dark. They stand now white skeletons, drowned by the rising level of water."

Owen Wister, *Harper's Magazine*, 1936

The battle over **water** in Jackson Hole is but one small chapter in the sordid tale of irrigating the arid West. Skirmishes here began almost immediately after settlers arrived, as homesteaders dug ditches off the Snake River and its tributaries to water their plots; these practices continue today, with issues over taxation and the rights of neighbouring states to local water remaining inflammatory issues. Much of the drama centres on the federal government's **Reclamation Service**, established in 1902 to oversee water development projects throughout the western states.

Immediately after being formed, members of the Reclamation Service began to survey and construct dams in the greater Yellowstone area, starting with the Shoshone Dam – known now as the Buffalo Bill Dam – outside Cody in 1904. In 1907, the Reclamation Service built the first **Jackson Lake Dam** out of logs. After its failure soon after, construction began on a larger concrete structure in 1910. There was little local opposition as this new dam was being built, especially since construction flooded the local economy with revenue, and an overall sense persevered that the rugged valley (and its citizenry) could only benefit from taming the land.

Within a few years of its completion in 1916, however, opinions began to change dramatically. The dam had bloated Jackson Lake into a caricature of its former self, destroying acres of forest and surrounding the lake with an unsightly ring of dead trees that took decades to clear. Even more insulting locally, the new dam did nothing to benefit farmers within Wyoming, as potato and beet farmers downstream in Idaho received all the **rights** to the pent-up water – rights they still retain today. The Reclamation Service's domineering management style angered residents as well, to the point that plans for damming Jenny Lake and several other rivers and lakes within Grand Teton and Yellowstone were all shouted down in subsequent years.

The role Jackson Lake Dam has played in limiting more dams in the region is arguably its most lasting legacy. A less comforting future legacy has been suggested by the recent warnings of **earthquake** experts. Though reinforced only three decades ago, seismologists believe the dam, located less than ten miles from the Teton Fault, would be destroyed by a major quake – something the fault, geologically speaking, is due for anytime. It's hard to forecast the exact effects of a wall of water six storeys high ripping down the Snake River, though there's little doubt that devastation would ensue.

a park campground, these include a gas station, a grocery/sporting goods store and a pair of restaurants and bars. If you're not spending the night or grabbing a meal, the chief reason for pulling in is Jackson Lake itself. The lodge's **marina** rents all manner of watercraft, from canoes and kayaks to motorboat and flat-bottomed deck cruisers, and also operates private fishing and sailing tours (see p.164 for details).

Of more interest to non-sailors is nearby **Signal Mountain Road**, a five-mile route leading 800ft up to the summit of Signal Mountain (7593ft). Laced with plenty of curves (trailers or RVs are not permitted), the ride up can be painfully slow, but the trip is well worth it, especially to view a sunrise or sunset. Separate car parks access two summit **viewpoints**: the first, Jackson Point Overlook, faces west towards the mountains and is the end of a fine hike (see **H32**, p.136), while the second, Emma Matilda Overlook, faces northeast towards its namesake lake. The views from both are unforgettable, with the Teton Range at its most majestic and Jackson Hole looking impossibly flat, its clusters of valley floor forest akin to continents adrift on a dusty ocean plain; also visible is the Gros Ventre Range ringing the valley to the east and, on particularly clear days, the Absaroka Mountains in Yellowstone to the north.

South to Jenny Lake

Less than a mile south of the Signal Mountain Road turn-off is **RKO Road**, named for the early Hollywood studio that used the area's dramatic backdrop to film an assortment of Westerns. Unpaved, the heavily rutted road is a bit of a slog (4WD recommended), crossing the sagebrush flats with wonderfully wide-open views east for 3.5 miles to a small parking area by the Snake River. Fishermen frequently use the route, but anyone can park by the water and hike the trails along this peaceful stretch of the river; it's a good elk-spotting area, as well as a simple way to experience the solitude of a float trip without actually getting out onto the water. If a 4WD vehicle is at your disposal, it's possible to follow **River Road**, which branches off south from RKO Road, about a dozen miles along the western shelf of the Snake River. An exceedingly rocky route also open to **mountain bikes**, it eventually rejoins Teton Park Road by the picnic area north of Taggart Lake Trailhead. Come October, the entire road closes until spring to protect the migratory path of local pronghorn.

Between the RKO Road entrance and North Jenny Lake Junction are two stellar viewpoints. The first, **Potholes Turnout**, focuses on the pockmarked plains to the south that are dotted with tiny depressions created by stagnant blocks of ice left behind by retreating glaciers. Slightly further south and on the opposite side of the road is **Mount Moran Turnout**, from which the fourth-tallest peak in the Teton Range looms across Jackson Lake. One of five glaciers still clinging to the flat-topped peak, aptly named Skillet Glacier, is clearly visible on Moran's front face, as is a black, vertical stripe at the peak called a diabase dike that's made of hardened magma some 775 million years old.

South again, past a dirt road leading north to a secluded **boat ramp** at Spalding Bay on Jackson Lake, is **Mountain View Turnout**, the final lay-by along this stretch.

Jenny Lake Scenic Loop

At **North Jenny Lake Junction**, the road splits, with Teton Park Road continuing its march southward at the same spot where a four-mile scenic loop branches off towards the mountains. This latter route, **Jenny Lake Scenic Loop**, is justifiably one of the most popular drives in the park since it accesses a string of glacial lakes – **Leigh Lake**, **String Lake** and **Jenny Lake** – each meriting a look on foot. Before reaching them, the wooded road cruises by **Cathedral Group Turnout**, a good place to brush up on the geological forces that created the singularly gorgeous scene before you. Boards explain the naming of the Cathedral Group – Teewinot Mountain, Mount Owen and Grand Teton, forming a massive, multi-faceted fortress from this view – and point out the five-storey-tall **fault scrap** visible beneath nearby Rockchuck Peak, clear evidence of the dramatic rising and falling still occurring along the Teton Fault.

Unless you're an overnight guest, there's little to see at high-end *Jenny Lake Lodge* south of here, but visitors with an hour or so to spare should take the road across from it to **Leigh and String Lakes Trailhead**. From the picnic area beside String Lake, an easy and scenic trail leads one mile alongside the narrow lake through woods to a picturesque view across the greenish waters of Leigh Lake; if you have more time, continue on to Bearpaw and Trapper Lakes (see H33, p.137). Becoming a one-way route south of *Jenny Lake Lodge*, the Scenic Loop next skirts the eastern edge of Jenny Lake before meeting back up with Teton Park Road. A **viewpoint** en route offers superb views across the lake up into Cascade Canyon, along with the option to scramble down the moraine ridge to soak your feet in the crystalline waters.

South Jenny Lake

Back to a single highway, Teton Park Road quickly passes the entrance to **South Jenny Lake**, a buzzing hub of activity around the lake's southeast shore. The main car park fills up fast during peak season, and most visitors hustle straight for the boat dock to rent kayaks and canoes or hop on the charming pontoon **ferry** across the lake (see p.164 for details). Taking off every fifteen minutes, the ride disembarks at the mouth of Cascade Canyon, from where the park's most popular trail leads to nearby **Hidden Falls** and, more strenuously, **Inspiration Point** high above Jenny Lake. Long lines can form at both docks in the afternoon, so either plan on completing the round-trip in the morning or skip the boat ride by hiking to (and/or from) the far boat dock along a moderate two-mile trail that hugs the lake's south and west perimeters (see **H34**, p.138 & **H47**, p.153).

Back near the parking area are two handy information centres. **Jenny Lake Visitor Center** (daily: mid May to early June 8am–5pm, early June–early Sept 8am–7pm, rest of Sept 8am–5pm; ☎307/739-3343) is housed in cosy Crandall Studio, built in 1925 as a gallery and store by local photographer/painter Harrison Crandall; it was moved here from its original setting by String Lake in 1995. It's a

---

A grand debate

In 1872, **Ferdinand Hayden** returned to Yellowstone with his band of cartographers, guides, artists and soldiers for a second exploratory tour of the region. Months earlier, President Ulysses S. Grant officially declared Yellowstone the world's first national park, and Hayden's expedition party spent the summer mapping close to 10,000 square miles of the region's terrain. To cover the huge expanse, his group split into northern and southern divisions, with Hayden's second-in-command, **James Stevenson**, leading the Snake River Division south down along Shoshone and Lewis Lakes and into Jackson Hole. Tagging along with this group was **Nathaniel "National Park" Langford**, a former member of the Washburn Expedition (see p.253) and now Yellowstone's first Park Superintendent. On July 28, fourteen expedition members set out to climb **Grand Teton** (13,770ft). Half of the group made it as far as the peak's Lower Saddle (11,200ft), and Langford and Stevenson certainly made it as far as Upper Saddle (13,160ft), as they were the first to officially report a man-made rocky enclosure found there, thought to be a native spiritual site. Both claim to have continued onwards a further 610ft up extremely technical terrain to the summit. Weeks later, an elated Langford gave a speech to the entire gathered expedition, proposing that Grand Teton's name be changed to Mount Hayden. Hayden proudly accepted, and so in a span of about two weeks the iconic peak was successfully conquered and also renamed.

Or so it seemed. Momentum for the name-change quickly fizzled out, and before the turn of the century, so did widespread belief in Langford and Stevenson's bold claim. In August 1898, six members of the Rocky Mountain Club began climbing

terrific place to visit not only for its information desk, relief map of the park and exhibits detailing local geology, but for its fireplace that's most welcome on chilly days. A few steps away, **Jenny Lake Ranger Station** (mid May to mid Sept, hours vary; ☎307/739-3343) dispenses backcountry permits along with climbing information. Rangers here are responsible for search-and-rescue missions, and a simple exhibit inside describes the most common causes of climbing accidents; according to rangers, 93 percent of accidents are due to human error as opposed to gear failure or acts of nature. Should you want to try climbing, headquarters for highly regarded **Exum Guides** is a short walk south across Cottonwood Creek (see p.168 for details). Also in the South Jenny Lake area is the popular tent-only *Jenny Lake Campground*, as well as **Jenny Lake Store**, good for a coffee and free copy of the *Jackson Hole Daily* newspaper.

South to Moose

Save for a pair of trailheads, there's not a whole lot of reason to stop on Teton Park Road south from Jenny Lake to Moose. The views along the entire eight-mile stretch are continually extraordinary, however, with nothing between the road and towering Grand Teton due west but sagebrush plains. **Lupine Meadows Trailhead**, 1.5 miles down an unpaved, but well-maintained side road, is a popular jump-off point for climbers, and also the best place to set out from if hiking well uphill to Amphitheater Lake and/or Garnet Canyon (see H35 & H36, p.138 & p.139). Some mountaineers stay at the **Climbers' Ranch** a few miles further south on Teton Park Road, a set of rustic cabins run by the American Alpine Club. Nearby **Taggart Lake Trailhead** is the starting point for hikes to Taggart and Bradley Lakes (see H37, p.139), both hidden behind the forested moraines – bumpy islands of green floating on the dry outwash plains – visible from the roadside parking area.

Grand Teton. Two stopped at Upper Saddle, while the remaining four – **William Owen**, **Franking Spalding**, **Frank Peterson** and **John Shive** – continued on, picking their way carefully to the top. Their path, known now as the **Owen-Spalding Route**, remains heavily used as the easiest, albeit still tricky, way up the summit. Atop the peak, the four members could not find any signs of prior human visitation; as per custom, they chipped their names into boulders and left behind a cairn as proof of their visit. Soon after, Owen published a story in the *New York Herald* describing his group's adventures and claiming that they were, in fact, the first to reach the peak; a public battle quickly ensued, with Langford defending his and Stevenson's claim. Inconsistencies in some of Langford's previous accounts – Langford wrote, for example, that the enclosure was actually on the summit, and not well below, as is the case – plus a complete lack of physical proof weakened his case, and Owen eventually won the war of words; ever since, his group has been recognized as the first to officially climb Grand Teton (of course, whoever built the lonely rocky enclosure in the Upper Saddle decades, or even centuries, earlier could very possibly have completed the climb long before the days of record-keeping).

As for other documented firsts, **Eleanor Davis**, vice-president of the Colorado Mountain Club, became the first female climber to top Grand Teton, in 1923. And in June 1971, **Bill Briggs** crested the summit, clicked into his skis and became the first maniac to ski down the Grand. Briggs now runs the ski school on the less death-defying terrain of Jackson's Snow King ski resort, roughly twenty miles south of his famed feat.

Northern Grand Teton

Along with its scenic viewpoints and handful of outstanding hikes, the northern third of Grand Teton is most notable for the amenities grouped around two main stopovers, **Jackson Lake Lodge** and **Colter Bay Village**. Both are located a short way north of Jackson Lake Junction, from where it's 24 miles via Hwy-191 to Yellowstone's southern border, the final third of which leads through **John D. Rockefeller, Jr. Memorial Parkway**. The area's main draw is Jackson Lake, humming with watercraft galore throughout summer. Boat ramps are located at Colter Bay Village and **Leeks Marina** further north until late August most years, by which point the water diet of Idaho farmers downstream has drained the lake-cum-reservoir to levels unsafe for docking and cruising.

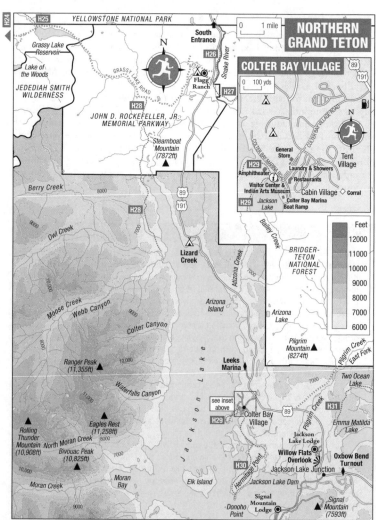

Jackson Lake Lodge and around

Just north of **Willow Flats Overlook** – one of the best spots in the entire Yellowstone region for moose spotting – **Jackson Lake Lodge** is the park's swankiest public area. *Jenny Lake Lodge* may be more expensive, but unless you're an overnight guest, there's little to see or do there. On the contrary, *Jackson Lake Lodge* boasts plenty of activity beyond its hotel rooms and cottages. Built by Rockefeller's Grand Teton Lodge Company, the main lodge was considered an eyesore by many upon its 1955 opening. The bluff-top, Gilbert Stanley Underwood-designed inn is certainly not as memorable as other national park masterpieces – Robert Reamer's *Old Faithful Inn* (in Yellowstone – see p.72) and Underwood's own *Ahwahnee Hotel* (in Yosemite) immediately come to mind – but the architect's blocky design here has survived its critics well with simple, Modernist grace. Closer to the main road, the complex is also home to **Grand Teton Medical Clinic** (daily: mid May to mid Oct 10am–6pm; ☎307/543-2514) and a **corral** featuring trail and wagon rides (May–Sept; ☎307/543-2811).

Jackson Lake Lodge warrants a stopover for its monumental **upper lobby**, where a series of massive picture windows line the southwestern wall, perfectly framing the Teton skyline beyond. Along the other three walls are wildlife prints by painter Carl Rungius – some of the originals hang in Jackson's National Museum of Wildlife Art (see p.206) – and nearby is the table where US and Soviet diplomats signed a statement of peace in 1989, helping end the Cold War. With plenty of couches, two large corner fireplaces, a coffee kiosk, free wireless internet and a newsstand downstairs, the common area is a relaxing spot to temporarily plug back into the outside world. For more substantial fare, two of the park's top **restaurants** – the diner-like *Pioneer Grill* and more expensive *Mural Room* (details on p.194) – are just steps away.

Accessed from the upper lobby, the lodge's large back **deck** features a stunning vista over Willow Flats, a brushy expanse that stretches between the lodge and Jackson Lake; the deck is without peer when it comes to **sunset** socializing in Grand Teton. A ranger is often posted here at dusk on summer evenings to answer questions and help scope out moose in the marshy meadows below, and it's a rare evening when at least one of the gangly creatures isn't spotted from a distance. The deck's *Blue Heron Lounge* also does a roaring trade, enabling visitors to enjoy local beers and huckleberry margaritas with the knockout view.

Lunch Tree Hill

An interpretive, paved **trail** north of *Jackson Lake Lodge*'s massive deck leads a quarter-mile up historic **Lunch Tree Hill**. Legend has it that during a picnic upon this hill in 1926, Yellowstone Superintendent Horace Albright helped convince John D. Rockefeller, Jr. – who had hiked up this same hill two years earlier with his sons – of the need to protect the mountains and surrounding valley as a national park (see box, p.89); thanks to the work of these two men, you don't need to be a millionaire to enjoy the unfettered hilltop view today. The first section of the trail, which eventually leads north to Colter Bay, is lined with placards detailing how features throughout Jackson Hole earned their names. If you're spending the night in the area, consider making the walk up at **dusk**, when Willow Flats' tiny sparrows come alive to swoop drunkenly about for insects while the Tetons, appearing lit from within, radiate with evening alpenglow.

Colter Bay Village and around

Though named after John Colter – the Lewis and Clark expedition member and daring trapper widely considered to be the first white man to explore the Yellowstone region (see p.252) – there's nothing particularly adventurous about **Colter Bay Village** at first glance. Built around huge parking areas a few miles north of *Jackson Lake Lodge*, the sprawling development is nonetheless a good place to run errands in the park. Dotted around several large car parks are a fairly well-stocked grocery and sports shop (daily: late May to Sept 6.30am–9.30pm), laundry facilities, public showers and gas stations. Further out on the village's edges are tent, RV and cabin accommodation and two serviceable restaurants.

Unappealing as Colter Bay Village looks, there are several worthwhile activities here. Foremost is a tour of **Native American artefacts** in the visitor centre's museum, while outdoor options start with the series of flat and well-marked **trails** that begin immediately nearby, offering superb mountain views as well as waterside opportunities to spot moose, osprey and an assortment of colourful ducks (see **H29**, p.134 & **H30**, p.135). Provided water levels are high enough, rental boats and tickets for lake cruises can be had at the nearby **marina**, while horseback rides head out from **Colter Bay Corral** – for details on each, see p.164 and p.167, respectively.

Colter Bay Visitor Center and Indian Arts Museum

Along with dispensing general information and backcountry permits, **Colter Bay Visitor Center** (daily: early Jun–early Sept 8am–7pm, early May to early Jun & early Sept–mid Oct 8am–5pm; ☏307/739-3594) is the meeting place for a handful of ranger-led walks and lectures, both inside and in a pleasant amphitheatre nearby, throughout the week in summer. The centre also shelves an impressive array of books on native cultures, a great primer for its free **Indian Arts Museum** one room over, itself a welcome surprise both for the quality of its collection and its atmospheric layout. Spread over several moodily lit levels, the works were purchased from collector David T. Vernon (1900–73) by Laurance S. Rockefeller in 1972, who then handed them over to the park for display. Not limited to regional tribes, the overarching theme is the utilitarian nature of native art – it's not enough for an item to look good, it also must serve a function. This ideal comes to life in the display case filled with impossibly intricate beaded sashes, pipe cases and tomahawk sheaths, along with the dozens of worn, yet beautiful moccasins shown nearby. Equally transfixing are the feathered Crow coup sticks, used by braves who would get close enough to enemies to tap them with one of these sticks – known as "counting coup", the ultimate test of courage – before retreating. The lower level hosts a studio where a rotating cast of native guest artists create and sell original pieces.

Leeks Marina to northern border

Hwy-191 follows the eastern shore of Jackson Lake as it steadily climbs north towards Yellowstone, and a string of picnic areas, along with a marina and campground, line the route. **Leeks Marina** is officially open from mid May to mid September, but its docks may close earlier in particularly dry years; sheltered in Pelican Bay and guarded by Moose and Cow Islands, the marina is named after pioneer Stephen Leek (see box opposite). With no rentals or campground, there's not a whole lot for the visitor who doesn't have a boat in tow, though *Leek's Pizzeria* here makes a decent pie (see p.193).

From the marina, Hwy-191 continues north through thick forests dotted with occasional meadows. Past *Lizard Creek Campground*, the northernmost such outpost in the park, the road climbs further before leaving Grand Teton and entering John D. Rockefeller, Jr. Memorial Parkway.

Father of the Elk

Stephen Leek, one of the most intriguing but least renowned of Jackson Hole's early settlers, arrived in the valley in 1888. Unlike most of his fellow transplants, Leek, an accomplished hunter, didn't take up homesteading, but instead set up shop as a hunting and fishing guide, expanding his operations over several decades from a humble tent by the Snake River to a large hunting lodge complete with tourist cabins and gas station near where Leeks Marina sits today. Eventually run with the help of his two sons, what was known as **Leek's Camp** is considered by some locals historians to be Jackson Hole's first dude ranch.

As is the case with most experienced hunters, Leek respected his prey, and he was one of the first local citizens to sound the alarm over the valley's dwindling **elk** population. By the early 1900s, several elements were working in tandem to destroy the elk's long-standing way of life, not the least of which was how Jackson Hole's ongoing homestead expansion was cutting off migratory paths and taking over important elk wintering grounds. Adding to this was the fact that without any federal oversight, poachers were running rampant, including the particularly devious **tuskers**, a group who would slaughter elk solely for their eye teeth – an item that, in a sad bit of irony, members of the fraternal Elks Club across the country paid handsomely to wear as ivory pendants. Outraged local citizens, including Leek, eventually managed to run the tuskers out of the valley, but they could do little when the brutal **winter of 1908–09** blew through. Combined with the decline of good grazing lands, the intense cold led to a gruesome mass starvation, with skeletal elk walking the streets of Jackson in search of anything green. Even after settlers realized the extent of the tragedy and began feeding the starving creatures hay, thousands of elk died off. Throughout the winter, Leek lugged about his camera – given to him by one of his wealthy customers, George Eastman of Kodak fame – and photographed the carnage.

The following spring, Leek toured with his **photos** and gave lectures on the need for elk preservation, earning him the nickname "Father of the Elk" and leading Wyoming to authorize $5000 for the purchase of winter feed. Soon after, the federal government became involved and created the **National Elk Reserve** in 1912 on the outskirts of Jackson. Pieced together from public and privately purchased lands, the refuge not only helped protect wintering elk, but also promoted the positive side of turning private lands over to the government for preservation, an idea that culminated in the creation of Grand Teton National Park nearly two decades later.

John D. Rockefeller, Jr. Memorial Parkway and around

Connecting Grand Teton to Yellowstone, **John D. Rockefeller, Jr. Memorial Parkway** is essentially an eight-mile stretch of highway surrounded by nearly 25,000 acres of forest. The parkway was established in 1972 to recognize the work of the legendary conservationist, who a played a critical role in the creation of not only Grand Teton, but several other national parks as well, including Acadia in Maine, Shenandoah in Virginia and Great Smoky Mountains in the Appalachians. As the road continues its climb out of Jackson Hole, there's little – save for the starting point of the hike out to Huckleberry Mountain along the Sheffield Creek Trail (see H27, p.133), and a turn-off explaining the still-evident **Huck Fire** of 1988 – in the way of diversion until **Flagg Ranch** (☎1-800/443-2311, ⊛www.flaggranch.com) a couple of miles from Yellowstone's South Entrance Station. Originally established as a tiny fort by the US army in the early 1900s, at the time in charge of Yellowstone's safekeeping, the resort was then operated as a dude ranch throughout much of the twentieth century. Today it's a family resort, most useful to passers-by for its gas station, convenience store and picnic area – the last of which is best enjoyed at the turnaround point of an easy amble along Flagg Canyon (see H26, p.132). Along with cabins and a campground (see p.187 for details), the resort runs horseback rides, guided fishing excursions and river trips, and has a restaurant open to the public. However, unless you're planning on rising early to either drive west on adjacent Grassy Lake Road or fish in the Snake River – there's a good trout hole just upstream of the bridge due south of Flagg Ranch – there's little reason to spend the night.

Flagg Ranch Information Station (daily: early June to early Sept 9am–3.30pm; ☎ 307/543-2327) by the main lodge is most useful for getting directions to Polecat and Huckleberry Hot Springs. Come winter, Hwy-191 ends at Flagg Ranch, once a buzzing launching point for **snowmobiles** in Yellowstone but now, due to stringent regulations, a veritable ghost town throughout the cold months, with only the occasional group or snowcoach pulling in.

Grassy Lake Road

From Flagg Ranch, **Grassy Lake Road**, also known as Reclamation Road, meanders 47 bumpy miles west to Ashton, Idaho. Along the way, the road leaves John D. Rockefeller, Jr. Memorial Parkway and enters Caribou-Targhee National Forest, skirting 10,000-acre **Winegar Hole Wilderness** along Yellowstone's southern border. Taking at least two hours to drive in the driest conditions, the heavily rutted dirt road is best tackled with a 4WD vehicle. While a few sights (as well as places to camp) are a short drive from Flagg Ranch, the ragged route is mainly used by those accessing Yellowstone's secluded **Cascade Corner** (see p.83) from the south.

One mile west of Flagg Ranch sits the tiny parking area for a trail leading to meadowside **Polecat and Huckleberry Hot Springs**, clothing-optional dipping spots used mostly by locals; some dedicated soakers even snowshoe into the springs in winter (ostensibly while clothed). Completely undeveloped, these natural springs are best visited with a knowledgeable local in tow, as otherwise you risk being scalded by dipping into the wrong spots. Past Polecat Creek, Grassy Lake Road turns to dirt as it soon passes the first of several rustic **camp sites** and the northern terminus of the **Glade Creek Trail** (see H28, p.133); for the next thirty-plus miles the road remains unpaved, leading through patches of woods, large marshy areas and lovely open meadows.

At **Grassy Lake Reservoir** itself, eleven miles west of Flagg Ranch, the road crosses over a 1930s-era dam built as a compromise to appease those who wanted to impound Yellowstone Lake's waters. Three separate trailheads just north of this reservoir lead to some of Yellowstone's most isolated attractions, including stunning Union Falls (see H25, p.131). Further on, Winegar Hole Wilderness just to the north is prime **grizzly habitat**, while other creatures to watch for in this wildlife-rich area include black bear, moose, fox, elk and waterfowl such as sandhill cranes and loons; it's a region also renowned for **wildflowers**. Approximately fifteen miles west from Grassy Lake Reservoir is arguably the road's prettiest sight, **Indian Lake** – covered in a blanket of lily pads, it's a wonderful picnic area where bald eagles and moose are commonly seen.

Continuing west, the road becomes paved within a few miles. If heading to Yellowstone's Cascade Corner, look for signs pointing towards **Cave Falls Road** soon after hitting the paved stretch. Beyond the turn-off, the road races through rolling Idaho farmland, with the sloping rear of the Teton Range clearly visible all the way to **Ashton**, a small town dominated by pair of grain elevators. From Ashton, it's fifty miles northeast on Hwy-20 and over Targhee Pass (7072ft) to West Yellowstone (see Chapter 12).

Day hikes

eyond the car parks and boardwalks lies Yellowstone and Grand Teton's greatest feature: the wilderness itself. There are nearly **1500 miles of trails** weaving through Yellowstone and Grand Teton, and no trip is complete without at least a long ramble or two. Regrettably, only a small percentage of visitors head out for a hike of any length, perhaps due to a mistaken assumption that mysterious gear and a secret set of backcountry skills are needed. Whatever the cause, buck the trend and dedicate as much time as possible to hiking; you'll be rewarded by stellar scenery and welcome solitude.

The shorter **interpretive trails** – such as the boardwalk loops through Yellowstone's main geyser basins – have been detailed within chapters 1 to 3. The fifty hikes discussed within this chapter and the next cover only a portion of the options in both parks, but offer a solid range for both first-time and veteran

"Leave no trace" hiking guidelines

- **Carry out all rubbish** If you pack it in, pack it out. Some hikers carry a small plastic bag and pick up items dropped by less considerate souls.
- **Stay on the trail** Walk single file and refrain from cutting switchbacks.
- **No souvenirs** Leaving no trace also means leaving all as you found it. Fallen antlers, wildflowers, driftwood and the like are not fair game and should be left where found.
- **Bury bodily wastes** Use the chemical toilets found at most trailheads – and if you get caught short on the return, bury waste at least six inches deep and one hundred feet from any stream or river. Carry a small plastic bag so you can carry out your toilet paper.
- **Stand aside for horses and uphill hikers** Horses and mules are common on many trails – step off the trail to let them pass. Uphill hikers have right of way.
- **Purify drinking water** Use a giardia-rated filter or purifier, or boil water for five minutes.
- **Camp away from water and trails** Ensure you're at least two hundred feet away from lakes and streams, and out of sight of nearby trails, if possible.
- **No "improvements"** Don't dig trenches, cut vegetation or build windbreaks or new fire rings.
- **Follow fire rules** Never light a fire where banned; where fires are allowed, use only existing fire rings. Burn only dead and felled wood.
- **Wash clean** Avoid putting anything (even biodegradable soap) in lakes and streams; carry your washing water 100–200 feet away.
- **Be bear-safe** See box on p.110.

visitors. Picking out the "best" hike within either park is impossible, as the spectrum of choice is simply too vast. Certain hikes are better for wildlife or dramatic vistas, however, and we've included a short **comment** at the start of each hike to help narrow down your choices. Generally speaking, you're best off picking a trail that's close to where your day begins or en route to your evening's destination – virtually every trailhead leads past something memorable, and there's

Bear awareness

There are an estimated six hundred **grizzly bears** – and nearly as many **black bears** – within Yellowstone alone, and you don't want to meet any of them up close. In both parks, sightings are monitored and posted at ranger stations and trailheads, and the risks of running into a bear are pretty low on heavily tramped trails. Despite the overall scarcity of **attacks**, bear-awareness is crucial to both humans and the local ursine population, so it's essential when hiking and camping to be vigilant, obey basic rules, know the difference between a black bear and a grizzly (the latter are bigger and have a humped neck – see p.266 for further details), know how to avoid dangerous encounters and understand what to do if confronted or attacked.

The cardinal rules

Be prepared by following the **cardinal rules**: store food and rubbish properly, make sure bears know you're present, don't approach or feed them and, if you find yourself approached by one, don't scream - and certainly don't run. When hiking, walk in a group (bears are less likely to attack if there are more than four people) and, since bears feel most threatened when surprised, make lots of noise by speaking or clapping as you traverse the wilderness (note, however, that popular tinkling "bear bells" are often not loud enough). Be especially alert and noisy when close to streams, in tall vegetation or when travelling into the wind, as your scent won't carry to warn bears of your approach; also, move straight away from dead animals and berry patches, both important food sources. Watch for bear signs – get out quickly if you see fresh tracks, diggings or droppings – and keep in the open as much as possible. Finally, report any sightings to a ranger upon your return.

As for **camping**, do so away from rushing water, paths and animal trails, and keep your site scrupulously clean. Store food and rubbish in a bear-proof canister, or hang it well away from your tent between two trees at least fifteen feet above the ground (many campgrounds have bear poles or steel food boxes). Never bury rubbish – bears will just dig it up – and certainly don't store it in or near your tent. Avoid smelly foods, including fresh, dried or tinned meat and fish, and never store food, cook or eat in or near your tent, as lingering smells may invite unwanted nocturnal visits. Aim to cook at least 100 to 200 feet *downwind* of your tent; freeze-dried meals and plastic bag-sealed food work best. Likewise, keep food off clothes and sleeping bags, and if possible, sleep in different clothes than those in which you ate. One technique worth considering is stopping to cook and eat dinner on the trail before arriving at your backcountry site, thus keeping the scent of food away from your overnight area.

Close encounters and attacks

Bears are wildly unpredictable, and experts can't seem to agree on the best tactics should an **encounter** occur; indeed, there's no guaranteed life-saving way of coping with an aggressive bear. Calm behaviour, however, has proved to be the most successful strategy in preventing an attack, for bears don't actually *want* to attack – rather, they simply want to know you're not a threat. Bears in the act of feeding little point in wasting an hour or two in the car heading to a different area before striking out.

If you follow the basic guidelines, hiking one of the less strenuous trails in this chapter should be quite easy, regardless of age or experience. If you prefer a **guided hike**, however, several local nonprofits and tour operators listed in Chapter 10 are happy to help; these aren't only for novice hikers, as visitors looking for information on specific subjects such as bear behaviour and geology also stand to gain a great deal from them. More **experienced hikers** may feel restricted by this chapter's day-hiking recommendations and can jump to Chapter 5, "Backcountry hiking and camping".

and mothers with cubs are particularly dangerous and prone to suspicion. When a bear makes woofing noises, snaps its jaw, puts its head down and ears back or moves toward you, it generally means it's pegging you as a target. A bear raised on its hind legs and sniffing is trying to identify you – and if it does so repeatedly, it's getting agitated.

Ideally, on first encounter you want to stand stock still, never engage in direct eye contact (perceived as aggression by the bear) and – absurd as it sounds – start speaking to it in low tones. Whatever you do, **don't run**, which simply sets off an almost inevitable predator–prey response in the bear; after all, a bear can manage up to 35mph, a speed you can't dream of. Instead, back away quietly and slowly at the first encounter, looking downward while speaking gently to the bear. If your subtle retreat seems to be working, make a wide detour, leave the area or wait for the bear to do so – and always leave it an escape route.

If you're **attacked**, things are truly grim. With grizzlies, playing dead – curling up in a ball, protecting your face, neck and abdomen – is the most effective response. Fighting back will only increase the ferocity of a grizzly attack, and there's no way you're going to win. Keep your elbows in to prevent the bear from rolling you over, and be prepared to keep the position for a long time until the bear loses interest. You may be subjected to one good blow and a few minutes of attention, and that's it – your injuries may still be severe, but you'll probably live. With a black bear the playing dead routine won't wash, though they're not as aggressive as grizzlies, and a good bop to the nose or sufficient frenzy on your part *may* actually send your furry attacker scampering off. Don't play dead with either species if the bear stalks or attacks while you're sleeping in your tent. In these cases, the bear would rather make a meal out of you instead of toss you around for amusement, so fight back with abandon – people who have survived such attacks have often had an uncommonly brave companion clatter the bear with something big and heavy.

Bear spray

The most prevalent anti-bear measure sold in stores throughout the region is **bear spray**, a mace-like pepper spray designed to be blasted into the face of an attacking bear. In no way does carrying such a spray substitute for the precautions detailed above, but as a last-ditch resort to avoiding an attack, it can be effective; we recommend carrying a pressurized canister ($30–50). Of course, for the spray to be effective it needs to be handy, so be sure to keep it either holstered on your hip or in an immediately reachable pocket. Rumours abound of some users spraying the deterrent on themselves and their gear, as one would insect spray – don't do this. Besides enduring the embarrassment of explaining why you've spent the last hour having your eyes hosed out, studies have shown the spray's scent might actually *attract* curious grizzlies. After purchasing, read all the enclosed instructions and be sure to test out the spray with a quick downwind blast.

Hiking practicalities

A backcountry use permit is not required for a day hike. This doesn't suggest, however, that hikers should head straight out without certain **prerequisites**. Along with a map, you'll want suitable footwear, plenty of water and food in case you're delayed on the trail, and – perhaps most importantly – warm and waterproof clothing. Fierce thunderstorms are common throughout summer in and around the parks, and it can snow here any month of the year, so always be prepared for the worst. For full details on footwear, clothing and what else to lug along, see p.147.

Staying on track

Trails throughout both parks are largely well maintained, with clearly posted **signs** detailing directions and distances at most junctions. Likewise, the majority of trailheads post directions and current trail conditions, and free **trail maps** providing a basic sketch of recommended day hikes are available at visitor centres. However, for any trip into the woods over a mile or two in length, you should bring along a detailed **topographic map**, as signs get blown down, knocked over by wildlife or simply vandalized; anyway, even seasoned hikers get disoriented on occasion. A variety of options are sold in the region's visitor centres and at most ranger stations – highly recommended are the series of waterproof maps by Trails Illustrated (National Geographic), as well as those by Beartooth Publishing. Trails Illustrated's map of Grand Teton (1:80,000; $12) is fine for the smaller of the two parks, but its overall Yellowstone map (1:168,500; $12) is designed on too large a scale to be of much use. Instead, choose one or more of its maps splitting Yellowstone into four equal-size quadrants (1:63,360; $12 each): Old Faithful, Mammoth Hot Springs, Tower/Canyon and Yellowstone Lake.

Safety

Hiking alone is only recommended for experienced trekkers, and even solo experts and groups should always leave a projected itinerary behind with someone. Heed the advice of rangers and sign in at all trailheads wherever you're expected to do so. The most common **safety issues** come down to errors of judgement rather than natural disasters, and most can be averted simply by making sensible decisions based on your level of experience. There are lots of fantastic hiking opportunities available in well-travelled areas with clearly marked trails, so you're better off sticking to these if your experience is limited. Remember, too, that a detailed topographic **map** and **compass** are only helpful if you know how to use them.

Mountain weather is notoriously unpredictable, and hail and snowstorms can arrive any time of year. **Hypothermia** is the top cause of hiking deaths; regardless of conditions when setting out, always pack a warm, waterproof layer and put it on *before* you get wet or cold. When hiking above treeline, you'll be completely exposed to the sun, in which case a lightweight long-sleeve shirt is a very good idea, in addition to hat and sunglasses. If **lightning** becomes a potential threat, swiftly head down below treeline; if you get stuck in the open, crouch between boulders or hunker down atop insulating material such as a foam sleeping mat. **Altitude sickness** can also be a concern to many – see p.30 for more information on adjusting to the region's high elevations.

Yellowstone's **thermal areas** demand special caution. When walking through a geyser basin, always stick to marked trails to avoid burns (or worse) by breaking through thin crusts covering boiling water. Never travel through thermal areas after dark, and remember that it's illegal to bathe in any waters completely of thermal origin (see p.169 for legal places to dip and soak). Certain trails require

Hydrothermal Yellowstone

The Yellowstone Caldera, a massive volcanic crater created by an epic explosion some 640,000 years ago, outlines one of the planet's most active volcanic hot spots. Thousands of annual earthquakes attest to the forces bellowing below, but it's Yellowstone's incredible array of hydrothermal features – including half the world's geysers – that best prove the vigour of the area's volcanic muscle. Most geologists don't expect the Caldera to blow again for thousands of years, so in the meantime the park's wonderland of sparkling hot springs, gravity-defying geysers and other magma-driven oddities will remain to mystify and amaze.

Whirligig Geyser ▲

Grotto Geyser ▼

Hot springs and geysers

Yellowstone's most common and visually splendid hydrothermal features are its **hot springs**, often called pools. Hot springs are sourced by boiling water heated by magma located only a few miles underground. Unlike geysers, there are no constrictions in the spring's underground plumbing, meaning the superheated water can circulate via convection and cool off before reaching an eruptive level. Along with the numerous springs bubbling by the park's busy boardwalks, pools ranging from deep puddles to giant-sized hot tubs dot the backcountry. Keep your distance, tread cautiously around them when forced to, and forget about taking a dip – these pools are scalding at best, deadly at worst.

There are more than three hundred active **geysers** in Yellowstone, by far the largest concentration on the planet. Essentially hot springs that erupt both water and steam, geysers are formed by a constriction within the spring's plumbing that prevents the superheated water from reaching the surface to cool; eruptions occur when groundwater forms bubbles that blow the water through vents at the top. Yellowstone's geysers appear in two basic forms: fountain geysers, which typically bubble up into a pool and gush water before subsiding; and cone geysers, which shoot a single jet upwards through a cone or nozzle formed by a steady accumulation of mineral deposits.

Colourful wonders

The most distinctive element of Yellowstone's ten-thousand-plus hydro-thermal features is their amazing range of **colours**. The brilliant shades of blues are caused by the refraction of sunlight off particles in the water, while the remaining palette of colours – reds, oranges, yellows, browns, purples – that ring springs and collect in runoff channels are brightly coloured algae and bacteria called **thermophiles**. The range of colour indicates a specific temperature range: green, brown and rust-red typically specify cooler water; brighter pink, yellow and orange, meanwhile, indicate hotter water, with some thermophiles living in temperatures over 170°F.

Mudpots, fumaroles and travertine terraces

Rudely burping and plopping away, you'll find children of all ages in the midst of giggle fits when standing by **mudpots**. These are hot springs with a limited, but highly acidic water supply, and depending on the amount of water available, they can range from a weak, soup-like consistency to thick pools of melted tar; they've also been known to expel dollops of hot mud onto bystanders, so be prepared to high-tail it should one get particularly raging. The bubbling within mudpots is caused by escaping gases – the reason they typically stink – rather than boiling temperatures.

Reaching temperatures as high as 280°F, **fumaroles** are the hottest type of hydrothermal feature. Like mudpots, they also run short of water as they ominously hiss steam through underground fissures that reach deep into molten rock below. Near Yellowstone's northern boundary, meanwhile, Mammoth Hot Springs' **travertine terraces**, while not classified as a distinct hydrothermal feature, nevertheless make up the park's most alien landscape. Beneath Mammoth's limestone is an extensive web of fissures and tunnels that forces acidic hot water up from the magma-heated underworld, depositing

▲ Orange Spring Mound

▼ Sapphire Pool

Fountain Paint Pot ▲

Riverside Geyser ▼

the rock's calcium carbonate as distinctive chalky-white mounds and terrace-like formations containing psychedelic, thermophile-generated streaks of brown, green, yellow and orange.

Must-see hydrothermal features

▶▶ **Abyss Pool** A 53ft-deep pool that, along with nearby Black Pool – likewise a stone's throw from Yellowstone Lake – makes a trip to West Thumb Geyser Basin essential. See p.76.

▶▶ **Fountain Paint Pot** A flatulent pool of bubbling mud in Lower Geyser Basin, watery in spring before growing thick towards summer's end. See p.69.

▶▶ **Grand Prismatic Spring** Yellowstone's largest spring is also its most vivid, a fierce blaze of near-neon blues, reds, yellows and oranges at Midway Geyser Basin. See p.70.

▶▶ **Lone Star Geyser** It's a pleasant five-mile round-trip hike or bike ride to this dramatic geyser, whose picturesque eruptions make it the park's most popular backcountry hydrothermal feature. See p.152.

▶▶ **Orange Spring Mound** This heaping mass of travertine along Mammoth's Upper Terrace Drive sports an orange coating wherever water continues to seep down. See p.49.

▶▶ **Riverside Geyser** Perched on the banks of the Firehole River, this beautifully sited crowd-pleaser erupts, on average, every six hours. See p.73.

▶▶ **Roaring Mountain** North of Norris and named after the growl of sulphurous steam pouring off it, Roaring Mountain's face is pockmarked with dozens of fumaroles. See p.61.

▶▶ **Sapphire Pool** The bright blue star of Biscuit Basin lives up to its name as well as any feature in the park. See p.74.

river crossings; for these, bring along a pair of lightweight, but sturdy sandals – it's foolhardy to cross slippery streambeds barefoot, and you'll regret it for hours if your boots become soaked – and either lock arms with a partner or use a walking stick for balance. Also be sure to unstrap your pack so you can slip out quickly should you fall. If a crossing seems particularly perilous or is over thigh-deep, don't think twice about turning back.

Encounters with large **animals** such as bears, elk, bison and moose demand awareness and respect (for details on bears, see p.110). As park rules state, you must stay at least 100 yards away from bears and at least 25 yards away from all other animals. You're far more likely to be bothered by biting insects such as **mosquitoes** and **ticks**, for which a strong repellent and long trousers are your best defences. Conduct a thorough body search for ticks after walking through brushy areas – these tiny insects can pass along Colorado tick fever and Rocky Mountain spotted fever (albeit very rarely). If you find one burrowing into your skin, grab it by the head with a pair of tweezers and yank it out.

Always take caution when **eating** or **drinking** in the wild. All water not taken from a tap, regardless of how clean the source appears, should be boiled for up to five minutes or pumped through a giardia-rated filter or purifier. And unless you're absolutely positive of your ability to pick out edible berries, plants and mushrooms in the wild, do not eat them – at least a half-dozen varieties of poisonous mushrooms grow in the parks, along with other dangerous plants such as water hemlock that are best avoided.

Hikes within Yellowstone

Busy as Yellowstone's roads can be, the more than one thousand miles of trails weaving through the park are often secluded and quiet. Certainly the further one travels from the roads, the more isolated the terrain becomes; on routes like the Thorofare Trail and those within Cascade Corner, it's easy to hike for a full day without spotting another person. But, even on the shorter and most popular paths, moments of seclusion are plentiful, along with scenes of idyllic beauty and virtually guaranteed opportunities for wildlife spotting.

Gallatin Corner

Rugged and constantly undulating, the trails in Yellowstone's under-visited **Gallatin Corner** lead into deep wilderness, while exceptional views avail

---

How difficult is the hike?

All the hikes in this guide have been given a difficulty rating in one of four categories:

Easy Generally a walk of up to a couple of hours on relatively smooth surfaces across flat or gently sloping ground.

Moderate A hike with some gradient but on well-maintained trails, taking up to several hours.

Strenuous A tougher proposition on fairly steep and occasionally rough ground, with a typical duration of several hours, if not more.

Very strenuous A trek of at least eight hours negotiating steep terrain on uneven ground.

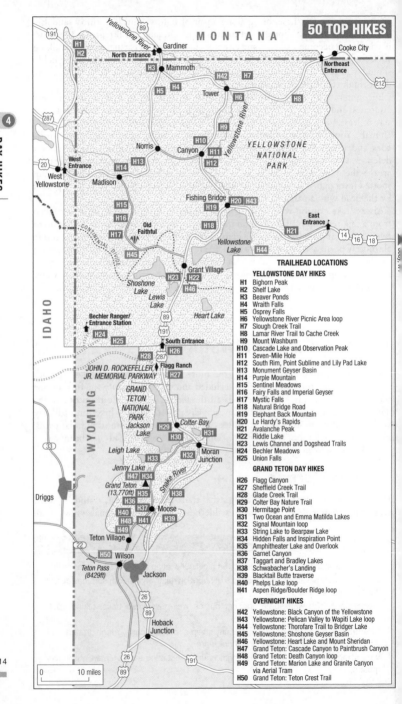

MONTANA

50 TOP HIKES

TRAILHEAD LOCATIONS

YELLOWSTONE DAY HIKES

- H1 Bighorn Peak
- H2 Shelf Lake
- H3 Beaver Ponds
- H4 Wraith Falls
- H5 Osprey Falls
- H6 Yellowstone River Picnic Area loop
- H7 Slough Creek Trail
- H8 Lamar River Trail to Cache Creek
- H9 Mount Washburn
- H10 Cascade Lake and Observation Peak
- H11 Seven-Mile Hole
- H12 South Rim, Point Sublime and Lily Pad Lake
- H13 Monument Geyser Basin
- H14 Purple Mountain
- H15 Sentinel Meadows
- H16 Fairy Falls and Imperial Geyser
- H17 Mystic Falls
- H18 Natural Bridge Road
- H19 Elephant Back Mountain
- H20 Le Hardy's Rapids
- H21 Avalanche Peak
- H22 Riddle Lake
- H23 Lewis Channel and Dogshead Trails
- H24 Bechler Meadows
- H25 Union Falls

GRAND TETON DAY HIKES

- H26 Flagg Canyon
- H27 Sheffield Creek Trail
- H28 Glade Creek Trail
- H29 Colter Bay Nature Trail
- H30 Hermitage Point
- H31 Two Ocean and Emma Matilda Lakes
- H32 Signal Mountain loop
- H33 String Lake to Bearpaw Lake
- H34 Hidden Falls and Inspiration Point
- H35 Amphitheater Lake and Overlook
- H36 Garnet Canyon
- H37 Taggart and Bradley Lakes
- H38 Schwabacher's Landing
- H39 Blacktail Butte traverse
- H40 Phelps Lake loop
- H41 Aspen Ridge/Boulder Ridge loop

OVERNIGHT HIKES

- H42 Yellowstone: Black Canyon of the Yellowstone
- H43 Yellowstone: Pelican Valley to Wapiti Lake loop
- H44 Yellowstone: Thorofare Trail to Bridger Lake
- H45 Yellowstone: Shoshone Geyser Basin
- H46 Yellowstone: Heart Lake and Mount Sheridan
- H47 Grand Teton: Cascade Canyon to Paintbrush Canyon
- H48 Grand Teton: Death Canyon loop
- H49 Grand Teton: Marion Lake and Granite Canyon via Aerial Tram
- H50 Grand Teton: Teton Crest Trail

0   10 miles

themselves along the region's mountain ridges. Wildlife sightings are frequent here as well, from moose browsing streamside to bighorn sheep clinging to the steep slopes of **Bighorn Peak**. The area's trailheads are accessed along the east side of US-191 north of West Yellowstone – a route that dips in and out of the park and skirts its entrance fee altogether – so consider hiking in this area if you're en route to or from Gallatin Valley and Big Sky (see p.222).

H1 Bighorn Peak

Ascending 3100 vertical feet in seven miles, this day-long trek is best suited to robust hikers acclimatized to the region's higher altitudes. The route described here follows the shortest, steepest route up 9930ft **Bighorn Peak**, beginning with a gradual climb along Black Butte Creek and through Gallatin Petrified Forest. At about the four-mile mark, the path switches gears considerably as it stretches into subalpine territory on the approach to the mountaintop, where an unforgettable panorama of Yellowstone's remote northwest wilderness awaits.

Beginning from the roadside trailhead, follow the **Black Butte Trail** as it meanders through forest alongside the northwest bank of its namesake creek. At the junction with the Dailey Creek Cutoff Trail about two miles in, continue uphill on the Black Butte Trail to your right. As you climb gently but consistently, be on the lookout for mule deer and moose; also keep your eyes peeled for slabs of petrified wood, a sure sign that you've entered **Gallatin Petrified Forest**. As the trail grade steepens a little over halfway to the summit, you may spot **bighorn sheep** and **bears** (most likely grizzlies). If the latter, exercise extra caution in autumn months as the giant creatures may be particularly aggressive due to the increasing dearth of whitebark pine nuts, the shortage of which is even more acute in this section of the park than in other areas.

Once you reach the Sky Rim Trail at 6.7 miles, the harshest climbing is behind you and you're only a short distance from Bighorn Peak, which sits atop Yellowstone's northwest border. From the summit, take in Sheep Mountain to the near northeast and the densely forested expanse of Gallatin National Forest to the north, as well as your path up (and back down) through the Gallatin River watershed to the southwest. After sufficiently soaking up the scenery, retrace your steps to Black Butte Trailhead.

Difficulty Very strenuous
Distance 14-mile round-trip
Estimated time 8–10hr
Season June–Sept
Trailhead location Map p.44. Black Butte Trailhead, just under 30 miles north of West Yellowstone on US-191.
Comments A steep climb to one of Yellowstone's least-visited promontories, with close looks at a petrified forest along the way; best hiked with a partner or group due to bear activity.

H2 Shelf Lake

Slightly less taxing than tackling Bighorn Peak, this hike to the **highest lake in Yellowstone** is a couple of miles longer and suitably rewarding; it also provides a chance to closely examine a recently burned landscape. Starting from well-marked **Specimen Creek Trailhead** on the east side of Hwy-191, the first six gently graded miles along the Specimen Creek Trail allow your leg muscles to loosen up – this entire section of the route climbs a mere one thousand

Difficulty Strenuous to very strenuous
Distance 16-mile round-trip
Estimated time 8–10hr
Season June–Oct
Trailhead location Map p.44. Specimen Creek Trailhead, just over 25 miles north of West Yellowstone on US-191.
Comments An all-day trek through a recently burned area to Yellowstone's highest lake.

vertical feet. About 1.5 miles from the trailhead, you'll find yourself amid the spot-burned remnants of 2007's **Owl Fire**, a conflagration caused by lightning that ultimately burned 2800 acres. Remain alert (especially on windy days) through this section, as dead branches snagged overhead may fall at any time.

At the four-mile mark, the trail crosses the North Fork of Specimen Creek and leaves the burned area behind; two miles beyond that at the junction with the Crescent Lake/High Lake Trail, continue following the north-leading Specimen Creek Trail to the left. From here, the path steepens considerably, although manageably, and once you arrive at meadow-lined **Shelf Lake** (9200ft) two miles later, your legs will have carried you from that junction another 1100ft into the heights of the Gallatin Range. With Sheep Mountain looming overhead to the northeast, a pair of picturesque **campsites** (WE5, WE7) are available here in the event you've planned ahead and wish to take your time returning to the trailhead; otherwise, follow the same path back to your vehicle.

Mammoth Hot Springs and around

The steamy travertine terraces of **Mammoth Hot Springs** are the main roadside attraction in the northwest corner of Yellowstone, but the best hikes hereabouts actually pass few thermal features. With several rivers and small ponds in the area, the featured backcountry attractions are wildlife and wildflowers, along with some attractive waterfalls. North of Mammoth, several trailheads line the dusty road to Gardiner, including the terminus of the narrow path within the **Black Canyon of the Yellowstone** (see **H42**), which ends in the affable town itself.

H3 Beaver Ponds

You almost certainly won't spot any beavers on the **Beaver Ponds Trail** – they're thought to be gone from this area – but you will pass a collection of lovely ponds while cutting through fields renowned for impressive wildflower displays. An added bonus is that this is one of Yellowstone's rare loop hikes that can be walked in a single morning or afternoon.

Starting from the northern end of Mammoth's Lower Terraces, the first several hundred yards of this hike are the steepest, climbing close to 400ft up Clematis Gulch along the **Sepulcher Mountain Trail**. At about the 0.75-mile point, you'll branch off to the north at a signed junction, following

> **Difficulty** Moderate
> **Distance** 5.2-mile loop
> **Estimated time** 2hr 30min–4hr 30min
> **Season** May–Oct
> **Trailhead location** Map p.46. At the southern edge of Mammoth, between Liberty Cap and the private stone house at the northern end of the Lower Terraces.
> **Comments** An easily followed hike great for spotting wildflowers and elk alike.

the Beaver Ponds Trail as it heads due north for a couple of miles before looping back towards Mammoth. Wildlife paths branch off in all directions from the main trail; to make sure you stay on the right route, look for orange blazes nailed high on tree trunks. As you approach the ponds at the loop's northern end, the trail dips in and out of shady woods – look for scars left by grazing elk on trunks of the area's aspen trees – and past a radio tower. The path **passes** by at least five ponds, so you'll want insect repellent handy if there's no breeze. Among the colourful flowers typically spotted here are delicate **Rocky Mountain iris** (the roots of which are poisonous) and gorgeous **yellow columbine**. After turning back to the south, the trail skirts the final, largest pond, home to the remnants of an abandoned beaver dam. Past here, the route crosses mainly high meadows dotted with sagebrush and, often enough, elk; take your time, as there are lovely views down to the town of

Gardiner to the north and dusty **Mount Everts** (7842ft) to the southeast. Toward trail's end, you'll walk alongside Old Gardiner Road, dipping down to its entrance behind *Mammoth Hot Springs Hotel*. From here, it's a short walk past the hotel and Yellowstone General Store back to the original trailhead to complete the loop.

H4 Wraith Falls

This trail to **Wraith Falls** is one of Yellowstone's shortest, and makes for a great short break while driving the Mammoth-Tower Road. Switching from dirt path to boardwalk and back again, the trail starts by cutting through somewhat marshy sagebrush meadows at the western end of the **Blacktail Deer Plateau**. Even on this brief jaunt, it pays to tote along your bear spray just in case, although you're far more likely to spot a bull elk, complete with majestic antlers. You get your first view of the falls after

Difficulty Easy
Distance 0.7-mile round-trip
Estimated time 30min
Season May–Oct
Trailhead location Map p.46. 5 miles east of Mammoth en route to Tower, half a mile past Lava Creek Picnic Area.
Comments An extremely short trail leading to the base of a nearly 100ft-tall cascade.

crossing Lupine Creek on a short wooden bridge; the trail then quickly twists up a moderate incline to a viewing platform with a head-on view of Wraith Falls. Fed by Lupine Creek and rushing down a 95ft-long rocky slide, the cascade is more pleasant than powerful, and appears ghostly (as implied by its name) under a full moon. After enjoying the view, return the way you came.

H5 Osprey Falls

Only those with stamina to spare will get to witness **Osprey Falls** as it plunges 150ft within narrow **Sheepeater Canyon**. Beginning from the roadside trailhead, the first three miles are easy as the route follows a bumpy service road that curls around the southern flanks of rounded **Bunsen Peak** (8564ft); the dirt road is open to mountain bikes as well. Around the southeast side of the peak, you get your first view into deep Sheepeater Canyon. After heading steeply downhill about a hundred yards, the road joins the **Osprey Falls Trail** and leads down into the canyon. As the wooden sign here notes, the trail beyond is indeed "steep and

Difficulty Strenuous
Distance 9-mile round-trip
Estimated time 3hr 30min–6hr
Season May–Oct
Trailhead location Map p.46. Bunsen Peak Trailhead, south of Golden Gate Canyon five miles from Mammoth en route to Norris.
Comments One of Yellowstone's top bike-and-hike options, with thundering, hidden falls a just reward for a steep downhill climb.

narrow", and if you've biked in, you'll have to dismount and lock up at this point.

Before beginning the long switchback descent to the **Gardner River** some 500ft below, the trail leads south along the canyon rim for about 0.25 miles, affording views of the bands of volcanic pentagonal columns protruding from the canyon walls. Once the trail begins its descent, the incline instantly turns steep and rocky; take your time on the more than mile-long climb to give your knees plenty of breaks. With the canyon being so narrow, you don't get a view of the mighty falls until turning a corner down by the banks of the river. The awe-inspiring falls thunder down a fifteen-storey drop, a cascade that results in large volumes of white water downstream in May and June; still, the waterfall remains impressive throughout summer. If you're confident in your footing, climb past the falls' spray for a rocky perch only a few feet from the rushing water. The walk back up is no picnic, however, so be sure to rest before retracing your steps to the trailhead over 4.5 miles away.

Tower-Roosevelt, Lamar Valley and around

Taking in Yellowstone's northeast quadrant, these hikes cover stupendous **Lamar Valley**, trout-rich **Slough** and **Pebble Creeks** to the north and the northern reaches of the **Yellowstone River**. While there are few thermal areas of note, wildlife abounds and the fishing along most rivers and creeks is superb. We've also included the popular hike up **Mount Washburn**, located roughly equidistant between Tower-Roosevelt and Canyon to the south.

H6 Yellowstone River Picnic Area loop

Starting from **Yellowstone River Picnic Area**, this looping path affords grand views down into the park's longest river around **Calcite Springs**, plus opportunities for spotting osprey and bighorn sheep. It's not a perfect loop – the final stretch back to the trailhead requires a walk alongside the Northeast Entrance Road – but the section of the hike away from the river, which leads through a varied landscape, makes it worthwhile.

Difficulty Moderate
Distance 3.7-mile loop
Estimated time 2–3hr
Season May–Oct
Trailhead location Map p.53. Yellowstone River Picnic Area on the Northeast Entrance Road, one mile east of Roosevelt Junction.
Comments A family-friendly loop hike with impressive, easily reached canyon views.

The trail begins by climbing steeply uphill, parallel to the road out to Lamar Valley, to the east rim of an area known as the **Narrows of the Yellowstone**. For the next 1.5 miles, the trail sticks close to the canyon's edge, the sulphuric smells of Calcite Springs on the opposite side of the river a constant companion. Look out also for the scores of cute **yellow-bellied marmots**, which dart among the rocks by the canyon edge and often approach hikers, though try and resist the temptation to feed them. Along with peering into the canyon to view the rows of **volcanic basalt columns** and, possibly, the nests of **osprey** and **peregrine falcons**, keep a sharp eye on the trail ahead for **bighorn sheep**; if they spot you first, they'll scamper further down the canyon and out of sight. As the trail nears the two-mile point, it turns east away from the river, giving a final view towards the columns guarding Tower Fall (no view of the cascades, however). The next mile leads mainly downhill, weaving through fragrant sagebrush meadows and past a small stand of aspen trees; **pronghorn** are commonly spotted grazing in the area, and **black bear** sightings are not infrequent. Upon reaching the Northeast Entrance Road, it's an unexciting 0.7-mile return walk west to the starting point.

H7 Slough Creek Trail

One of the finest backcountry trips for anglers in Yellowstone, the **Slough Creek Trail** is equally popular with backpackers, particularly for autumn colours and plenty of elk-spotting opportunities. The wide path weaves its way more than ten miles from the trailhead to Yellowstone's northern border –

Difficulty Moderate
Distance 4 to 20-mile round-trip
Estimated time 2–12hr
Season May–Oct
Trailhead location Map p.53. Just before *Slough Creek Campground*, a couple of miles down the gravel road off the Northeast Entrance Road five miles east of Roosevelt Junction.
Comments Superb fishing opportunities and a broad, attractive valley make this a very popular trail.

across which sits the private **Silver Tip Ranch**, which runs frequent pack and wagon trips down the trail. Should you want to hang around overnight to explore further, seven backcountry campsites line the trail; all need to be booked far in advance as fishermen tend to scoop them up quickly.

The trail's first half-mile is entirely uphill and weeds out the unfit – unless they've chosen to ride horses in, of which there is ample and odorous evidence along the trail. After flattening out, the trail leads through a lightly forested zone before dipping slowly down to Slough Creek, just under two miles from the trailhead. This attractive, broad valley area is known as the **First Meadow**; the trail, passing Buffalo Fork Junction and the dilapidated Slough Creek Patrol Cabins, cuts through the meadow, with smaller paths across the tall grass offering access to the river. Five miles from the trailhead is the **Second Meadow** and the first set of backcountry campsites, while three miles further on is the **Third Meadow**, also complemented with a set of campsites and arguably the finest fishing destination. There's no real goal for day-trippers, so hike out as far as you wish, then simply follow your footsteps back.

A second option, seven miles from the trailhead, is to follow the **Bliss Pass Trail** six strenuous but stunning miles east over Bliss Pass (9250ft) to switchback down to the **Pebble Creek Trail** and back south to the Northeast Entrance Road. This makes for a very rewarding 21-mile trip, though you'll either need to arrange for a shuttle or hitch a ride back to the trailhead at Slough Creek.

H8 Lamar River Trail to Cache Creek

This relatively flat trail allows visitors used to lugging cameras and binoculars to leave the heavy equipment behind for a few hours and get out onto the floor of **Lamar Valley**, where a bison-eye view of "North America's Serengeti" awaits. Along with **bison**, you might see **coyote**, **pronghorn** and **mule deer**, and if you visit soon after dawn you may even hear a wolf pack howling in unison.

From the trailhead's car park, the hiking path immediately crosses **Soda Butte Creek** on a simple wooden bridge. Past the bridge, game trails lead off in multiple directions, so stick to the most clearly defined path following the flow of the creek. After

> **Difficulty** Moderate
> **Distance** 6-mile round-trip
> **Estimated time** 2–4hr
> **Season** May–Oct
> **Trailhead location** Map p.53. Soda Butte Trailhead (also known as Lamar River Trailhead), 16 miles east of Roosevelt on the Northeast Entrance Road.
> **Comments** Leave the roadside wildlife watchers behind as you encounter Lamar Valley's fauna close up.

hoofing up the ridge forming the edge of the creek's ancient riverbed, you'll cross onto Lamar Valley's sagebrush floor; don't be surprised if a bison blocks your path at some point, necessitating a wide looping detour around the trail.

Just over a mile in, you'll meet a stock trail after the first Y-junction. A right turn leads southwest on the **Specimen Ridge Trail** to a ford of the Lamar River half a mile away; head left instead, sticking to the southeastern **Lamar River Trail** (which doesn't actually reach its namesake river until four miles on) as it traces the lower shoulder of Mount Norris (9985ft) to the east. For nearly two miles, the trail leads uphill at an easy angle, through the grassy lower end of Lamar Valley that binoculars can't reach from the road; the opposite hillsides here may be heavily fire-scarred, but it remains an equally beautiful and, away from the roads, more peaceful stretch of the valley.

Soon after passing high above an obvious, white thermal stretch tucked into woods off the Lamar River, the trail reaches the second Y-junction. To the left is the **Cache Creek Trail**, which heads east, then northeast along the creek for more than twenty miles, eventually crossing Republic Pass (10,491ft) and dipping into Shoshone National Forest and Cooke City beyond. Head right instead, sticking to the Lamar River Trail, which leads south and down an often-muddy slope to **Cache Creek** itself. The creek's rocky riverbed is a perfect place to break for a picnic or a couple of hours fishing, with plenty of washed-up logs on which to relax before returning the way you came. The first of more than a dozen backcountry campsites (3L1) along the Lamar River Trail is here as well, though the rest are located across the creek, a thirty-foot ford not recommended until late June at the earliest. To return to Soda Butte Trailhead, walk back the way you came.

H9 **Mount Washburn**

Rangers often rate the trip up **Mount Washburn** (10,243ft) the best bet for those who have time for only one hike, and it's hard to argue with them. A 1500-foot uphill trek the entire way, hikers are rewarded with some of the best **panoramic views** of the park; in addition, **bighorn sheep** are frequently spotted en route. Two paths lead up the peak from the Grand Loop Road between Canyon and Tower: one leaves from **Chittenden Road Trailhead** on Mount Washburn's north side, while the other begins at **Dunraven Pass Trailhead** on the mountain's south side. Described

> **Difficulty** Strenuous
> **Distance** 5-mile round-trip
> **Estimated time** 3–5hr
> **Season** June–Sept
> **Trailhead location** Map p.53. 1.4 miles up Chittenden Road, located 6 miles south of Tower Fall on the Tower-Canyon section of the Grand Loop Road.
> **Comments** Stupendous views, bighorn sheep and a central location make this one of the park's top hikes.

below is the first route, as it's mountain bike-accessible and slightly shorter, but details are similar should you choose Dunraven Pass Trailhead, from which the trek runs one mile longer. If you're in a group with more than one car, consider leaving a vehicle at both trailheads so you can hike up one side of the peak and down the other.

From the end of Chittenden Road, the wide 2.5-mile trail up the north side of Mount Washburn (the tallest peak in its namesake range and the remnant of an extinct stratovolcano) never gets overly steep; taking frequent breaks, groups with kids and less fit hikers should find the journey manageable. As with any other alpine zone, the **flora** hereabouts is particularly delicate – look for blue lupine, pink monkey flowers and violet shooting stars – so always stay on the trail. The route is exposed, so pack warm and waterproof gear, and start heading down at the first sign of a storm. Atop the peak sits a three-storey **lookout tower**, complete with restrooms and indoor/outdoor viewing platforms. Diagrams here point out major sights in the park, including the Grand Teton itself 75 miles to the south, visible on clear days.

Canyon and around

The **Canyon** area lays claim to the finest compact network of trails within the park. South of the **Grand Canyon of the Yellowstone**, a tight set of trails offer the option of creating a variety of loops varying from an hour in length to a full day or more, while the canyon's north side includes hikes up **Mount Washburn** (see H9 for a shorter route) and the excellent trail to **Seven-Mile Hole**. Furthermore, trailheads located north towards Tower and west towards Norris lead to several **backcountry lakes**, including Cascade (H10), Grebe, Ice, Wolf and Cygnet Lakes.

H10 Cascade Lake and Observation Peak

Starting a mile north of Canyon Village, this hike has nothing to do with the Yellowstone River or the surrounding canyon area; instead, it's a journey tailor-made for **wildflower** lovers, along with peak-baggers looking to crest **Observation Peak** (9397ft), a steep uphill climb from **Cascade Lake**. Beginning from the edge of Cascade Picnic Area, a flat trail leads straight west into scrubby woods, where a sign-in box sits one hundred yards in. Check the recent postings: **grizzlies** are known to forage trailside, and should previous hikers that day mention a bear sighting, it's advisable to skip the trail and head elsewhere. Just beyond, the trail cuts alongside a large circular meadow where hawks circle overhead and moose may be spotted nibbling on creekside willows. After hopping over a few of these small streams, the route intersects with the **Cascade Creek Trail**, which leads 1.7 miles south to the Canyon-Norris Road. Turn right to continue west to Cascade Lake, crossing through a tangle of new growth and burned lodgepole creaking in the wind before entering a second, narrower meadow. If it's rained lately, things can get fairly muddy from here to the lake, as the meadow turns marshy and the trail crosses over crystal-clear Cascade Creek on a short footbridge. The lake itself can be a bit of a letdown (particularly if conditions are cloudy), what with its southern half ringed by a forest of dead trees. However, there are typically several types of wildflowers in bloom throughout summer, including yellow glacier lily and purple, bell-shaped sugarbowl.

There are also three **backcountry sites** by the lake, useful if you're planning to fish — the little lake holds grayling and cutthroat trout, as does **Grebe Lake**, a four-mile hike west − or make a more leisurely climb up Observation Peak. Starting from the north end of Cascade Lake, the trail to the summit takes in 1650 vertical feet in three miles, meaning it's a steady climb the entire way; bring plenty of water as well, as there's no dependable source en route. The panoramic views from atop the aptly named peak are spectacular, with the southern view of Hayden Valley particularly enchanting.

> **Difficulty** Moderate to strenuous
> **Distance** 5-mile round-trip to Cascade Lake, 11-mile round-trip to Observation Peak
> **Estimated time** 2–3hr for lake, 7–9hr for peak
> **Season** May–Oct
> **Trailhead location** Map p.57. Cascade Picnic Area, a mile north of Canyon Village on the Canyon-Tower Road.
> **Comments** An easy hike to a small lake through attractive, wildflower-filled meadows, with the option of tacking on a stiff peak hike.

H11 Seven-Mile Hole

The steep hike down the **Grand Canyon of the Yellowstone** to **Seven-Mile Hole**, an idyllic spot deep in the canyon that's well suited for a riverside picnic or an overnight stay, is another top candidate in the "If you only have time for one hike" category − provided you have the stamina for the long, precipitous uphill climb required on the return. Along with passing two of the park's tallest waterfalls, the trail leads by a beautiful lofted meadow, through an active thermal area and down to the banks of the trout-rich Yellowstone River, with views of the canyon's gorgeous multicoloured walls along the way.

> **Difficulty** Strenuous
> **Distance** 10-mile round-trip
> **Estimated time** 5–8hr
> **Season** May–Oct
> **Trailhead location** Map p.57. Glacier Boulder Trailhead, near Inspiration Point on one-way North Rim Drive.
> **Comments** Tough on the knees, this steep downhill slog passes two epic waterfalls en route to an idyllic spot by the Yellowstone River.

The trail starts by weaving through the woods for a quarter-mile before reaching the deep canyon's north rim. There's no view of Lower or Upper Falls – both are hidden by a few bends upstream – but the canyon walls are striking enough on their own. Continuing alongside the rim's edge, the trail takes just over a mile to reach a clear view across the canyon to **Silver Cord Cascade**, the tallest waterfall in Yellowstone (its height is listed between 800–1000ft, depending on whether one includes the rocky waterslide at its base). The thin fall lives up to its name later in the day, when the afternoon sun turns the narrow stream into a metallic arrow shooting down through the smallest of gaps. Past here, the trail – dotted with pieces of volcanic obsidian – dips back into the lodgepole forest for a peaceful, if dull stretch, where your sole companion will be the creaking of trees; you'll more than likely have to crawl under, or hop over, recently fallen pines across the trail. Just before reaching the junction with the **Mount Washburn Trail** at the 2.7-mile point, the path parallels a lovely grassy meadow with views of its namesake peak to the north. Continuing towards Seven-Mile Hole, the trail reaches the canyon edge again in about a half-mile.

Now the real work begins, as the trail heads downward nearly 1500ft in just over two miles. The trail doesn't switchback much, instead leading steeply downhill across plenty of crumbling rocks. Unlike the bare walls upstream, the sides of the canyon here are heavily forested, with large swathes of green reaching down to the riverbank. A couple of minutes further on, you'll cross straight through a shadeless, bright-white **thermal zone** featuring a handful of small bubbling springs and steaming vents. Past the thermal area is a backcountry site (4C1), by the river on its own path; soon after this, photogenic **Twin Falls** can be seen across the canyon, a streak of white water and attendant green plant life cascading 135ft between pink and rust-red canyon walls. After passing a second backcountry site (4C2) located trailside, the trail finally spills out into **Seven-Mile Hole** itself before terminating across tiny **Sulphur Creek** at the best of the backcountry sites (4C3), spectacularly located on a flat spot 100ft above the roaring river. As fishing is allowed downstream of Silver Cord Cascade, the area boasts superb fly-fishing for native cutthroat, sometimes found clustered in Sulphur Creek's bathtub-sized pools.

Once you've finished basking in your destination, you'll have to return the way you came; don't forget to fill up on filtered or purified water in the creek or river beforehand.

H12 South Rim, Point Sublime and Lily Pad Lake

This hike along the **Grand Canyon of the Yellowstone** is only one of several great options within the spider's web of trails along the canyon's south rim. Some worth-while detours have been noted, and if you have the time we recommend walking the entire **South Rim Trail**, starting from Wapiti Trailhead near Chittenden Bridge and looping back via the Clear Lake Trail. The following route takes in the South Rim Trail's unpaved eastern half, beginning from bustling **Artist Point** – from here, leave the crowds behind by heading up the trail to the

Difficulty Moderate
Distance 2.5-mile round-trip
Estimated Time 1–2hr
Season May–Oct
Trailhead Location Map p.57. Ribbon Lake Trailhead, accessed from Artist Point parking area.
Comments One of many fine trips along the Grand Canyon of the Yellowstone's scenic south rim.

east. For the next mile, the path briefly rolls up and down steep terrain, alternating between forest and the canyon edge before reaching **Point Sublime**, marked by a rough fencepost defining the trail's end. There are several superb, unobstructed views of the canyon along the way, its walls streaked in dramatic hues of pink, orange and rust-red, and dotted with ridges atop which lodgepole pines cling to life on the narrowest of knife-edges. As the trail literally forms the canyon edge at points, this hike is not recommended for visitors with children.

After relaxing at Point Sublime – a pretty, if less spectacular look east at the forested walls of the canyon downstream – begin heading back the way you came. This time, however, when passing the **Ribbon Lake Trail** junction at the halfway point, turn south to visit tiny, but attractive **Lily Pad Lake** less than five minutes down the trail. Just before reaching it, you'll pass a sign-in box; there's no need to register if you're just going to Lily Pad Lake, but check anyway for any recent wildlife reports. The lake itself is more of a pond, attractively topped with hundreds, if not thousands of pads; you may not want to linger, however, as mosquitoes here can often be ferocious.

From Lily Pad Lake, either return the way you came, or expand the hike by heading further east to **Ribbon Lake** and the brink of **Silver Cord Cascade** beyond (better viewed across the canyon on **H11**); you can also walk west to **Clear Lake**, which despite its name is rather green-tinged. If heading toward the latter, you'll pass through a large thermal area featuring large **mudpots** along the way.

Norris and Madison junctions

Offering campgrounds but no commercial services, **Norris** and **Madison** are the two most low-key junctions on the park's Grand Loop Road. Nor are there many marked hiking trails between them, though the two most popular routes are listed below. More trails can be reached by heading west from Madison towards West Yellowstone, including a short jaunt to **Harlequin Lake** and another hike on the relatively flat **Gneiss Creek Trail**, which starts along the Madison River and cuts northeast through Madison Valley to a trailhead on Hwy-191, fourteen miles away. Crossing several creeks along the way, this is a great choice for anglers seeking solitude, though there's only one backcountry campsite (WA1) throughout the entire stretch.

H13 Monument Geyser Basin

Starting south of the Gibbon River Bridge – around which several thermal features puff away – this short ramble leads to a bizarre backcountry geyser basin. The trail begins by following the river upstream for a quarter-mile, passing pockets of lily pads floating in the stream's calmest corners. Once the trail breaks from the river, the path begins a moderately sharp zigzagging route up to the geyser basin. Along the way, you'll earn nice views of **Gibbon Meadows** due north – the river looking like a twisted blue ribbon as it lazily floats through its namesake meadows – and snowcapped Mount Holmes in the background. Up top, the trail flattens out as

Difficulty Moderate
Distance 2-mile round-trip
Estimated Time 1–2hr
Season May–Oct
Trailhead Location Map p.59. Due south of the Gibbon River Bridge, about 5 miles south of Norris and 8 miles north of Madison.
Comments Take a short break to visit this small backcountry geyser basin, located atop a short but steep climb south of Gibbon Meadows.

you enter **Monument Geyser Basin**, located a mile from the trailhead. A narrow, chalky strip 200 yards long, the basin features steaming vents and small sizzling pots, along with a series of strange, chimney-shaped sinter cones that lend it its name. It all seems transported from another planet, or even some monochromatic book by Dr Seuss. While most of the skinny cones have been sealed, the biggest, known as **Thermos Bottle Geyser**, still manages to let off steam, though it will also close soon. Do not travel beyond the basic log and stone boundaries set up at trail's end, as you could easily break through crust and burn your foot. Once finished with your exploration, retrace your steps to the trailhead.

H14 Purple Mountain

This hilltop hike certainly isn't one of Yellowstone's finest trails, but views from the peak are nonetheless worth the effort; what's more, it's handily located within walking distance of nearby *Madison Campground*. Starting from the Madison-Norris Road due north of Madison Junction, the trail immediately snakes into a new-growth forest and travels alongside a dry ravine (bring plenty of water, as there's no reliable trailside source throughout). For more than three miles, the trail climbs 1500ft up **Purple Mountain** at a

> **Difficulty** Strenuous
> **Distance** 6.5-mile round-trip
> **Estimated Time** 3–4hr
> **Season** May–Oct
> **Trailhead Location** Map p.59. Small roadside parking area 100 yards north of Madison Junction.
> **Comments** Excellent views across Yellowstone's west-central region.

remarkably consistent pace through a "lodgepole desert" landscape that supports the tall and narrow trees and little else. At least you'll get plenty of shade, and the trail is smooth throughout, meaning running shoes or sturdy sandals are suitable should you want to leave your boots behind. From the peak of the tall hill, views include Gibbon Valley to the north and Firehole Valley, its steaming streams rising from a host of geysers and pools, to the south. Further off are clear shots of regional mountain ranges, including the Absarokas, Madison and, on the clearest of days, even the Tetons far to the south.

Old Faithful and around

The hikes in this section cover the 33-mile stretch of road from Madison southeast to West Thumb, with **Old Faithful** located at the halfway point. The area is home to the world's greatest collection of thermal features, with hikes accessing notable backcountry geysers and springs that many visitors never get to see. All the mainly boardwalk-based geyser basin trails, including the entire **Upper Geyser Basin**, are covered in detail in Chapter 2, while the popular **Lone Star Geyser Group** is described as part of a longer hike to the backcountry **Shoshone Geyser Basin** (H45) in Chapter 5.

H15 Sentinel Meadows

Starting from the parking area at the end of **Fountain Flat Drive**, this relaxed hike kicks off by following an old gravel road; biking is allowed along this stretch all the way to Fairy Falls Trailhead (H16), though you'll likely see more anglers on their way to fishing spots along the Firehole River, which the road crosses 0.3 miles in. Sizzling nearby and constantly discharging into the rivers is **Ojo Caliente Spring**, surrounded by a stone circle intended to keep people away; as its Spanish name ("Hot Eye") implies, the boiling spring is indeed toasty (200°F).

> **Difficulty** Easy to moderate
> **Distance** 4-mile round-trip
> **Estimated Time** 2–3hr
> **Season** May–Oct
> **Trailhead Location** Map p.68. At the end of Lower Geyser Basin's Fountain Flat Drive.
> **Comments** Walk attractive meadows where bison roam in early summer, en route to visiting the remains of a historic bathhouse.

Just past the bridge across the river, the **Sentinel Meadows Trail** (no bikes allowed) breaks off to the west, heading downstream alongside the river through a grassy field carpeted, in June and July, with purple, yellow and white wildflowers. After cutting away from the river, the trail begins its path through **Sentinel Meadows**, a favourite grazing spot of bison in mid July before most migrate to their summer habitat in Hayden Valley. Some of the best views of the beautiful meadow are just past a pair of backcountry sites (OG1, OG2), as the trail crests a small hump.

Looking across the green expanse from here, the obvious focal points are three massive thermal mounds known as **Flat Cone**, **Mound Spring** and **Steep Cone**, each puffing away like a steam engine. From the hump, it's just over a half-mile, partly through patches of new-growth forest, to the spring known as **Queens Laundry**. The bubbling blue pool was officially named by Superintendent Philetus W. Norris in 1880 after the brightly coloured clothes early park workers hung in the nearby bushes while "gambolling like dolphins in the pools". The roofless **log hut** that stands nearby is actually a National Historic Site; built by Norris in 1881 as a bathhouse, the unassuming ruin has the distinction of being the first building constructed for public use in any national park. Swimming is no longer allowed hereabouts, so after taking a break, follow your footsteps back to the trailhead.

H16 Fairy Falls and Imperial Geyser

This hike makes for an easy trip out to one of the region's loveliest and tallest falls, with the option of tacking on an extra 1.5-mile round-trip to visit one of Yellowstone's most beautiful backcountry geyser pools. From the roadside trailhead, the hike begins by crossing the **Firehole River** on a steel bridge before following an old road for a mile. This section is open to bikes as well, allowing for a **bike/hike** option to shorten the overall trip time. As the road passes to the south of Midway Geyser Basin, you get a good view of colourful **Excelsior Geyser** along the way. At the one-mile point, the trail to **Fairy Falls** branches off to the west (no bikes allowed), leading 1.5 miles through a forest of naturally reseeded lodgepole pines, varying in height from 4 to 18ft and proving the fires of 1988 were but a temporary setback. Halfway to the falls is a **backcountry site** (OD1) that's one of the closest such sites to a trailhead in the park. The last few hundred yards approaching the falls are the most dramatic, with charred tree trunks standing guard over a green-carpeted forest floor and the steep, craggy edge of the Madison Plateau looming to the south. It's off this rocky face that Fairy Falls itself plummets, a wispy yet dramatic 197ft plunge between white-grey rocks that lands in a calm, perfect pool at its base.

> **Difficulty** Moderate
> **Distance** 5-mile round-trip to Fairy Falls, 6.5 miles to Imperial Geyser
> **Estimated Time** 2–4hr
> **Season** May–Oct
> **Trailhead Location** Map p.68. Fairy Falls Trailhead, just south of Midway Geyser Basin.
> **Comments** Moderate terrain, graceful falls and a stunning backcountry geyser make this a must-do amble.

While many visitors snap their photos and begin heading back, it pays to continue onwards to a series of geysers 0.7 miles further ahead. If it's been raining recently, be prepared for plenty of mud and insects; still, **Imperial Geyser**, the biggest of the bunch, is worth the effort. Framed by the rounded humps of **Twin Buttes**, the geyser first became active in the mid 1920s, spouting as high as 80ft into the air. It quickly became a visitor favourite, even earning its name in a newspaper contest to drum up publicity for Yellowstone. However, the geyser went dormant soon after, and hibernated for nearly four decades before erupting again at smaller heights. Still active, the geyser continues to change dramatically, and at the time of writing it consisted of a large, beautiful blue pool with hints of green, spouting up in five-foot boiling bursts towards its centre; also look for a hot tub-sized gurgling mudpot and several steaming nearby vents that have erupted in the past. From here, it's possible to head north a few miles along the Imperial Meadows Trail to visit **Queens Laundry** and **Sentinel Meadows** (**H15**), a side-trip that can be turned into a long loop or, better yet, a one-way hike if a second car is left at the end of Fountain Flat Drive. If neither is an option, return the way you came past Fairy Falls to the original trailhead.

H17 Mystic Falls

Mystic Falls is a reward for those willing to leave the visitor-clogged boardwalks of Biscuit Basin behind. After viewing the geysers and pools here, find the trail to the falls at the west end of the boardwalk. A half-mile walk through a low coniferous forest (regrowth from the 1988 fires) lands hikers at a fork. To continue the easy hike to the 70ft-high falls, take a left along the Firehole River and follow the rumble of the water for another 0.2 miles.

Heartier hikers should take a right at the fork and climb the steep switchbacks of a deeply carved cliff for a marvellous vista of **Biscuit Basin**. Lined with raspberries and huckleberries, the path is as sweet in berry

> **Difficulty** Easy to moderate
> **Distance** 1.4-mile round-trip to Mystic Falls, or 3-mile loop to Biscuit Basin vista
> **Estimated Time** 1hr 30min–2hr 30min
> **Season** May–Oct
> **Trailhead Location** Map p.68. West end of Biscuit Basin boardwalk, about 2 miles north of Old Faithful.
> **Comments** A short jaunt to spectacular falls, with an optional high-climbing loop that lends a great overview of Biscuit Basin.

season as it is steep. Expect grey jays, tiny chipmunks and fat golden-mantled ground squirrels as trailside companions. From the top, the scattered debris of Sapphire Pool 500ft below is visible; this geyser exploded violently in August 1959, four days after a 7.5 magnitude earthquake disrupted numerous thermal features in the vicinity and created Earthquake Lake northwest of West Yellowstone (see p.219). In the distance, buildings around Old Faithful can be seen along with various jets and steam clouds from every part of the valley. The loop eventually begins to drop in altitude on a less-steep set of switchbacks just above the falls; watch for loose gravel along the steep drop-offs.

To extend this hike, the Mystic Falls loop connects with trails to **Summit Lake** (7.2 miles) and **Fairy Falls** (9.2 miles one-way; **H16**).

Lake Village, Fishing Bridge and the East Entrance

These hikes cover a large swathe of the park around Yellowstone Lake's northern and eastern shores, from the area around Lake Village east to Fishing Bridge and along the twisting East Entrance road. Much of the area is prime **grizzly country**, particularly narrow and beautiful **Pelican Valley** and the nearby shores of Yellowstone Lake around **Mary Bay**; trail closures due to bear activity are possible, so keep an eye out for signs. See the box on p.110 for details on necessary precautions.

H18 Natural Bridge Road

Natural Bridge Road, leading to a 51ft-high natural arch with a 29ft span, begins on the north side of the Bridge Bay boat launch parking area (Bridge Bay campers can also access the path from the campground). The well-maintained trail traces the curve of the marina's bay, eventually leading west through a mature coniferous forest. The path then merges with a closed road that once allowed cars direct access to the fragile bridge. Today this blacktop is an easy walk for families with buggies (strollers), or for less sure-footed travellers.

The road forks into a loop, with the rock bridge at its far end. The feature formed when **Bridge Creek** meandered into underground cracks in the volcanic soil; frost and freeze cycles loosened debris, letting the stream carry away rubble over the years and leaving the isolated strip of rock above. It was discovered in 1871 by the Hayden Survey party, and eventually opened to the public ten years later when a trail was constructed across the top of it. A later proposal to build a narrow road on the bridge would have made for palm-sweating fun for early car tourists, but was never acted upon. These days, signs encourage visitors to stay off the frail volcanic rock altogether.

For a different look at the geological oddity, a rocky trail summons energetic hikers to zigzag up the steep cliff about 60ft. At the top, carved stairs offer access to the shallow creek that runs through the arch; straddling the trickle allows a great photo op for those who stayed below to take pictures of their companions, high above and framed by the bridge.

Difficulty Easy
Distance 3-mile round-trip
Estimated time 1hr–1hr 30min
Season May–Oct
Trailhead Location Map p.78. *Bridge Bay Campground*.
Comments A sweat-free stroll out to delicate, explorable Natural Bridge.

H19 Elephant Back Mountain

As Lake Village is only a short walk away, this loop up the slopes of **Elephant Back Mountain** is particularly popular both early in the morning and after dinner with overnight guests and workers alike. If you're not spending the night at Lake Village, there's space for a handful of cars on either side of the road at the trailhead. Though you'd have to try pretty hard to get lost off this trail, stop at the provided sign-in box anyway to check for any **bear updates** – the animals have been known to frequent the area, and the trail sometimes closes late in the season as a result. From here, the path briefly starts uphill before flattening out for around a third of a mile through thick lodgepole pine forest. This section makes for a nice preamble to the strenuous loop that begins at the intersection ahead.

Difficulty Moderate to strenuous
Distance 4-mile loop
Estimated time 2–3hr
Season May–Oct
Trailhead location Map p.78. Between Lake Village and Fishing Bridge Junction along the Grand Loop Road.
Comments A rewarding loop that'll make you work to earn unforgettable views over Yellowstone Lake.

Head left at the junction for a slightly shorter uphill slog, following the trail as it cuts back and forth uphill some 800ft, giving the occasional peek out to Yellowstone Lake along the way. After sweating it up to the top, the trail flattens and leads to an open 180-degree **vista**, complete with a pair of rustic benches. Directly below is *Lake Yellowstone Hotel*, while to the east the Absaroka Mountains march alongside the gigantic lake to the horizon. Once you've taken in the remarkable scenery, the trail loops further back into the woods before circling back down to the junction and the trailhead beyond.

H20 LeHardy's Rapids

Parts of the **Howard Eaton Trail** predate Yellowstone's Grand Loop Road as one of the earliest main sightseeing routes within the park. Today, many sections of this extensive trail network are found in close proximity – a little too close, in many cases – to the Grand Loop. One stretch of the historic trail that's mostly out of sight (and earshot) of auto traffic, however, is this four-mile section between **Fishing Bridge Trailhead** and **LeHardy's Rapids** (known in some local quarters as LeHardy Rapids), just north of Yellowstone Lake. Here the Eaton Trail parallels the bucolic banks of the Yellowstone River and winds through open meadows and forests of lodgepole pine, some of which endured the flames of 2008's **LeHardy Fire**, which burned nine thousand acres in the area.

> **Difficulty** Moderate
> **Distance** 8-mile round-trip
> **Estimated time** 4–5hr
> **Season** May–Oct
> **Trailhead location** Map p.78. Fishing Bridge Trailhead, just east of Fishing Bridge Junction along the East Entrance Road.
> **Comments** A gentle stroll along the banks of the Yellowstone to whirring rapids famed for waterfowl and, in spring spawning season, leaping trout.

Begin from the parking area at Fishing Bridge Trailhead, from which the Howard Eaton Trail hugs the east bank of the Yellowstone for a short time before cutting away from the water toward a service road; soon enough, the path winds its way back toward the river. As you walk northward along the flat and well-defined trail, keep a look out for **bears**, which frequent this area in search of fresh catches from the trout-filled river; waterfowl such as **pelicans**, **swans** and **goldeneye ducks** can also often be prevalent. Aside from LeHardy's alluring white water, the main attraction here is the chance to see **cutthroat trout** leaping above the rapids' current in spring in an effort to spawn a few miles upstream in the Fishing Bridge area – a spectacle for which it's worth braving early-season mud along the trail.

It's possible to continue along the Howard Eaton Trail as far north as **Wapiti Lake Trailhead**, near the South Rim of the Grand Canyon of the Yellowstone, although its distance from Fishing Bridge Trailhead (15 miles) all but ensures a night spent along the way unless you have a ride or second vehicle waiting at hike's end. This further section of trail also features more climbing and direct sun exposure than the relatively easy, shaded four-mile section profiled here.

H21 Avalanche Peak

Though out of the way for many (save those heading to or from Yellowstone's East Entrance), this tough trail basically leads straight up nearly 2000 vertical feet to the top of **Avalanche Peak** (10,566ft). The towering peak boasts some of the park's finest views, making it – along with Mount Washburn (see H9) and Mount Sheridan (see H46) – an essential trip for peak junkies. As the final ascent is completely exposed, do not attempt this hike in foul, or even potentially foul, weather; to avoid the region's frequent summer afternoon storms, head out as early as possible. Furthermore,

> **Difficulty** Strenuous
> **Distance** 4.5-mile round-trip
> **Estimated time** 3–4hr
> **Season** June–Oct
> **Trailhead location** Map p.64. Across the road from Eleanor Lake on the East Entrance Road, 20 miles east of Fishing Bridge.
> **Comments** A tough, but suitably rewarding slog featuring some of the best panoramic views of Yellowstone and beyond.

although the once-plentiful whitebark pines on the peak's slopes have fallen prey to mountain pine beetles and blister rust disease, the remaining purple-brown cones are still a bear's favourite snack, making this prime **grizzly country** come September and October. Check at the trailhead sign-in box for updates and be prepared for possible trail closure.

The first mile climbs steadily but easily through a pleasant forested landscape before dipping through a cleared avalanche slide area strewn with wildflowers into early autumn. Past here, the trail becomes progressively tougher, initially granting good views of aptly named **Top Notch Peak**, then swinging back for the long climb up Avalanche Peak, bare as a newborn's backside from its countless eponymous slides. The last quarter of a mile is the toughest, much of it leading directly across a scree slope littered with lopsided, loose rocks. Work your way carefully along the ridgeline to the peak, where stunning 360-degree views of the park and Wapiti Valley to the east await. For those confident with their **off-trail** skills, it's possible to drop down the northeast side of the peak's bowl and swing back around to the trail, but most hikers should choose to follow their original path back down.

West Thumb and the South Entrance

Covering the 22-mile stretch of road between **West Thumb** and Yellowstone's **South Entrance**, the following hikes lead to Yellowstone's largest, most dramatic backcountry lakes. Along with the day hikes detailed below, energetic visitors should consider taking the superb overnight hikes to **Shoshone Geyser Basin** (**H45**) and **Heart Lake/Mount Sheridan** (**H46**) detailed in Chapter 5; at 20 miles and 23 miles, respectively, either trek can be completed in a *very* long day.

H22 Riddle Lake

Crossing the Continental Divide, this undemanding out-and-back trail leads to pleasant **Riddle Lake**, whose name comes from a fur-trapper myth about a body of water that flowed into both the Pacific and Atlantic Oceans. On early maps, several different bodies of water throughout the region were named Riddle in honour of this puzzling feat, but by the 1870s only this lake remained officially Riddle. In reality, the lake eventually drains into the Atlantic Ocean by way of its outlet named, of course, **Solution Creek**.

> **Difficulty** Easy
> **Distance** 5-mile round-trip
> **Estimated time** 2hr
> **Season** July–Oct
> **Trailhead location** Map p.75. 2.3 miles south of Grant Village, just past the Continental Divide sign on the east side of the road.
> **Comments** An easy ramble to the shores of a little backcountry lake; best hiked in a group due to frequency of bears.

Closed until mid July due to grizzly activity, the trail leads northeast into the woods from its roadside start, heading through lodgepole forest dotted with large patches of burned trees and the occasional clearing. For the first couple of miles, the route marches uphill ever so slightly, with signs of post-fire renewal all about. Before reaching the lake, the trail cuts across, and then along, a beautiful meadow that bleeds into marsh by the lake's northwestern shore. This is prime area for **moose** and bird **spotting** (including sandhill cranes), so don't forget your camera. From here, you can continue along the lake's northern edge; however, the trail soon peters out and rangers typically forbid travel any further east of the lake due to the prevalence of bears in the area. You're best off sitting down – or even splashing in the shallow waters on hotter days – to take in the serene scene, complete with broad-shouldered Mount Sheridan framing the background.

H23 Lewis Channel and Dogshead Trails

One of the park's few true loop hikes, this route takes in Lewis Lake, the scenic Lewis River Channel and Yellowstone's largest backcountry lake, Shoshone Lake, all within a half-day's journey. From the trailhead, the first 1.5 miles of the Lewis Channel Trail aim flatly northwest through resurgent woods originally scarred from the 1988 fires before crossing a sandy wash that's often wet early in the season;

soon enough, the route turns southwest to meet **Lewis Lake**. Next, the trail rises up and down along the lake's northern shore – the towering Tetons clearly visible to the south – before cutting inland to hook up with the mouth of the **Lewis River Channel**. For nearly four miles, the trail follows the channel upstream to the north, leaving it only to round the occasional marsh. It's an idyllic stretch of water, popular with fishermen and kayakers, and also a good place to watch osprey and eagles dive-bomb for trout.

> **Difficulty** Moderate to strenuous
> **Distance** 11-mile loop
> **Estimated time** 5–7hr
> **Season** May–Oct
> **Trailhead location** Map p.75. 5 miles south of Grant Village, due north of Lewis Lake on the west side of the road.
> **Comments** A rare Yellowstone loop hike with nice views of both Lewis and Shoshone Lakes.

The channel ends (or, more truly, begins) at **Shoshone Lake**, where the trail also ends in a junction; turning left (west) leads to Shoshone Geyser Basin 8.5 miles away (see **H45**). Instead, take a right onto the **Dogshead Trail** for the second half of the hike. Before heading back, however, take the time to visit the shores of Shoshone Lake via the path to backcountry campsite 8S1. The passage leads to a rocky beach perfect for a picnic, while just a few steps away sits an A-frame cabin that's home to the **Shoshone Lake Ranger Station**; the lucky rangers stationed here patrol the area on kayak. Once breaktime ends, continue following the Dogshead Trail as it heads southeast along a portion of the Continental Divide Trail, cresting several good-sized hills over the next 3.5 miles. There's very little shade hereabouts as most of the forest is young re-growth from the 1988 fires, so be sure to bring sunscreen and a hat. After crossing Dogshead Creek – dry by late July – the final 1.3 miles is the hike's least interesting leg, following a flat gravel service road back to the trailhead.

Cascade Corner

Isolated and with few roadside sights, there's not much to do in Yellowstone's Cascade Corner but hike. The area's two most popular trailheads are **Bechler Ranger Station** and **Cave Falls**, though several worthwhile hikes begin north of **Grassy Lake Road** as well. Wetter than the rest of the park, trails here remain soggy and insect-infested throughout most of summer, meaning the best hiking is to be had from mid August until September, once the meadows dry out and the insect populations die down. River crossings, required on many Cascade Corner trails, are also less dangerous at this time.

H24 Bechler Meadows

It would be a sin to visit Cascade Corner and not hike to **Bechler Meadows**. This long but flat route not only loops through the gorgeous meadows, but also passes a couple of small waterfalls en route. Indeed, the hike starts at wide **Cave Falls** (see p.83), then heads upstream along the western bank of the raging **Bechler River** on its **namesake trail**, which tumbles down rocky chutes and tosses logs about like matchsticks before reaching the confluence of the Bechler and Falls Rivers. Past this river junction, the trail passes small

> **Difficulty** Moderate
> **Distance** 15-mile round-trip
> **Estimated time** 6–8hr
> **Season** July–Oct
> **Trailhead location** Map p.64. Cave Falls parking area at the end of Cave Falls Road.
> **Comments** A superb hike along the Bechler River to a loop route through lovely Bechler Meadows.

but fierce **Bechler Falls** about a mile from the trail's start. Above the falls, the river calms considerably, its surface still as glass.

In less than a mile, the trail comes to the first of many junctions; turn right (east) and stick to the trail hugging the Bechler River. Two miles ahead you hit another junction, this time with Rocky Ford Cutoff – turn right (east) again to continue on the Bechler River Trail, fording the ice-cold river at a spot around fifty yards wide; this crossing should not be attempted until the river calms, typically by late July. Beyond the ford, the trail leaves the river and cuts through an open grassy meadow – a small taste of things to come – to a junction with Mountain Ash Creek Trail a mile onwards. Turn left (north) and continue along the Bechler River Trail for another three miles, hopping across a couple of small creeks, then up and down a series of wooded hills to another junction.

This junction, nearly eight miles from the trailhead, is the gateway to Bechler Meadows, meaning it's time to leave the Bechler River Trail behind by turning left (west) onto the **Bechler Meadows Trail**; should you head northeast on the Bechler River Trail through Bechler Canyon, it's 3 miles to Colonnade Falls, 7.4 miles to Three Rivers Meadows and 24.3 miles to Old Faithful. The Bechler River at the junction is all but unrecognizable from the frothy torrent at the hike's start, and just past backcountry site 9B2 is a shorter, but just as icy, river crossing. You're now among the majestic meadows themselves, following a narrow path over two miles through a waving sea of knee-to-waist-high grasses; bear left at the junction with the cutoff path to the Boundary Creek Trail. Keep your eyes peeled for **moose**, **herons** and **sandhill cranes** – but even without any wildlife spotting, the wide meadows are breathtaking, **Ouzel Falls** faintly visible to the north as the **Tetons** arc into the southern horizon. Towards the southern end of the meadows, past a few islands of trees, you'll cross over a wobbly **suspension bridge** and soon after head back into the woods. At the next junction, head left (southeast) onto **Rocky Ford Cutoff**, which leads just under a mile back to the day's first river crossing and your original inbound route.

H25 Union Falls

This trail to **Union Falls** is perhaps the finest hike in Yellowstone's remote Cascade Corner. At 250ft, the waterfall is one of the highest in the park – and a leading candidate for the most breathtaking, formed by the explosive confluence of two streams that happen to join at the top of a massive cliff. The effect is loud, dramatic and exceptionally photogenic.

There are several approaches to the falls, but the following route is the most direct. From the trailhead, the **Mountain Ash Trail** cuts through a marshy zone, reaching the **Falls River** at the 1.2-mile mark. You'll

Difficulty Moderate
Distance 16-mile round-trip
Estimated Time 7–9hr
Season July–Oct
Trailhead Location Map p.64. Picnic area on the west side of Grassy Lake Reservoir Dam, 10 miles west of Flagg Ranch along bumpy Grassy Lake Road.
Comments A long day hike or leisurely overnight trip showcasing one of Yellowstone's most stunning waterfalls.

need to carefully ford the river, which will be swift even when shallow. Just past the ford is a junction with the Pitchstone Plateau Trail – continue hiking northwest here along the Mountain Ash Trail, climbing steadily for several miles. This old roadbed, once referred to as **Marysville Road**, was used by Mormons as they settled within Jackson Hole over a century ago (look closely for wagon ruts carved into the stone), a better alternative to the more treacherous crossing of Teton Pass, which required settlers to drag a tree behind their wagon to keep it from descending faster than the horses.

Four miles from the Falls River, a steep decline leads to a ford across **Proposition Creek**; after less than a mile, take the spur trail northeast to Union Falls, a route that requires you to wade through **Mountain Ash Creek** a short distance up the trail. There are two backcountry campsites near the trail junction between the creek and the Morning Falls tributary (9U4 and 9U5). A side trail to **Morning Falls** can be explored by following the maintained path from the campsites for about half a mile along the tributary. At this point, the trail to Union Falls becomes unmaintained, slippery and potentially muddy as it follows several small falls and cascades. If planning an overnight trip, the **campsites** here are ideal spots to pitch a tent, provided they haven't been taken over by Boy Scouts, who have a large camp nearby at Grassy Lake Reservoir. Explore the final two-mile trail to Union Falls at your leisure – at the very end of the trail is a rewarding overlook of Union Falls – then return the way you came.

Hikes within Grand Teton

It seems the **Teton Range** was designed for hiking – a tight clutch of stunning peaks ribbed with canyons, themselves sheltering picturesque creeks and bird-filled forests. Trails such as those at Hermitage Point and Hidden Falls/Inspiration Point are perennially popular with visitors, but many excellent paths, like the Phelps Lake loop and Blacktail Butte traverse, are much less frequented, with abundant wildlife to boot.

John D. Rockefeller, Jr. Memorial Parkway

Most visitors simply race through **John D. Rockefeller, Jr. Memorial Parkway**, the thin strip of protected land that connects Yellowstone and Grand Teton. The area, however, is more than just a divider between the parks on a map – the parks' ecosystems merge here, too. Driving through southbound, visitors will notice a drop in altitude from Yellowstone to Grand Teton, as well as a decrease in the ratio of pine to aspen trees. The most striking transition, however, is Yellowstone's steadily recovering southern region, scorched by great wildfires nearly 25 years ago, as it melds into the lush Jackson Lake area.

H26 Flagg Canyon

If you're looking to pry yourself from your car, stretch your legs for a few hours and perhaps even enjoy a picnic during your drive between Yellowstone and Grand Teton, this easy out-and-back stroll along the Snake River's **Flagg Canyon** remains a solid choice in late spring, summer and well into autumn. Despite its easy trailhead access right off Hwy 89/191, the path maintains a low profile given the relatively light use it gets from visitors speeding through the Rockefeller Parkway en route to the parks' more recognized destinations.

Difficulty Easy
Distance 5-mile round-trip
Estimated time 2–3hr
Season May–Oct
Trailhead location Map p.104. South Gate Picnic Area, 1.6 miles north of Grassy Lake Road junction on Hwy 89/191.
Comments A mild stroll along one of the Snake River's many scenic canyons.

Flagg Canyon is composed of a **rhyolitic lava flow**, through which the Snake River has carved a path over time. Don't despair over the hike's first 0.4 miles, during which the trail swings more closely to the highway than the river; as you continue southward, the path begins to hug the river and its striking canyon more closely along its west edge as it follows a mostly flat route through lush meadows and lodgepole pine forest. You may also experience chance **wildlife sightings** above you (bald eagles); at eye level (moose, elk); on the ground (squirrels); and in the river waters below (goldeneye ducks, Canada geese, otters).

Continue straight at the junction with Polecat Creek Trail at the 1.3-mile point, after which you'll spot **charred trees** across the river – these mark the perimeter of 1988's massive Huck Fire, one of the hottest wildfires to scorch the Yellowstone region that summer. A little further on, just short of the two-mile mark, look for a small feeder creek streaming down the canyon's walls that joins the Snake in a flurry of **small cascades**. A half-mile on, you'll know you're about to reach the hike's turnaround point once you drop slightly and walk along the left side of a willow-fringed pond, finally coming to a bridge over the park highway. Across this bridge is a **picnic area** near Flagg Ranch's riverside units that makes a nice spot for a snack or lunch before heading back the way you came.

H27 Sheffield Creek Trail

The **Sheffield Creek Trail** winds through the wreckage and regrowth of the 1988 Huck Fire, climbing steadily to a lookout tower high atop Huckleberry Mountain. This area is part of **Bridger–Teton National Forest**, and though the trail is maintained with some regularity, the number of dead trees that have fallen across the path since the last chainsaw crew visited may be daunting for hikers not in the mood for a trail game of "over and under".

The fire, which started when high winds blew a tree across a power line, has allowed for a unique trail, as the views from this high area are spectacular and not blocked by branches. The first hour of the hike is a steep

Difficulty Strenuous
Distance 10.6-mile round-trip
Estimated time 7–9hr
Season June–Oct
Trailhead location Map p.104. 0.6 miles south of the Flagg Ranch turn, at Sheffield Creek sign. Follow the road for a half-mile across the concrete-bottomed stream to the camping/parking area.
Comments A steep and rugged climb through burned areas up to Huckleberry Mountain's lookout tower.

1200ft climb through low, thick new-growth forest. As the elevation rises, the number of gnarled and sculpture-like burned trees still upright also increases. The crest of the mountain, by contrast, was untouched by the fire, offering a completely different kind of beauty as you walk through a thick forest in the prime of its life.

There are upwards of twenty small runoff streams and several eco-zones along the trail, making it ideal for animal spotting. Below the teetering lookout tower, the lush, rolling meadows make for great moose and elk habitat. Grouse and other birds are plentiful among the new growth, and signs of deer and bear presence can be found along all parts of the trail. Be sure to summit the final climb to the **lookout tower**, perched tentatively upon a spectacular outcropping of weathered rock. The Forest Service does not usually allow access into the building, but the near-panoramic view from its porch is still worth the climb. Once you've sufficiently absorbed the vista, return back down to the trailhead along the same route.

H28 Glade Creek Trail

A terrific trail for those exploring the **John D. Rockefeller, Jr. Memorial Parkway** area, this path offers hikers the chance to view wildlife and intriguing topography at the northern end of Jackson Lake, while also allowing visitors the freedom to scale the hike's length according to their schedule and ability. The trailhead has no amenities, so be sure to make a pit stop at **Flagg Ranch Resort**, where camping, lodging, eateries, a gas station and a convenience store are all available.

The gentle trail begins in a burned stand of aspen trees that are magnificent in their dalmatian-like charring pattern; you're soon led closer to the Snake River plain as you drop in elevation to about 50ft above the river's wetlands. The main river channel is still a half-mile to the east, but the wildlife viewing – everything from bald eagles to black bears – from this elevation can be excellent. Three miles along the southbound trail, cross the unmarked border into Grand Teton National Park. About five miles in, the trail climbs and strays inland from Jackson Lake to intersect with the **Owl Creek Loop Trail**, accessible by kayak or canoe for those seeking a multi-sport adventure. 2.5 miles further south is a good turnaround point at a patrol cabin; access to Jackson Lake is also available here. Expect heavy mosquitoes along this trail until cooler autumn weather arrives and bears become a greater deterrent. As this is a simply routed out-and-back hike, turn and retrace your steps to the trailhead at any time.

Difficulty Easy to moderate
Distance Up to 16-mile round-trip
Estimated time 1hr to full day, depending on distance
Season Aug–Oct
Trailhead Location Map p.104. At Flagg Ranch, follow Grassy Lake Road 4 miles west. Trailhead is on south side of road.
Comments An isolated trail following the route of the Snake River to the northern edges of Jackson Lake.

Jackson Lake, Colter Bay and around

In many ways, **Jackson Lake** is as much a centrepiece of Grand Teton National Park as its namesake peak. Speedboaters, sailors and kayakers may flock in droves, but the low-lying areas around Jackson Lake offer plenty of activity for landlubbers as well. Each of the hikes listed in this section offers top-notch vistas of the majestic Teton Range, while providing hiking options that vary in length and topographic challenge; each also offers the chance to distance yourself from summer crowds.

H29 Colter Bay Nature Trail

Behind **Colter Bay Visitor Center**, a paved trail strikes off to the northwest, soon becoming a well-marked dirt path leading past an amphitheatre where ranger talks, evening gatherings and Sunday morning religious services all take place. Runners seeking a short jog will enjoy this option, as the **Colter Bay Nature Trail** offers little elevation change and is hard-packed without much ankle-twisting glacial till. Consider visiting this accessible path early to beat the hordes of tourists that claim it later in the day; also consider that during morning hours, the nearby marina is less noisy, thereby increasing your chances of seeing wildlife.

Difficulty Easy
Distance 2-mile loop
Estimated time 45min–1hr 30min
Season May–Oct
Trailhead Location Map p.104. Colter Bay Visitor Center.
Comments A short figure-eight stroll through the woods strung along Jackson Lake's shore, with easy lake access.

Past the amphitheatre, the trail follows an isthmus to what becomes an island when the lake runs high, creating a figure-eight path. One of this trail's best features is its easy and frequent access to **Jackson Lake**: families can explore stretches of beach and examine splendid driftwood sculptures deposited on the shore, and there are well-placed picnic tables at the northernmost part of the trail should you fancy a scenic snack. Finally, be sure to bring along a camera, as views of the Grand Teton and Mount Moran straight ahead are marvellous in any season. When it's time to make your way back, simply retrace your steps.

H30 Hermitage Point

Escape nearby traffic by slinking away to Colter Bay and its lovely network of trails. After viewing the incredible native artefacts inside Colter Bay Visitor Center (see p.106), lace up your hiking boots and experience what makes this a truly special area: **Hermitage Point**, extending south from Colter Bay into the southeastern part of Jackson Lake. Beginning at a maintenance road at the southern end of the parking area, these trails allow for anything from a half-hour jaunt to a full-day trip, and you can pick and choose your own route. The trail suggested here, a 9.4-mile jaunt, sticks to the Jackson Lake shoreline.

Difficulty Easy to moderate
Distance 9.4-mile round-trip
Estimated time 4–5hr
Season May–Oct (certain sections open in winter)
Trailhead location Map p.104. Colter Bay, at south end of parking area.
Comments A serene walk through the woods of the Hermitage Point peninsula, with wonderful lakeside views of the Tetons.

Since the trailhead is near Colter Bay's stables, there's often horse traffic on the trails nearest the parking area. Families find that the small loops at the trail's beginning make for good driving intermissions, so also expect lots of foot traffic during the hike's first half-mile. However, crowds often quickly thin out once the trail enters the thick forest and passes the beaver lodge in Heron Pond.

Deposits left behind by receding glaciers created the Hermitage Point peninsula, which has several ponds where small ice fields continued to settle once the glaciers dissipated. The trail only rarely climbs or dips as it hugs the shore of Jackson Lake, but it still manages to lead hikers through a few **distinct eco-zones**. Thick coniferous forests filled with red squirrels dominate most of the area, but the southern end is home to sagebrush meadows and Uinta ground squirrels. The trail also explores a low wetland meadow and fantastic swan ponds on the east side of Hermitage Point.

For a bracing treat, take a dip in chilly **Jackson Lake** at the southernmost tip of Hermitage Point (also a perfect lunch spot); indeed, the photographic opportunities here are unparalleled. Mount Moran and the Grand Teton tower above the lake's western shore, and the cobbled beach is fun to explore. Finally, return to Colter Bay the way you came.

H31 Two Ocean and Emma Matilda Lakes

This hike past **Two Ocean Lake** is a good choice for those looking to wear away a winter's worth of rust. There are a series of trails in the area, and the route suggested here is a loop around Two Ocean Lake that climbs to a high lookout at its halfway point, then cuts past **Emma Matilda Lake** back to the often-buzzing trailhead.

Though sporadically closed to protect nesting **trumpeter swans**, it's possible to complete the loop back around Two Ocean Lake's southern shore (an equal distance to

Difficulty Moderate
Distance 9.5-mile loop
Estimated time 4–5hr
Season June–Oct
Trailhead location Map p.104. Two Ocean Trailhead. 1 mile northwest of Moran Junction, take paved Pacific Creek Road to unpaved Two Ocean Road; follow it for 2–3 miles to the trailhead.
Comments Far from the park's central, crowd-pleasing paths, this excellent hike leads to grand views and prime wildlife viewing opportunities.

the trailhead). For a more strenuous challenge, however, continue from the western tip of Two Ocean Lake up to **Grand View Point**. The mile-long trail heads uphill via smartly graded switchbacks through a coniferous forest that supports dozens of bird species, including chickadees, yellow warblers and the occasional raven. Once at the top, you're rewarded with areas boasting **360-degree vistas**, from which views include Bridger-Teton National Forest to the east and the storied Teton Range to the west.

After resting, head downhill for 1.7 miles to a junction of trails leading to Jackson Lake Lodge, Christian Pond and the southern shore of Emma Matilda Lake; this last option loops back to the trailhead, now just 2.7 miles away. The trail slowly gains back most of the altitude lost on the hike down from Grand View Point, placing hikers on a bench overlooking crescent-shaped Emma Matilda Lake. The lake is named for the wife of William Owen, one of the men sharing the controversial honour of making the first recorded ascent of Grand Teton in 1898 (see box, p.102).

While the lake looks enticing from above, the trail never diverges to allow access to the water. Atop the bench, there's little topographic change as you're led through a lightning-fire area known for bear activity; be sure to take precautions. As the trail drops back down toward Two Ocean Lake, it leads through lovely meadows, and, with one mile left, the trail splits: following it to the right leads you around the south side of Emma Matilda Lake, and to the left is your starting point, Two Ocean Lake Trailhead.

H32 Signal Mountain loop

Nearly all visitors to the summit of **Signal Mountain** drive the paved, winding road to the top, so it's quite likely you'll end up sharing this trail with only a few others, in addition to the odd elk or moose you find browsing along the way. This is a terrific hiking option if you visit Grand Teton in one of the shoulder seasons – its relatively **low elevation** (Jackson Point Overlook atop Signal Mountain sits at only about 7600ft) makes this a smart option when snow still covers the Tetons in spring, while bugling elk and turning aspens help make this a particularly special part of the park come late September.

Find a **parking spot** along Signal Mountain Road near the trailhead, then begin walking

> **Difficulty** Moderate
> **Distance** 5.5-mile loop
> **Estimated time** 3–4hr
> **Season** May–Oct
> **Trailhead location** Map p.95. Turn onto Signal Mountain Road from Teton Park Road; trailhead is located at small lay-by approximately 1 mile ahead.
> **Comments** A quiet hike with a variety of charms: potential wildlife sightings, lush meadows and forests, wildflowers galore and jaw-dropping views of the Tetons.

in an easterly direction through lodgepole pine forest, passing to the right of a lily pad pond as you go (this is one of the most likely spots to spot **moose** along the way). In practically no time you reach a trail junction, at which you bear right; you'll return in a few hours via the path on the left. The trail is fairly level as it passes through a heavily foliaged meadow with a great view of Mount Moran to the west. It then veers to the left of two small ponds before climbing slightly into stands of lodgepole and aspen.

1.75 miles from the trailhead, bear right again at the loop's second junction; it's here you begin your assault on the summit another mile up the trail. Climb steadily through a forest of Douglas fir that soon spills out briefly into a wildflower-strewn meadow. It's then back into the forest for a series of switch-backs that lead to **Jackson Point Overlook**, from where you can absorb the otherworldly view of the spiky Tetons with those who have made the drive up.

For the return trip, backtrack down the switchbacks to the trail junction one mile down, where this time you'll follow the path to the right. Enjoy continued views of the Tetons across Jackson Lake, many of which are framed by groves of pine and aspen, as you pass over easily scaled ridges along this section of the loop. Once you reach the first junction you encountered on the way up, bear right to reach your vehicle.

Teton Park Road and Jenny Lake

The inner loop road of Grand Teton, officially known as **Teton Park Road**, delivers visitors to the base of the immense peaks above **Jenny Lake**. Some of the finest, most enjoyable hiking in the park can be found on the trails weaving around the Jenny Lake area, where it's easy to feel miniscule among the sublime landscape of jaggedly towering peaks and U-shaped canyons.

H33 String Lake to Bearpaw Lake

Hiking high up into the Tetons is an unmiss-able experience, but you don't have to embark on a Herculean trek to enjoy the park's scenic backcountry wonders. One of Grand Teton's finest flat hikes begins at **String Lake Picnic Area** along **Jenny Lake Scenic Loop**. String Lake itself is a family favourite, as it's shallow enough to actually warm up by midsummer; it also boasts several small beaches. The trail is busy for the first mile, full of families exploring the narrow lake's eastern shoreline while looking

> **Difficulty** Easy
> **Distance** 8-mile round-trip
> **Estimated time** 3hr 30min
> **Season** May–Oct
> **Trailhead location** Map p.95. Leigh and String Lakes Trailhead.
> **Comments** A scenic lakeside path that leads to several campsites at the base of the Tetons.

out for moose and grouse. At the one-mile point, the flat path divides; take the Portage Trail, then veer towards Leigh Lake Trail/Bearpaw Lake at the next marker. You may well find the trail is yours alone for the rest of the way in all its panoramic glory.

From here, continue along the eastern shore of **Leigh Lake**, dotted with forested islands and duck-topped boulders exposed in the sometimes white-capped water. You'll mainly find expert paddlers at this picturesque lake set at the base of the soaring Tetons, as the portage from String Lake weeds out recreational canoeists. The north end of Leigh Lake's shoreline was burned in a fire in the early 1980s, so the smaller pines here are very dense, obscuring the lake from sight for the first while. Eventually the path enters a large meadow and splits in three directions: a right turn leads to a campsite on the eastern shores of **Bearpaw Lake** (at a beach bordering a play-land of boulders scattered in shallow water); a left turn takes you toward the tip of Leigh Lake and its volunteer-staffed patrol cabin; and straight ahead goes to additional campsites set along the western shore of Bearpaw Lake. Take the last of the three options and continue about a half-mile past the campsites to the Trapper Lake campsite, set back from the trail under tall trees. Just when it seems the trail has ended without ever offering a peek at **Trapper Lake**, a beaver pond spillway appears, splashing noisily into the tiny, very private lake; a favourite of fisherman, trout rise hungrily to the surface when a hatch is on. Spend some time poking around the shore and climbing the boulders scattered at the base of the mountains, then return the four miles to the trailhead.

H34 Hidden Falls and Inspiration Point

This is widely regarded as Grand Teton National Park's signature short hike, and with good reason – this brief journey into the Tetons allows you to take in a **boat trip**, a photogenic **waterfall** and a **spectacular overlook of Jenny Lake**. To begin, the majority of hikers board the **Jenny Lake Ferry** (see p.164) from the East Boat Dock across the water to the trailhead; should you wish to add distance to the short hike, consider the 2.4-mile jaunt around the lake's southern point, saving the boat trip for the way back. From the Jenny Lake Ferry

> **Difficulty** Moderate
> **Distance** 2-mile round-trip via ferry; 4.5 using ferry one-way
> **Estimated time** 1–3hr
> **Season** June–Oct
> **Trailhead location** Map p.95. East boat dock at Jenny Lake.
> **Comments** Stupendous up-close views of the Tetons and a shimmering cascade await just across the water from South Jenny Lake's hubbub.

parking area, this easy addition hugs the lake's southern shore, diving in and out of the sun and past thickets of edible thimbleberry bushes.

From the west boat dock, a gentle climb leads to **Hidden Falls**. Despite exposed roots and tricky rocks, most visitors should be able to make the walk without too much trouble. The falls, cloaked by forest on their approach, are spectacular, as is the view to the peaks above. Keep your packs closed, however, as this area is frequented by bears, so much so that the Park Service has deemed it a **picnic-free zone**. As well as looking out for bears, scan the nearby cliffs for red and white helmets – Exum Mountain Guides use the area as a practising ground. From the falls, it's a strenuous 0.4-mile slog up 200ft on a rock-strewn trail to **Inspiration Point**. It's well worth it, however, for the singular perspective the spot provides of Jenny Lake, Jackson Hole and even the Gros Ventre Range across the valley floor. The trail continues into the mountains as the Cascade Canyon Trail (see H47), but to get to the west boat dock, return to Hidden Falls and follow the signs from there.

H35 Amphitheater Lake and Overlook

Built in the 1920s by two Jackson Hole businessmen years before the Civilian Conservation Corps constructed the bulk of the Park Service paths, this trail from Lupine Meadows Trailhead to **Amphitheater Lake** is one of the oldest and best in the park. You'll feel it for days – the trail gains more than 3000 feet of elevation in just over four miles – but you'll remember it forever. Just don't make this your first hike at this elevation, as you'll want a few days to adjust before you take on such a steep challenge.

Throughout much of summer, wildflowers greet you at **Lupine Meadows Trailhead**, becoming denser as the trail winds gradually upward through a sloped moraine to the

> **Difficulty** Very strenuous
> **Distance** 10-mile round-trip
> **Estimated time** 6–8hr
> **Season** July–Oct
> **Trailhead location** Map p.95. Lupine Meadows Trailhead. Take the signed, unpaved road 1 mile south of South Jenny Lake Junction for another mile to the parking area.
> **Comments** Find your subalpine hiking rhythm on this demanding but well-graded climb up to a high mountain cirque set at treeline.

junction with the **Valley Trail** at 1.7 miles. From here, the switchback-happy trail begins to seriously climb, reaching a second junction – **Garnet Canyon Trail** (see H36) – after an additional 1.3 miles and 1000 vertical feet. Stick to the **Amphitheater Lake Trail** by veering right, climbing another two miles and 1200ft via nineteen occasionally shaded zig-zags to trail's end. Boulder-lined **Surprise Lake** sits at the 9500ft mark, tucked in a cirque at the base of **Disappointment Peak**. You can expect to see ice during most of the year, so a refreshing dip won't cross your mind – but there are a few designated camping spaces here (which require procuring a permit ahead of time). Amphitheater Lake is only a short distance beyond; to reach it, continue along the north side of Surprise Lake around the tree-covered slope dividing the lakes. Beyond Amphitheater Lake itself is **Amphitheater Overlook**, which looks out at Delta Lake and up to Teton Glacier, Disappointment Peak and the Grand Teton.

If you're feeling particularly robust, return to **Garnet Trail junction** two miles down the trail and bear right into **Garnet Canyon**, described in detail below. Otherwise, retrace your earlier path down to Lupine Meadows Trailhead.

H36 Garnet Canyon

While this hike shares its first three miles with the Amphitheater Lake Trail (profiled above), its ultimate destination, **Garnet Canyon**, is more easily reached and, to many who visit it, just as striking. Note that the final 0.6 miles described here, which lead to a lovely area known as the Meadows, require minor **route-finding skills**.

Begin by following the directions noted above toward Amphitheater Lake; once you reach the **Garnet Trail junction** at the 3-mile mark, bear left, at which point you'll have already scaled over 1600ft of steep Teton incline. Once on Garnet Canyon Trail, climb a short distance before entering deeply sunken Garnet Canyon itself, with the imposing eastern face of **Nez Percé** (11,901ft) towering further up the canyon. Continue onward along the path, which eventually turns rocky as it traverses scree-strewn slopes; its maintained section ends near **Cleft Falls**, 1.1 miles after Garnet Trail junction. At this point, a series of **rock cairns** point your way through a boulder field to a little-used trail along Garnet Creek. Just over half a mile beyond the end of the maintained trail, you reach the **Meadows**, originally named for a lush carpet of wildflowers since partially buried by a 1951 landslide. Enjoy a snack and catch a glimpse of **Spalding Falls**, an 80ft cascade near the west end of the Meadows, before retracing your boot imprints back to Lupine Meadows Trailhead.

Difficulty Strenuous
Distance 8.2–9.4-mile round-trip
Estimated time 4–6hr
Season July–Oct
Trailhead location Map p.95. Lupine Meadows Trailhead. Take the signed, unpaved road 1 mile south of South Jenny Lake Junction for another mile to the parking area.
Comments Revealing deep canyon landscapes, this less taxing companion hike to the Amphitheater Lake slog merits a few hours of its own.

H37 Taggart and Bradley Lakes

Not quite a perfect loop, this hike is a fairly straightforward ramble past two of the attractive **glacial lakes** – Taggart and Bradley – that dot the Tetons' eastern escarpment. From the trailhead car park, the dusty trail starts flat, cutting under a row of power lines to the first of several well-marked junctions. Turn right for the most direct route to Taggart Lake, 1.5 miles away. As elsewhere in the park, the region's geological history quickly makes itself known as you head up the moraine separating the lake from the

Difficulty Moderate
Distance 5-mile loop
Estimated time 2–4hr
Season June–Oct
Trailhead location Map p.95. 2 miles north of Moose Entrance Station, directly off Teton Park Road.
Comments An instructive hike to two glacial lakes, highlighting the region's glacial history and post-fire landscapes.

russet sagebrush flats to the east. An oasis of green, the moraine's rich soil is home to stands of Engelmann spruce, lodgepole pine and aspen. Scars from a major fire in 1985 likewise abound, with charred trunks shooting pencil-straight up into the sky as you approach the second fork in the trail. Head left for the final half-mile to **Taggart Lake** (6902ft), named after a member of the Hayden Survey of 1872.

Following the lake's eastern edge, the trail follows a northerly uphill route, offering fine views into the mouth of **Avalanche Canyon**, through which the glacier that scooped out Taggart Lake's basin once travelled. After cresting the moraine separating the two lakes, the path leads down through thick forest untouched by fire to striking **Bradley Lake** (7022ft), smaller than Taggart and named after another member of the Hayden Survey. Several paths lead directly down to the water, with many of these trails leading to spots secluded enough for a quick skinnydip on the warmest of days. It's possible to continue heading north around the lake to hook up with the **Amphitheater Lake Trail** (see **H35**) 1.5 miles onwards; otherwise, to complete the hike it's a mostly downhill, mile-long hike south on the **Bradley Lake Trail** (turn left at the trail junction) back to the main trail junction due east of Taggart Lake. From here, you'll retrace your steps just over a mile back to the trailhead.

Moran Junction to Moose Junction

While the dry southeast section of the park may pale in comparison to the peaks and lakes of the Tetons in terms of pure visual drama, there are still a few fine trails where it's worth getting your boots dusty. One of the best treks heads up **Blacktail Butte**, rising from the sagebrush flats east of Moose; another memorable stroll at **Schwabacher's Landing** drops down from those same flats to the Snake River, where you can see first-hand what the local beaver and osprey population is up to.

H38 Schwabacher's Landing

Not every hike needs to be a workout; sometimes one can be nothing more than exploration, like this choose-your-own-adventure hike at **Schwabacher's Landing**. A popular fishing spot, Schwabacher's features an ecosystem not represented in other Grand Teton hikes. The Snake River here rarely consists of one channel – in fact, it's been historically difficult for engineers to build bridges over the Snake for the way it divides and braids in unpredictable ways each season. Its capricious nature also makes a detailed hiking itinerary here all but impossible.

Angler trails provide pathways to explora-

Difficulty Easy
Distance Varies
Estimated Time Varies
Season April–Oct
Trailhead Location Map p.95. Follow Hwy 89/191 4.1 miles north of Moose Junction to Schwabacher's Landing, then follow gravel road to parking areas near Snake River.
Comments A rare, unscripted foray into the bottoms of the Snake River drainage.

tion here. Follow a trail to the north and you may come across giant **beaver lodges** and remnants of various dams they've industriously constructed. As high water frequently washes away their old engineering projects, these creatures are always busy, and many of the felled trees sport fresh gnaw marks. Though generally nocturnal, beavers can occasionally be spotted in broad daylight, so keep your eyes and ears open; if a beaver sees you first, it may loudly slap its flat tail against the water as a warning to others in the vicinity.

While exploring the river bottoms, you're likely to spot a **bald eagle**. Once ravaged by DDT and other human-related perils, these birds have made an impressive comeback. Another flying predator hereabouts is the **osprey**; smaller than an eagle, it's no less avid a fish-catcher. Brown above and white below, osprey are often seen flying aerodynamically with a fish facing forward in their talons. Also evident is the region's volcanic history, with rhyolite and obsidian often found mixed in with other stones washed down from the Yellowstone caldera. Remember that rocks, along with driftwood, belong to the park, and cannot be taken home.

H39 Blacktail Butte traverse

This hike is best if you exploit a shuttle system to save major backtracking. Leave one car at trail's end at the **Blacktail Butte** climbing wall, the first major parking area just north of Moose along the east side of Hwy 89/191; drive the second car south to Gros Ventre Junction, then northeast to the junction leading north to **Mormon Row**. Head north five miles along unpaved Mormon Row to the gate (which is sometimes closed), park off the road and begin the hike here.

> **Difficulty** Moderate to strenuous
> **Distance** 4.5 miles one-way
> **Estimated time** 2hr
> **Season** June–Oct
> **Trailhead location** Map p.88. Mormon Row, five miles north of junction with Gros Ventre Road.
> **Comments** An overlooked gem revealing terrific views of Jackson Hole.

Pass through the gate and proceed through meadows lined with aspen trees. Due to a preponderance of **bison trails**, things can get a bit confusing, but aim for the trail to the right that heads straight up the spine of the butte. This rocky uphill trail lends insight into the geological history of Blacktail Butte: an ice age anomaly, it's an outcropping of rock so hard that glaciers divided around it. Much of the upward slope is glacial till – rocks left behind when the ice scraped off its earthen luggage and ground down into fist-sized cobbles.

Follow the steep course up an 800ft climb. When you stop to catch your breath, use it as an excuse to gaze at the scene east of you: the town of Kelly, the mass of Sleeping Indian behind it and Gros Ventre Slide at his feet. Beyond the enormous slide area are the aptly named Red Hills, which follow the contour of the Gros Ventre River. From this high vantage point, try to spot the historic fields of Mormon Row to the north and east of Blacktail Butte, where the irrigation ditches and patterns of old fields contrast with the land not cleared of sagebrush and native vegetation by the settlers. These days, the valley's main inhabitants are bison (the black spots in the fields below) and pronghorn (grey spots).

At the **summit** of the butte, the trail flirts with thick, deep woods before moving into quiet meadows. The top features roads once used by ranchers, watering holes for their cattle, an unmarked cowboy grave and even a rumoured airplane crash site. Sightings of the re-introduced **grey wolf** are also becoming increasingly common up top. The trail cuts northwest across the top of the butte, eventually depositing you on the west side at large vertical slabs of rocks where climbing fanatics gather. A few yards more, and the trail finally reaches the valley floor; from here, it's a short jaunt north to your vehicle.

Laurance S. Rockefeller Preserve

Beautifully maintained and smartly routed, the hiking trails within **Laurance S. Rockefeller Preserve** are as singularly exceptional as the Preserve's visitor centre (see p.90) and, indeed, the land itself. The small network of trails here was opened to the public in 2007 once the Preserve's 1100 acres were transferred to the National Park Service from the Rockefeller Trust, and these paths never suffer from overuse thanks to the policy of allowing no more than fifty or so cars into the Preserve's parking area.

4

DAY HIKES | Hikes within Grand Teton

With walls of Teton rock towering above to the west and unforgettable views across cobalt-blue **Phelps Lake**, this eminently enjoyable seven-mile loop has become, in the eyes of those who have experienced it, one of Grand Teton's **premier day hikes**. Minimal steep sections and a sandy beach along Phelps Lake's north shore help make this a terrific option for anyone looking to while away a morning or afternoon (or both) in a section of the park yet to be discovered by the majority of visitors.

Difficulty Moderate
Distance 7-mile loop
Estimated time 3–4hr
Season May–Oct
Trailhead location Map p.88. Laurance S. Rockefeller Preserve parking area.
Comments If you're looking for wilderness-like quietude, a beautiful mountain lake and a sandy lakeshore in the shadow of the Tetons, you've come to the right place.

Begin from Laurance S. Rockefeller Preserve's parking area; try to **arrive before 11am** to avoid having to wait for a vehicle space. After winding around the Preserve's visitor centre and crossing a footbridge over Lake Creek, follow the **Lake Creek Trail** to the left at the junction where it begins, along with its counterpart, the Woodland Trail (you'll wrap up your loop later in the day by returning on the latter path). Immediately enter a wooded landscape as the trail climbs very gently, near at times to **Lake Creek** itself. After a half-mile, the path crosses occasionally paved, occasionally busy Moose-Wilson Road; another half-mile on, you'll pass a sizeble, grassy meadow on your left and, not much later, a conveniently placed **restroom**. You're now within striking distance of Phelps Lake, so when you reach its perimeter trail, go right and choose from numerous choice vantage points affording championship-calibre vistas across the water.

Upon departing this most photogenic of rest stops, rejoin the **Phelps Lake Trail** and begin following it counterclockwise around the lakeshore. As it passes distinctive **buck-and-rail fences** indicating the former boundary of the Rockefeller property, the path stays near the water's edge but rarely dips down alongside it. Further along the lake's northeast shore, about three miles from the trailhead, note the trio of inviting backcountry campsites perched above the shoreline to the right and reached by short spur paths. Continue another half-mile or so to what may be Wyoming's finest **beach**, a sandy strand along Phelps Lake's north shore that's ideal for a picnic lunch, a brave dip into the lake's waters or even an afternoon nap. This section of the lake is also accessible via a slightly shorter, but quite steeper hike originating from Death Canyon Trailhead.

Back on the Phelps Lake Trail and now continuing west a very short distance, bear left at the junction with the **Valley Trail** (which leads to Death Canyon and its same-named trailhead). The half-mile or so that follows is the hike's most sharply graded as it ascends a lateral moraine to reach a junction with the **Open Canyon Trail**. From here, it's another mile through densely wooded terrain (known to be prime **black bear territory**) to the junction with a short spur trail leading down to **Huckleberry Point**, another top lakeshore vista on a hike rife with them. Metal boardwalks built to protect neighbouring wetlands lead from near Huckleberry Point's access path along the Phelps Lake Trail to another junction, this one recognizable as the Lake Creek Trail via which you originally reached Phelps Lake. To enjoy an alternative route back to the trailhead, continue just under half a mile to the junction with the **Woodland Trail** and turn right. Spend your final 1.2 miles ambling through alternately open and wooded terrain, again crossing Moose-Wilson Road (0.7 miles after joining the Woodland Trail) en route to the Preserve's parking area.

H41 Aspen Ridge/Boulder Ridge loop

Making for a slightly shorter day out than the Phelps Lake loop described above, this delightful hike gently heads up, over and around glacial moraines just south of Phelps Lake. Expect to share the **Aspen Ridge** and **Boulder Ridge Trails** with very few others, as most Rockefeller Preserve visitors seem to stick to the Lake Creek and Woodland Trails.

Start from the parking area and follow the same route to Moose-Wilson Road as detailed in H40. Just after crossing the road, bear left onto the Aspen Ridge Trail, which rises and dips through forests of **aspen** and young **lodgepole pine**, and where the enveloping calm may have you thinking you've been somehow transported into deep wilderness, miles from the nearest road. Some 2.5 miles from the parking area, you reach a ridge featuring **far-ranging views** of both Open and Granite Canyon, as well as Mount Hunt. The trail then drops down the morainal ridge to an intersection with the Lake Creek Trail in about three-quarters of a mile; once it comes into sight, take time to enjoy the vista across gorgeous **Phelps Lake** before continuing.

From the Phelps Lake Trail/Woodland Trail junction, it's just a tenth of a mile along the latter to your turn onto the Boulder Ridge Trail, which begins climbing right away. A half-mile along, the trail forks: the two branches join together again within 0.2 miles, so either one is fair game. Note the massive **boulders** here – house-sized glacial erratics carried to this spot by enormous flows of ice eons ago. Just over half a mile after the two forks converge, the Boulder Ridge Trail meets the Woodland Trail, on which you enjoy the final 0.8 miles en route to the parking area.

> **Difficulty** Moderate
> **Distance** 6-mile loop
> **Estimated time** 2–4hr
> **Season** May–Oct
> **Trailhead location** Map p.88. Laurance S. Rockefeller Preserve parking area.
> **Comments** An enjoyable, slow-paced route through quiet woodland and forest filled with aspen groves and glacier-hauled boulders.

5

Backcountry hiking and camping

A n indisputable highlight for adventure-seeking visitors to the parks will be a night or more spent out in the wilds, waking early on a frosty morning to the echoing sounds of howling wolves or bugling elk. Only a slice of Grand Teton and even less of Yellowstone can be seen from roads and short interpretive trails, and leaving this so-called frontcountry behind to enter the **backcountry** is a thrilling trip that any able-bodied person should consider. From isolated thermal areas like those in Yellowstone's Shoshone Geyser Basin to a high-altitude traverse amid the mighty Tetons, some of the region's finest highlights require a long yet rewarding trip to view them.

While the idea of heading off into the hills with your tent may sound appealing, keep in mind that there are certain **responsibilities** you take on when doing so. The reason that so many cliché backcountry camping mantras – "good campsites are found, not made", "take only pictures, leave only footprints" – exist is that the advice they offer continues to be ignored. Perhaps the core axiom of the backcountry is to always **pack out what you pack in** – or more, if you come across someone else's litter. Also, unless you want to run the risk of starting a wildfire, check to see if **fires** are permitted at your backcountry campsite; if they are, only use dead, downed wood.

Backcountry hikers are also advised to read the introduction to Chapter 4, "Day hikes", for details on **maps**, hiking **safety** and more.

Backcountry information and practicalities

The top source for **backcountry information** in the region are the rangers of Yellowstone and Grand Teton National Parks. Armed as they are with the latest info, most will gladly share choice bits of insider knowledge to inquisitive visitors. If things aren't too busy at the ranger station or backcountry office where you arrange your required backcountry **permit**, feel free to linger and ask the attending ranger for his or her advice on trails and destinations. Before leaving, check weather forecasts and ask about any potential hazards along your intended route, such as recent bear sightings or swift-rushing rivers you may need to ford.

Remember that black bears and grizzlies can be encountered virtually anywhere in the backcountry; see the box on p.110 for advice on being **bear-aware** throughout your treks.

Yellowstone: backcountry camping and permits

Dispersed camping within Yellowstone's backcountry is prohibited; however, with over 300 **designated backcountry sites**, you should have little problem finding the perfect place to pitch your tent. A free **permit** specifying your assigned sites and nights is required; these can be obtained from the ranger stations and backcountry offices listed in the box, below. Permits can be collected no earlier than 48 hours in advance of your trailhead departure, and if time allows, rangers can often help narrow down your choices with their personal picks. Since a mere fraction of visitors venture into Yellowstone's backcountry, it's rarely a problem to procure a **reservation**. However, for the most popular sites – around Yellowstone and Shoshone Lakes and the northern half of Lamar Valley, in particular – you may want to make one in advance. These cost $20, and can be made by post or in person for the upcoming season beginning April 1; reservation sheets with mailing addresses can be downloaded from the park's website (⑩ www.nps.gov/yell) or you can call the main backcountry office to request one (☎ 307/344-2160). Reserved permits must be collected in person by 10am on the day of your trip's start, at which point you'll also be required to watch a half-hour video on backcountry safety.

Grand Teton: backcountry camping and permits

As in Yellowstone, free **permits** are required for any overnight trip into Grand Teton's backcountry, with two dozen **designated backcountry sites** around the park's lakes, including Jackson, Leigh, Phelps and Holly. Unlike Yellowstone, however, the remaining permits are issued for **camping zones**, trailside regions high in the Tetons where dispersed camping is allowed. As long as you follow the rules – which include camping at least 200ft from lakes and streams and staying out of sight from the trail whenever possible – you're free to pitch your tent wherever you'd like within each zone. These high-altitude areas are often used by climbers and scramblers sticking close to their rocky routes, but hikers are welcome to overnight as well. Throughout summer, permits can be picked up at Craig Thomas (Moose) and Colter Bay Visitor Centers (see p.90 & p.106) or Jenny Lake Ranger Station (see p.103); in other seasons, permits are only available at Moose. One-third of individual campsites and all group sites can be **reserved** in advance, and with fewer spaces than Yellowstone to choose from, you may want to consider this option, especially if you're planning an expedition for July or August. Reservations are taken from January 1 to May 15 for the year ahead; these cost $25 and

---

Yellowstone backcountry permit offices

As Yellowstone covers such a large area, you're best off picking up your **permit** (and the handy advice that goes with it) at the station closest to where your trip begins. That said, all the following offices can issue backcountry permits when open. During the off-season, call ☎ 307/344-2160 to have your permit issued.

- Bechler Ranger Station
- Bridge Bay Ranger Station
- Canyon Visitor Center
- Grant Village Visitor Center
- Mammoth Visitor Center
- Old Faithful Ranger Station
- South Entrance Ranger Station
- Tower Ranger Station
- West Yellowstone Visitor Information Center

may be made in person, via fax (⑤307/739-3438) or by post (Grand Teton, Permits Office, PO Drawer 170, Moose, WY 83102). For more information, call ⓣ307/739-3309 or visit ⓦwww.nps.gov/grte. You must pick up your reserved permit by 10am on the first day of your backcountry trip or your spot may be given to someone else.

Campfires, cooking and food storage

Open **fires** are only permitted in fire rings at designated sites. If sitting before a fire is key to your camping experience, work with a ranger to find such a spot, as a good percentage of backcountry sites in the more popular areas of Yellowstone are fire-free; open fires are likewise prohibited at many of the designated sites – and banned within all alpine camping zones – in Grand Teton. **Backpacking stoves**, however, are permitted at all sites, and they are easily the quickest, most efficient way to cook meals. It's a good idea to stock up on stove fuel in one of the gateway towns before venturing into the parks.

Upon arriving at your backcountry camping area, one of the first orders of business should be **storing your food properly**. Extra pack weight notwithstanding, it's easiest to simply carry all your food and personal hygiene items (toothpaste, sunscreen, lip balm, deodorant, et al) in a **bear-resistant canister** deep in your pack. Failing this method, look around for a **food storage pole** – typically a log lashed high up, parallel to the ground between two trees – provided at most campsites around one hundred yards from the tent area. If there's not one to be found, search out a sturdy branch at least fifteen feet off the ground and five feet out from the trunk, and **hang your food** stash from that. To do this, you'll need to bring your own rope and stuff sacks, and be sure to also include any and all scented personal items. Note that all cooking and eating should be done in this area as well to keep food odours away from your sleeping area. Finally, remember to *never* eat or store food near, let alone inside your tent.

Water and waste disposal

Before leaving on any hike of distance, talk to rangers and study maps to get up-to-date info on accessible **water**. On some hikes, you'll pass creeks and springs every few hundred yards, while on others – particularly late in the season, when runoff has dissipated – you'll need to conserve greatly or pack an extra bottle or two. Regardless of how fresh and clean water in the backcountry looks, it should be boiled for five minutes or processed with a giardia-rated purifier or filtration system available from any shop where camping gear is sold. **Giardia**, a waterborne protozoan that leads to chronic diarrhoea, abdominal cramps, fatigue and loss of weight, is a problem in backcountry water supplies; to avoid catching it, refrain from drinking directly from rivers and streams. After all, you never know what unspeakable acts animals – or irresponsible people – have performed in them further upstream.

As for **litter**, it's a very simple guideline: If you pack it in, pack it out. Some popular backcountry areas have very basic pit toilets, but where none exist, be sure to **bury human waste** at least six inches in a so-called cathole, one hundred feet minimum from the nearest water supply and camp. Similarly, you should urinate far from the trail and any water source, preferably on rocky ground to avoid damage from animals digging about after you leave. Used tampons should be packed out. Finally, don't use **soaps or detergents** (even biodegradable varieties) anywhere near lakes and streams; fellow backcountry visitors using water purifiers or filters downstream won't appreciate your actions at all. Instead, when cleaning yourself, dishes or clothes, carry water at least one hundred feet (preferably two hundred) from the water's edge before washing.

Backcountry equipment and packing

Balance is the crucial element when deciding what **equipment** to take on a backcountry trip. Take too much and your back might never forgive you; carry too little and a trip can be ruined by hunger, sleep deprivation, weather or some similar inconvenience (or disaster). You'll have to figure out via trial and error the tricky balance between weight and what's essential, but a few ways you can help yourself is by sticking to lightweight foods, avoiding cans, paring down your wardrobe to the bare minimum and choosing a slender paperback over your collected works of Shakespeare.

Clothing

It's not uncommon to have breakfast while temperatures are below freezing, only to eat lunch under the sun at close to 80°F. You'll therefore want to pack a full complement of **layers**, starting with long underwear. Convertible trousers that unzip into shorts are a good choice for your next layer – especially if you'll be fording rivers – along with a T-shirt or two. You should also carry a **waterproof jacket**, **fleece top** and lightweight **winter hat** and **gloves** in case the weather turns nasty. Though more costly, you'll be most comfortable in layers made from polypropylene or a similar **synthetic** material, as these tend to wick moisture away as you sweat; cotton clothing, while undeniably comfortable when dry, will quickly chill you to the bone in a cold breeze once dampened. For the same reasons, avoid cotton **socks** and splurge on a couple of pairs of wool (or synthetic, wool-like) socks instead.

Also worthy of a spending spree are sturdy **hiking boots** geared toward the Rockies' unforgiving terrain. Be choosy when shopping around, as your main considerations should be whether you'll be more comfortable in **heavy-duty** boots or something **lightweight**. If you don't plan on spending days on end scrambling about in the backcountry, it may be best to go for a fairly light, flexible pair. However, if you're heading out on a longer expedition and plan on carrying a heavy pack throughout, it's probably best to invest in high-cut waterproof boots with strong soles. Most importantly, **break in** your new boots by walking (or even hiking) in them for several weeks before your trip to avoid the scourge of all hikers: **blisters**. Finally, when packing your first-aid kit, don't forget to include pieces of blister-covering **moleskin**, just in case (though a piece of well-placed duct tape has been known to work nearly as well).

Basic gear

It's worth investing some thought and financial resources to ensure that you have the basic **hiking and camping equipment**, and that you know how to use it all. First up is a sturdy **backpack** in which to store and transport your gear. Once you've narrowed down the size you're after, concentrate on fit, making sure the pack's maze of straps is properly explained in order to maximize its efficiency. **Tents** are available in a near-bewildering array of sizes and styles, but for most, a two-person, three-season tent in the five-pound range will be the smartest and most economical choice. As for a **sleeping bag**, anything that can't stuff down to about the size of a basketball or smaller is likely too bulky. Unless you're winter camping, however, there's no need to blow hundreds of dollars on a space-age design that will keep you warm in a thirty-below blizzard; rather, invest in a good backpacking bag rated to twenty degrees. Lastly is a **sleeping pad**. Inflatable pads stuff down small, while foam rolls are cheaper, lighter and easier to use, albeit not quite as soft. Either type will provide a layer of warm

Personal preferences dictate exactly what you'll need to take on a hiking trip, but the following checklist should point you in the right direction.

Day hiking

- Map
- Water
- Strong hiking shoes or boots
- Wool or synthetic-wool socks
- Waterproof jacket
- Sturdy water bottle(s) or reservoir
- Sunscreen
- Sunglasses
- Hat
- Bear spray
- Snacks and emergency food
- First-aid kit (with moleskin)
- Binoculars (optional)
- Camera (optional)

Essential overnight gear

- All of the above
- Waterproof tent
- Food (including emergency supply)
- Water purifier or filter
- Stove and fuel
- Pots, pans and utensils
- Sleeping bag
- Sleeping pad
- Long-sleeve shirt
- Warm, long trousers
- Long underwear
- Warm, lightweight hat and gloves
- Camp shoes (sandals work best)
- Insect repellent
- Waterproof matches or lighter
- Pocketknife
- Headlamp or flashlight (with extra batteries)
- Rubbish bags
- Toilet paper
- Soap/personal hygiene items
- Stuff sacks and plastic zipper bags
- Bear-resistant canister for food storage
- Backcountry permit
- Fleece or down jacket

Additional overnight gear

- Lightweight tarp or tent groundsheet
- Books, playing cards, etc
- Small trowel
- Journal and pen
- Fishing gear (and licence)
- Field guides
- Rope or nylon cord
- Flask

insulation between yourself and the earth, helping you rest far more comfortably than you would without one.

Overnight hikes

The following list of **overnight hikes** is a mere introduction to the region's vast backcountry, covering everything from the deep, desert-like Black Canyon in north Yellowstone to the snowy alpine reaches of the Tetons' highest ridges. Most of these hikes can be completed in a few days; avid backpackers looking for lengthier options should note that several of the day hikes described in Chapter 4 can be strung together or forged deeper into wilderness.

H42 Yellowstone: Black Canyon of the Yellowstone

This one-way trip in the northern reaches of Yellowstone tracks the mighty **Yellowstone River** as it flows northwest out of the park through the colourful walls of the **Black Canyon of the Yellowstone**. The entire stretch could be tackled in one very long, sweat-soaked day, but we've stretched it into a three-day hike to offer plenty of time for wildlife watching (best in early summer) and relaxing in the shade; the route slices through the warmest area in the park, making it a good choice when snow covers most other Yellowstone trails. Ample opportunities for catching trout in the Yellowstone and its tributaries add yet another great excuse for taking the slow road.

The first day covers seven miles, allowing time to pick up backcountry permits and arrange transportation from your ending point in Gardiner; you'll either need to leave a second shuttle car in town or fix a ride to **Hellroaring Creek Trailhead**. From here, the path leads steeply down 500ft in one mile to a suspension bridge crossing high above the Yellowstone; black bears are commonly spotted here, so remain aware. Beyond the bridge, you'll pass the Coyote Creek Trail and another junction with the **Hellroaring Creek Trail**. It's possible to continue straight to ford the Yellowstone, but the crossing is exceedingly dangerous. Instead, head northeast on the Hellroaring Creek Trail to the stock bridge 1.8 miles away. Once across, you'll loop back down alongside Hellroaring Creek, past a small **ranger patrol cabin** and duck-filled pond to backcountry site 2H1, a mile detour off the main trail at the confluence of Hellroaring Creek and the Yellowstone River; with a sandy beach nearby, this is a great place to spend the night.

Day two covers around twelve miles, starting with a climb into a beautiful high meadow; the numerous shed antlers strewn about prove that elk frequently enjoy the area as well. As you climb, you're afforded great views to the river below, with snowcapped peaks on the horizon. Three miles in, the path crosses **Little Cottonwood Creek** (stock up on water here), then **Cottonwood Creek** a mile onwards; trout are often easily spotted in both waterways. You're now within the Black Canyon proper, its dark walls looming across the opposite shore. Three miles further, after crossing into Montana from Wyoming, the trail passes a junction with **Blacktail Deer Creek Trail** before going past pretty **Crevice Lake** and over **Crevice Creek** on a sturdy footbridge. A short way onwards is **Knowles Falls**, a squat and powerful rush of the river dropping some 15ft. Another mile west sit two nice campsites: 1Y2, tucked up against a near-vertical canyon wall, and 1Y1, set on a big bend in the river and boasting its own sandy beach area.

Difficulty Strenuous	
Distance 22 miles one-way	
Estimated time 3 days	
Season May to early Oct	
Trailhead location Map p.53. Hellroaring Creek Trailhead, 15 miles east of Mammoth and 4 miles west of Roosevelt on the Grand Loop Road.	
Comments Apart from thermal features, this trip takes in nearly all the park's varied landscapes, from high plains to deep forests and river valleys.	

Continental Divide Trail

Stretching 3100 miles through New Mexico, Colorado, Wyoming, Idaho and Montana between the United States' northern and southern borders, the **Continental Divide Trail** (CDT) squiggles like a child's drawing along the way, and with a full thirty percent of its route still unmarked, it requires plenty of backcountry navigation skills to complete. Most hikers take it one section at a time, though some speed-hikers have completed the span in less than ninety days, presumably not stopping for many photos along the way. The CDT enters **Yellowstone** from Idaho's Caribou-Targhee National Forest to the west, and exits nearly 70 trail miles later into Wyoming's Bridger-Teton National Forest; sights along the way include Old Faithful, Shoshone Geyser Basin (see H45) and Heart Lake (see H46); after heading east of Grand Teton National Park, the trail cuts through Wyoming's Wind River Range, home to some of the finest scenery in all the Rockies. For more information, visit both Ⓦwww.cdtrail.org and www.cdtsociety.org.

Your third and final day takes in five miles of hiking beside and above the river, cutting through a semi-desert environment surrounded by beautiful "painted" canyon walls. Unlike anywhere else in Yellowstone, this area makes you feel as if you've been transported to one of Utah's national parks. Upon reaching **Gardiner**, the trail dumps out by *Rocky Mountain Campground*, from where it's half a mile to a true post-hike reward: a burger and milkshake at *Steve's Corral Drive-Inn* (see p.231).

H43 Yellowstone: Pelican Valley to Wapiti Lake loop

An excellent choice for fit wildlife watchers, this long overnight trek weaves through heavenly **Pelican Valley** before cutting north along a loop cresting at **Wapiti Lake** deep in Yellowstone's backcountry. Home to meadows, forests, lakes and numerous rivers, the area is a magnet for wildlife – wolves, bison, moose, elk, osprey and sandhill cranes are all regularly spotted in and around the valley. Of most interest (and concern) are **grizzly bears**, of which there are many hereabouts. Indeed, Pelican Valley comprises some of the finest grizzly habitat in the country, and is therefore heavily managed; the valley is **closed** to hikers between early

> **Difficulty** Strenuous
> **Distance** 30-mile round-trip
> **Estimated time** 2 days
> **Season** Early July to Oct
> **Trailhead location** Map p.64. Pelican Valley Trailhead, along an unpaved road accessed 3 miles east of Fishing Bridge Junction.
> **Comments** A long but flat journey through some of the finest grazing and hunting grounds for megafauna in the park.

April and early July to give bears the liberty to hunt spawning trout in peace, while all hiking is likewise banned between the hours of 7pm and 9am from early July until early November. Though not required, rangers strongly recommend hiking in groups of four or more and never hiking this area solo.

Due to the presence of bears, there are no backcountry campsites within or just out of Pelican Valley, necessitating a long trek out to the first series of sites. While day hikers can travel out as far as they feel comfortable before returning, overnighters must cover close to **fifteen miles** to reach a site; this isn't an exceedingly difficult task, however, as the trail remains relatively flat throughout.

From the trailhead, the hike begins by cutting three miles through patches of forest and past the Turbid Lake Trail to the winding, blue ribbon that is **Pelican Creek** (no fishing allowed). To continue north, you'll need to ford the shallow creek before tramping 1.6 miles through grassy meadows to the start of the **Astringent Creek Trail**. This trail forms the western half of a long and narrow creek-side loop, and from here it's eight miles due north to **Wapiti Lake** – the first two-thirds on the Astringent Creek Trail and the last third on the **Broad Creek Trail**. Along the way, you'll cut through numerous narrow meadows and pass by **White Lake** and **Tern Lake**, both worth a quick detour for potential looks at moose and waterfowl. Sitting at the top end of the loop, Wapiti Lake itself is rather plain, but it's a convenient overnight spot with two backcountry sites (4W2 and 4W3; wood fires allowed). Should these two sites be booked, there are several more sites back to the south and west.

On day two, 9.5 miles out of a total 15.5 miles are spent heading south on the **Upper Pelican Creek Trail**, paralleling the previous day's route a mile to the east. The first four miles up to the turn-off for the **Fern Lake Patrol Cabin** are nearly identical, crossing through a mix of burned and old-growth forest. Afterwards, however, the focus changes a good deal as the trail follows (and several times, fords) Pelican Creek downstream past numerous thermal areas; the biggest of the bunch, the **Mushpots**, include large bubbling cauldrons of mud alongside springs and steaming vents. A little over a mile south of here, the trail intersects with the Pelican Creek Trail, from where it's 1.7 miles southwest back to the junction with the Astringent Creek Trail. From this point, simply retrace your previous day's footsteps just over four miles to complete the trip.

H44 Yellowstone: Thorofare Trail to Bridger Lake

If your idea of a good time is taking a **boat ride** across Yellowstone Lake, then hiking for two days through a river valley to an area further from roads than anywhere else in the US outside of Alaska, this is the expedition for you. The route along the **Thorofare Trail** described here provides efficient access to the upper Yellowstone River valley, and by hiring a backcountry water taxi (call ☎ 307/242-3893; service operates mid June to mid Sept) out of **Bridge Bay** to drop you

Difficulty Strenuous
Distance 50-mile round-trip
Estimated time 4–5 days
Season mid-July to early Oct
Trailhead location Map p.64. Bridge Bay Marina.
Comments A flat two-day trek through the valley of the Upper Yellowstone River to an uncommonly remote corner of the park.

and your gear off at the mouth of **Columbine Creek** along the southeast shore of Yellowstone Lake, you'll shave 18 round-trip miles off the hike from its traditional starting point at Thorofare Trailhead along the East Entrance Road. Note that this route includes numerous **stream crossings** that, in all but the wettest years, should be manageable after mid July; nevertheless, be sure to exercise necessary caution when fording any swift currents, and ask a ranger about water levels before setting out.

Once you disembark from your water taxi and onto *terra firma* near Columbine Creek, your first few hours along the Thorofare Trail are largely devoid of long-range views while you walk through thick lodgepole pine forest untouched by the area's fires of 1988 and 2003. Some 6.5 miles in, around Terrace Point, the path opens up into meadows offering a **panorama** of the upper Yellowstone River valley. A couple of miles further on is the hike's first stream crossing at **Beaverdam Creek**, which may be swift and knee-deep even after mid July. The nearby meadows frequently see moose, elk and sandhill cranes; **grizzlies** also hang out in the meadows and forest beyond Beaverdam Creek, so don't hesitate to make a minor racket announcing your presence wherever thick stands of pines prevent long-range visibility. Two miles south of Beaverdam Creek (about 10.5 miles from the boat drop-off spot), you arrive at Lower Ford Junction; campsite 6B1 (closed until mid July) is nearby. If you didn't get too late a start, you can press on another 2.5 miles or so down the trail to campsite 6C1, just before Trapper's Creek, for your first night's stay.

The next morning, ford knee-deep **Trapper's Creek** and hike through more regenerating forest to **Turret View Meadow**, where you'll enjoy a terrific view of Turret Mountain to the east. At the 17-mile mark, the route necessitates yet another knee-deep ford at **Mountain Creek**. The ensuing six miles after Mountain Creek become extraordinarily scenic as the trail passes through more meadows and forest, and on a few occasions, right by sharp bends in the Yellowstone River; as you move through this country, look west across the river for fine views of Two Ocean Plateau. About 21 miles from Columbine Creek, you'll cross **Cliff Creek**, usually relatively shallow by late July.

From here, it's two more miles to the **Thorofare Ranger Station** just north of Yellowstone's southeast border, and another two miles to **Bridger Lake**, a true portrait of backcountry serenity ringed by grass and pines. If you wish to camp within the confines of Yellowstone, go right at the trail junction just before the ranger station and look for campsites 6T1 and 6T2 another mile up Thorofare

Creek; otherwise, seek out campsites at any likely spot adjacent to Bridger Lake, which lies within Bridger-Teton National Forest's Teton Wilderness.

Considering how far you've trekked out here, you may want to take an **extra day** to soak in the solitude of this remarkably isolated region before heading back northward on the Thorofare Trail to catch your return water taxi.

H45 Yellowstone: Shoshone Geyser Basin

One of the first places that grabs the attention of long-haul hikers as they pore over Yellowstone maps is **Shoshone Lake**. Far enough from roads to be tantalizing wild, but close enough to reach within a day, this is the largest lake in the lower 48 with no direct road access. This hike targets one of its highlights, **Shoshone Geyser Basin**. Sitting at the farthest point from a road by the lake's far western edge, its pools, small geysers and mudpots make up the largest backcountry thermal area in the park. There are several

Difficulty Strenuous
Distance 20-mile loop
Estimated time 2 days
Season mid-June to Sept
Trailhead location Map p.75. Lone Star Trailhead, 3.5 miles east of Old Faithful.
Comments Take in both the biggest backcountry lake and backcountry geyser basin in Yellowstone.

routes to it, with the following overnight hike beginning from the north at **Lone Star Trailhead** and finishing to the northeast at **DeLacy Creek Trailhead**. This loop enables you to cover fresh ground on the return, but to complete it you'll either need to have a second car waiting at DeLacy Creek or hitch a ride between the two trailheads, located six miles apart on the busy, narrow road between Old Faithful and West Thumb.

From Lone Star Trailhead just upstream from narrow **Kepler Cascades**, it's 2.5 miles to **Lone Star Geyser Group**; this is the hike's easiest portion, following a flat roadbed also popular with bikers. Sporting a tall, steep cone, Lone Star Geyser itself is a firm favourite of geyser gazers, erupting regularly every three to four hours upwards of 50ft. To witness one of its thirty-minute long eruptions, check either the logbook at the trailhead or at the Old Faithful Visitor Education Center for a rough timetable, then plan accordingly. Past the geyser, the trail narrows and crosses a footbridge over the Firehole River, then weaves though a combination of pretty meadows and sparse woods for 3.5 miles to **Grants Pass**; though not a particularly steep climb, snow can be knee-deep along this portion until mid June. From here, the trail tumbles down at an easy pace for two miles, passing junctions with the Bechler River Trail and a stock trail that loops north around Shoshone Geyser Basin. The basin features more than one hundred thermal features and not a single boardwalk or sign, so while you may have the entire area to yourself, always stick to solid ground, tread lightly and watch your step – you're a long way from help should you burn yourself.

An **advance reservation** is recommended to spend the night at one of the three backcountry sites in the area; closest is 8R5, while similarly lakeside 8T1 is to the south and 8G1 is in a meadow below Grants Pass to the north. After re-exploring the geyser basin in the morning light, you'll trace the northern shores of Shoshone Lake for nearly nine miles along the **North Shoshone Trail**; its first half passes mainly through forest, while its latter half is routed by a backcountry **ranger cabin** before opening up to nice views across the lake. There are nine backcountry sites along this stretch, but the majority are saved for boat access only. Near the trail's end, you'll have to hop across or ford slender **DeLacy Creek** before reaching its namesake trail; from here, it's an easy three-mile hike northward alongside the creek (look for plentiful waterfowl, along with the occasional moose) and back to the main road.

5

H46 Yellowstone: Heart Lake and Mount Sheridan

This out-and-back overnight hike to **Heart Lake** and up nearby **Mount Sheridan** (10,305ft) is a fantastic first choice for an overnight trip into Yellowstone's backcountry. The distance covered is reasonable – indeed, hikers in top shape can make it in one extremely long day – and its rewards are great, with plentiful wildlife, backcountry geysers, lakeside campsites and stupendous views from one of Yellowstone's finest peaks. The entire area is closed to hikers until July as a bear management area, so take all necessary precautions, including carrying bear spray.

Difficulty Strenuous
Distance 23-mile round-trip
Estimated time 2 days
Season July–Sept
Trailhead location Map p.75. Five miles south of Grant Village on the east side of South Entrance Road.
Comments A memorable overnighter that takes in backcountry hot springs, a delightful lake and arguably the park's finest panoramic viewpoint.

The first several miles, shooting through forest half-burned in 1988, are flat and easy. Signs of new growth abound in the form of 5 to 12ft-tall lodgepole pines, while squirrels dart among the scattered logs. At the 3-mile point, the trail skirts around the charred hulk of **Factory Hill** (9601ft), still quite bare since the pre-fire stands of Engelmann spruce that once covered the slopes take much longer to rebound than other native trees. At this point you'll also begin smelling the telltale scent of sulphur, and soon enough you'll pass the first of many bubbling springs on, and just off, **Witch Creek**. The trail then follows the flow of the creek all the way to Heart Lake, located 7.5 miles from the trailhead. The final mile or so is mainly downhill, crossing several times over warm Witch Creek and past a collection of pretty, greenish-blue pools. Having reached the lake's northern end, the trail splits at **Heart Lake Ranger Station**. A left turn heads east and around the lake to a series of trails leading deeper into the backcountry. Instead, turn right towards Mount Sheridan and walk along the rocky beach rimming the lake's northwestern shore. Six **backcountry campsites** are strung just off the water here; best are 8H2 and 8H3, the only two that allow wood fires.

One of this hike's main selling points is that you can now set up camp, leaving your heaviest gear behind before hoofing it up Mount Sheridan, though it's best to save the ascent for the morning to avoid the chance of an afternoon thunderstorm. It's an extremely tough slog at any time of day, climbing 3000ft in just under four miles; there's no dependable water source along the way, so purify or filter sufficient supplies at Heart Lake. The trail's switchbacks are mainly out in the open, so you're soon rewarded with progressively better views. Halfway up, massive **Yellowstone Lake** comes into view, giving an extra boost for conquering the peak's final alpine leg through several hundred yards of crumbling rocks, as well as a narrow ridge crossing. Along with patches of snow that usually stick around right through the summer, there's a **fire lookout tower** atop the peak, built in 1932 and restored in the 1990s. Should the attendant be in a chatty mood, he or she might be willing to point out some of the highlights from the panoramic view – including Grand Teton to the south and Mount Washburn (see **H9**) to the north – and discuss the day-to-day details of fire-spotting. After regaining your energy, your return trip is simply all the way back to your camp and the trailhead along the same route.

H47 Grand Teton: Cascade Canyon to Paintbrush Canyon

This classic Teton loop makes for a fine overnight jaunt into the park's alpine wilds, beginning at the mouth of Cascade Canyon, forking north to Lake Solitude then returning down Paintbrush Canyon, with an overnight stay at Holly Lake. The first portion of the trip follows Grand Teton's most popular hike to **Hidden Falls** and **Inspiration Point** beyond, reachable via the Jenny Lake Ferry (see `H34` for additional details).

After you reach Inspiration Point, you'll leave most of the crowd behind as Cascade Creek ushers you through its namesake canyon. Note the many rockslides, or talus slopes, created by the expansion and contraction of frost, which works boulders free throughout the year. This nearly five-mile stretch of trail leads through the canyon's

Difficulty Strenuous
Distance 19.5-mile loop
Estimated Time 2 days
Season Late June to early Oct
Trailhead location Map p.95. West Boat Dock on Jenny Lake.
Comments A well-travelled loop through some of Grand Teton's finest wilderness scenery, complete with a night at an alpine lake.

bottom, with Mount St John (11,430ft) to the north and Teewinot Mountain, Mount Owen and the Grand Teton to the south. At trail's end, head north at the T-junction with the North Fork Cascade Canyon Trail (part of the **Teton Crest Trail** – see `H50`) for a steady 1200ft elevation gain over the next three miles toward incomparably beautiful **Lake Solitude** (9035ft), rung with a thick necklace of alpine fir and whitebark pine. Due to the shadow cast by the cirque surrounding it, ice remains atop the lake well into July. Should you wish to turn this hike into a lazier two-nighter, the North Fork Cascade Canyon backcountry camping zone is due south of the lake.

Leaving Lake Solitude, the trail climbs steeply up and over **Paintbrush Divide**, at 10,720ft the highest point on the Teton Crest Trail. From here it's all downhill, with peaceful **Holly Lake** – reached via a left turn on a cutoff trail less than two miles after Paintbrush Divide – presenting an ideal spot to set up camp after a long and demanding day on the trail. Camping here is relegated to three designated sites lakeside, though there are large backcountry camping zones (Upper Paintbrush Canyon and Lower Paintbrush Canyon) along the trail to the west and east. From Holly Lake, follow the trail down Paintbrush Canyon, 4.5 miles east through thick woods, then veer south for 1.3 miles along String Lake to the northern tip of Jenny Lake. Trace the shoreline path to the southeast for a little over two miles back to the South Jenny Lake parking area.

`H48` Grand Teton: Death Canyon loop

Death Canyon is the second largest canyon within the Tetons, trailing only Webb Canyon at the range's northern end. This 26-mile hike affords ample opportunity to ponder not only its singular beauty, but the epic scale of its glacially eroded U-shape and 2.5 billion-year-old walls.

Starting from popular **Death Canyon Trailhead**, the hike's first mile heads up to **Phelps Lake Overlook** (see p.90). From this scenic viewpoint, a 400ft descent lands you squarely in bear and moose territory as you follow the trail into Death Canyon. Once within the canyon, its impossibly towering

Difficulty Very strenuous
Distance 26-mile round-trip
Estimated Time 2–3 days
Season Late June to early Oct
Trailhead Location Map p.95. Death Canyon Trailhead, southwest of Moose and 1.5 miles off Moose-Wilson Road on a rocky, unpaved road.
Comments A long but rewarding trek that hits several of the park's backcountry highlights.

walls reveal layers of Precambrian gneiss, schist and pegmatite, while huge Engelmann spruce shade the canyon floor in a protective canopy. As you climb steadily, a small log **patrol cabin** sits near the four-mile mark, originally constructed during the Civilian Conservation Corps era of the 1930s as a shelter for men constructing trails, and still used today by backcountry rangers. Provided there are no approaching storms, continue the counterclockwise loop by pointing your boots toward **Static Peak** (11,303ft), named for its propensity to be struck by lightning. With a quick ascent of 3000ft in just four miles, the switchbacks on this portion of the trail challenge all comers, cresting at the highest point on any maintained trail in the park (10,800ft).

The route then skirts the west slope of Static Peak along the **Alaska Basin Trail**. Just under a mile northwest of Static Peak, go left at a fork in the trail and dip steeply before gently climbing to the cluster of tiny **Basin Lakes**; you're now outside the national park's boundaries and in **Jedediah Smith Wilderness**, where **camping permits** are not required and you won't be hindered by camping zones. Just north of Basin Lakes is one of the trail's major junctions, where you turn left and head west on the **Teton Crest Trail** before scaling the **Sheep Steps** switchbacks to the pass by **Mount Meek** (10,681ft), your re-entry point into Grand Teton. From here, it's on to the renowned **Death Canyon Shelf**, a bumpy 3.5-mile stretch of trail with stunning mountain views and a thankfully negligible elevation change. Dispersed **backcountry camping is allowed** all along Death Canyon Shelf, and with sunsets casting a warm alpenglow on nearby Grand Teton, the area contains some of the most memorably sited camping spots in the entire region, although water sources up here are sparse. At **Fox Creek Pass** at the southern end of the shelf, turn off Teton Crest Trail and onto **Death Canyon Trail**, heading downhill 5.4 miles east through **upper Death Canyon** back to the patrol cabin to complete the loop. This last area is also zoned for backcountry camping and features easy access to the creek that runs next to the trail.

H49 Grand Teton: Marion Lake and Granite Canyon via Aerial Tram

This relatively short overnighter offers a rare opportunity to have yourself and your gear hoisted over 4100ft up into the Tetons. To take advantage, board Jackson Hole Mountain Resort's **Aerial Tram** at Teton Village (see p.212 for details) to be whisked the better part of a vertical mile in just under ten minutes; once you hit the trail with fresh legs at 10,450ft, you'll be glad you paid for the privilege. From there, it's a short first day (6.2 miles) to **Marion Lake** – a jellybean-shaped gem at the base of Housetop Mountain

> **Difficulty** Moderate to strenuous
> **Distance** 16-mile loop
> **Estimated time** 2 days
> **Season** Late June to early Oct
> **Trailhead location** Map p.86. Valley Trailhead at Teton Village.
> **Comments** Let the tram do your early climbing before you penetrate scenes of signature Teton grandeur.

(10,537ft) that's a coveted backcountry camping destination – before a 9.4-mile descent the next day back to Teton Village via scenic **Granite Canyon**.

After disembarking from the giant red flying box and strapping on your pack, follow the adjacent trail down a gusty ridge half a mile down to a junction. Turn right here and immediately enter Grand Teton National Park as you drop further into a talus-filled cirque. The trail soon climbs out of the cirque before descending into the upper South Fork of Granite Canyon; it then bends northwest before meeting the Middle Fork Cutoff Trail 3.5 miles from the tram platform. Bear left here and prepare to climb over the next 0.6 miles toward the **Teton Crest Trail** junction, where you'll head right. After a quick descent, prepare to begin one of this hike's few truly stiff climbs, 600ft over just under a mile up to a saddle. As you top the saddle, seek out the underused **Game Creek Trail**, which leads half a mile up to a ridge affording long-range looks down the west side of the Tetons and across Caribou-Targhee National Forest into Idaho.

Back on the Teton Crest Trail, drop steeply from the saddle and continue less than half a mile to the junction with North Fork Granite Canyon Trail, from where it's 0.6 miles up a steep bench to **Marion Lake**; at 9240ft, the lake is a full 1200ft lower than where the Aerial Tram dropped you earlier in the day. As you prepare to settle in for the evening, look for three **campsites** just east of the lake.

The next day, return to the junction with **North Fork Granite Canyon Trail** and go left, following it along its 500ft descent over the course of a mile-plus to its junction with the Open Canyon Trail; expect to cross Granite Creek's North Fork, as well as a pair of feeder creeks, during this short stretch. The next junction (with Middle Fork Cutoff Trail) is less than a mile ahead, after which the trail slips in and out of thick woods while traversing slopes strewn with talus and other assorted avalanche debris. It's at this point that your two-day expedition really finds its groove, with the ensuing 4.7 miles through **Granite Canyon** a full production of lush, wildflower-studded meadows and thick, coniferous forests backed all the while by the dulcet sounds of burbling **Granite Creek**.

At the bottom of the canyon, turn right at the **Valley Trail** junction to follow its route (gently climbing and descending at times) over 2.5 miles back to Teton Village.

H50 Grand Teton: Teton Crest Trail

The epic **Teton Crest Trail** runs from near Teton Pass, west of the tiny outpost of Wilson, all the way north to Paintbrush Canyon, covering the southern half of the Teton Range. Its route is composed mainly of the western portions of several loop trails that lead deep into the mountains and use the range's canyons as gangplanks on which to march into the highlands. The official length of the trail is just over 35 miles, but a seemingly endless combination of connecting trails lets hikers add on routes to their heart's content (and, possibly, their lungs' discontent).

Difficulty Very strenuous
Distance 35.4 miles one-way
Estimated Time 5 days
Season Late June to early Oct
Trailhead Location Map p.95. Phillips Canyon Road Trailhead on Hwy-22 east of Teton Pass (if hiking northward); String Lake Picnic Area (if hiking southward).
Comments Explore the best of the Tetons' alpine highlands on one of the greatest destination trails in the US.

Choosing to travel **southbound** gets the route's toughest climbs out of the way soonest, and also covers the most awe-inspiring scenery at the get-go. Conversely, the **northbound** route described below lets hikers ease into the hike with more of a warm-up early on. Either way you travel on this rugged path, you'll want to establish some sort of **shuttle**, whether it be cars left at both ends, working with a car-shuttle service or simply arranging for a taxi to pick you up at an appointed time (for details on these last two options, see box opposite).

Most Teton Crest Trail hikers spend four nights on the trail and aim for about eight miles per day; considering the weight of a full pack and the often-demanding terrain, this seems to be a reasonable goal – even for experienced, acclimatized hikers. Travelling south to north, begin at **Phillips Canyon Road Trailhead**, just downhill from **Glory Slide** halfway up the east side of Hwy-22's sharply graded Teton Pass. A gentle climb up Phillips Pass (8932ft), tracing the west side of Jackson Hole Mountain Resort's **Rendezvous Mountain**, lands hikers at the Middle Fork of **Granite Canyon**, a good spot for a first night's camp at 7.8 miles. Zigzag past the North Fork and back uphill to Marion Lake (see H49), then past Spearhead Peak (10,131ft) to Fox Creek Pass, where trails from Death Canyon and Fox Creek converge. Continue north across the fantastic **Death Canyon Shelf** (see H48) and camp at its northern end on night two.

Grand Teton hiking shuttles and taxis

If you're planning a hike in Grand Teton that ends far from where you begin and you don't have two cars at your disposal, a handful of Jackson **shuttle and taxi services** can help you retrace your steps once you hit your hike's finish line. Try Holly Frank Shuttle Service (☎307/690-9390) if you'd like your vehicle moved from your starting trailhead to your finishing one while you're on the trail; if you prefer an old-fashioned cab ride back to your car at the end of your trek, contact Teton Taxi (☎307/733-1506) or Snake River Taxi (☎307/732-2221).

On your third day, begin by hiking up and over **Mount Meek Pass**, then down the Sheep Steps, following the curve of **Alaska Basin**. Heading north from **Basin Lakes**, the next landmark is **Sunset Lake**, a little jewel just east of the trail. Heading up and over **Hurricane Pass**, don't miss **Schoolroom Glacier** at about the 20-mile mark; having received its name as a "textbook" example of an alpine glacier, it features a perfect moraine where rocks and debris have been pushed by the glacier, and around which an eroded outlet offers a stream. After descending into the **South Fork of Cascade Canyon**, look for a place to pitch your tent in the area's backcountry camping zone for night three.

Day four is your last strenuous day of hiking. Follow the trail through the **North Fork of Cascade Canyon** to lovely **Lake Solitude** (see H47), crowned by an embrace of rocks towering 1000ft above. Take a rest at the lake, as the next leg of the trail ascends the highest point along the entire route, **Paintbrush Divide** (10,720ft); soon after, dig in for one last night on the downhill slope at one of the campsites near **Holly Lake**. Your final day's journey is an easy six-mile descent down gorgeous **Paintbrush Canyon** to **String Lake Picnic Area**.

Summer activities

D riving around the parks in **summer**, you'll pass by dirt-encrusted cars and trucks so overloaded with gear they look like modern-day prairie schooners. Kayaks and canoes hug roofs, while bikes hang from trunk racks and fishing poles dangle out of open windows. These visitors have the right idea, as Yellowstone and Grand Teton offer a wealth of **outdoor activities**. **Hiking** is the most popular pastime, with day and overnight options covered in detail in chapters 4 and 5. Close behind and steadily growing in popularity, **fly-fishing** in the region's celebrated rivers is a dream come true for many. Spin-fishermen, **boaters** and **paddlers** are all drawn to the depths of the parks' largest lakes, on excursions running the gamut from leisurely, hour-long trips to extended overnight expeditions into water-accessible areas of the backcountry. Grand Teton's Snake River is the only major waterway in either park open to float trips (gentle rides in large rafts), but thrilling **whitewater-rafting** trips can be taken just outside the parks in all directions. **Swimming** is another option in some of the calmer waters, including two popular swimming holes in Yellowstone heated by surges of thermal runoff.

On firmer ground, long-distance **cycling** on Grand Teton's bike paths and less congested minor roads makes for a scenic (and potentially sweaty) workout, while Yellowstone is home to numerous service roads leading bikers past backcountry geysers and photogenic rock formations. As most hiking trails are open to stock animals as well, the opportunities for **horseriding** are far greater; guided backcountry trips into the most isolated corners of the parks can be arranged, though most visitors opt for short trail rides leaving from one of several park-run stables. Most adventurous of all, **rockclimbing** in Grand Teton draws mountaineers from across the globe, and courses are offered by two of the finest climbing schools in the country.

Fishing

Yellowstone alone has more than two hundred fishable streams, and a roll call of the park's most famous is enough to get **fly-fishers** everywhere running for their waders. Best known are the **Yellowstone** and **Madison Rivers**, with Slough Creek and the Lamar and Firehole Rivers leading a secondary pack of at least a dozen equally eminent streams. In Grand Teton, the **Snake River** takes top honours, while more of the country's finest "blue-ribbon" trout streams await only a short drive from either park, including a collection of "**forks**" that could alone justify a week-long fishing trip: the Henry's Fork west in Idaho, the Clark's Fork north of Cody, the Buffalo Fork east of Moran Junction and the South Fork south of Jackson. Not only are all these rivers impossibly scenic – nowhere else can one fish surrounded by steaming geysers, within a long cast of grazing bison or in the shadow of a range as impressive as the Tetons – they're also home to vast populations of trout, including the prized native cutthroat, which is strictly catch-and-release within Yellowstone (see box, p.81).

A wide range of hatches on these rivers requires a well-stocked fly box, and as conditions depend greatly on seasonal variables, your best bet upon arrival is to stop by one of the many superb local **fly-fishing outfitters** (see box, p.160). Even if you already have everything you need for a day in or on the water, it pays to purchase a few flies or a spool of tippet, as spending just a couple of dollars frees up knowledgeable staff members to answer questions on current hot spots and which flies to try first. Hiring a **guide** for the day may be pricey, but being taken straight to some of the best locations – along with the opportunity to pepper a local expert with questions – is worth the expense to most. Indeed, a successful strategy is to hire a guide for the first day or two of fishing, then head out independently with newly gained know-how. Guides can also be hired at the main **marinas** in both parks for fishing in Yellowstone and Jackson Lakes.

Within Yellowstone

Save for a few major exceptions, Yellowstone's **fishing season** runs from the Saturday of Memorial Day weekend (typically the last weekend in May) until the first Sunday in November. A **Yellowstone National Park fishing permit** is required; Wyoming or Montana licences are *not* valid. Permits can be purchased at all ranger stations, visitor centres and general stores; the cost is $15 (for a three-day permit), $20 (seven-day) or $35 (season). Each permit comes with an eighteen-page guide listing the numerous fishing regulations, and it's vital that you read and understand them all. Some of the most important rules include: no lead sinkers or barbed hooks (pinch down barbs with pliers); only artificial lures and flies – meaning no minnow, worms or foodstuff allowed; all **lake trout** caught in either Yellowstone Lake and River (and the latter's tributaries) must be killed; and, all native fish – cutthroat trout, Arctic grayling and mountain whitefish – are strictly **catch-and-release**.

For the most part, if you can reach a **river** in Yellowstone, you can fish it. However, good places to look for easy access are the numerous riverside picnic areas, where you'll be able to find a shady place to park as well. For a detailed review of Yellowstone's rivers and hatch cycles, *The Yellowstone Fly-Fishing Guide* by Craig Mathews and Clayton Molinero (Lyons Press) is comprehensive, concise and highly recommended.

Early in the season, the finest fishing is on the park's west side, where rivers tend to clear quickest from winter snowmelt. Fishermen flock to the **Firehole River** on opening day, a spectacular dry-fly stream weaving through some of the park's largest geyser basins; it's as tricky as it is beautiful, however, as the rainbow, brown, brook and cutthroat trout in the river are accustomed to the presence of anglers and, therefore, wilier than most. By mid July, the constant rush of thermal waters raises the Firehole's temperature to 80 degrees in spots, limiting fishing until early September. To the north, the slender **Gibbon River** is also worth trying early in the season, and best fished along its wider stretches south of Norris. Formed by the confluence of the Gibbon and the Firehole, the celebrated **Madison River** flows west from Madison Junction in wide curves along the road to West Yellowstone, from where it cuts north to Hebgen Lake. Among other types of fish, the Madison is renowned for large brown trout, most often caught in early June or, better yet, late September and early October, when the river is surrounded by bright autumn foliage.

The star of the central and northern reaches of the park is the **Yellowstone River**, a waterway so complex and varied that entire books have been written on

Fly-fishing gear and guides

The following outfitters run **guided trips** on rivers within Yellowstone, Grand Teton and the surrounding national forests, and most of them also arrange lessons. The going rate for a full-day trip for one or two anglers ranges from $375–450 and generally includes gear and instruction (if needed), transportation and a packed lunch. All the outfitters listed also run well-stocked **shops** filled with the expected array of rods, lines and leaders, along with cases of hand-tied flies, guidebooks and maps (often free) to top fishing spots. The general stores within both parks stock a limited selection of flies and supplies as well, but you're better off stopping at one of the following dedicated fishing shops.

Cody

North Fork Anglers 1107 Sheridan Ave ⊕307/527-7274, ⊛www.northforkanglers .com. Cody's top fishing shop, fully stocked and featuring reasonably priced guided trips on the North or South Fork of the Shoshone, the Clark's Fork of the Yellowstone or into Yellowstone itself.

Gardiner

Parks' Fly Shop 202 Second St S ⊕406/848-7314 ⊛www.parksflyshop.com. In business since 1953, this excellent outfitter runs float trips on the Yellowstone River north of the park boundary, along with a variety of wading trips that include backcountry jaunts to smaller tributaries within the park itself. Pick up free fishing maps at the shop detailing top spots within Yellowstone, as well as on Montana's Gallatin and Missouri Rivers.

Grand Teton

Snake River Angler Dornan's in Moose ⊕307/733-3699 or 1-888/ 998-7688, ⊛www.snakeriverangler.com. At the very least, anglers should drop in here to pick up the *Jackson Hole Moosepaper* ($1 donation), filled with hatch charts and regional river maps. Located steps from the Snake River and stocked with dozens of useful fly varieties, guided trips here focus on the Snake, Green and South Fork Rivers; early

fishing this single river alone. To protect what is the finest cutthroat fishery in the country, fishing is not allowed on the river north of Yellowstone Lake until July 15, and several stretches are closed permanently, including the portion stretching several miles north from Mud Volcano, as well as Chittenden Bridge downstream to Silver Cord Cascade. As the longest undammed river in the lower 48, the Yellowstone boasts an estimated two hundred miles of tricky trout water, with prime fishing inside the park found on the stretch north from Fishing Bridge to Mud Volcano (the permanently closed area at LeHardy's Rapids excepted), as well as throughout much of the Black Canyon of the Yellowstone (see H42, p.148). Outside the park, numerous access points line the highway as it traces the Yellowstone from Gardiner fifty-plus miles north to Livingston.

To the west of the Yellowstone River, the **Gardner River** and its many tributaries (including Panther, Indian and Obsidian Creeks) make for relatively easy fishing for non-native brook trout; the Gardner is the one river in the park where children eleven years old and younger may fish with worms as bait. To the east of the Yellowstone River and accessible via the Northeast Entrance Road en route to Cooke City, both the **Lamar River** and its tributary, **Soda Butte Creek**, begin attracting serious anglers in swarms by late July; by mid August, grasshoppers also begin thronging the meadows bordering these rivers, giving skilled feather-throwers the joy of catching cutthroats and rainbows on large terrestrial flies. Another popular late-summer stream is **Slough Creek**, which flows into the Lamar to the north and is easily accessed near its eponymous campground; its best summer excursions up to Yellowstone's west side rivers, as well as autumn trips to Lewis Lake in the southern part of the park, are also offered.

Jackson and around

Jack Dennis Fishing Trips 70 S King St ⊤307/690-0910, ⓦwww.jackdennis.com. Along with flies and supplies, stop into this shop around the corner from the town square to pick up the free, information-packed *Western Fishing Newsletter*. A long list of guided float and wading trips around the region are offered, along with lessons and seminars that include a two-hour casting class ($125 for two people) on a private, trout-stocked pond.

Westbank Anglers 3670 N Moose-Wilson Rd ⊤307/733-6483 or 1-800/922-3474, ⓦwww.westbank.com. On the banks of the Snake River three miles south of Teton Village, this well-stocked shop and outfitter organizes trips to trout hotspots around the world. Local trips focus on the Snake, Green and South Fork Rivers, with guided trips into Yellowstone also on offer.

West Yellowstone

Blue Ribbon Flies 305 Canyon St ⊤406/646-7642, ⓦwww.blueribbonflies.com. With a solid reputation among locals and frequent visitors, Blue Ribbon Flies' guides lead a wide variety of excursions, including wading day-trips in Yellowstone, floats down the Madison, dry fly-fishing on nearby Hebgen Lake and extended "Road Trips" ($3400–4000 for two) that hit a host of rivers throughout the region.

Bud Lilly's Trout Shop 39 Madison Ave ⊤406/646-7801 or 1-800/854-9559, ⓦwww.budlillys.com. A smartly stocked shop that also leads guided trips into Yellowstone, as well along the Madison outside the park and on the Henry's Fork in nearby Idaho; trips on the latter two rivers can be waded or floated in drift boats.

Jacklin's Fly Shop 105 Yellowstone Ave ⊤406/646-7336, ⓦwww.jacklinsflyshop.com. This centrally located shop boasts a huge selection of flies, along with a crew of experts to help you pick out the current best. Outfitted trips head out along the Madison, Henry's Fork and all of Yellowstone's top streams.

fishing, however, requires at least a two-mile hike out, with conditions improving the further you're willing to walk (see **H7**, p.118).

As for fishing on **lakes** within the park, the two most accessible are **Yellowstone** and **Lewis Lakes**, each home to a boat launch (see p.163 for rental information). Shore fishing from Yellowstone Lake can be decent at times, but to hunt down the largest lake and cutthroat trout, you'll want to fish by boat; the best time to fish the big lake is immediately after the annual season's June 15 opening. Historically fishless, Lewis Lake to the south now supports populations of brook, brown, cutthroat and lake trout, and both spin- and fly-fishermen can have luck casting from the shore soon after its ice melts off in mid June; throughout the rest of summer, fishing here is best by boat, and October can be a particularly fruitful time to try the lake once brown trout begin spawning. Connected to Lewis Lake by a three-mile channel, **Shoshone Lake** has the same fishing schedule and populations of fish, though its remote location ensures that it sees far fewer anglers. Other fine backcountry fishing lakes include: **Grebe** and **Wolf Lakes**, themselves the headwaters of the Gibbon River and home to large populations of catch-and-release Arctic grayling, as well as rainbow trout; **Trout Lake**, a one-mile hike north of the Northeast Entrance Road where great cutthroat and rainbow fishing becomes available on July 15; and **Heart Lake**, a wonderfully isolated spot to reel in lake and cutthroat trout south of Yellowstone Lake, accessed via an overnight hike (see **H46**, p.153) and, like Trout Lake, open for fishing on July 15.

Whether on a lake or river, a **Wyoming fishing licence** is required to fish in Grand Teton; for non-residents of the state, these cost $14 for a one-day permit, or $92 for a year's access. In the park, licences can be purchased at Snake River Angler (see box, p.160), as well as Signal Mountain Lodge, Flagg Ranch Lodge and the marina and store at Colter Bay Village. You are responsible for following all regulations, including closures and catch limits, so carefully read the pamphlet that comes with each licence.

The pride of fly-fishing in Grand Teton is the scenic **Snake River**, teeming with native cutthroat trout. Unlike Yellowstone's streams, the Snake is fishable via drift boat, letting anglers cover more water in a few hours than could possibly be fished in several days of wading and walking along the banks. Unless you have your own boat, however, you'll likely have to hire a guide to float down the river, a relatively expensive proposition (see box, p.160). Some of the best spots from which to cast from the banks or in which to wade include the boat launch areas around Schwabacher's Landing and Deadmans Bar, along with the parking area at the end of bumpy RKO Road south of Signal Mountain (see p.100). Note that only artificial flies and lures can be used on the Snake and most of its tributaries from the Jackson Lake Dam south to Wilson Bridge outside the park. The river is open to fishing year-round, though all cutthroat caught between November and March must be released. Runoff clouds up river clarity throughout May and June, and the best fishing occurs mid July to mid October. Other popular trout rivers either in or just outside Grand Teton include: the **Gros Ventre River**, particularly above and below Lower Slide Lake; **Flat Creek**, south of the park within the National Elk Refuge; the **South Fork**, south of Jackson; and the **Buffalo Fork**, east of Moran Junction in Bridger-Teton National Forest.

Anglers also flock to Grand Teton's lakes in great numbers, using both fly and spin rods. Most are ice-free by early June, though all (save **Jackson Lake**) remain open to fishing year-round. Fishing on the latter is nevertheless prohibited only throughout October, in order to protect spawning Mackinaw lake trout; throughout most of summer, its best fishing is by boat as visitors troll deep down for the largest fish. Unlike at Yellowstone Lake, lake trout are welcome in the lake and need not be killed upon capture. **Phelps**, **Taggart** and **Bradley Lakes** all host healthy populations of cutthroat and lake trout, though **Jenny** and **Leigh Lakes** draw more fishermen since they're much more accessible to those in inflatable tyre innertubes and canoes.

Boating

From kayaking along the shoreline in Yellowstone Lake's isolated lower "fingers" to buzzing about Jackson Lake on a pair of waterskis, **boaters** have several renowned lakes on which to play within Yellowstone and Grand Teton. The Snake River is the sole major river with boat access, but when you add in the seemingly endless supply of rivers and lakes in the neighbouring national forests, it's no surprise that the greater Yellowstone ecosystem is celebrated for its boating. For the thrills of a **whitewater rafting** trip, you'll have to head out of the parks; there are quality stretches on the North Fork of the Shoshone River outside Cody, the Yellowstone River north of Gardiner and the Snake River south of Jackson, but the region's most thrilling adventures are found on the Gallatin River in its namesake valley (see p.222). If you're interested in a guided canoe or kayak trip in the parks, see the "Activity-based tours" section on p.197.

A **permit** is required for all vessels – including inflatable tyre innertubes – in the parks. In Yellowstone, these can be obtained at most of the entrance stations, as well as the Grant Visitor Center and Bridge Bay Ranger Station. In Grand Teton, permits can be purchased at any of the marinas, as well as the Craig Thomas Discovery and Visitor Center at Moose. Fees for non-motorized vessels are $10 for a one-week permit and $20 for an annual; motorized permits cost double. Permits purchased in Yellowstone are honoured in Grand Teton, and vice versa. Be sure to visit the parks' websites for information on other **regulations and requirements**.

Within Yellowstone

In the early days of Yellowstone tourism, visitors could escape the dusty confines of their stagecoach to cross **Yellowstone Lake** on the steamboat *Zillah*, plonking down $2.50 to arrive at *Lake Yellowstone Hotel* in style. Nowadays, boating in the park is much more of a do-it-yourself affair, with only **Bridge Bay Marina** at the northern end of Yellowstone Lake offering rentals and dockage (late May to mid Sept 8am–5pm; ☏ 307/344-7311). Typically covered in ice patches through May, the massive lake is no place for beginners, so unless you're confident in your boating skills, don't head out without a guide. Also, always stay close to shore when paddling as conditions can change almost instantaneously – capsizing in the numbing waters can be potentially fatal. **Rental** options at Bridge Bay Marina include rowboats ($10/hr, $45/day) and slightly larger outboard motor-boats ($47/hr), along with 22ft ($152 for two hours) and 34ft ($196 for two hours) powerboats. If you're interested in a **guided boat tour**, one-hour voyages on the *Lake Queen II* ($14.25) depart several times daily. More adventurously, backpackers travelling by foot, canoe or kayak can call ahead to arrange a **backcountry shuttle** ($152/hr; ☏ 307/242-3893), a water taxi that will drop you across the massive lake. There are more than three dozen boat-accessible **backcountry campsites** edging the lake, allowing for overnight to week-long kayak and canoe trips; advance reservations for these sites are recommended, and booking procedures are the same as with backcountry hiking sites (see p.145). Note that there's another, far less popular boat launch (without dock) at the southwest end of Yellowstone Lake at Grant Village.

To the south towards Grand Teton is roadside **Lewis Lake**, the third-largest lake in the park and the only other one with a boat launch; canoes, kayaks and motor-boats are all allowed. From the north end of Lewis Lake, it's possible to paddle upstream via the Lewis Channel to **Shoshone Lake**, the largest backcountry lake in the contiguous United States. The Lewis Channel is the only stream in the park open to kayaks and canoes (no boats), and while the first two miles are easy, the final mile is shallow and rocky, and requires getting into the frigid water to drag your vessel upstream – waders and river shoes are highly recommended. The effort is well worth it, however, as paddling the shorelines of Shoshone Lake and spending a night or more at one of twenty backcountry sites scattered along its rim is an experience not easily forgotten. Due in part to the short season – the lake doesn't become ice-free until mid June – the sites here are extremely popular, making advance reservations essential (see p.145). As with Yellowstone Lake, conditions on Shoshone Lake can change rapidly, so only experienced paddlers should launch upon it without a guide.

Canoes, kayaks and boats are prohibited on all other rivers in the park, including the entirety of the Yellowstone until it flows north out of the park at Gardiner.

Within Grand Teton

Much more so than Yellowstone, boating is high on **Grand Teton**'s list of popular activities. For starters, non-motorized float trips *are* allowed on the **Snake River**. These popular half-day excursions are a relaxing way to view the landscape as you meander past elk and moose and beneath soaring eagles, the Teton Range towering splendidly to the west. Two of the best **operators** are Snake River Kayak and Canoe ($45; ☏1-800/529-2501, ⓦwww.snakeriverkayak.com), whose guides raft groups thirteen miles through Grand Teton, and Snake River Anglers ($58; ☏1-888/998-7688, ⓦwww.snakeriverangler.com), floating twelve miles from Moose to Wilson Bridge south of the park; both operators' trips depart three times daily. If you're without a guide, a **permit** is required (same fees as Yellowstone); these are sold at visitor centres in Moose, Colter Bay and Flagg Ranch and should only be purchased by experienced rafters and kayakers – the Snake River is a deceptively difficult waterway to navigate.

Boats are banned from all other rivers within Grand Teton, but they are allowed on ten of the park's largest lakes, a luxury that certainly doesn't hurt boating's popularity in the park. Among these ten lakes, motorized boats (but no jet skis) are permitted only on **Jackson** and **Jenny Lakes**, with engines limited to ten horse-power on the latter; elsewhere, canoes, kayaks and inflatable tyre innertubes are allowed on Phelps, Emma Matilda, Two Ocean, Taggart, Bradley, Bearpaw, Leigh and String Lakes, in addition to Jackson and Jenny. For one of the best paddles in the park, put in at String Lake and paddle north onto spectacular Leigh Lake; a short portage is required between the two, and there are several backcountry campsites set around Leigh Lake for overnight stays.

For those without a boat in tow, there's still a good amount of tour and rental choices. Beginning in the southern part of the park, Adventure Sports (☏307/733-3307) at Dornan's in Moose rents out canoes and one- or two-person kayaks for $48 per day, including all necessary equipment to load them onto your vehicle. Up Jenny Lake Road, the most popular boat trips in the park are the **ferry rides** across Jenny Lake to Cascade Canyon Trailhead (daily: early July to mid Aug 7am–7pm, June to early July & mid Aug to early Sept 8am–6pm, mid- to late May & early to late Sept 10am–4pm; $10 return, $7 single; ☏307/734-9227). In addition, one-hour scenic cruises around the lake are offered for $15, while canoes and kayaks ($15), as well as small motorboats ($28), can be rented at hourly rates. To the north, two marinas on busy Jackson Lake offer tours and rentals, with similar rates for canoes and kayaks to those at Jenny Lake. **Signal Mountain Lodge Marina** (late May to mid Sept, hours vary; ☏307/543-2831 ext. 250) rents out a variety of motored watercraft on an hourly basis, including runabouts ($55), eight-person pontoons ($77) and deck cruisers ($99) with room for up to ten passengers. A bit further up the road, **Colter Bay Village Marina** (June–Aug; ☏307/543-2811) hosts narrated tour cruises (90min) for $26, with three-hour breakfast ($36) and dinner ($57) excursions also available. Just north of Colter Bay, **Leeks Marina** (mid-May to mid-Sept, potentially earlier in dry years) has a boat launch and docks, but no rentals.

Bicycling

Bicyclists may have arrived in the Yellowstone region first – the park's first bike tourists date back to 1883 – but the car has long been king of the road, and on the whole the main highways within Grand Teton and particularly Yellowstone make for poor **bicycling**. The narrow, paved shoulders are inconsistent, with traffic (including lane-hogging RVs) constantly zipping past and easily distracted drivers enjoying the vistas and searching for wildlife instead of focusing on the road. All in all, highway riding here in high season is a recipe for disaster, though plenty of so-called bikepackers – long-haul bicyclists – manage to avoid the above litany of hazards on tours each year. For the average day-tripping bicyclist, there's a solid selection of lesser-driven routes and old service roads open to bikes in both parks. If you're unable to tote along your own two wheels, reasonably priced **rentals** are available in most of the gateway towns, as well as from Bear Den Gift Shop at Yellowstone's Old Faithful Village and Adventure Sports at Dornan's in Moose, Grand Teton. Unless specified, riding on hiking trails is strictly forbidden in the parks.

Within Yellowstone

The best time to ride the roads in Yellowstone is from late March to late April, when several long sections of the park's **highways** have been cleared of snow but still remain closed to automobile traffic; the main drawback to this strategy is that a majority of park amenities remain shuttered at this time of year. If set on a long road ride within the park in summer, the best portion of **highway** to tackle is the 47-mile stretch from Mammoth east to Tower and onwards to Cooke City, one of the straightest sections with fair visibility throughout; the highway from West Yellowstone to Grant Village via Old Faithful (also 47 miles) is likewise better than most, although dangerously narrow shoulders persist in spots. There is growing sentiment for additional off-highway bike paths in this region of the park, but plans so far remain in the earliest idea stages.

Off the main highways, more than a dozen unpaved side roads a mile or longer make for excellent mountain biking. Among these, top choices are **Old Gardiner Road** (five miles one-way), a wildlife-rich route across the sagebrush flats between Mammoth and Gardiner, and **Blacktail Plateau Drive** (seven miles one-way; see p.51); both of these routes are open to cars as well, while the remainder are open to bikers and hikers only. Two such hiking/biking paths – the service road up **Mount Washburn** (five miles round-trip; **H9**) and **Natural Bridge Road** (three miles round-trip; **H18**) – are covered in detail in Chapter 4, "Day hikes".

The toughest of all bike-accessible dirt roads in Yellowstone is six-mile **Bunsen Peak Loop Road**, starting south of Golden Gate Canyon and leading east and then north around its eponymous peak to a trailhead south of Mammoth Hot Springs Corrals; at the near-halfway point, you can lock your bike and make the steep climb down to Osprey Falls (**H5**) to complete the finest hike/bike combination in the park. **Fountain Freight Road** (five miles one-way), heading from the end of Fountain Flat Drive south to Fairy Falls Trailhead, is another terrific bike route with access to hiking trails: along with paths to Sentinel Meadows (**H15**) and Fairy Falls (**H16**), the old service road passes alongside Midway Geyser Basin. South of here, starting adjacent to *Old Faithful Inn* and heading 1.5 miles north to Morning Glory Pool is perhaps the park's most popular bike route, a paved path through Upper Geyser Basin leading past several signature geysers, including Castle, Grotto and Riverside Geysers. Last is the partially paved **Lone Star Geyser Road** (2.5 miles one-way), which begins at Lone Star Trailhead a couple of miles southeast of Old Faithful; tracing the beautiful Firehole River, this trek is best timed to witness one of Lone Star Geyser's dramatic eruptions (see **H45** for details).

For **rentals** and **information** on Yellowstone bike trails, stop into the excellent **bike shop** inside Bear Den Gift Shop (☎307/545-4825), part of the *Old Faithful Snow Lodge* complex, where the helpful staff also makes repairs. $35 gets you a hybrid bike, helmet and lock for a 24 hour period; hourly ($8) and half-day ($25) rates are also available, in addition to kids' bikes, trailers and even gloves.

Within Grand Teton

With heavy and fast traffic on Grand Teton's **Hwy-191** making for uncomfortable road riding during high season, bikers instead flock to several **quiet, long and scenic roads** where interaction with cars is minimal in the southeast section of the park, as well as a popular paved **bike path** running adjacent to Teton Park Road between Dornan's (in Moose) and South Jenny Lake. The latter option is set well off the main road but still enjoys the same peerless views throughout its gently rolling eight-mile (one-way) route; if you're looking to have a little more space to yourself, you'd do well to head east on Antelope Flats Road from Hwy-191 for a **thirteen-mile loop** encompassing the sagebrush plains and roaming bison herds of Mormon Row, Gros Ventre Road and the village of Kelly, one of the finest easy-paced rides anywhere; tack on two extra miles to the total mileage if Dornan's is your starting/ ending point. It's also possible to cobble together itineraries over fifty miles in length using Gros Ventre Road as a base, including trips leading up and past the Gros Ventre Slide (see p.93) within Bridger-Teton National Forest. A few miles past the slide area, the road turns to dirt, giving mountain bikers fifteen more potholed and scenic miles to explore. Other terrific mountain-biking roads in (or beginning in) Grand Teton include: **Shadow Mountain Road**, weaving through national forest lands north of Antelope Flats; **Grassy Lake Road**, a rough, nearly fifty-mile stretch slashing between Grand Teton and Yellowstone; and rutty and rustic **RKO/ River Road** (see p.101) in the central region of the park.

Adventure Sports (☎307/733-3307) within the Dornan's complex in Moose is the park's top resource for bicycle **rentals** and **information**, with a wide variety of bikes available at rates starting from $36 per day, including full suspension and hybrid electric types; a helmet is included in all rentals. For additional options, as well as a wealth of mountain-biking trails in its outlying area, head to **Jackson** due south of the park (see p.210).

Horseriding

In tune with the region's cowboy and ranching traditions, "stock" animals – mainly **horses**, but also mules and even llamas – are permitted on the majority of trails in Yellowstone and Grand Teton. As these large animals can't help but damage paths, overnight stock use is banned until trails are dry enough to absorb the animals' weight, typically the end of June. Should you want to take anything from a long day-trip to a week-long backcountry adventure, numerous operators are licensed to do so, including several dude ranches in or bordering Grand Teton. Those bringing their own horses should check park websites, where details on everything from grazing requirements to backcountry stock camps are listed. Most visitors, however, seem content to saddle up on shorter nose-to-tail-style **horseback rides** leaving from concessionaire-run stables within both parks – riders must be at least eight years old and 4ft tall, and there's a weight limit of 240lb.

Within Yellowstone

One-hour ($38) and two-hour ($58) **trail rides** depart from three corrals within Yellowstone, each managed by Xanterra (☎307/344-7311). The busiest corral (early June to mid Sept) is next to *Roosevelt Lodge*, from where trips lead north across the rolling sagebrush hills of the Northern Range. Other options from Roosevelt include stagecoach rides (five daily; $12) and the **"Old West Dinner Cookout"** (see p.192) each evening, for which rates start at $55 per adult, including horseback ride and steak dinner. The corral at Canyon (mid- June to early Sept) offers rides through pretty meadows and alongside Cascade Creek, while Mammoth Hot Springs Corral (mid- May to mid Sept) opens earliest but offers rides covering the least inspiring terrain. For an **overnight pack trip**, Yellowstone Wilderness Outfitters (☎406/223-3300, ⓦwww.yellowstone.ws) in West Yellowstone is one reputable outfitter in the area, and while such trips aren't easy on the wallet – Yellowstone Wilderness Outfitters charges $1400 per person for a four-day trip to Heart Lake, among myriad other trip options – they're certainly memorable.

Within Grand Teton

Grand Teton Lodge Company operates corrals (June–Aug; ☎307/543-3100) at *Jackson Lake Lodge* and Colter Bay Village. There's not much difference between the two, with simple one-hour ($36) and two-hour ($54) **trail rides** departing daily from both; a **breakfast wagon ride** is also offered three times each week at *Jackson Lake Lodge*, for which advance reservations are required.

If an afternoon of riding is not nearly enough, there are several working **dude ranches** in and just outside the park. Two of the finest are **Triangle X Ranch** (☎307/733-2183, ⓦwww.trianglex.com), located across the highway from Cunningham Cabin along Hwy-191, and **Gros Ventre River Ranch** (☎307/733-4138, ⓦwww.grosventreriverranch.com), just outside the park's southeast boundary on the way to Lower Slide Lake. Both ranches offer all-inclusive week-long stays, including meals and horseriding, starting at $1600–1700 per person in high season. You may be able to negotiate a shorter stay early or late in the season, and pack trips can also be arranged.

Rock climbing and scrambling

While opportunities for climbing in Yellowstone are very limited, Grand Teton is a premier destination for **climbing** enthusiasts, and the sight of the **Tetons** is enough to get many non-climbers thinking about roping up and having a go as well. These jagged peaks are laced with routes, from fun scrambles to challenging climbs suited solely to expert climbers. Snow and ice climbs are possible, but the majority of routes follow hard granite, a trustworthy surface that's one of the Tetons' finest attributes. Accessibility is also a plus here, although you'll still need to lug your gear on lengthy warm-up hikes to reach the start of most climbs.

Within Yellowstone

Older and rounded over by millions of years of erosion, the mountains within **Yellowstone** are not known for climbing, itself a prohibited activity within the crumbly confines of the Grand Canyon of the Yellowstone. Most of the tallest peaks, including Mount Washburn (**H9**, see p.120), Avalanche Peak (**H21**, see p.128) and Mount Sheridan (**H46**, see p.153), can be scaled with little or no scrambling involved. The **Absaroka Mountains** attract a handful of backcountry alpinists each year, particularly around **Eagle Peak** – the tallest in the park at 11,358ft – on Yellowstone's isolated southeast border, but these routes take several days of hiking to reach. The only accessible area in which to play around within park boundaries is the **Hoodoos**, a field of boulders a short drive uphill from Mammoth en route to Norris. A couple of very small car parks here access the rocks, some close to 20ft tall, providing a few hours worth of scrambling fun.

Within Grand Teton

Climbers tackle **Grand Teton**'s fusillade of peaks year-round, but the most popular climbing period is from early July until mid September, by which time much of the high-altitude snow will have melted. The obvious goal for many is the summit of **Grand Teton** itself – at 13,770ft, it's the second-highest mountain in Wyoming and one with a colourful climbing history (see box, p.102). There are numerous established routes leading up "the Grand", all of them technical and requiring the appropriate equipment. Even inexperienced climbers, however, can summit the majestic peak on a three- or four-day introductory **climbing course**, provided they pass each day's requirements.

Two excellent mountain guide services work the park. Closest is **Exum Mountain Guides** (☎307/733-2297, ⓦwww.exumguides.com), which operates a summer office located steps away from Jenny Lake's boat dock across Cottonwood Creek. The company's namesake, Glen Exum (1911–2000), pioneered the difficult **Exum Ridge** up the southwest side of Grand Teton at the age of 19, without the use of ropes and while wearing football cleats. Down in Jackson, **Jackson Hole Mountain Guides** (☎307/733-4979, ⓦwww.jhmg.com) is similarly reputable. Both companies offer a variety of rock-climbing courses, along with guided climbs cresting all the major summits; winter trips, including backcountry skiing and snowboarding, are also available. The most popular basic climbing courses run over two to four days and culminate in an ascent of the Grand Teton ($775–855, more for a private guide); those with climbing experience can join a one-day expedition ($555–675). Both companies maintain base camps beneath Grand Teton at around 11,000ft.

Beside Grand Teton, other popular climbs in the range include: **Middle Teton**, featuring a half-dozen routes of varying difficulty, including a non-technical route to the top with a fair amount of scrambling; **Cascade** and **Death Canyons**, both lined with a variety of challenging wall climbs; and **Mount Owen**, the toughest to conquer among main Teton peaks. A tall lump of rock across the Snake River, **Blacktail Butte**, is an even more popular climbing spot, where a car park just north of Moose Junction on Hwy-191 offers immediate access to a near-vertical sport-climb up a limestone face.

For detailed route information, the best overall book is *A Climber's Guide to the Teton Range* by Leigh Ortenburger and Reynold Jackson (Mountaineers Books). **Permits** are not required for mountaineering, but climbers planning on camping en route must obtain a free backcountry camping **permit** (see p.145 for details). From June until September, these can be procured at **Jenny Lake Ranger Station** (mid-May to mid-Sept, hours vary; ☎307/739-3343) near Jenny Lake Visitor Center; headquarters for the park's climbing rangers, this should in any case be your first stop for information and advice on routes and conditions, especially since snow may persist until August on certain passes. During the rest of the year, permits are available at **Craig Thomas Discovery and Visitor Center** in Moose.

A final valuable source for not only information but also accommodation (and possibly climbing partners) is the **Climbers' Ranch** (☎307/733-7271, ⓦwww.americanalpineclub.org), a cluster of shared cabins off Teton Park Road a couple of miles south of Jenny Lake. Run by the American Alpine Club, the bunk accommodations are rough (everything, including bedding, must be supplied yourself), but the nightly rate ($10 for AAC members, $20 for non-members) leaves little room for complaint; only climbers are eligible to stay. In the park, Moosely Seconds (☎307/739-1801) within the Dornan's complex sells and **rents** climbing shoes, ice axes, crampons and other invaluable climbing gear.

Swimming

Swimming in the parks is a matter of thinking before you leap. Whether in a lake or river, pond or creek, the majority of water in the region is simply too **cold** for a comfortable swim on all but the hottest of days. Conditions in some cases, moreover, can stretch beyond the uncomfortable and into the dangerous: averaging a frigid 45 degrees throughout the year, survival time once immersed in **Yellowstone Lake** is estimated to be only twenty minutes. Swift and filled with underwater hazards, the region's rivers are equally treacherous and unforgiving, and **drowning** is the second-leading cause of accidental death in the parks after car accidents.

All that said, a swimsuit should still be packed alongside your thermal underwear. If you don't mind your feet squishing into a murky river bottom, many of Yellowstone's smaller backcountry lakes and creeks are suitable for a quick, mid-hike dip come July and August; alternatively, if you're up for a splurge, *Mammoth Hot Springs Hotel* has cabins with their own private hot tubs. Best of all are two superb natural swimming and soaking areas in Yellowstone – a pair of rivers with segments warmed by the onrush of nearby thermal waters. The more northern of the two, the **Boiling River** within the greater Gardner River (see p.228), is accessed via a flat dirt path about a half-mile from the parking area along the highway two miles north of Mammoth. Equally popular is the **Firehole Swimming Area** along the Firehole River in the park's western section (see p.67), with limited parking available along Firehole Canyon Drive. No lifeguards are stationed at either location, and each spot requires swimsuits. Both close at dusk and throughout early summer until the rivers have calmed enough from snowmelt highs, and only the Boiling River stays open through winter for those brave enough to soak in subzero air temperatures.

To the south within John D. Rockefeller, Jr. Memorial Parkway are the similar, though less frequently used, bathing areas at **Polecat** and **Huckleberry Hot Springs** near Flagg Ranch (see p.107). In **Grand Teton**, swimming is allowed in all the park's lakes, though their icy-cold temperatures will send most visitors scurrying for the nearest hot shower. **Phelps**, **String**, **Leigh** and **Jenny Lakes** all have sandy beach areas, however, with shallower waters that go from cold to pleasantly cool later in summer. *Jackson Lake Lodge* has a **pool** open to hotel guests and those staying within Colter Bay Village, and younger kids will have fun splashing around **Kelly Warm Spring** on Gros Ventre Road to the southeast (see p.93). Swimming in the **Snake River**, however, is dangerous and not recommended.

Soaking directly within a hot spring – known as "hotpotting" – is both illegal and foolhardy. Several unfortunate bathers, including park employees supposedly in the know, have died after slipping into the wrong spring. To soak safely, head to the naturally fed pools at excellent **Chico Hot Springs** (see p.233), 45 minutes north of Gardiner, or more rustic **Granite Hot Springs** ($6; ☏307/734-7400, ⓦgranitehotsprings.mountainmancountry.com), an equal distance south of Jackson on Hwy-191.

Winter activities

Blanketed in snow between November and April, **Yellowstone** takes on a
whole new appearance in **winter**: a silent and strange world of white
where waterfalls freeze in mid plunge, geysers blast towering plumes of
steam and water into the chilly air, and buffalo, beards matted with ice,
stand around in frost-coated huddles. Elk, coyote, bighorn sheep and, most
popularly, wolves, likewise tough it out in the park, and can be spotted relentlessly searching for enough sustenance to power them through the season.
Indeed, aside from hibernating bears, humans are the one summertime fixture
whose presence decreases most dramatically. On average, 150,000 visitors enter
Yellowstone in winter − about one-sixth of the park's total visitation in any
given August.

There are two major explanations for this huge drop-off. First is that by early
November, all but two of Yellowstone's five entrance gates are **closed** to car traffic,
with only Gardiner's North Entrance and the isolated Northeast Entrance near
Cooke City − accessible only from Gardiner throughout winter, in any case −
remaining open. All other major entrances remain open to over-snow traffic,
namely **snowmobiles** and **snowcoaches**, or human-powered cross-country skis
and snowshoes. The second reason for limited visitation is, simply enough, the
weather. In a region where summer snowstorms aren't entirely uncommon,
winter is long and unforgiving. Lower in altitude, the area around Mammoth
tends to be less snowy than the rest of the park, attracting elk and other creatures
to its more accessible grasses. Deep snowdrifts four feet and up are typical in other
areas, and throughout the park sub-freezing temperatures are the norm.

All that said, with some smart pre-planning and the right cold-weather gear, a
winter visit to Yellowstone makes for a magical encounter, and one that's
markedly different than summer. **Wildlife-spotting** opportunities are superb, and
the list of viewable attractions is long. **Mammoth Hot Springs** and **Lamar
Valley** are both reachable by car along the open northern road, while over-snow
shuttles can access many sights along the northern section of the Grand Loop
Road, including steaming **Roaring Mountain**; the same is true of all sights along
the nearly one-hundred-mile southern section of the Grand Loop, including the
Grand Canyon of the Yellowstone, **Old Faithful** and **Midway** and **West
Thumb Geyser Basins**. Plus, unlike the busy summer season, you'll share these
sights with only a handful of other hardy visitors, allowing you plenty of time to
loiter and soak in the wonderfully crisp views.

To the south, **Grand Teton** presents a similar situation in winter. Visitor
numbers are similarly reduced, as is the availability of facilities − only **Craig
Thomas Discovery and Visitor Center** at Moose remains open, with all other
park-run operations shut for the season. However, the park's main artery −
Hwy-191 − remains snowploughed, negating the need for snowcoach

Winter road closures

The most important changes within the parks during winter are **road closures**. In **Yellowstone**, the vast majority of roads remain unploughed, with only the road from Gardiner to Cooke City via Mammoth Hot Springs kept open year-round to automobile traffic; all other roads close by early November, and remain so until late April or early May. As a result, the only way to see most of the park – including Old Faithful and Canyon – is by booking a guided snowcoach or snowmobile tour. To the south, Hwy-191 cutting north to south through **Grand Teton** remains open from Jackson all the way to Flagg Ranch throughout winter; conversely, several of the park's secondary roads – namely, Moose-Wilson Road, Antelope Flats Road and most of Teton Park Road – are closed to automobile traffic until the snow melts in spring.

Outside the parks, some lesser state highways close during heavy snowfall, but for the most part, highways and passes remain open in all but blizzard conditions. The one notable exception is Hwy-212 east of Cooke City, including the Beartooth Highway, which closes in mid October and doesn't reopen until at least mid May. This closure makes **Cooke City** the literal end of the road for no less than half the year, barring access to Yellowstone from Billings or Cody to the east.

Keep in mind that roads that do remain open and ploughed both inside and outside the parks are often snow-covered and icy, and most are not maintained at night; see p.25 for **winter driving tips**, along with regional **road hotline numbers** useful for current road conditions.

transportation and allowing easy access to dozens of **cross-country** and **snowshoe trailheads**, along with roadside **views** of the snowcapped Tetons. Indeed, what Grand Teton lacks in terms of teeming wildlife and bizarre thermal features, it makes up for with stunning mountain vistas. Save for a summer sunset, the Tetons never look better than on a crisp snowy day, when the brilliant blue winter sky contrasts sharply with the white, frosted peaks.

Of course, winter activities in the region aren't limited to the parks. Along with more obscure cold-weather pursuits such as dogsledding or winter fly-fishing, visitors flock to the region for its extraordinary **downhill skiing** and **snowboarding** at Jackson Hole Mountain Resort, Big Sky and Grand Targhee. See the outlying town chapters for detailed looks at these resorts, along with details on other winter activities outside the parks.

Winter practicalities

Roads aren't the only services in the region that shut down during winter (see box above). As early as the day after Labor Day, businesses in the parks' gateway towns begin closing, remaining shuttered for up to eight months until it's time to ramp up again for summer. Within the parks, the majority of visitor centres, hotels, campgrounds and restaurants begin closing in late September (some even earlier), with nearly all of them boarded up by the time most park roads are gated shut in early November. In Yellowstone, only **Albright Visitor Center** in Mammoth Hot Springs (daily 9am–5pm; ☎307/344-2263) and **Old Faithful Visitor Education Center** (daily Dec–March 9am–5pm; ☎307/344-2750) stay open during winter, while in Grand Teton, Moose's **Craig Thomas Discovery and Visitor Center** (daily 9am–5pm; ☎307/739-3399), is the only such facility to not shut down; all three continue to run a limited schedule of ranger programmes throughout winter. Visitor centres in both Jackson (see p.203) and West Yellowstone (see p.217) also remain open.

Due in large part to downhill skiing, a large chunk of Jackson's **accommodation** options remain open year-round; the other gateway towns, however, have much less to offer in winter. The latter is also true within the parks, with the only winter lodging options in Grand Teton being Dornan's *Spur Ranch Cabins* and *Triangle X Ranch*. In Yellowstone, only the hotel and campground at Mammoth Hot Springs and *Old Faithful Snow Lodge* remain open. (For further details on these overnight options, see Chapter 8, "Accommodation".) Places to **eat** are equally limited, with only three choices inside Yellowstone: the relatively plush dining rooms at *Mammoth Hot Springs Hotel* and *Old Faithful Snow Lodge* (reservations recommended at each) and the latter's fairly forgettable *Geyser Grill* snack bar. The general store at Mammoth Hot Springs sells snacks and drinks, and by and large remains open throughout the snowy season (daily 9am–6pm), though it may be closed on Sundays, holidays and during particularly slow times; at any rate, you're best off stocking up on supplies before arriving. Grand Teton's winter dining situation is similarly thin, with the excellent *Pizza Pasta Company* at Dornan's in Moose maintaining limited hours in winter (daily 11.30am–3pm & 5–7pm; ☎307/733-2415 ext 300). For more information, see Chapter 9, "Eating and drinking".

Winter wildlife watching

Winter wildlife watching in the parks is a unique experience, made all the more enriching by the lack of summer crowds. Visitors, however, should take into account that those animals that haven't migrated or hibernated are locked in a continuous struggle to take in more energy than they expend to stay alive in the tough, often arctic conditions. Take extra caution to not spook or stress animals by keeping your distance – no photo is worth wasting an animal's precious energy reserve.

Bison, often rimed with a coat of frost or a blanket of freshly fallen snow, are one of the stars of the winter season. Constantly on the move in search of food, herds are sometimes spotted travelling single file through chest-deep snow to conserve energy. Using their strong neck muscles as an engine, bison use their massive foreheads as shovels to reach greenery buried underneath snow. As with bison, **elk** scratch out a perilous living among whatever vegetation they can reach, constantly scraping away at snow with their front hooves. While the biggest grouping of elk in the region can be seen in the National Elk Refuge just north of Jackson (see p.206), Yellowstone's Northern Range is home to a huge, if more dispersed, herd, and upwards of 15,000 elk winter in the park. Though spotted virtually everywhere, both elk and bison tend to gather at warm thermal and riverside locations, where the ground's heat melts away the snow – and superb settings for photos await – as plumes of steam frame the enormous, frosted animals. **Moose**, whose long legs have adapted to walk through high snow, are no longer very prevalent in Yellowstone; however, they're commonly spotted both in Grand Teton – look around Buffalo Fork Meadows, south of Moran Junction – and in surrounding areas such as the Gallatin's riverbanks in Big Sky and the ski slopes of Jackson Hole Mountain Resort. Other larger mammals commonly spotted come winter include **bighorn sheep**, visible in Gardner Canyon north of Mammoth and along Hwy-191 entering Big Sky, and the ubiquitous **coyote**, sporting puffed-up winter coats that make them look brawnier than their summer selves.

Among large predators, **grizzlies** and **black bears** are smart enough to curl up and wait out the winter months by hibernating. Though uncommon, bears do awaken on occasion for a wander; in Yellowstone, they have been spotted out of their dens every month save for January. Interestingly, females give birth to cubs (typically two) in their den while in a semiconscious state between mid January to early February, but return to sleep for two months as their cubs nurse and slumber. Meanwhile, bears' competition – **wolves** and **mountain lions** – maintain higher profiles in winter. Though mountain lion sightings are exceedingly rare year-round, your best chance of spotting a wolf is in winter when packs hunt and feed on elk – upwards of ninety percent of their winter diet – and launch into their February mating season; listen closely around this time for the shortened howl of a male wolf wooing a rival pack's female for a clandestine rendezvous. Highway closures throughout the majority of Yellowstone aren't much of a hindrance for wolf spotting, as the road from Mammoth to Cooke City cuts through the territories of several packs, some of which seasonally migrate to the area due to the Northern Range's shallower snow and wintering elk herd. As in summer, wolf sightings are most common at dawn or dusk, when they're most active. To increase your chances of tracking a pack, consider one of the perennially popular winter **wolf-watching trips** presented by the Yellowstone Association Institute (see p.196 and *The wolves of Yellowstone* colour section).

Ospreys, sandhill cranes and peregrine falcons all soar away to warmer temperatures come autumn, but **bald eagles** – easily spotted when perched in stands of leafless cottonwood trees lining riverbanks – **trumpeter swans**, **American dippers** and dozens of other species stick around through winter. Perhaps most visible are **ravens**, who have opportunistically learned not only to follow wolves on the hunt – thirty or more hungry ravens accompany most wolf kills – but also stake out car parks and other areas where humans gather. Remarkably, ravens have taught themselves to unzip backpacks, and many stories exist of snowmobilers or winter campers returning from a short hike to find their gear ransacked, with the best bits of food lifted by one of the wily scavengers.

Snowcoach tours

Along with snowmobiles, the only other motorized vehicles permitted on unploughed roads within Yellowstone are **snowcoaches**. The park's original Canadian-built machines, popular in their homeland where ploughed roads were less common, were first allowed into the park in 1955, and until recently visitors still had a chance (albeit rare) of seeing one of these dark red or banana-yellow Bombardiers – looking like the love child of a tank and a school bus – still rumbling over park roads. Nowadays, snowcoaches entering Yellowstone are converted small buses, vans or SUVs with the tyres removed and large skis added to the front and treads to the back. As comfortable as a normal bus ride, including heat (something snowmobiles obviously can't provide), these modern coaches are used for both day-tours as well as general winter transportation into and through the park. Shuttles depart daily (mid-Dec to early March) from Mammoth, West Yellowstone and Flagg Ranch, with most stopping at Old Faithful; confirm before booking that your trip will be on a modern coach, as the older models are cramped and rumble loud enough to require earplugs.

For those looking for **transportation** into or through Yellowstone, the park's concessionaire, Xanterra, is the best option (☎307/344-7311, ⊛www.travel yellowstone.com). Costing between $55–70 per person, the company operates daily **one-way trips** to Old Faithful from Mammoth (7.30am), West Yellowstone (noon) and Flagg Ranch (12.30pm), along with onward journeys from Old Faithful (most of which require an overnight stay); **round-trip tours** are also available to the Grand Canyon of the Yellowstone from Mammoth ($125) and

Old Faithful ($130). In any case, all of Xanterra's regularly scheduled trips are considered tours as well, though just how much information you get depends on that day's driver and the patience of your fellow passengers; stops are made for wildlife spotting (and restroom visits), as well as for quick walks around the likes of Fountain Paint Pot.

Unlike the excursions described above, **dedicated tours** don't transport park employees and trailhead-bound skiers/snowshoers, making them often a better choice for visitors simply hoping to get a day-long look at Yellowstone in winter. These tours spend more time at sights along the way and include guides who – relying as they do on tips and good word of mouth for business – are typically more helpful and informative. West Yellowstone is the primary hub for snowcoach tours heading into the park, with average rates hovering around $100–110 per person for a round-trip to Old Faithful, and about $10 more to Canyon – top **operators** include Back Country Adventures (☎406/646-9317 or 1-800/924-7669, ⓦwww.backcountry-adventures.com) and Yellowstone Vacations (☎406/646-9564 or 1-800/426-7669, ⓦwww.yellowstonevacations.com).

See the box on opposite for details on a winter use plan proposal that, at the time of writing, could potentially **ban snowcoaches** from entering Yellowstone.

Winter activities

A major element to enjoying **winter activities** in Yellowstone and Grand Teton is pre-planning. Unlike summer, when you can quickly stuff a daypack with necessities before hopping on a bike or hiking a trail, most snowy sports in the parks are gear-intensive and often require a reservation, guide or shuttle trip. The most popular activities are **cross-country skiing**, **snowshoeing** and **snowmobiling**, all of which require warm winter gear along with equipment readily available for rent in the region; we've broken down each of these activities in detail on the following pages.

In terms of popularity, second-tier winter activities in the parks include **ice-skating** – rinks and skates are available to guests at both *Mammoth Hot Springs Hotel* and *Old Faithful Snow Lodge* – and **ice-climbing** up frozen waterfalls in Grand Teton's backcountry; check with Exum Mountain Guides (ⓦwww.exumguides.com) for details on the latter. In Yellowstone, the **fishing** season ends the first Sunday in November and doesn't start again until Memorial Day weekend. Fishing in Grand Teton, however, is allowed year-round on portions of the Snake River north of Moran and south of Moose (catch-and-release from Nov–March), while all the park's lakes, including Jackson Lake, are open to ice-fishing throughout winter. For more information on fishing, see Chapter 6, "Summer activities".

Snowmobiling

There's no leisure activity in Yellowstone more contentious these days than **snowmobiling.** Once these noisy, speedy machines arrived in the park in the 1960s and proliferated exponentially over the ensuing three decades – pumping up local economies in the process – it was clear that a showdown between "sledheads" and snowmobile opponents was inevitable. Today, restrictions have tightened considerably, with potentially more on the immediate horizon (see box opposite), and while park visitors are no longer allowed to ride off alone into the sunset, one hand steering while the other grips a full can of beer, it's still possible to have plenty of good times riding along nearly two hundred miles of ploughed roads within Yellowstone. Indeed, whether you love snowmobiles or loathe them, it's hard to deny that riding one can be exhilarating fun.

As official park concessionaire, Xanterra (℗1-866/439-7375, ⓦwww.travel yellowstone.com) is the only option for a guided **snowmobile tour** starting inside Yellowstone. Embarking shortly after sunrise, an all-day tour taking in either Old Faithful or the sights around Canyon and Lake Villages (from *Mammoth Hot Springs Hotel*) or the Grand Loop's southern section (from *Old Faithful Snow Lodge*) costs $275 per snowmobile (one or two riders) and includes everything from helmet down to toe warmers. Outside the park, the overwhelming majority of tours start from West Yellowstone, and while these often get going slightly later in the morning (8–9am), they're also more affordable, ranging between $200–220 for

Yellowstone's snowmobile controversy

Once **snowmobiles** were first allowed into Yellowstone in 1963 – the machines remain forbidden in most national parks, including Glacier in northern Montana – winter in the park became largely defined by the machines' loud rumblings and gasoline-soaked fumes, with as many as seventy thousand sleds entering the park annually by the mid 1990s. Though most visitors obeyed traffic laws and stayed on designated roadways, tales of rowdy riders were legion, ranging from brazen "sledheads" zipping along at twice the maximum 45mph speed limit to groups heading off-road to buzz past bison and other wild game. To many concerned park officials, visitors and observers, conditions had spiralled out of control: naturalists argued that the pollution and noise caused by snowmobiles were dangerously stressing wildlife during an already difficult season for them; skiers and snowshoers were frustrated by the machines' adverse effects on solitude and quiet; and many rangers were weary of chasing out-of-control groups. A winter use plan issued in 2000 proposed to **ban snowmobiles entirely**, an idea that was embraced by many – including the Clinton administration and the vast majority of US citizens polled on the issue – and the era of motorized sleds in Yellowstone seemed at an imminent end. Lawsuits and a change of administration in the White House, however, helped revoke the outright ban – much to the pleasure of West Yellowstone, the self-described "Snowmobile Capital of the World", which relies greatly on the trade.

Since the early 2000s, all snowmobiles entering Yellowstone have been required to use the **quietest and cleanest-burning** technology available (presently meaning four-stroke engines), with a **limited number** of machines allowed in the park per day (originally 720, currently 318). Furthermore, under the stricter rules, sledders have been required to be led by a professional **guide**, whose main responsibility is to ensure everyone stays single file on the road, keeps a safe distance from wildlife and generally behaves. While both sides were less than euphoric about these compromises (particularly snowmobile-rental businesses in the park's gateway communities), they did manage, at least for a time, to ease tensions between ardent snowmobile proponents and opponents.

However, with Yellowstone's current interim winter use plan expiring at the end of the 2010-2011 winter season, the uneasy truce that had settled around the snowmobiling skirmish is a memory: if no new management plan is approved, *all* over-snow vehicle (OSV) access to Yellowstone will cease, beginning in 2011–12. Alternatives being batted around at the time of writing range wildly from a complete ban of all OSVs to an increase in the number of snowcoaches and snowmobiles permitted daily, to even ploughing the road to Old Faithful from the north while also allowing a limited number of OSVs through the park's South Entrance. A **decision** is expected sometime in 2011, ostensibly before the season's first heavy snowfall, so visit the park's website for updates.

day-long trips, including clothing; respected operators include Back Country Adventures (☎406/646-9317 or 1-800/924-7669, ⓦwww.backcountry -adventures.com) and Two Top Snowmobile Rental (☎406/646-7802 or 1-800/522-7802, ⓦwww.twotopsnowmobile.com).

Regulations within Grand Teton are similar to Yellowstone in that four-stroke engines are also mandatory and numbers are limited (140 sleds per day); however, guides are not required. This is partly due to the fact that only one trail in the park, a section of the six-hundred-mile **Continental Divide Snowmobile Trail** (CDST; ☎307/739-3614 for information on trail conditions), is open to snowmobiles. Riders in Grand Teton are allowed to cut off the CDST onto frozen Jackson Lake, but only to access areas for ice-fishing. Located directly on the CDST just east of the park, *Grand Teton RV Resort* (☎307/733-1980 or 1-800/563-6469, ⓦwww.yellowstonerv.com) offers non-guided half-day snowmobile packages starting at $100–125 (including helmet and clothing), as well as guided tours from $225–240; rates are per person.

Outside the parks are well over five hundred additional miles of groomed snowmobile terrain, mainly within the neighbouring national forests where regulations are far less stringent. West Yellowstone and Cooke City are the area's two most snowmobile-friendly towns – see their respective chapters for further details.

Cross-country skiing and snowshoeing

Snowcoach and snowmobile tours allow visitors to view the parks' winter wonderland from roads, but the best way to fully immerse yourself in the region's winter landscape is on a pair of **cross-country (Nordic) skis** or **snowshoes**. With only the sound of your breath and the squeaking snow beneath as you huff along through a sparkling, snowy paradise dotted with panoramic views, steamy thermal features and abundant wildlife, park exploration on foot is an unforgettable experience for those who give it a go. Neither activity requires a great deal of experience, provided you're in decent shape – if you can walk, you can snowshoe with today's advanced models, and cross-country skiing is nowhere near as difficult to pick up as downhill (Alpine) skiing. However, don't even think about heading out without being properly prepared and outfitted: winter in the Rockies is unforgiving, and the odds of someone finding you trailside in an emergency are remote. Always check in with a ranger or an information desk for a current weather report and to leave an itinerary, and wear several adjustable layers of waterproof clothing, along with sunscreen and glasses/goggles; other critical steps include bringing extra clothes and food, and travelling in a group. While free basic **maps** to winter trails are available at ranger stations and visitor centres, those heading beyond viewable distance of the road should also take a compass and a detailed topographic map. For other ideas on backcountry tips and what to bring, see the box on p.148.

Off-road trails are not groomed in either park, though more often than not a path will have already been blazed ahead of you. Trails are typically flagged with orange tree markers, but check with a ranger or local ski shop employee for advice on the easiest paths to follow if you're worried about losing your way. Etiquette requires that downhill skiers have right-of-way; when snowshoeing, be sure to travel beside ski tracks rather than directly on them.

Within Yellowstone

While pretty much every path within Yellowstone is open for exploration to expert sliders and winter hikers, there are three main options for diving into the park's backcountry on established winter trails. Easiest is the series of trails

The wolves of Yellowstone

Sitting by the roadside in Yellowstone watching a wolf pack in pursuit of its prey – or just waking to a hair-raising, early morning howl – are unforgettable experiences, and ones that park visitors were deprived of for seventy years. It's hard to overestimate the importance of the successful return of wolves to the region, and the re-introduction programme has been one of the National Park Service's brightest success stories, cementing Yellowstone's reputation as the country's top area for wildlife-watching.

Re-introduction

Effective cullers of crowd-pleasers like elk and mule deer, **grey wolves** (*canis lupus*) lived in and around Yellowstone until their extermination in 1926 — the culmination of a period that saw these native "devil's dogs" trapped, poisoned and shot at almost every opportunity. In the 1940s, forward-thinking wildlife biologist **Aldo Leopold** advocated re-introducing wolves to restore the Yellowstone ecosystem's precarious balance; a half-century of heated debate ensued, and on January 12, 1995, fourteen Canadian wolves were trucked in under Gardiner's Roosevelt Arch, with another 27 following by 1996. Each animal was radio-collared, kept in acclimatization pens hidden throughout **Lamar Valley**, and fed a steady diet of elk, deer, moose and bison that had died around the park. Several more years of transplants were scheduled but soon cancelled as the programme became an instant success. By 2003, 173 wolves – a high-water mark – were living in Yellowstone, and although the population has dropped and levelled off in the time since, they continue to remain protected under the US Endangered Species Act.

Grey wolves up close

Despite the name, the coat of a grey wolf can range from snow white to midnight black; males can weigh upwards of 130 pounds, while females top out at 110. A wolf's life is not an easy one, and fatal wounds sustained by taking on much larger prey are common – the **average lifespan** of a grey wolf in the wild is only 3 to 4 years. Typically only the pack's alpha female is allowed to get pregnant, giving **birth** in April to an average of

Radio-collering offspring of re-introduced wolves ▲

Wolf playing with pups ▼

five pups. The entire pack takes turns caring for the young and bringing food to the den, as well as sticks and colourful bits of trash for cubs to play with. These exceptionally **territorial** animals will attack and kill intruding wolves, including renegade Romeos hoping to poach a lesser female to start a new pack.

Yellowstone wolf packs

At the time of writing, fourteen packs roam in and out of Yellowstone, with an overall population hovering around a hundred. Due to the high density of prey, pack **territories** around Yellowstone are small by wolf standards – less than fifty square miles – making the park, and its elk-rich Northern Range in particular, the most reliable place in the world for observing wolves in the wild.

Social creatures by nature, wolves live in packs ranging in size from six to over thirty, led by an alpha male and female who keep other pack members in line. Tracking the groups is fascinating, with coups and the natural deaths of alphas leading to splinter groups and other packs taking control. The **Druid Peak Pack**, for example, long dominated Lamar Valley before losing its Northern Range territory to upstart packs and eventually disbanding in 2010.

Along with territory size, pack numbers depend on the main food source. For example, the ranks of bison-hunting, non-Northern Range groups such as **Mollie's Pack** have grown larger in order to take down the massive animals; up to fourteen wolves have been seen biting and hanging from a bison at one time. Elk are easily the most common **prey**, though mule deer, moose, beaver and – most controversially – domestic cattle on neighbouring ranchlands are also hunted.

▲ Wolves feeding on mule deer

▼ Wolves kissing

Wolf-watching

Wolf-watching has become a fascinating addition to the Yellowstone experience, and numerous organizations (including the Yellowstone Association Institute, see p.196) lead spotting expeditions. A telescope or set of high-powered binoculars are essential, with wolves more often than not sighted half a mile away or further. Winter is the best time for wolf-watching, when packs ferociously hunt elk and, to a lesser extent, bison struggling to survive the frigid cold; also, wolves' coats show up more clearly silhouetted against a snowy background, making winter the prime spotting season. Since wolves are most active around dawn and dusk, you'll need to be on their schedule to increase the chances of seeing one; the majority of sightings occur before 8am.

Unless you get word of a recently seen pack or fresh kill elsewhere, your best bet is to explore the year-round Northeast Entrance Road leading through Lamar Valley, which cuts through the range of around a half-dozen packs. You're sure to pass Yellowstone's most hardcore wolf-watchers – some working for the official Yellowstone Wolf Project, others just enthusiasts – and most will happily fill you in on the latest news and perhaps even let you peek through their telescopes. Along with roadside spotting parties, other **telltale signs** that wolves might be near include flocks of ravens, herds of elk fleeing in fear and, most obviously, that inimitable wolf howl.

As with other wild animals, it's your responsibility to not interact with wolves; a fed wolf is a dead wolf, so always carry any food scraps or rubbish away with you. Should a wolf approach – a rare, but not unheard-of occurrence – get into the closest car and drive away.

Grey wolf and ravens feeding on a kill ▲

Wolf-watchers with telescopes ▼

Grey wolf ▼

Winter camping

The only designated campground within both parks to remain open all through the winter is at Mammoth Hot Springs. **Backcountry camping** is allowed, however, with many regulations similar to those in summer. Permits are required and can be picked up at visitor centres at Mammoth, Old Faithful and Moose. As in summer, it's essential to be prepared for all conditions, keeping in mind that night-time temperatures of -30°F are routine. Frostbite and hypothermia are obvious **dangers**, as are avalanches, snow-covered thermal features, stream and lake crossings, and hungry wildlife (proper food storage is required throughout winter). See the guidelines and advice at the start of Chapter 5, "Backcountry hiking and camping", for more information, and take into account that you'll want to pack additional winter gear, including ski wax, an equipment repair kit, avalanche beeper and probe, and extra warm clothing (which should be kept dry at all costs). Finally, and perhaps most dauntingly, wood fires are not allowed in the backcountry in winter, meaning that your camping stove will be your sole heat source.

located off the park's sole ploughed road (connecting Gardiner and Cooke City), on which enthusiasts can drive to trailheads themselves; basic maps (Mammoth, Tower, Northeast) covering this stretch are available free at visitor centres and Bear Den ski shops (see p.178). Some of the more popular trails hereabouts include the mainly flat, 3.5-mile (one-way) **Barronette Trail**, which follows the old road to Cooke City and weaves in and out of conifer forest beneath its eponymous peak, and the more difficult eight-mile (one-way) **Blacktail Plateau Trail**, which begins a short drive east of Mammoth and climbs close to 1000ft over its first six miles, rewarding skiers and snowshoers with wonderful views and ample wildlife spotting.

A second option within Yellowstone is to book a ride on a snowcoach and disembark at a trailhead along one of the park's unploughed roads. There's a cluster of fine trails located around Canyon, but the park's most popular trail network is in the Old Faithful area; rather than attempting to camp in the backcountry's subzero temperatures after a full day of exploring, skiers and hikers can instead bed down inside the warm *Old Faithful Snow Lodge*. Among the dozen-plus trails around Old Faithful, those leading to **Fairy Falls** and **Mystic Falls** are among the most used, as is the **Lone Star Geyser Trail**, a lovely nine-mile round-trip to the frequently eruptive geyser set along the spectacular Firehole River.

The final network of winter trails within Yellowstone are reached from West Yellowstone, detailed on p.221.

Within Grand Teton

Given that Grand Teton's main roadway is ploughed all the way from Jackson to Flagg Ranch, there are dozens of places to set off from for a memorable day of snowshoeing or Nordic skiing. Note, however, that for the protection of both people and animals, several zones within the park are closed in winter, including the Snake River floodplain and all areas above 9900ft. For more information on winter closures, stop in at the Craig Thomas Discovery and Visitor Center at Moose, where you can also get current trail and weather updates, as well as join a ranger-guided snowshoe hike (daily 1.30pm; reservations required, snowshoes provided; $5 donation; ☎307/739-3399).

One of the flattest places to zip along in the park is **Teton Park Road**, which remains unploughed for thirteen miles between the car park at Taggart Lake Trailhead and *Signal Mountain Lodge* between November and April. Groomed on occasion, this stretch of road along the base of the Tetons allows for several different tours. From the southern trailhead, options include the short, albeit difficult four-mile **Taggart Lake Loop** (covering part of H37; see p.139) and the easier eight-mile loop to the southern edge of **Jenny Lake**. From the northern trailhead at *Signal Mountain Lodge*, you can tramp along the shores of **Jackson Lake** or test your stamina by huffing up **Signal Mountain Road**, a twelve-mile round-trip gaining close to 800ft elevation en route.

To the north, **Colter Bay** is open to easy exploration aside (or on) frozen Jackson Lake and past Swan Lake and Heron Pond; even further north at the edge of Yellowstone, some of the area's best and most secluded trails head out from **Flagg Ranch**. Along with routes exploring the Snake River valley, you can also head out from Flagg Ranch on the easy 2.5-mile **Polecat Creek Loop**. Toward the southern end of Grand Teton, access points to a host of fine trails are strung along **Moose-Wilson Road**. Just north of Teton Village (home to its own ten-mile Nordic ski track; see p.213), the road closes for winter, offering access to a couple of flat, snowy miles along pretty Lake Creek. From the northern parking area on Moose-Wilson Road, hardy skiers and hikers can huff up to Phelps Lake Overlook (see p.90), a five-mile round-trip gaining close to 600ft.

Rentals and tours

While you'll want to pack winter attire for Nordic skiing and snowshoeing, lugging your own gear along is not a necessity as **rental equipment** is readily available. In Yellowstone, *Mammoth Hot Springs Hotel* and *Old Faithful Snow Lodge* each host a Bear Den Ski Shop (☎307/545-4825) where gear can be rented by the half- and full day. Rates are very affordable, with snowshoes at $15 per day and skis/boots/pole packages available for $18.50. Both shops also offer ski repair and waxing services, as well as cross-country ski **lessons** – expect to pay around $58 for a two-hour group lesson including the aforementioned gear package. In Grand Teton, the sole rental option is the Trading Post (☎307/733-2415) at Dornan's near Moose, with rates similar to those in Yellowstone.

As for **tours**, Xanterra runs a limited selection of cross-country ski and snowshoe trips in Yellowstone ranging from $45 for an afternoon ski trip from Old Faithful to Fairy Falls to a full-day "Grand Canyon Ski Tour" ($140) starting from either Mammoth or Old Faithful. Within Grand Teton, several companies run cross-country and snowshoe tours led by naturalists; two of the top operators are Hole Hiking Experience (☎307/690-4453 or 1-866/733-4453, ⓦwww.holehike.com), offering half-day ($95), full-day ($130) and ambitious five-day ($1100) tours, and Rendezvous Backcountry Tours (☎307/353-2900 or 1-877/754-4887, ⓦwww .skithetetons.com), charging $200 for one-day cross-country ski tours.

Details on additional rental and tour services in the gateway towns are listed in their respective chapters.

Listings

Listings

8 Accommodation 181

9 Eating and drinking 189

10 Park programmes and tours 195

8

Accommodation

I f you're looking to stay in either park with a roof overhead, **accommodation** will be your trip's biggest expense; it can also be the biggest hassle if you don't plan ahead. While good for the concessionaires that manage Yellowstone and Grand Teton's lodging, the blend of limited supply and high demand does not serve visitors very well, and for the most part you'll have to pay more for less, with plain, motel-style rooms going for mid-range hotel room prices. Cabins are common as well, but while some look like classic log structures from the outside, don't expect to find a wood-burning stove surrounded by cosy, hand-carved hardwood furniture on the inside – again, think "basic motel room" and you probably won't be let down. With high rates of staff turnover from summer to summer, service (particularly in Yellowstone) can be spotty, and in-room amenities are rather basic – phones are rare, while TVs, radios and bathrooms stocked with jetted tubs are non-existent.

All caveats aside, **staying in the parks** still makes sense. Rooms may not be the most memorable, but the lodges themselves and the surroundings often are, and being able to take a post-dinner hike on a nearby trail to spot wildlife at dusk or enjoy a natural feature in solitude easily justifies the extra money spent. The convenience of being near the action – and avoiding having to drive back and forth from the gateway towns – is tough to beat; after a long day spent exploring, all you'll really want from your room is a place to sleep anyway. All lodging options within both parks are listed in this chapter, and deciding which **area** to stay in depends mostly on your itinerary.

Pitching a tent in the great outdoors is easily the top accommodation bargain in the region, and choosing to camp in or outside the parks is a no-brainer. **Campgrounds** in both parks are reasonably priced ($12–20; $5–8 for walk-in sites), and while perhaps not always the quietest or most bucolic of places, they are nonetheless convenient and well run. Fireside ranger programmes (see p.196) are held in many park campgrounds, and star natural attractions and good hiking trails are rarely far away. And with a great number of sites operating on a first-come, first-served basis, you won't need to plan months ahead – provided you arrive in the morning and not in the middle of a busy holiday period, you should be able to find a site at all but the most in-demand campgrounds. During the busiest times, check in at an entrance station or visitor centre, where rangers will have current information on site availability and can help point out campgrounds you should try first. The alternative to staying at established campgrounds is to camp in the **backcountry** for free, though you'll need a permit – to say nothing of proper gear and preparation; see Chapter 5 for more details. Bear in mind that rough camping by the roadside or in your car/RV in a car park is not permitted, and rangers and police officers will not hesitate to cite and evict violators.

Most lodges and campgrounds in both parks are closed during **winter**; see Chapter 7 for details.

Yellowstone

All indoor **accommodation** within Yellowstone is run by **Xanterra** (☎307/344-7311 or 1-866/439-7375, ⓦwww.travelyellowstone.com), which also manages facilities in well over a dozen other national and state parks. **Reservations** – available by phone and online – are strongly recommended for visits in the June to September period, and are essential over public holiday weekends. Note also that all rooms within Yellowstone are **non-smoking**. Bottom-end **rates** can be fairly reasonable, with some of the simplest cabins available for as little as $69 per night; the occasional bargain (particularly in off-season months such as May and October) can even be had at the park's historic lodges, *Old Faithful Inn* and *Lake Yellowstone Hotel*.

Xanterra also manages nearly half of Yellowstone's twelve **campgrounds**. Reservations at *Bridge Bay*, *Canyon*, *Grant Village*, *Madison* and RV-only *Fishing Bridge* should be made as far ahead as possible; inconveniently, Xanterra's website does not offer online camping reservations, so call one of the company's numbers above. The park's other seven campgrounds, operated by the National Park Service, are available on a first-come, first-served basis, so arrive early in the day for the best campsite pickings in high season, as many can fill up between the hours of 10 and 11am. Camping stays are limited to fourteen days total between July 1 and Labor Day (first Monday in September), and thirty days the rest of the year. All campgrounds have toilet facilities (flush unless otherwise noted), but pay **showers** are only available at *Canyon*, *Fishing Bridge* and *Grant Village*. RV sites are available at all Yellowstone campgrounds, but only *Fishing Bridge* has capabilities for hook-ups; also, the use of generators is banned at *Indian Creek*, *Lewis Lake*, *Pebble Creek*, *Slough Creek* and *Tower Fall*. A limited number of $5 hiker/biker sites are available at all campgrounds for those arriving under their own steam.

Hotels and cabins

Canyon Lodge and Cabins Open early June to late Sept. As with the nearby campground, this accommodation's best selling point is its central location only half a mile from the Grand Canyon of the Yellowstone. Starting as a tent camp in 1883, the area has always been one of the most popular bases for visitors, and it's a shame that the current configuration of rooms and cabins can't compete with options at Lake and Old Faithful Villages for atmosphere or aesthetic design. Tucked behind the long, squat and shamelessly dated *Canyon Lodge* – home to a restaurant, lounge, deli and cafeteria, but no actual lodging – is a set of desultory-looking cabins dating from the 1950s–60s, all en suite. Most affordable are the bare-bones Pioneer Cabins, a relative bargain at $73 per night; larger and slightly better-decorated cabin units range from $99–173. The spruce rooms ($173) in the nearby c.1990s *Cascade* and *Dunraven Lodges* are far more appealing, and each has its own bathroom.

Grant Village Open late May to early Oct. This uninspired development – the southernmost in the park – has drawn plenty of criticism for both its lack of style and lack of empathy with its surroundings. Completed in the mid 1980s, the architecture is reminiscent of countless suburban condominium complexes that sprouted up across the country at the same time, with three hundred small motel-style rooms ($157) divided evenly among six two-storey buildings. Of course, there's plenty to see and do in the immediate area, as rooms are only a stone's throw from Yellowstone Lake's southwest shore; considering rates here, however, you may be better off pitching a tent at nearby *Grant Village Campground*.

Lake Lodge Cabins Open early June to early Oct. Just along the road from *Lake Yellowstone Hotel* are 186 well-priced cabins all with their own bath. Despite the somewhat misleading name, none have a lakeside location; rather, units are lined up behind the log-built *Lake Yellowstone Lodge*, a 1920s facility featuring a cafeteria, small bar, gift shop, guest laundry and two huge fireplaces, as well as a lake-facing deck that's a serene place to curl up with a book. There's a stark trade-off in your choice of cabins, as those handiest for the lodge are shadeless, while those back towards the forest (sections H and J) are larger and enjoy more peaceful surroundings. The cheapest options, Pioneer and Frontier Cabins ($69–99), are basic with one double bed, while the more spacious Western Cabins have two doubles and can accommodate four people ($173).

Lake Yellowstone Hotel and Cabins Open mid-May to late Sept. Located on the northwest shore of the big lake, with sections dating as far back as 1891, *Lake Yellowstone Hotel* is the oldest standing building in the park. It's a grand, buttercup-yellow exercise in colonial-style architecture that's reminiscent of an overgrown Southern plantation mansion (not a little misplaced in the northern Rockies), and rocking on a wicker chair on its lakeside deck while looking across the blue water is an unforgettable way to relax after a long day of hiking or sightseeing. Rooms are on the small side, but comfortable and decked out in cheery colours. Prices range from $150 a night for rooms in the newer, less atmospheric annex to $225 for a lake-view room in the original section. The hotel's interior is generally bright and airy, and its lobby's Sun Room, which looks directly over the lake, is one of the finest places in Yellowstone for an evening drink. On the opposite side of the hotel from the lake are about one hundred shadeless boxes posing as cabins ($134), and although each has its own bathroom, plus two double beds and quick access to the main hotel's common areas, the *Lake Lodge Cabins* a short jog up the road are a nicer, much better-value option.

Mammoth Hot Springs Hotel and Cabins Open mid-May to early Oct and late Dec to early March. Located at the north end of the park and built in the 1930s, the exterior of this wooden structure is sprightlier than the rather dull rooms inside; behind the hotel, the nearly one hundred cabins (summer only) were also begun in the 1930s and are pleasant enough, if undistinguished. The trade-off for this mediocrity is that rates can be quite reasonable, with the cheapest of the hotel rooms ($87) and cabins ($79) sharing a bathroom; rooms or cabins with private bath cost an additional $30. Other options include a pair of larger suites with king-size beds, sitting room and cable TV ($439), and a small handful of cabins with

fenced-in hot tub at the front ($213). While the main hotel building boasts a cosy lobby and its attached Map Room – worth a look for the 18ft-wide US map composed of fifteen different types of wood – many visitors actually prefer to stay in one of the cabins for a little extra privacy. It's also worth noting that along with *Old Faithful Snow Lodge*, this hotel is one of only two Yellowstone winter accommodation options, and the only one of the two accessible by car.

Old Faithful Inn Open early May to early Oct. Spending at least one night in the Old Faithful area is really a must, ideally in a rustic room (some with own bath) at the stunning *Old Faithful Inn*. Nearly all its rooms have been remodelled in recent years, and those without a bathroom cost as low as $99 per night (add $30 for private bath). Larger rooms and suites, some with two king-size beds and a sitting room, range from $129–239. If possible, request a room in the *Old House* – the original 1904 building – as they are the most atmospheric. Regardless of where you end up, this is the most coveted accommodation in the park, so book as far in advance as possible, especially for summer stays.

Old Faithful Lodge Cabins Open mid-May to late Sept. Built in the 1920s, the log-and-stone *Old Faithful Lodge* is the closest building to Old Faithful itself in the Upper Geyser Basin. There are no rooms in the actual lodge building, but over one hundred cabins line up behind it with some of the cheapest rates in the park. Budget Cabins ($69) are little more than a plain motel unit, with shared bath and showers located a short walk away in the lodge building's public restroom. The nicer, en-suite Frontier Cabins ($113) are a tad more polished; if you're a light sleeper, however, be sure to pack earplugs to counteract the thin walls.

Old Faithful Snow Lodge and Cabins Open late April to late Oct and mid-Dec to early March. Along with *Mammoth Hot Springs Hotel*, the *Snow Lodge* provides Yellowstone's sole winter accommodation (although it's not car accessible throughout the snowy season); unlike at Mammoth, the cabins here are open in winter and offer the park's most affordable winter rates. Opened in 1998, the lodge is by far the most modern in the park, and, since it was designed to fill a pressing need for good winter accommodation around Old Faithful, there's very little wasted space on soaring ceilings that would otherwise cost a fortune to keep heated. The result is an exceedingly cosy place, complete with charmingly snug lobby (with fireplace), comfortable seating areas and a terrific bar and restaurant (see p.191). Rooms inside the lodge ($204) feature plenty of light-coloured woods and contemporary bathrooms, while the two varieties of en-suite cabins on offer – duplex Frontier Cabins ($99) dating back several decades, and the quieter, c.1990s Western Cabins ($149) with larger windows – make for relatively good value.

Roosevelt Lodge Cabins Open early June to early Sept. Located a short drive from Lamar Valley and Tower Fall, *Roosevelt Lodge* and its surrounding area was supposedly Theodore Roosevelt's favourite in the park. Fittingly, the wonderful, ranch-like main building named for him here blends in well, featuring unfinished log columns, an attractive restaurant and bar, two log fireplaces and rocking chairs on the outside deck. The latter overlook rows of 82 rustic cabins, whose relatively isolated location away from the park's most crowded villages accounts for much of their appeal. Very basic Roughrider Cabins ($69) are little more than wooden shelters with two beds and a wood stove, sharing communal bathroom facilities; en-suite Frontier Cabins, meanwhile, feature motel-like accommodation ($113) and sleep four.

Campgrounds

Bridge Bay 3 miles south of Lake Village; 7800ft. Open late May to mid-Sept; 432 sites; $19.50. The park's largest campground is located in a sun-scorched open area, although shade increases the further back you venture toward the forest; you may even find a site high enough for a lake view in one of two tent-only loops. Handy for Bridge Bay Marina, it's an ideal choice for anglers and boating enthusiasts. The nearest pay showers and coin laundry are four miles away at *Fishing Bridge RV Park*. Reservations available.

Canyon Adjacent to Canyon Village; 7900ft. Open early June to early Sept; 272 sites; $19.50. One of Yellowstone's larger campgrounds, densely forested *Canyon* also features the most tent-only sites, many

of which are clutched a bit too closely together for comfort. Its central location and nearby amenities are more convenient than most, however: it's not far from the park's most photographed view (along the south rim of the Grand Canyon of the Yellowstone), while also within walking distance of restaurants, stores, pay showers and a coin laundry. Reservations available.

Fishing Bridge RV Fishing Bridge; 7800ft. Open mid-May to late Sept; 250 sites; $28. Due to frequent bear activity in the area, *Fishing Bridge* only welcomes hard-sided campers; reservations are essential throughout summer. Pay showers, coin laundry, gas and a general store are all nearby. Check the park website for updates on the campground's ageing electrical hook-up system, which was out of service in 2010. No maximum stay limit.

Grant Village Grant Village 7800ft. Open late June to early Oct; 425 sites; $19.50. While this vast campground is spread across a dozen loops and can get very crowded, its shady and cleverly designed sites maintain a certain privacy, boosting its appeal as an alternative to Grant Village's humdrum lodging. Restaurants, gas, general store, pay showers and coin laundry are all nearby. Reservations available.

Indian Creek 8 miles south of Mammoth Hot Springs; 7300ft. Open mid-June to mid Sept; 75 sites; $12. *Indian Creek* is one of the park's most quiet and rustic campgrounds, with sites dotted around two loops in a lightly wooded forest. There's good fishing nearby in the Gardner, Panther and Obsidian Rivers. Chemical toilets. First-come, first-served.

Lewis Lake 10 miles north of South Entrance; 7800ft. Open mid-June to early Nov; 85 sites; $12. Yellowstone's southernmost campground features plenty of quiet and shade, along with easy access to Lewis Lake; it's spread over four loops (all first-come, first-served), including one particularly appealing walk-in loop. Chemical toilets.

Madison Just west of Madison Junction; 6800ft. Open early May to late Oct; 277 sites; $19.50. Situated near the junction of the Madison and Firehole Rivers, this pleasant spot is predictably popular among anglers, with paths leading down to the Madison behind the campground. No showers or laundry are immediately nearby, but West Yellowstone is only a 30min drive west. Reservations available.

Mammoth Just outside Mammoth Hot Springs en route to Gardiner; 6200ft. Open year-round; 85 sites; $14. This dusty sagebrush plot sits right beside the busy highway, giving it the park's least desirable campground setting. Still, it boasts a few benefits: Mammoth's amenities are only a half-mile away, elk routinely prance through and, for the supremely hardy, it's the only park campground open in winter. First-come, first-served.

Norris Just north of Norris Junction; 7500ft. Open late May to late Sept; 116 sites; $14. Pleasantly forested sites are dispersed across three loops at this mid-sized campground elevated above the Gibbon River. Best is Loop A, with several sites within steps of the burbling brook. Trails lead to Norris Geyser Basin less than a mile away. First-come, first-served.

Pebble Creek 9 miles west of Northeast Entrance; 6900ft. Open mid-June to late Sept; 32 sites; $12. Set by the side of the creek, but not far off the highway at the eastern end of Lamar Valley, this is an immensely popular spot among Soda Butte Creek fishermen towards the second half of summer. With direct access to a selection of fine trails, day-hikers also like to set out from here. Chemical toilets. First-come, first-served.

Slough Creek 5 miles east of Tower-Roosevelt Junction, then 2.5 miles off Northeast Entrance Road; 6250ft. Open late May to late Oct; 23 sites; $12. Located down a dirt road, this is one of the most popular campgrounds in Yellowstone among fly-fishermen, who begin flocking here in July and continue to fill it until September. Its ideal location beside Slough Creek also offers access to several excellent backcountry trails. Chemical toilets. First-come, first-served.

Tower Fall Adjacent to Tower Fall; 6600ft. Open late May to late Sept; 31 sites; $12. Located up a steep and curvy half-mile road, this is a poor choice for RVs, with no room for anything over thirty feet. It's terrific for tent

---

Saddle up

Provided you're happy to spend good portions of your day on horseback, staying at a **dude ranch** is the closest city slickers can get to living the cowboy life short of signing on for a cattle-tending job. The Yellowstone region is liberally dotted with these establishments (also known as "guest ranches") – some of which put guests to work mucking out stables at dawn, others taking a less taxing approach by offering leisure activities (horseriding, fly-fishing and fancy breakfasts) that just happen to be centred on a ranch. Prices vary wildly depending on the level of luxury and season – cheaper summer options in basic, rustic cabins with no-frills communal meals can start at under $150 per day (including horses and meals), while ranches providing more opulent accommodation will set you back twice that, if not more. Packages are typically organized by the week, though shorter options are sometimes available.

There are no actual dude ranches within **Yellowstone**, but drive out of the park in any direction and you'll quickly cross paths with arched gateways and dirt roads leading down to stables and a main house. A good area to check first is the true cowboy country of **Wapiti Valley** east of Yellowstone en route to Cody, where a top pick is *Crossed Sabres Ranch* (℡307/587-3750 or 1-888/587-3750, ⓦwww.crossedsabresranch.com). **Gallatin Valley** north of West Yellowstone is also home to several fine options, including *320 Ranch* (℡406/995-4283 or 1-800/243-0320, ⓦwww.320ranch.com) adjacent to the Gallatin River. As for **Grand Teton**, a handful of dude ranches reside within or just outside park boundaries, most notably year-round *Triangle X Ranch* (℡307/733-2183, ⓦwww.trianglex.com), which has been operated by the same family for four generations. Just across the park's southeast border is *Gros Ventre River Ranch* (℡307/733-4138, ⓦwww.grosventreriverranch.com), a more sophisticated enterprise with swanky log cabins, gourmet grub and plenty of fine trout water nearby.

A helpful resource is the **Dude Ranchers' Association** (℡307/587-2339 or 1-866/399-2339, ⓦwww.duderanch.org), which offers recommendations and bundles of information.

campers, however, and its off-highway location, not far from both Lamar Valley wildlife viewing and *Roosevelt Lodge*'s summer amenities, afford it a unique niche among Yellowstone campgrounds. Chemical toilets. First-come, first-served.

Grand Teton

Started by the Rockefeller family over half a century ago, Grand Teton Lodge Company (GTLC; ☎307/543-2811 or 1-800/628-9988, 🌐www.gtlc.com) is the official concessionaire for **accommodation** within its namesake park, running facilities at *Colter Bay Village*, *Jackson Lake Lodge* and *Jenny Lake Lodge*. Unlike Yellowstone, however, where Xanterra holds a monopoly on all park accommodation, there are a handful of private in-holdings also offering overnight options in Grand Teton, including *Signal Mountain Lodge*, *Dornan's Spur Ranch Cabins*, *Moulton Ranch Cabins*, *Triangle X Ranch* (see box, p.185) and, in neighbouring John D. Rockefeller, Jr. Memorial Parkway, *Flagg Ranch*. **Reservations** are advised for all properties, and ideally should be made several months in advance for summer stays.

Other than the lowest-end offerings at *Colter Bay Village* and *Moulton Ranch*, you won't find much under $100 a night within Grand Teton, so **camping** is often the best option for budget travellers. The park's five campgrounds (none open year-round) operate on a first-come, first-served basis; tent sites cost $20 per night. *Signal Mountain* and *Lizard Creek Campgrounds* are managed by *Signal Mountain Lodge* (☎307/543-2831 or 1-800/672-6012, 🌐www.signalmountain lodge.com), while the remaining three are run by GTLC. *Jenny Lake Campground* is the park's most popular and can reach capacity as early as 9am; a few others fill daily in July and August, so plan to arrive in the morning to claim the best possible spot. The only camping facility with showers ($4) is *Colter Bay Campground*, and the maximum allowable stay at park campgrounds is fourteen nights (seven nights at *Jenny Lake*). In addition, Flagg Ranch just north of the park has a campground, with other options in surrounding National Forests – Grassy Lake Road west of Flagg Ranch and Gros Ventre Road east of Gros Ventre Slide are two of the closest places to look. **RVs** are allowed at all campgrounds other than *Jenny Lake*, though full hook-ups are only available at the trailer villages at Colter Bay and *Flagg Ranch*; both *Signal Mountain* and *Lizard Creek* have a 30ft limit.

Visitor centres can advise on accommodation and camping **availability**, with recorded information available on ☎307/739-3603.

Hotels and cabins

Colter Bay Village Cabins GTLC. Cabins open late May to late Sept, tent cabins early June to early Sept. The largest of Grand Teton's villages is home to 166 cabins, along with dozens of canvas-roofed "tent cabins" – on the rustic side, but nonetheless one of the more reasonably priced places to stay in the park. The actual cabins, laid out suburban-style along several narrow roads, are often dowdy and less than inviting, and come in several variations: basic one-room units with shared bathroom ($65), one-room cabin-splits with private bathroom ($119–165) and two-room cabins with connecting bathroom ($179–219). None have kitchen facilities, and walls are very thin, meaning that unless you reserve the entire cabin – most are split into two units – you may hear your neighbour's every move. A cheaper alternative is to stay in one of the basic log-and-canvas tent cabins, each with four bunk beds, a wood-burning stove and outdoor barbecue grill and picnic table; bring your own bed linens, as none are supplied. These good-value units cost $52, with each additional person $6 extra. Guest amenities include internet on a shared computer at the check-in office, along with access to the pool at *Jackson Lake Lodge*.

Dornan's Spur Ranch Cabins Moose
☎ 307/733-2522, ⓦ www.dornans.com. **Open all year.** Boasting breathtaking views of the Tetons and set near the Snake River, this private ten-acre in-holding has been owned and operated by the same family since its early days as a homestead. Along with a restaurant, wine shop and grocery and outdoor stores (see p.91), Dornan's offers year-round lodging in its log-built Spur Ranch Cabins. Each of the dozen one- and two-room cabins is decked out with attractive lodgepole pine furniture, a fully equipped kitchen and private bathroom; the two-bedroom cabins can accommodate up to six people. Built in the early 1990s and renovated in 2010, these units are immensely popular, so book as far ahead as possible, especially for stays during high season. Cabin rates are $186 (for a one-bedroom) and $265 (two-bedroom) mid-May to mid-October with a mandatory three-night minimum, and $125 and $175 respectively during the rest of the year.

Flagg Ranch Resort ☎ 307/543-2861 or 1-800/443-2311, ⓦ www.flaggranch.com. **Open mid-May to late Sept.** Nestled in light pine forest between Grand Teton and Yellowstone, this resort can't claim the arresting mountain views enjoyed by other lodges to the south, but it occupies a strategic location that allows easy access to both parks – or a nice stopover in between – all while offering a full range of services. Accommodation is in well-appointed cabins ($179–189), each fitted with one or two king-size beds, coffee-maker and private bathroom with full-size tub, while the main log-built lodge has a restaurant and bar.

🏃 **Jackson Lake Lodge GTLC. Open late May to early Oct.** Set just north of Jackson Lake Junction, this legendary lodge enjoys a peerless view of the Tetons from above the marshy expanse of Willow Flats, and even if you're not bedding down here for the night, the place still demands a visit. Those who do stay overnight pay a premium for the epic setting, with the least expensive of the lodge's 37 rooms starting at $229, while those with mountain views start at $289. Rooms are on the plain side, but are decently sized with two comfortable double beds plus private bath; a handful of more impressive suites are offered in the $625–775 range. In front of the lodge on

both sides of the huge parking area sit 350 beige-and-green Classic Cottage units, comfortable and surprisingly pleasant considering their subdivided design; rates are equal to those in the main lodge for non-view and view units, as well as for larger suites. If staying in a Classic Cottage, be sure to request one with a chair-outfitted patio. Free wireless internet access is available in the lodge's upper lobby.

Jenny Lake Lodge GTLC. Open late May to early Oct. Grand Teton's premium lodging and dining property boasts outstanding service to accompany its 37 luxury log cabins, each with its own huge pine bed, private bath and patio with rocking chairs. While the serene setting isn't as grand as *Jackson Lake Lodge*'s bluff, the main building and string of cabins are only a quarter of a mile from the north shore of its namesake lake, and all are within easy walking/riding distance to several excellent trails. *Jenny Lake Lodge*'s stratospheric rates – single-room and duplex cabins cost $620 per night, while rates for suites shoot as high as $885 – are somewhat tempered by the fact that breakfast and a five-course dinner are included, along with horseback rides and free use of the lodge's bicycles. Note that reservations for this high-end property are made on a separate number (☎307/733-4647).

🏃 **Moulton Ranch Cabins Mormon Row** ☎ 307/733-3749, ⓦ www.moultonranch cabins.com. **Open late May to late Sept.** Only steps away from the oft-photographed barns along unpaved Mormon Row (and still owned by a descendant of the original barn builders), this is one of the few privately owned parcels of land remaining in the area. While the owners decamp for Idaho in the winter, throughout summer they live in the main building and manage five lovingly maintained cabins around it. Three of the units have been built fairly recently, while the other two date back more than a century – one is the original homestead building, and the other was formerly used for grain storage. The smallest cottage fits two snugly and rents for $89 nightly, while the largest sleeps up to six and goes for $229. Reserve well ahead, as many of the units (particularly the larger ones) get snatched up as far as one year in advance.

Signal Mountain Lodge and Cabins ☎ 307/543-2831 or 1-800/672-6012, ⓦ www.signal mountainlodge.com. **Open early May to mid-Oct.**

Located on the southeast shore of Jackson Lake, this lodge offers a range of accommodation choices, all only steps from the water; all are also on the dated side, although some visitors may appreciate certain units' retro atmospherics. Least desirable are the bland, motel-style Country Rooms ($175), each with one or two king-size, private bathroom, microwave and mini-fridge. A much smarter buy are the one- and two-room Rustic Log Cabins ($132–198), more airy than those at Colter Bay and sleeping up to six people. Best of all are the two-room Lakefront Retreats ($254–274) at the far end of the property, which feature kitchens and shared decks offering outstanding views across the lake.

Campgrounds

Colter Bay Colter Bay Village; 6800ft. Open late May to late Sept; 368 sites; tent sites $20, walk-in sites $8, RVs $42–55. Large and utilitarian, this campground features loop after loop of heavily wooded sites that, fortunately, are divided into separate tent and RV zones. The wealth of facilities available at Colter Bay Village includes stores, a marina, restaurants, stables and a network of excellent nature trails.

Flagg Ranch John D. Rockefeller, Jr. Memorial Parkway; 6900ft. ☏307/543-2861 or 1-800/443-2311, ⊛www.flaggranch.com. Open late May to mid-Sept; 175 sites; tent sites $35 for two adults, RVs $60 for two adults, add $5 per additional adult. With a hundred of the sites here reserved for trailers, this is the campground best suited to RV-driving visitors; most tent campers will want to stay here only if *Lizard Creek* in Grand Teton to the south or *Lewis Lake* in Yellowstone to the north are fully booked. The wooded campground is close to good fly-fishing on the Snake River, while facilities include pay showers, laundry, full RV hook-ups and a nearby grocery and restaurant. Reservations available.

Gros Ventre 5 miles northeast of Gros Ventre Junction; 6600ft. Open early May to early Oct; 355 sites; tent sites $20, RVs $40. Though

certainly not the most beautiful, the largest campground in Grand Teton sprawls out along eight loops near the cottonwood-lined banks of the Gros Ventre River, less than twelve miles from Jackson. One of the fifty-site loops is tent-only, and generators are barred from the campground's southern half; many other parts of this dry, sagebrush-covered area, however, are ideal for RVs. Given its size and somewhat distant location from the park's main attractions, it's always the last to fill, if it does at all.

Jenny Lake South Jenny Lake; 6800ft. Open mid-May to early Oct; 59 sites; tent sites $20, walk-in sites $8. Laid out in a sparingly wooded area close to Jenny Lake and its dock, these are the most coveted campsites in Grand Teton, and you'll need to plan ahead (and have lucky timing) to stake one out. Its popularity stems from the absence of RVs, as well as its picturesque setting, relatively small size and proximity to some of the most popular hiking trails in the park.

Lizard Creek 8 miles north of Colter Bay Village; 6850ft. Open mid-June to early Sept; 60 sites; tent sites $20, walk-in sites $5. Located on a small peninsula at the north end of Jackson Lake, this somewhat secluded campground can feel forlorn by the end of the summer, when the lake hereabouts has drained. Before then, however, the superbly shaded sites set along two loops – one for tents, one for RVs – are a great find, offering striking views over the lake and beyond; best of all, the campground rarely fills.

Signal Mountain Signal Mountain Lodge; 6800ft. Open early May to mid-Oct; 86 sites; tent sites $20, RVs $49. A fantastic lakeside campground with a fair amount of pine tree shade to boot, *Signal Mountain* boasts a few small sites with lake views, although you'll need to arrive early – or move early on your second day – to nab one; the whole campground can fill to capacity before noon in high season. Facilities at the nearby lodge include gas, groceries, restaurants and bar, and it's a short walk to the beach and marina.

Eating and drinking

ew visitors return from a Yellowstone and Grand Teton vacation bragging about all the amazing meals they've enjoyed within the parks. The town of Jackson hosts a line-up of **cuisines** both gourmet and eclectic, but the rest of the region tends to lean on a menu heavy on grilled steaks and wild game, pan-fried trout and grilled burgers, all served with the ubiquitous side of fries or mashed potatoes. There are a handful of notable restaurants within both parks featuring high-end food (with prices to match), and while the ambience in these can be superb, overall quality is subject to spottiness, particularly in early summer when newly imported staff members are busy learning on the job. Diner-style platters and fast-food meals can be found in most major park villages, and more often than not are fairly, rather than exorbitantly, priced. No trip to the parks is complete without sampling a locally sourced huckleberry sundae or milkshake – available at one of the many **ice-cream** stands typically found in general stores and lodges.

If cooking tent-side, it pays to load up on supplies before heading into the parks. **Supermarkets** in the gateway towns stock all but the most exotic ingredients, while the general stores in Yellowstone and Grand Teton are strong on snacks and beverages, including beer and liquor, but far less reliable for fresh meats and produce. For a **picnic** lunch, there are several delis and snack bars in both parks offering takeaway food, while packed lunches – usually including a sandwich, fruit, chips and beverage – can often be ordered the night before from most establishments.

Yellowstone

Operated by Yellowstone concessionaires, the park's snack bars and restaurants aren't particularly cheap, but considering the lack of competition, they're not hideously expensive, either. Along with the do-it-yourself and takeaway approaches, there are three options for eating in the park: diner-style meals inside one of the **general stores**; basic food at one of the self-serve **cafeterias** or **cafés**; and, full-blown meals at one of several lodge **restaurants**. The sit-down restaurants share many of the same items – including similar breakfasts, vegetarian dishes and drink/dessert menus – but to keep things varied, each maintains its own list of house specialties. There's not a lot of price difference among the restaurants, where you can expect to pay $15–25 per main course; however, the dining rooms inside *Lake Yellowstone Hotel*, *Old Faithful Snow Lodge* and *Old Faithful Inn* are the clear standouts for food and ambience, while the barbecue grub at *Roosevelt Lodge* is a family favourite. All restaurants are likewise open for lunch and breakfast, generally offering a breakfast buffet that includes fresh fruit, cereals, pastries and standard cooked items in the $12 range. Note that **reservations** are essential for dinner during summer at all lodge restaurants – call ☏307/344-7311 or 1-866/439-7375.

Hours vary at the dozen or so **Yellowstone General Stores** (Ⓦwww.visit yellowstonepark.com), located at busy points throughout the park, though most stay open 7.30am–9.30pm throughout summer; the Mammoth store is the park's sole shopping option in winter, with limited hours. Only a sliver of the stores are given over to actual groceries, however, since souvenirs of all shapes and sizes – along with books and limited outdoor goods – take up most of the space. Several park stores also have **soda fountains** slinging burgers, fries, ice-cream cones and shakes to rows of customers on stools, and you'll be hard-pressed to *not* strike up convivial conversation with servers and fellow visitors at these old-fashioned diners.

Unlike at Grand Teton, there are no real standout spots in Yellowstone to linger over a **drink** while enjoying the view; if hoping for just that, you're best off lugging along a bottle of wine and plastic cups on a short stroll for an alfresco nightcap. The best atmospheres for an indoor drink in the park are the bars at *Old Faithful Inn* and *Old Faithful Snow Lodge*, or the colonial-style Sun Room inside *Lake Yellowstone Hotel*; the lounge inside *Canyon Lodge*, while certainly relaxed, has anachronistic decor better suited to Rat Pack-era Las Vegas than a contemporary national park.

Canyon

Canyon's General Store, where you'll also find the excellent soda fountain detailed below, is one of the better spots in the park to hunt down fresh produce. All other food options in the village are located along the extended length of hopelessly dated *Canyon Lodge*.

Canyon Cafeteria At the far southern end of *Canyon Lodge* is this workaday cafeteria, serving breakfast, lunch and dinner and featuring a reasonably priced buffet throughout the day. A la carte dinner items include country fried steak and roast turkey, with rice bowls and lasagne also available; nothing's over $10.

Canyon Lodge Dining Room Set at the opposite end of *Canyon Lodge* from the *Cafeteria*, the village's priciest dining option is a low-key affair where bison *asada* ($13.95) and sautéed trout ($16.75) prove almost as popular as the house specialty, prime rib *au jus* ($23.95 for a 14oz cut); a trip to the large salad bar is an extra $4.50. Burgers (about $10) dominate the lunch menu, while the straightforward breakfast buffet runs $12. The adjacent lounge, meanwhile, is worth a look (and possibly a drink) if only to indulge in its comically misplaced furnishings, most notably the space-age bachelor pad ceiling fixtures looming overhead like giant asterisks.

Canyon Soda Fountain The most inviting of the park's general store soda fountains, Canyon's old-fashioned dining counter is brighter than similar offerings found elsewhere around Yellowstone, and is a much stronger bet than the nearby *Cafeteria*. Unsurprisingly, the menu's heavy on burgers – including a triple-patty monstrosity with cheese for $15 – but lighter options are also available, including the requisite salads for about $10. Breakfast is available until 10.30am.

Grant

As with its accommodation scene, it's difficult to get excited about **Grant Village**'s utilitarian eating options. Even Grant General Store is a letdown, with its *Grant Village Grill* taking a drab fast-food approach rather than a more affable soda fountain route.

Grant Village Grill Best left alone, the area's least desirable option offers the usual line-up of burgers and fries (under $7), although the availability of ice cream and milkshakes helps ease the sub-mediocrity.

Grant Village Restaurant Despite being poorly signed off the adjacent road, the village's largest dining hall bustles at breakfast, lunch and dinner. Breakfast is built around a la carte items and an $11.50 buffet; lunch is a condensed version of the dinner menu, which focuses on steaks, chops and seafood, plus a few meatless options ($17–24). Simple boxed breakfasts and lunches are also available for $8.95.

Lake House Restaurant An informal spot located along the lakeshore – a short walk downhill from Grant Village's lodging centre – that's open for breakfast and dinner only. Mornings see a fairly priced buffet, while dinner consists of sliders (mini-burgers), sandwiches and salads; prices hover around $10 per item.

Lake and Fishing Bridge

Lake Village is the hub of dining activity on Yellowstone Lake's north shore; elsewhere, nearby Fishing Bridge has a good soda fountain, though there are no sit-down options available at Bridge Bay.

Fishing Bridge Soda Fountain A nice spot for a simple meal, the cosy soda fountain in the rear of Fishing Bridge General Store boasts warm ambience and a no-frills menu. Everything's under $10, from omelettes and French toast in the morning to burgers and sandwiches in the afternoon; an equally relaxed coffee counter sits adjacent.

Lake Hotel Dining Room Set in a large and airy colonnaded hall with the best views of any Yellowstone restaurant, and boasting fine service and an adventurous menu, *Lake Hotel Dining Room* has no shortage of inviting attributes. Signature mains such as bison osso bucco ($28.50) and vegetarian ratatouille risotto ($14.75) are crowd-pleasers, while main-sized salads are also available for $15 and under. The lunch menu holds onto some of these gourmet flourishes at lower prices, while breakfast includes a la carte items along with a buffet ($13.50) that's more robust than those in other park dining rooms.

Lake Lodge Cafeteria Inside the attractive main log building at *Lake Lodge* is one of the park's casual cafeterias popular with families; hit-and-miss mains include chicken and trout, both fried and around $10 a plate, including sides.

Mammoth Hot Springs

In a separate building across from *Mammoth Hot Springs Hotel*, you'll find both of the area's eating options, *Terrace Grill* and *Mammoth Dining Room*. Mammoth General Store, one building

further, is good for coffee or ice cream, but no full meals are available.

Mammoth Dining Room Although not quite on a par with the fine-dining rooms at Old Faithful and Lake, *Mammoth*'s dinner menu possesses some singular touches, including huckleberry brie chicken ($16.75) and linguine *fromaggio* ($13.95); strongly consider saving room for a Yellowstone Sundae ($5.75), made with rich huckleberry ice cream draped over a piece of crumb cake. Lunch items are $10 and under, while breakfast offers the standard buffet ($11.50) along with fairly priced a la carte choices. Just off the restaurant, a comfortable lounge has wireless internet access. Note that this is the only place to eat in Mammoth come winter, when reservations are required.

Old Faithful

Dining options here are divided evenly between the three lodges within view of the famed geyser – *Old Faithful Inn*, *Old Faithful Lodge* and *Old Faithful Snow Lodge*. The *Snow Lodge* is the newest of the bunch, open throughout winter and featuring the park's top bar.

Obsidian Dining Room Located on the ground floor of Yellowstone's most modern inn, *Old Faithful Snow Lodge*'s fine year-round restaurant features the park's most urbane dining experience, where service is attentive and the beer list is remarkably rich with regional brands. Top evening specialities include bison short ribs ($18) and the excellent wild boar tenderloin ($30); lunch is only available in winter. Breakfast options mirror those found at other park restaurants, while the attached *Firehole Lounge* is Yellowstone's swankiest bar, with several wines available by the glass, along with craft beers on draught and top-shelf whiskeys. Dinner reservations recommended in winter.

Old Faithful Inn Dining Room Though both the food and service can vary unpredictably from excellent to mediocre, reserving a table here at the park's highest-profile restaurant – memorably defined by the *Old House*'s distinctive burl wood columns – is worth the gamble. Notable mains such as trout cooked in pecans and lemon butter ($16.75) compete with a nightly dinner buffet ($23.75) encompassing prime rib and several sides. Buffets are also offered

Best bets: eating and drinking

Best cheap eats

Yellowstone *Canyon Soda Fountain*. See p.190.

Grand Teton *Pioneer Grill*. See p.194.

Cody *Our Place*. See p.244.

Cooke City *Buns 'N' Beds Deli, BBQ & Cabins*. See p.236.

Gardiner *Steve's Corral Drive-Inn*. See p.231.

Jackson *Creekside Meats, Market & Deli*. See p.207.

West Yellowstone *Running Bear Pancake House*. See p.220.

Best splurge dining

Yellowstone *Obsidian Dining Room*. See p.191.

Grand Teton *Jenny Lake Lodge Dining Room*. See p.194.

Cody *Irma Restaurant*. See p.244.

Cooke City *Beartooth Café*. See p.236.

Gardiner *Antler Pub & Grill*. See p.231.

Jackson *Silver Dollar Grill*. See p.208.

West Yellowstone *Oregon Short Line*. See p.220.

Best bars

Yellowstone *Firehole Lounge*. See p.191.

Grand Teton *Blue Heron Lounge*. See p.194.

Cody *Silver Dollar Bar*. See p.244.

Cooke City *Beartooth Café*. See p.236.

Gardiner *K-Bar and Cafe*. See p.231.

Jackson *Snake River Brewing*. See p.209.

West Yellowstone *Eino's Tavern*. See p.219.

at lunch ($13.50; bbq chicken sandwiches and trout) and breakfast ($11.50; park standard) as well, though you might be better off ordering from the menu at both meals. The nearby *Bear Paw Deli* has cheap snacks and sandwiches, while the attached *Bear Pit Lounge*, outfitted with etched glass panels, is a fun place to toast a nightcap.

Old Faithful Lodge Cafeteria Closest to the geyser itself – and in dire need of a design makeover – the dowdy *Old Faithful Lodge Cafeteria* offers serviceable mains costing no more than $10: trout amandine, bison meatloaf, sandwiches and salads. The cafeteria's finest attribute is its covered outside deck, lined with rocking chairs that look directly out to Old Faithful only one hundred yards away. Breakfast here comes courtesy of *Old Faithful Lodge Bake Shop* adjacent to the *Cafeteria*, where an open counter offers jumbo cinnamon rolls and muffins for well under $5.

Tower-Roosevelt

Roosevelt Lodge's dining choices are Yellowstone's most distinctive, featuring a cowboy theme that youngsters happily latch onto. A few miles south at Tower Fall, the tiny snack bar inside the General Store serves only ice cream and beverages.

Old West Dinner Cookout While it's hard to miss the whiff of Disney-like orchestration to the Old West-style cookouts organized by Roosevelt Corrals, they nonetheless make for a fun evening of food and entertainment, especially for families. Depending on whether you arrive at the outdoor cookout spot via horseback or covered wagon, prices are $55 or $80 per person ($10 less for kids 11 and under). Once at the feeding ground, guests – or for these few hours, "dudes" – enjoy a 12oz slab of steak and other country fare, including deliciously sweet baked beans; fireside sing-alongs of old western nuggets make up the entertainment. Available mid June to early Sept; call ahead for reservations and vegetarian meal requests.

Roosevelt Lodge Dining Room This mild-mannered dining room in the small and rustic *Roosevelt Lodge* has about two dozen plain tables set between wood columns, with a menu big on bbq meats; dinner prices top out at $24 for a massive portion of baby back ribs. Lunch sees a flurry of burgers and bbq sandwiches ($8–9) along with smaller portions of the aforementioned dinner favourites, while breakfast is the expected mix of pancakes and egg dishes, along with *huevos carnitas* – all $10 and under.

Grand Teton

As with its accommodation, restaurants in Grand Teton are split between park concessionaire-run establishments and privately operated ones. Given this competition, restaurants here are, on the whole, better than in Yellowstone, if still pricey, with the gourmet option at *Jenny Lake Lodge* the runaway choice for most exclusive. Taking top honours for an evening drink with **mountain views** is *Blue Heron Lounge*'s back deck at *Jackson Lake Lodge*, although the vistas from the lakeside deck at *Signal Mountain Lodge* and the lofty patio at Dornan's *Pizza Pasta Company* are also top-notch.

If staying in Grand Teton for more than a couple of nights, consider driving into nearby **Jackson**, home to the region's finest array of restaurants and bars (see Chapter 11 for details). Campers cooking outdoors will likewise want to stop in the town to stock up on groceries at one of its large supermarkets.

Colter Bay and Leeks Marina

Located side by side, the two restaurants at Colter Bay Village are Grand Teton's least inspired choices, both for their setting and food. To the north, the sole dining choice en route to *Flagg Ranch* is a fun pizza parlour at Leeks Marina.

Café Court The cheaper of the two options at Colter Bay is this circular eatery, where young staffers sling out adequate burgers, hot and cold sandwiches, and a small selection of pre-made salads; the bland pizzas and dodgy-looking Mexican mains are best avoided. Pretty much everything costs around $8 or under, with bottled beer also available.

John Colter's Ranch House A smarter option than *Café Court* next door, this family-friendly restaurant offers filling takes on breakfast standards (pancakes, eggs) and lunch staples (sandwiches, salads, burgers) for generally no more than $12. Dinner also mostly toes the regional line with fried chicken ($18) and wild salmon ($19), although the "you-catch-it, we'll-cook-it" trout offer ($12) is certainly unique and may well prove irresistible to anglers.

Leek's Pizzeria The thick pizzas ($13–22) at this lake-adjacent pizzeria are fine enough, although the mellow mood and fine views from the outside deck might be its biggest draw; calzones, pasta dishes, sandwiches and salads are also on offer. Open daily while the marina is open (typically late May to early Sept).

Flagg Ranch

While rarely a destination in its own right, *Flagg Ranch* makes a convenient pit stop for hungry, car-bound visitors travelling between Grand Teton and Yellowstone.

Bear's Den Restaurant Inside the resort's main lodge building, this intimate spot dishes out sauteed trout ($20), beef stew ($13) and three kinds of steaks ($26–34), alongside a limited wine list. Full breakfasts and a menu of extensive lunch items (all under $11) are also available, while a seat near the fireplace in the attached *Burnt Bear Saloon* is the perfect place for a post-dinner drink and chat.

Jackson Lake Lodge

The park's most famous lodge is home to two terrific restaurants and a bar with unparalleled views, all located off the second floor's grand lobby.

Blue Heron Lounge The park's prime spot for a sunset drink also serves small plates ($6–7) nightly, encompassing everything from chips and salsa to mozzarella olive focaccia. Find a spot at the enclosed bar or recline on the back deck with a craft beer or cocktail, all the better to watch hues of blue, pink and purple glow off Mount Moran across Jackson Lake.

Mural Room This sizeable restaurant is aptly named for the Old West murals covering one side wall, with huge picture windows affording mind-bending views of the Tetons on the other. While certainly no bargain – a few mains are priced at $33 and up – the dinner menu comprises an array of meat and seafood dishes, including such unique concoctions as molasses-spiced elk loin. Lunch mains ($11.50–14) are nearly as inventive, and there's a superb breakfast buffet ($14.50) on offer each morning. Reservations available on ☎307/543-3463.

Pioneer Grill Open all day and home to one long snaking counter, this often-buzzing room is a park classic, with clever takes on standbys such as meatloaf (bacon-wrapped; $16) and turkey sandwiches (served on croissant with sun-dried tomato/pesto spread; $8.75) that far outshine the diner's absence of views. Unless you've got a team in tow to help you mount an assault on the hilariously messy ice-cream-and-cookie dessert called the Mount Owen ($7.25), go the simple route and top things off with a marshmallow-rich Teton Treat (under $2). Come morning, the un-missable breakfast item is the fluffy pair of huckleberry pancakes served with blueberry syrup ($7.50).

Moose

Moose's dining options are located across the Snake River in the privately owned Dornan's complex, where along with the choices listed below, *Moose Trading Post & Deli* is a great place to grab sandwiches for nearby hiking, biking and rafting outings.

The Chuckwagon A summer-only outdoor affair known for all-you-can-eat sourdough pancakes ($9.75) at breakfast and heaping platters of ribs, bbq chicken, steak or trout – all served with loads of sides – at dinner ($18.50–25). The riverside picnic tables make for wonderful dining spots, although the food at lunch and dinner can be hit-and-miss.

The Pizza Pasta Company This cheery spot bakes delicious calzones ($9) and pizzas ($16), along with pastas, meatball sandwiches and salads. Although there's a full bar inside, most visitors head to the upstairs deck set in the shadow of the Tetons, where an alfresco pizza paired with a bottle of wine from the superb Wine Shoppe next door is a local post-hike tradition.

Teton Park Road

Surprisingly, no dining options exist around bustling South Jenny Lake, save for snacks and coffee at the small *Jenny Lake Store*. Rather, the sole options found along twenty-mile Teton Park Road are to the north, either at swanky *Jenny Lake Lodge* or further up the road at the more down-to-earth *Signal Mountain Lodge*.

Jenny Lake Lodge Dining Room The park's most sophisticated dining venue features a rotating fixed-price menu for breakfast and dinner, plus a remarkably affordable ($10–13) a la carte approach at lunch. Breakfast is $22, while dinner prices include wine pairings and range wildly depending on the main course and wine varietal: a grilled elk chop with an Italian chianti runs a mere $49, while braised beef short ribs paired with a Bordeaux will set you back $125. As can be expected at such premium pricing, service is impeccable; jackets are recommended for dinner, and reservations (☎307/733-4647) are required for breakfast, lunch and dinner. Request a window-side table, if available.

The Peaks A bit on the musty side, *Signal Mountain Lodge*'s dinner-only restaurant features a menu rich with the region's standard meat and fish fare ($23–31) alongside the odd vegetarian main (ratatouille, $20). Its best attribute, however, may be the extraordinary views across Jackson Lake. Call ☎307/543-2831 for reservations.

Trapper Grill Next door to *The Peaks*, *Trapper Grill* has a solid breakfast menu anchored by a range of omelettes and skillet meals ($10–11); lunch and dinner consists of the standard range of burgers, salads and sandwiches, all in the $8–14 range. Nearby, the one-room *Deadman's Bar* has one of Grand Teton's few televisions, though most visitors will find that its lakeside deck provides far better entertainment.

Park programmes and tours

C onsidering the wealth of must-see sights and tantalizing outdoor activities within the parks, it's easy to overlook the **ranger programmes** on offer. Don't, as attending even the shortest programme can add great overall insight, plus the opportunity to grill Yellowstone and Grand Teton's finest for insider know-how. Easiest to attend are the lectures and walks organized by the main visitor centres, which are on the short side but still packed with useful tidbits on all sorts of subjects. Similarly, **fireside chats** held throughout the summer at nearly all park campgrounds are worth attending, both for the congenial atmosphere – don't be surprised if an older ranger wills everyone into a sing-along session – and the informative lectures. Free and fun, these programmes require no reservations, allowing you to simply show up and take part.

If you're looking to delve more deeply into a particular topic or activity, you'll need to do some advance planning. With topics ranging from ancient supervolcanoes to re-introduced wolves, it comes as no surprise that several organizations concentrate on comprehensive **interpretive tours** and **courses**, as well as **activity-based tours**. Leading the charge is the phenomenal **Yellowstone Association**, offering more than four hundred field seminars and guided trips per year; attending any of them can turn out to be a trip highpoint. Along with letting you hobnob with like-minded visitors, guides are exceedingly knowledgeable and plugged into the local network, where news such as recent wolf or grizzly sightings travels fast. Quality gear is supplied as well, giving access to items such as expensive telescopes.

Several companies in the area also offer **general tours** of both parks. As most of them attempt to cover too much territory in too short a time, they're only advisable for visitors without their own transportation.

Ranger programmes and evening entertainment

Along with the **ranger programmes** listed below, the main visitor centres in both parks offer an excellent selection of lectures, films and short ranger walks. These include programmes such as tours around Old Faithful's Geyser Hill, a ten-minute lecture at Artist Point at the Grand Canyon of the Yellowstone and a wildflower walk along the floor of Jackson Hole; we've listed some of the best examples throughout the park tour chapters. Most programmes run from early summer until Labor Day (first Monday in September), with a limited selection available during the autumn and winter seasons – check park websites or the newspapers handed out at entrance gates for current listings. Fireside chats provide most of Yellowstone and Grand Teton's **evening entertainment**, though park hotels will often run slide shows or hire an evening piano player; the various bars throughout both parks, meanwhile, can be pleasant stops for chatting over a nightcap.

Fireside chats Held in amphitheatres and firepits within walking distance of most campgrounds throughout Yellowstone and Grand Teton, ranger-hosted fireside chats are a terrific way to end a day of exploration. Usually at least an hour in duration, these discussions/slideshows cover all manner of subjects, from geological history to wildflower spotting; weekly schedules are clearly posted at each campground. Most kick off around 9–9.30pm, save for the more family-oriented discussions at Norris in Yellowstone and Lizard Creek in Grand Teton, which generally start a couple of hours earlier. Bring a torch or headlamp for

the walk back, and wear warm clothing – the fires are typically small and used more for atmosphere rather than as a heat source. **Junior Ranger Program** Geared toward youngsters whose family plans to be in Yellowstone for at least a few days, the park's Junior Ranger Program is open to all kids aged 5–12. For $3, each child receives a twelve-page activity guide featuring a wildlife-spotting checklist and a list of objectives, including goals such as hiking a trail and attending a ranger programme. The programme is headquartered at the Madison Information Station, though kids can join at most visitor centres and ranger stations. Upon completing the requirements, participants are then "sworn in" by a ranger in a quick and fun ceremony, and receive one of three patches depending on age and season. Grand Teton runs a similar programme ($1) out of its Craig Thomas (Moose) and Colter Bay visitor centres through which participants aged 8 –12 can earn a "Young Naturalist" patch.

Yellowstone Association

The **Yellowstone Association** (☎307/344-2294, ⓦwww.yellowstoneassociation.org) is an invaluable resource for all park visitors, from first-timers to lifelong Yellowstone devotees. The nonprofit organization operates in partnership with the National Park Service, with all net proceeds funnelled directly into the park; since the Association's founding in 1933, it has provided Yellowstone with nearly $25 million in educational services and products.

For several decades, the Yellowstone Association **Institute** has offered courses on the park's natural and cultural history. Headquartered at the Buffalo Ranch in Lamar Valley, classes typically run one to four days in length and are led by a cast of experts that include local biologists, naturalists and professors, as well as highly respected authors and artists. Along with popular **field seminars** on wolf-watching and wildlife photography, an extensive selection of more esoteric courses covering the likes of bats, wilderness essay-writing and even Yellowstone's "ghost hotels" have been offered at various points – check the Association's website for a current listing. Course rates start at around $200, with discounts given to members (see below). Also available are a selection of **multi-day backcountry trips**, on which visitors hike alongside expert locals such as park historian and waterfall expert Lee Whittlesey, as well as private, topic-specific interpretive tours of the park ($495 per day for up to five participants; larger groups welcome). For overnight courses, you can either **stay** in a rustic three-person cabin at the Buffalo Ranch ($30 per night; propane heater provided; bring your own bedding or sleeping bag) or arrange your own accommodation in a park hotel or campground.

Even if you won't be joining a class or seminar, consider becoming a member either online or at any of the nearly dozen Association-operated bookstores scattered across the park and in gateway towns. Tax-deductible **membership** rates start at $35, and with the Park Service limping through continued budget cuts, the money will certainly be well spent.

PARK PROGRAMMES AND TOURS

Ranger Adventure Hikes From mid June until September, rangers in both parks lead several hikes that go far beyond the average boardwalk tour both in distance and depth of discussion. These free excursions head anywhere from three to eight miles into the backcountry at an easy pace as rangers stop frequently to answer questions and point out important natural features. Top picks include the steep trail up Avalanche Peak (**H21**, see p.128) and the mellower Beaver Ponds loop (**H3**, see p.116), both in Yellowstone, and a pleasant amble through Grand Teton's Laurence S. Rockefeller Preserve to Phelps Lake (containing elements of **H40**, see p.142). Most hikes begin no later than 8.30am, while reservations are always recommended and often required; consult park newspapers and websites for details and current offerings.

Interpretive tours and courses

Offering much more than simply general tours that stick to the highways and boardwalks within the parks, the companies and NGOs listed below specialize in **interpretive tours and courses** that zero in on a particular animal, historical subject or geological oddity. Scores of outfitters throughout the region lay claim to leading expert-run excursions within Yellowstone or Grand Teton, and while many of them undoubtedly do, the following all come highly recommended and can be counted on for an enjoyable time spent exploring and learning.

A Naturalist's World ☎406/848-9458, ⓦwww.tracknature.com. Based in Gardiner, A Naturalist's World focuses on the art of animal tracking. Co-owner James Halfpenny has written several books on the subject (as well as the superb *Yellowstone Wolves in the Wild* – see p.273), and is regarded as one of the country's pre-eminent trackers. Halfpenny leads most of the classes, including several winter courses when animal tracks in the snow are far easier to follow; rates start at $225 for a two-day course.

Teton Science Schools ☎307/733-1313, ⓦwww.tetonscience.org. Split between a wooded main campus north of Kelly near Grand Teton's eastern border and a much newer set of buildings less than two miles from Jackson, Teton Science Schools features courses ranging from multi-day seminars to year-long graduate programmes. Founded in 1967, the organization's immensely popular "Wildlife Expeditions" programme (☎1-877/404-6626) offers biologist-led half-day ($125–135) and full-day tours ($175–295) within Grand Teton and Yellowstone. Multi-day tours themed around the likes of winter wolf-watching and the autumn mating season are also offered.

Yellowstone Safari Co. ☎406/586-1155 or 1-866/586-1155, ⓦwww.yellowstonesafari.com. Founded by Bozeman-based naturalist and historian Ken Sinay in 1990, Yellowstone Safari Co.'s upbeat private tours aren't particularly cheap – a full-day interpretive tour of Yellowstone starts at $650 for two, with rates rising about $100 for each additional guest – but each can be custom-designed. Half-day to multi-day safaris within the park are offered, as are snowshoe tours in winter and overnight backcountry hiking tours along the Bechler River and through the Black Canyon of the Yellowstone in summer.

Activity-based tours

While the interpretive tour companies listed above can also organize **backcountry hiking** trips, we've included a handful of additional hiking outfitters below, along with companies dedicated to boating and biking. Details on **fly-fishing outfitters** that conduct day-trips or longer excursions can be found in the box on p.160; likewise, for more information on the two exceptional **climbing schools** leading trips in Grand Teton, see p.168.

Big Wild Adventures ☎406/848-7000, ⓦwww.bigwildadventures.com. Based north of Gardiner in Emigrant, Montana, Big Wild Adventures runs nearly a half-dozen summer hiking trips deep into Yellowstone's backcountry, along with expeditions penetrating the wilds of the nearby Absaroka and Wind River Mountains. Prices for a week average $1700 per person, including food, all gear, guides and transportation to the trailheads and back, but you can save $200 by bringing your own hiking equipment or booking two trips in one year.

Rendezvous Backcountry Tours ☎307/353-2900 or 1-877/754-4887, ⓦwww.skithetetons.com. Based in the tiny community of Alta, Wyoming, due west of Grand Teton National Park, Rendezvous operates day and overnight tours into the park in both summer and winter. Hiking trips in summer are led by naturalist guides and range from casual half-day ambles over six miles ($225) to three-day treks along the renowned Teton Crest Trail ($585). More unique are the company's winter offerings, particularly its multi-day cross-country ski and snowshoe extravaganzas ($540–1170) that allow participants to stay in private yurts fitted with bunk beds, kitchens, wood-burning stoves, propane lanterns and private latrines, all set above 8000ft along powdery Teton routes. Rates include meals but no gear rentals.

Snake River Kayak & Canoe ☎307/733-9999 or 1-800/529-2501, ⓦwww.snakeriverkayak.com. Jackson's top provider of paddling adventures offers a long list of guided tours in the area, including whitewater adventures on the Snake River south of Jackson ($75–125) and several Yellowstone Lake tours that range from memorable sunset paddles ($125) to four-day expeditions ($950); multi-day trips to Lewis and Shoshone Lakes ($400–850) are also offered throughout summer. Trip guides are affable long-time locals, while a kayak rolling clinic ($45) – offered in a heated, indoor pool – is a terrific way to get comfortable in your own vessel before taking to the currents yourself.

Teton Mountain Bike Tours ☎307/733-0712 or 1-800/733-0788, ⓦwww.tetonmtbike.com. This Jackson-based company operates bike tours up to five days in length in the parks and the surrounding national forests. Shorter trips include an easy eight-mile pedal across Antelope Flats ($60) and a tour of the Old Faithful area running up to fifteen miles ($150); rates include bikes and transportation to and from Jackson.

General park tours

Since most visitors explore the parks with their own transportation in non-snow seasons, there's not an overwhelming need for **general park tours** in summer. The excursions offered by the following companies are mostly hurried loops through a section of Yellowstone or Grand Teton; these tours may cover a lot of territory in a relatively short amount of time, but they leave little scope for exploration or investigation, and they're best left for those without transportation or with very little time to spend in the area. For tours starting outside either park, you'll need to tack on the parks' entrance fee to the overall price if you haven't purchased a pass. For winter tours, see Chapter 7, "Winter activities".

Buffalo Bus Touring Company 415 Yellowstone Ave, West Yellowstone ☎406/646-9564 or 1-800/426-7669, ⓦwww.yellowstonevacations.com. Operated by Yellowstone Vacations, these tours pile visitors into banana-yellow buses and whisk them around the park's Upper and Lower Loops. A tour of one loop costs $65 (both loops, $120), with free hotel and campground pick-up available.

Grand Teton Lodge Company ☎307/543-2811 or 1-800/628-9988, ⓦwww.gtlc.com. The schedule of narrated bus tours offered by Grand Teton's main concessionaire is surprisingly thin, with only a half-day excursion around Grand Teton ($38) and a full-day Yellowstone version ($68) available; each is offered three times weekly in high season.

Gray Line of Jackson Hole ☎307/733-4325 or 1-800/443-6133, ⓦwww.graylinejh.com. Picking up from all accommodation within Jackson and Teton Village ($10 extra for the latter), Gray Line runs full-day narrated bus tours of Grand Teton and Yellowstone's Lower Loop. Excursions are priced at $115, with a $15 discount for booking both.

Xanterra ☎307/344-7311, ⓦwww.travelyellowstone.com. Yellowstone's biggest concessionaire runs several park tours, most departing from accommodation centres at Mammoth, Lake and Old Faithful Villages. The overly ambitious "Yellowstone in a Day" outing ($68) takes 10.5 hours to complete the Grand Loop's circuit; other options include a five-hour "Photo Safari" ($81) and a two-hour sunset drive around Yellowstone Lake, each of which rolls along in a historic 1937 touring bus.

Out of the Parks

Out of the Parks

⑪ Jackson and around..201

⑫ West Yellowstone and Big Sky............................215

⑬ Gardiner and the Paradise Valley........................228

⑭ Cooke City and around 234

⑮ Cody and around 238

Jackson and around

Named in 1829 for renowned trapper and mountain man Davey Jackson, **Jackson Hole** is a broad river basin, hemmed in by the Gros Ventre mountains to the east and the Tetons to the west; it measures 48 miles north to south and varies between five and ten miles across. In the nineteenth century, "Hole" was a noun often employed to describe high mountain valleys, and indeed the Rockies were once peppered with "Holes". Tucked in at the south end of Jackson Hole is the town of **JACKSON**. To describe Jackson as an anachronism in the cowboy state of Wyoming is to put the situation mildly: art galleries, fine restaurants, flashy boutiques and gift stores dominate many retail spaces here, and it's fair to say that not everyone who visits is terribly enamoured of the moneyed-vacation culture upon which the town thrives. Happily, however, much of the laidback neighbourhood surrounding the tiny downtown still consists largely of simple cottages, betraying little evidence of the vast fortunes tied up in local real estate.

Clogged with visitors throughout summer, Jackson sits a few miles east of the Snake River, a similar distance south of Grand Teton National Park and 57 miles south of Yellowstone's South Entrance. Winter, while more sedate, draws heavy ski and snowboard crowds; Jackson's in-town ski hill is **Snow King**, while the more famous **Jackson Hole Mountain Resort** is a twenty-minute drive northwest of town, with a cluster of accommodation and services at **Teton Village** based at the bottom of its slopes. Bordering Grand Teton National Park, the resort's runs are wild enough to attract the occasional foraging moose, but visitors should save their wildlife spotting for the lifts, as they'll have plenty of other obstacles – boulders, bumps and steep bowls – to worry about while skiing or snowboarding. A third ski area, easy-going **Grand Targhee**, is about an hour's drive away near the Idaho border.

There's no question the Jackson area has become quite affluent since the 1990s, and spearheading this evolution from Wild West to Mild West has been a spate of openings by a number of **high-end hotels**, none bigger than Teton Village's slopeside *Four Seasons*. In town itself, dozens of art galleries line downtown streets, and the range of eating and nightlife options is easily the region's widest – and priciest. Unlike in similar Western glamour destinations such as Aspen, Sun Valley and Park City, however, Jackson's super-rich dress and act like regular folk, and in the main live in relative seclusion on ranches several miles from town. Thankfully, an outdoors-oriented atmosphere of jeans, shorts and fleece jackets still rules the day, and locals are generally friendlier than you'd expect from a place where they're often outnumbered by tourists.

JACKSON

East Gros Ventre Butte

Flat Creek

Snow King

EATING AND DRINKING

Billy's	3
Bubba's Bar-B-Que	10
The Cadillac Grille	3
Café Genevieve	6
Creekside Meats, Market & Deli	1
The Merry Piglets	2
Million Dollar Cowboy Bar	4
Pearl Street Bagels	8
Rendezvous Bistro	12
Silver Dollar Bar	5
Silver Dollar Grill	5
Snake River Brewing	11
Thai Me Up	9
Town Square Tavern	7

ACCOMMODATION

49er Inn and Suites	H
The Alpine House Inn & Cottages	B
Amangani	I
Anvil Motel	C
Jackson Hole Lodge	G
The Lexington at Jackson Hole	A
The Lodge at Jackson Hole	K
Painted Buffalo Inn	F
Rendezvous Bistro	
Sundance Inn	E
The Wort Hotel	D
Wyoming Inn of Jackson Hole	J

Teton Theater

Police Station

Center for the Arts

Jackson Hole Twin Cinema

Jackson Hole Museum

TOWN SQUARE

Teton County Fairgrounds

Library

Albertsons supermarket

0 — 200 yds

● ⓘ National Elk Refuge, National Museum of Wildlife Art (3 miles), Grand Teton (5 miles) & Airport ▲

● ⓘ Wilson, Teton Village, Jackson Hole Mountain Resort & Grand Targhee ▲   ▼ Hoback Junction

Arrival, information and getting around

Jackson's charming **airport** is actually within Grand Teton National Park, eight miles to the north. AllTrans provides **airport shuttle** service ($16 one-way to Jackson, $26 to Teton Village; ☎307/733-3135 or 1-800/443-6133, ⓦwww .jacksonholealltrans.com), as does a host of **taxi** services charging around $32 for a ride to Jackson and $55 to Teton Village; try Teton Taxi at ☎307/733-1506. The **Jackson Hole and Greater Yellowstone Visitor Center**, 532 N Cache St (daily: May–Sept 8am–7pm; rest of year 9am–5pm; ☎307/733-3316, ⓦwww.fs.fed.us/jhgyvc), has an ATM, restrooms, a good bookstore and loads of local information. Indeed, it's an experience in itself, with excellent taxidermy displays and helpful staff representing a variety of agencies, including the Jackson Hole Chamber of Commerce and the National Park Service. Very nearby, **Bridger–Teton National Forest Headquarters**, 340 N Cache St (Mon–Fri 8am–4.30pm; ☎307/739-5500), has details on hiking and camping in the nearby Gros Ventre.

Transport around Jackson Hole is provided by START buses (☎307/733-4521, ⓦwww.startbus.com), which run along five colour-coded routes from roughly 6.30am–10pm daily; grab a timetable on board or from the information centre, however, as service varies seasonally. Rides within the town of Jackson are free, while trips to Teton Village are $3 single.

Accommodation

Jackson's **accommodation** scene is split in two, with a large chunk located in town and another, smaller set of lodges huddled around the ski slopes in Teton Village. During the busy summer season, there are very few bargains to be had in town, while the odd deal can be found at one of the mainly high-end options by the slopes. Conversely, once skiers and snowboarders start arriving, slopeside rooms are at a premium, while in-town rates drop by up to thirty percent, meaning a basic motel room can become an exceptional value come winter. If you're here to **ski or snowboard**, it's easy enough to stay in town and commute to *Jackson Hole Mountain Resort*, though many find the convenience of sliding straight to the lifts worth Teton Village's higher winter rates.

Town Square Inns (☎1-800/483-8667, ⓦwww.townsquareinns.com) manages several hundred rooms spread over four mid-range motel properties in central Jackson, and is worth contacting if you can't find a room yourself at any of the places recommended below. *Jackson Hole Resort Lodging* (☎307/733-3990 or 1-800/443-8613, ⓦwww.jhrl.com) manages a full range of accommodation around Teton Village, from basic motel rooms to condos, townhouses and larger cabins.

What little **hostel** accommodation and **camping** there once was in Jackson itself has fallen by the wayside in recent years. The nearest hostel is now in Teton Village (see below), while those looking to pitch a tent will similarly have to trek well out of town, either to Grand Teton's huge *Gros Ventre Campground* (see p.188) or a pair of easily accessed Forest Service facilities, *East Table Creek* and *Station Creek* (both $15), perched alongside the Snake River about 25 miles south.

Prices listed below reflect the lowest available rate for a double-occupancy room.

Jackson

49er Inn and Suites 330 W Pearl Ave
☎307/733-7550, ⓦwww.townsquareinns.com.
This downtown motel is nothing fancy, but the rooms, decorated in a combination of rustic Western decor and standard motel fittings, are much larger than average. Extras include two very large hot tubs and a skimpy continental breakfast. A few two-room suites are available for larger groups. Summer $85, winter $66.

The Alpine House Inn & Cottages 285 N Glenwood St ☎307/739-1570 or 1-800/753-1421, ⓦ www.alpinehouse.com. Offering cosy B&B accommodation at its original property and newer one- and two-bedroom cottages a few blocks up the street, this delightful country inn is owned and managed by a pair of amiable former winter Olympians. The main house is a Scandinavian-feeling place decked out in blonde timber, with a comfortable reading room and terrific cooked breakfasts worth looking forward to. Their packages – including ski passes or cross-country expeditions – are also good value. Summer $175 (inn) and $325 (cottage), winter $145 and $275.

Amangani 1535 North East Butte Rd ☎307/734-7333 or 1-877/734-7333, ⓦ www.amangani.com. One of only two US properties operated by Singapore's renowned Aman Resorts group, *Amangani* vies with Teton Village's *Four Seasons* for the most luxurious accommodation in the entire region. Its stunning temple-like structure – built from redwood and sandstone, and set high on a butte between town and the slopes – features window-side tubs in every suite, not to mention a heated cliff-side pool. With *nightly* rates ranging between $875–1700 year-round, however, only those with money to burn need consider.

Anvil Motel 215 N Cache St ☎307/733-3668 or 1-800/234-4507, ⓦ www.anvilmotel.com. Situated at one of the busier intersections in town, the *Anvil*'s rooms are small but still in good shape, and the mini-fridge and microwave in each room are useful bonuses. Summer $87, winter $55.

Jackson Hole Lodge 420 W Broadway ☎307/733-2992 or 1-800/604-9404, ⓦ www.jacksonholelodge.com. A range of units is available at this motel-lodge, located about four blocks west of Town Square. Standard rooms are small with either one or two king-size beds, while studio and one-bedroom suites all have full kitchen facilities and can sleep up to six people. Guest amenities include free wireless internet, heated indoor pool, two whirlpool tubs and a sundeck and sauna. Summer $149 (standard) and $269 (suite), winter $89 and $129.

The Lexington at Jackson Hole 285 N Cache St ☎307/733-2648 or 1-888/771-2648, ⓦ www.trapperinn.com. Formerly known as the *Trapper Inn*, this four-building hotel underwent a recent renovation to encompass an even wider range of lodging, from standard rooms ($199) to a full quota of suites ($299) that now make up more than half the property's rooms; all of the former include mini-fridges and microwaves, while a chunk of the latter includes kitchens and fireplaces. There's also laundry and an indoor heated pool and whirlpool, as well as a terrific breakfast spread included in nightly rates, plus free wireless internet. Call or check website for rate deals, as management often prices them by availability.

The Lodge at Jackson Hole 80 Scott Lane ☎307/739-9703 or 1-800/458-3866, ⓦ www.lodgeatjh.com. A little over one mile from the Town Square, this pleasant hotel attracts an equal mix of business clients and vacationing families. It's spread across three attractive log-and-stone lodge buildings, with touches like elk-antler lamps adding life to the good-sized, chain-hotel rooms. There's a buffet breakfast each morning, along with free wireless internet, laundry facilities, a workout room and a heated indoor-outdoor pool. Summer $259, winter $119.

Painted Buffalo Inn 400 W Broadway ☎307/733-4340 or 1-800/288-3866, ⓦ www.paintedbuffaloinn.com. A fairly centrally located mid-range inn with clean facilities. There's nothing particularly outstanding about the 137 standard rooms, but the large heated indoor pool, free wireless internet access and continental breakfast, and on-site lunch café are all welcome amenities. Summer $178, winter $87.

Sundance Inn 135 W Broadway ☎307/733-3444, ⓦ www.sundanceinnjackson.com. This small, basic motel claims a very central location and 25 convenient ground-floor rooms, along with a pair of two-bedroom balcony suites ($219) upstairs that can also be rented as a single gargantuan unit. It's not uncommon to find fruit and pastries set out in the lobby by the friendly managers. Summer $129, winter $79.

The Wort Hotel 50 N Glenwood St ☎307/733-2190 or 1-800/322-2727, ⓦ www.worthotel.com. Built in 1941, the *Wort* is the most venerable – and best – high-end property in town, full of the kind of Old West style many Jackson visitors come seeking;

look no further than each room's micro-detailed door carving for evidence. The old hotel also boasts a comfortable lobby complete with grand staircase, as well as an excellent restaurant (see p.208) and lively bar (see p.209). Rooms and suites are furnished with enormous lodgepole pine beds topped with enough pillows to build a fort, while plush bathrooms sport full-size tubs. Summer $359, winter $229.

Wyoming Inn of Jackson Hole 930 W Broadway ☎ 307/734-0035 or 1-800/844-0035, ⓦ www.wyominginn.com. One of Jackson's better upper mid-range options, the *Wyoming Inn* is completely non-smoking and has complimentary airport shuttle, wireless internet and chocolate chip cookies (and, in winter, soup), plus laundry facilities and a brand-new on-site restaurant. Rooms are tidy, and all suites include a gas fireplace and whirlpool tub; a huge log fireplace gives the high-ceilinged lobby a cosy lodge vibe. Summer $300, winter $120.

Teton Village and around

The Alpenhof Lodge ☎ 307/733-3242 or 1-800/732-3244, ⓦ www.alpenhoflodge.com. A classic Bavarian lodge offering 42 handsomely appointed guest rooms, some with fireplaces and balconies. Amenities include two on-site restaurant options, free wireless internet, heated outdoor pool, hot tub, sauna and a ski shop and spa; an extra-special bonus for canine enthusiasts is the lodge's "Director of Guest Services", Sam the golden retriever, amiably patrolling the lobby. Nightly rates depend on occupancy, but generally hover around $230 year-round, with lower pricing available in shoulder seasons.

Four Seasons Resort Jackson Hole ☎ 307/732-5000, ⓦ www.fourseasons.com /jacksonhole. Even if you're not a guest, Teton Village's largest (and newest) slopeside structure is worth a peek for the rough-hewn stones and native artefacts in its main lounge. Elegant rooms feature marble bathroom fittings and leather couches, while the heated outdoor pool, massive fitness centre and spa, and full ski concierge services are all to be expected for nightly rates starting at $395 in winter and $625 in summer.

The Hostel ☎ 307/733-3415, ⓦ www .thehostel.us. An excellent slopeside budget choice with a raft of terrific amenities thrown in, including a lounge with fireplace, TV and games room, ski lockers and tuning room, microwave oven, coin-operated laundry, and ping-pong, pool and foosball tables; wireless internet is an extra $5. Each private room, containing either four twin bunks or two twins combined, is rented as a unit; all rooms have private bath, and no minimum stay is required. Nightly rates vary somewhat by season though bunk rooms average $25–28 year-round, with double-twins going for an average of just under $80.

The Inn at Jackson Hole ☎ 307/733-2311 or 1-800/842-7666, ⓦ www.innatjh.com. More affordable than most other Teton Village inns (particularly in winter), this lodge has nearly one hundred mid-size standard rooms, along with a few lofts. There's a heated outdoor pool and whirlpool tub, as well as laundry, free wireless internet, an on-site ski tuning shop and the village's popular Japanese restaurant, *Masa Sushi* (see p.208). Summer $199 (standard) and $229 (loft), winter $169 and $219.

The town and around

The main street running east–west through **Jackson** is bustling Broadway, while Cache Street is the north–south divide. Most of the bars, restaurants and services are within four to six blocks of the junction of these two streets, itself the site of Jackson's inviting **Town Square**, a block-wide park marked by an arch of tangled elk antlers at each corner; visitors crowd its lawn and paths for a corny nightly shootout staged here in summer (6.15pm; free). Old West-style boardwalks line the streets that fan out from the square, most filled with low-slung wooden buildings housing galleries, restaurants, boutiques, outfitters and, for those looking for wax figures of celebrities, the bizarre tourist trap that is Ripley's Believe It or Not.

About a fifteen-mile drive to the northwest along Moose-Wilson Road, there's not a great deal to actually see within the hodgepodge cluster of Western lodges and alpine chalets that make up **Teton Village** – though there's plenty of all-season outdoor activity in the immediate area, along with a small handful of worthy eating options. The tiny hamlet of **Wilson**, five miles west of Jackson en route to Teton Village, is of little interest apart from a notable bar and an excellent restaurant; beyond Teton Village is Grand Teton National Park's least-accessed gateway, Granite Canyon Entrance Station, described in detail on p.88.

Jackson Hole Museum

The obligatory Old West exhibit space in town is the small **Jackson Hole Museum** (late May to mid Sept Mon–Sat 10am–6pm, Sun noon–5pm; $3; ☎307/733-2414, ⓦwww.jacksonholehistory.org). Located a short walk from the Town Square at 105 N Glenwood St and topped by a covered wagon, it's no high-end historical venue; the artefacts inside the two-room museum, however, are still diverting enough to warrant a short visit. The collection kicks off with items associated with the local Tukudeka (Sheepeater) tribe, including more than a dozen samples of the type of beads they would trade. Colourful and surprisingly modern-looking, the prized beads – known as "foo-faw" by natives – came from glassworks in China, Italy, France and the former Czechoslovakia. The era of the Mountain Man is similarly represented, with plenty of beaver-hunting gear and traps on display, along with looks at homesteading and early tourism. The collection ends with a nod to locally filmed movies, most notably John Wayne's *The Big Trail* (his first starring role) and *Shane*.

The National Museum of Wildlife Art and National Elk Refuge

Less than three miles north of town along the highway is the hillside **National Museum of Wildlife Art** (Mon–Sat 9am–5pm, Sun 11am–5pm; $12; ☎307/733-5771, ⓦwww.wildlifeart.org, discount coupon available on website), an impressive global collection that trails only Cody's Buffalo Bill Historical Center for best museum in the region. Opened in 1994, the sandstone fortress exhibits a winning mix of classic landscape works alongside bright, modern concoctions such as John Nieto's Day-Glo portraits of a coyote, buffalo and wolf; a number of temporary exhibitions also roll through, so check the museum's website for current showings. The German-born Carl Rungius (1869–1959) is given the most space, with dozens of canvases ranging from his melodramatic early works to the more vivid wildlife paintings featuring abstract backgrounds that he moved on to later in life. Of equal note is the recreated studio of local painter John Clymer (1907–1989), packed with marvellous Western ephemera. Likewise look for the permanent collection documenting the travails of the American bison; it's anchored by Robert Bateman's extraordinary "Chief", which depicts a life-size bull ready to stampede through a foggy canvas.

Elk are obviously the lead attraction across the highway from the museum at the **National Elk Refuge** (☎307/733-9212). Established in 1912 (see p.107 for background), the refuge protects nearly 25,000 acres of prime winter habitat, used by upwards of five thousand elk (and over eight hundred bison) that begin migrating here in November. The animals have literally had to be kept alive through the winter months ever since the town's expansion left them cut off from vital winter feeding areas. Today, forage vegetation is seeded and cultivated on the Refuge, and during the harshest months up to thirty tons of alfalfa pellets are fed to the animals each day. From mid December until early April, you can take an hour-long **sleigh ride** ($18) along Refuge grounds to watch and photograph the elk up close; these tours start from the Jackson Hole and Greater Yellowstone Visitor Center (see p.203). Alongside elk and bison, the Refuge hosts creatures large and small, ranging from moose, bighorn sheep and coyote to nearly 175 species of birds, including trumpeter swans that fly up from the marshes surrounding Flat Creek, just north of Jackson's visitor centre.

Flat Creek is also a favourite for fly-fishermen between August and October; for more on local trout, stop by the **National Fish Hatchery** (free), located just off the highway at the northern end of the Refuge. Around 500,000 cutthroat are raised here annually, and it's possible to watch them spawn one by one between April and June. There's also a free **stocked pond** on site that's ideal for kids, with a catch limit of one trout per day. See p.161 for further details on Jackson-area fishing.

Eating

Jackson's **restaurants** are more or less split between family favourites and fancier spots, with increasingly few options otherwise. Most establishments are located within easy walking distance of Town Square and, regardless of price, have a generally laidback vibe.

Teton Village's **slopeside dining** breaks down in a similar manner. Along with the pricier options reviewed below, there's a decent range of smaller cafés – such as *Cafe 6311* in the Bridger Center and *Village Café* in the Mountainside Mall – that offer quick and affordable breakfasts and lunches. Up the mountain, classy *Couloir* sits atop the gondola route, as does *The Deck*, a more casual destination good for a relaxed drink.

Phone numbers are listed for establishments where it's advisable to reserve ahead.

Jackson

Billy's 55 N Cache St. Attached to the much more sophisticated *Cadillac Grille* (see below), this is nonetheless a cheery place to sit on a barstool and tuck into an enormous cheeseburger ($7 including fries) amid 1950s diner ambience. Open daily for lunch and dinner.

Bubba's Bar-B-Que 100 Flat Creek Drive. The best place in town to gorge on baby back ribs, sandwiches, burgers and steaks, all fairly priced. A 6oz New York steak is dubiously listed among the menu's "Diet Specials", but at least there's a gigantic salad bar ($8) to graze through. Bubba's is also a popular spot for breakfast – you can get a huge omelette with grits, biscuits and coffee for around $10. Open daily 6.30am–9pm.

The Cadillac Grille 55 N Cache St ☎ 307/733-3279. Lovely Art Deco restaurant across from the Town Square offering the same huge burgers as *Billy's*, but also buffalo, wild boar, caribou, antelope and seafood starters for $14–25. The attached bar often hosts a terrific happy hour. Open daily for lunch and dinner.

Café Genevieve 135 E Broadway ☎ 307/732-1910. Housed in a distinctive log cabin listed on the National Register of Historic Places, this welcoming spot cooks up breakfast (all-day), lunch and dinner daily. Lunch is mainly sandwiches and salads ($8–12), while dinner choices range from the usual Rocky Mountain fare – seared Idaho trout ($17), a bacon-wrapped pork chop ($18) – to more offbeat offerings such as shrimp and grits ($19).

Creekside Meats, Market & Deli 545 N Cache St. If heading northbound out of town, don't miss the chance to duck into this nondescript market for a takeaway sandwich. Choose from a number of top-shelf specialty sandwiches ($6–9) listed on the menu, or design your own doorstop lunch by marking your ingredient choices on a sheet provided at the counter, then handing it over to the kitchen staff. A few tables are available if you'd rather eat immediately. Open daily until 3pm; closed Sun in winter.

The Merry Piglets 160 N Cache St ☎ 307/733-2966. Come for the tasty, if unspectacular Mexican mains ($11–20) such as *carnitas* tacos and shrimp enchiladas, and stick around for the vibrant atmosphere and generously sized margaritas, themselves pairing nicely with pretty much anything on the food menu. Open daily for lunch and dinner.

Pearl Street Bagels 145 W Pearl Ave. A constantly hopping spot adored for its fine cappuccinos and, of course, fresh bagels that range from tomato-herb to cinnamon-raisin; there's an outpost in nearby Wilson as well. Free wireless internet. Open daily 6am–6pm.

Rendezvous Bistro 380 S Broadway ☎307/739-1100. This locally heralded alcove on the outskirts of town is known for pork *adobo* ($19), steak frites ($32) and grilled *ahi* tuna ($26), plus inventive nightly specials ($20–36) such as curry lamb stew. A good selection of affordably priced wines add to the bistro's allure. Open daily for dinner.

Silver Dollar Grill The Wort Hotel, 50 N Glenwood St ☎307/733-2190. Although the *Silver Dollar Grill*'s outstanding corn chowder is the menu's justifiable star starter, there are plenty of exceptional main courses also worth pausing your diet for: buttery, pecan-crusted trout ($21); an orange-marinated pork chop ($22); and not least of all, a truly enormous elk burger served on a parmesan bun and topped with brie ($18). Open daily for dinner.

Thai Me Up 75 E Pearl Ave ☎307/733-0005. Wyoming may not be known for Asian fare, but this bustling restaurant is a strong indicator that Jackson locals and visitors refuse to subsist exclusively on trout, bison and mashed potatoes. A range of delightful stir-fry vegetable and noodle dishes ($14–17) – all available with tofu, chicken, beef or shrimp – is well presented, with takeaway and delivery available. Open daily for dinner, weekdays for lunch.

Teton Village and Wilson

The Alpenrose The Alpenhof Lodge, Teton Village ☎307/733-3242. Serving dinner only, the *Alpenhof*'s fine dining restaurant features an extensive wine list and a menu specializing in fondue ($30–42 for two people), along with Western exotica (bison *pfeffer* steak, $35) and modern twists on Old World favourites (*Jägerschnitzel*, $26). Upstairs, the Tyrolean *Alpenhof Bistro* offers far more moderately priced sandwiches, salads and soups for lunch and dinner, plus plenty of seasonal ambience: a cheery log fire come winter and a sunny outdoor patio throughout summer.

Couloir Bridger Gondola summit, Teton Village ☎307/739-2675. Ascend to 9095ft for a four-course mix-and-match meal ($85) anchored by a number of mains, including the chef's specialty, smoked tenderloin of buffalo; you can also make arrangements for the "Chef's Table" option, which seats you and three others in *Couloir*'s kitchen itself. Open for dinner Fri–Sat, with an expanded schedule during the winter holiday season. Reserve well ahead.

Gamefish Snake River Lodge & Spa, Teton Village ☎307/732-6040. Eclectic takes on regional standbys – maple-glazed pork medallions, mint pesto-rubbed lamb rack – populate *Gamefish*'s array of offerings; just be prepared for main-course prices ($30–42) that range nearly as high as the neighbouring peaks. If you'd rather graze for less, small plates ($15 and under) such as a pulled elk quesadilla and even fish and chips are available. Dinner only.

Masa Sushi The Inn at Jackson Hole, Teton Village ☎307/733-2311. Set in a cosy upstairs nook, this consistently thronged Japanese spot prepares two-piece sushi orders ($4.50–6), *udon* bowls ($10–14) and full dinners such as teriyaki chicken and tempura shrimp ($14–18). Open for dinner Tues–Sun.

Nora's Fish Creek Inn 5600 W Hwy-22, Wilson ☎307/733-8288. A popular hangout adored throughout Jackson Hole for generously sized breakfasts of pancakes and omelettes, as well as moderately priced lunches and dinners built around tried-and-true favourites such as prime rib, salmon and trout. Desserts are homemade and especially worth saving room for. Open daily.

Nightlife and entertainment

The year-round tourist trade has made Jackson's nightlife scene the liveliest in Wyoming, but to get the most out of it, it helps to know what's happening on which night, since people tend to pack out one or two places and abandon the rest. Check the free *Jackson Hole Daily* (Ⓦwww.jhnewsandguide.com) for details on live bands and special happy hour sessions. Up in Teton Village, the raucous *Mangy Moose* fills quickly once the lifts shut down, while the mellower **bar 6** at the *Alpenhof Lodge* (see p.205) is better suited to quiet chats.

Beyond pints and pool cues, Jackson has a pair of centrally located **cinemas**: the c.1941 single-screen Teton Theatre (Ⓣ307/733-4939, Ⓦwww.jackson holecinemas.com), just off the Town Square; and Jackson Hole Twin Cinema (same phone and website), across from the post office on Pearl Avenue. Other local cultural activities of note include the varied list of programs (such as dance and theatre) at the **Center for the Arts**, 240 S Glenwood (Ⓣ307/733-4900, Ⓦwww.jhcenterforthearts.org), as well as Teton Village's stalwart **Grand Teton Music Festival** (Ⓦwww.gtmf.org), an annual summer-long series of classical music concerts.

Jackson

Million Dollar Cowboy Bar 25 N Cache Drive Ⓣ307/733-2207. Corny as it may be, just about everyone who visits Jackson ducks in at least once to this hugely touristy Western-themed watering hole. Rites of passage include sitting on one of the saddles at the bar, getting out on the dance floor, shooting pool at one of several tables or even indulging in a little karaoke. Cover most nights is $3–5, with live bands every Fri and Sat.

Silver Dollar Bar *The Wort Hotel*, **50 N Glenwood St** Ⓣ307/733-2190. A fairly relaxed and casual hotel tavern serving fine martinis and margaritas, as well as a limited food menu; don't waste your time counting the silver dollars embedded in the bar-top – there are over two thousand. Call or check the *Wort*'s website for the bar's entertainment schedule, which ranges from mellow country bands to bluegrass. No cover charge.

Snake River Brewing 265 S Millward St. Less than a ten-minute stumble from the Town Square, this lively brewpub is packed solid nightly with locals who lovingly consider it a second home. Mains such as pastas and pizzas run in the $12–15 range and won't send you home hungry, but it's the exceptional desserts and, unsurprisingly, the award-winning beers, that seal the deal. No smoking.

Town Square Tavern 20 E Broadway Ⓣ307/733-3886. With a sizeable patio perched above Broadway and overlooking Town Square, this watering hole is a good place to sit under the stars and knock a few back. The menu sticks to standard-issue pub grub ($7–10), but it's hard to go wrong with a three-hour happy hour (4.30–7.30pm), four pool tables and no cover for regular live entertainment.

Teton Village and Wilson

The Mangy Moose Teton Village Ⓣ307/733-9779. Liberally strewn with Western bric-a-brac, the *Moose* is Jackson Hole's legendary ski-bum hangout, famed for its après-ski happy hours that blurrily segue into rowdy evenings of live rock or reggae. The alfresco upstairs patio is a choice spot most anytime, and while the food isn't the greatest you'll find slopeside, the weekend brunch (10am–2pm) is worth a shot. Cover charges vary wildly depending on performer, though $5–20 is usually a safe bet.

Stagecoach Bar 5755 W Hwy-22, Wilson Ⓣ307/733-4407. A great dive bar that's worth the seven-mile drive from Jackson for its renowned Thursday Disco Night – in the event you packed your c.1977 leisure suit, you're encouraged to wear it – as well as the weekly Sunday appearance by the World Famous Stagecoach Band, featuring none other than Grand Teton skiing pioneer Bill Briggs (see p.103). There's also a terrific happy hour every Tuesday.

Summer activities

More so than in winter, when the local ski resorts buzz with life, **summer activities** in Jackson revolve around the options found within Grand Teton and, to a lesser extent, Yellowstone further to the north. There's still plenty to do hereabouts, however, outside of those activities listed in chapters 4 to 6.

Rafting

There's no doubt that coasting along while gazing up at the magnificent Tetons is a quintessential summer experience here, so we've listed the best companies for relaxing **raft trips** within Grand Teton National Park on p.163. Thrill-seekers, meanwhile, will want to opt for **whitewater-rafting** trips on the Snake River well south of town, where after leaving Jackson Hole, the river's canyon constricts the waterway to produce mostly Class III rapids. You can get drenched throughout summer and even into early autumn, though the Snake's runs are most thrilling (and coldest) from mid May to June. Jackson's top river outfitter is Snake River Kayak & Canoe, 260 N Cache St (☎307/733-9999 or 1-800/529-2501, ⊛www .snakeriverkayak.com), with Dave Hansen Whitewater, 515 N Cache St (☎307/733-6295 or 1-800/732-6295, ⊛www.davehansenwhitewater.com) being another reliable choice. Expect to pay $65–75 for a half-day run, including transportation and waterproof outerwear.

Fishing

The Snake River and its tributaries boast plenty of superb spots to try your hand at **fly-fishing** outside the national parks (see pp.158–162 for details on fishing *in* the parks). Meandering through the National Elk Refuge north of town, **Flat Creek** – Wyoming's sole fly-only waterway – opens to fishermen for three months every August. It's a tricky creek, requiring quiet stalking from the banks and a good selection of dry flies, but its location and beauty are hard to beat. Other worthy rivers in the Jackson area include the stretch of the **Gros Ventre River** below Slide Lake and the **Hoback River** as it flows through its eponymous canyon south of Jackson.

See p.160 in Chapter 6, "Summer activities", for details on Jackson's best fly-fishing shops and outfitters, from which you can also purchase a **Wyoming fishing licence**, required to fish the area's innumerable streams and lakes.

Mountain biking

As **mountain biking** is forbidden on most Yellowstone and Grand Teton trails, dedicated riders must stick closer to Jackson for fat-tyre excitement. Fortunately, there's a wealth of choices, starting with the trails at **Jackson Hole Mountain Resort**, where riders can use the Teewinot Lift to access seven miles of trails catering to all levels of expertise. At the time of writing, the resort was constructing a new five-mile trail network, with an expected completion date of summer 2011. For now, most locals still choose to stick closer to town and ride the slopes at Snow King, part of a free extensive trail network known as the "Backyard Trails"; at the base of the mountain, the **Cache Creek Trailhead** is one of the finest jump-off points, with access to a twenty-plus-mile loop connecting Cache Creek and Game Creek. Also at Cache Creek Trailhead, riders can hop onto the eight-mile Tiny Hagen/Putt-Putt Loop, a route featuring thrilling single-track biking.

The above only scratches the surface for off-trail riding. For more information and/or **bike rentals** ($25–35/day), call in at Jackson's Hoback Sports, 520 W Broadway (☎307/733-5335, ⊛www.hobacksports.com), which runs guided **bike tours** in the Jackson Hole area for $55–85 including equipment, and also sells useful maps of local bike trails. For tours around the Jackson Hole area ranging

1–5 days, contact Teton Mountain Bike Tours (☎307/733-0712 or 1-800/733-0788, ⓦwww.tetonmtbike.com).

Horseriding

Those who fancy **riding horses** can saddle up for a mellow one- or two-hour journey through mountain meadows with Teton Village Trail Rides ($35–55; ☎307/733-2674, ⓦwww.tetonvillagetrailrides.com). More customized rides are available through Mill Iron Ranch, ten miles south of Jackson near Hoback Junction (☎307/733-6390 or 1-888/808-6390, ⓦwww.millironranch.net), which runs trips ($50–160) ranging from simple two-hour trail rides to full-day rides complete with steak dinner and even fly-fishing.

Winter activities

With the region's best range of snowy activities, Jackson makes a prime winter destination, whether or not you choose to head north into the national parks. **Snowshoeing**, **Nordic skiing** and **snowmobiling** each bring in a small share of visitors, but downhill skiing and snowboarding are by far the biggest draws. There could hardly be more contrast between the **three ski resorts**: **Jackson Hole Mountain Resort** is the area's premier mountain with a huge vertical drop and terrain best suited to upper intermediate to expert downhillers, while on the west side of the Tetons, **Grand Targhee** has minimal development and mind-boggling

Jackson Hole's backcountry

Few places, if any, in North America reward **backcountry skiers and snowboarders** as much as Jackson Hole. The backcountry **gates** at Jackson Hole Mountain Resort (JHMR) access merely a portion of the explorable off-piste areas in Bridger-Teton National Forest and Grand Teton National Park, where a wonderland of natural bowls, chutes and thigh-burning runs up to 4000ft in length await. It's also an extremely dangerous area, with none of its wild acreage patrolled and deadly avalanches far too common; if you don't have a partner as well as the appropriate safety equipment and experience, don't even think about heading beyond resort boundaries.

The most popular entry gate, atop Rendezvous Bowl, leads into Cody Bowl and Rock Springs Bowl, from where it's possible to ski back into the lower Hobacks – and for which hooking up with one of JHMR's backcountry **guides** (☎307/739-2779 or 1-800/450-0477) is highly recommended. A full-day tour for a group of four is priced at $795, while a half-day for a similarly sized group costs $665 (morning) and $380 (afternoon). For additional backcountry experience, JHMR operates a few excellent multi-day backcountry **camps** ($450–1100) each winter, covering safety equipment and etiquette along with plenty of off-piste exploring. JHMR also offers guided trips around nearby **Teton Pass** (8429ft), a favourite local backcountry entry point. Accessed via a car park on Hwy-22 just west of Wilson, firmly packed walking leads into a mountain playground of powder-packed bowls than can often be skied as late as June; Jackson Hole Mountain Guides (☎307/733-4979 or 1-800/239-7642, ⓦwww.jhmg.com) also operates one-day tours in this area for $140–285.

A final option (if you've saved your money) is a day of **heli-skiing** into the Snake River, Hoback, Teton and Gros Ventre Ranges with High Mountain Heli-Skiing ($1050/person/day, includes lunch; ☎307/733-3274, ⓦwww.heliskijackson.com), which typically consists of six long, heart-pumping runs totalling 12,000–15,000 vertical feet. However you choose to head out-of-bounds, be sure to check **current conditions** at ⓦwww.skireport.com/wyoming/jacksonhole.

snow statistics. The third choice is smaller, family-friendly **Snow King**, best for night skiing options.

To **rent** ski gear in Teton Village, head for the Bridger Center; visitors can choose from K2, Salomon and Atomic packages at JH Sports Ski Shop (☎307/739-2649), while Hole in the Wall Snowboard Shop (☎307/739-2689) offers demo packages with the latest Burton and Salomon boards. Daily rental rates range from $37.50–54 at both shops, with 20 discounts available by booking in advance at ⓦwww.jacksonhole.com. In Jackson proper, Hoback Sports at 520 W Broadway (☎307/733-5335, ⓦwww.hobacksports.com) carries a full range of quality skis and boards, with rates slightly less than those at Teton Village.

Jackson Hole Mountain Resort

Famed as a top destination for the true skiing or boarding connoisseur, **Jackson Hole Mountain Resort** (☎307/733-2292 or 1-888/333-7766, ⓦwww.jackson hole.com) more than earns its accolades. This *is* a special mountain, arguably the best in the country for confident intermediates and advanced skiers and boarders to challenge themselves on run after run. A full fifty percent of its terrain is rated expert-only, and it boasts an unparalleled vertical drop of 4139ft; many a slider has stepped up to the slopes cocky, only to be left quickly humbled. Respect both the slopes and your abilities, though, and you're in for an epic day exploring the resort's potent mixture of terrain, from silky groomers and deep powder-fields to precipitous bowls and unpatrolled backcountry – just don't expect to wake up feeling pain-free the next morning.

The 2500 acres of Jackson Hole's skiable terrain divides into three areas: moving from right to left on the trail map, there's **Apres Vous Mountain**, the **Casper Bowl** area and much-vaunted **Rendezvous Mountain**, each progressively more difficult. The resort's new **Aerial Tram** – known as "Big Red" to locals and frequent visitors – zips skiers 4139ft up to the spectacular, windblown summit of Rendezvous Mountain (10,450ft) in nine minutes. Once at the top, a snowy nirvana spreads below, including the heralded **Hobacks**, where nothing is off-limits and some two thousand vertical feet of powder fields await. A less speedy trip up the mountain is the eight-person **Bridger Gondola**, which drops off below **Casper Bowl**; here you'll find some of the finest intermediate terrain at the resort, including long, groomed runs such as Easy Does It and Moran Woods, a superb spot to test your tree riding skills. To the north, it takes two quad lifts to access relatively under-skied Apres Vous Mountain (8481ft), a good bet on busy days – especially **Saratoga Bowl**, which hides powder stashes after the rest of the mountain is ridden out. Beyond the resort's five boundary gates lies some of the finest accessible **backcountry** skiing and snowboarding on earth (see box, p.211).

Going for $91 in the heart of the winter season, and $59–78 early and late in the season, **lift tickets** at Jackson Hole are certainly no bargain. Equally frustrating is the fact that multi-day packages don't offer much in the way of discounts; in fact, the only way to really save is by buying one of the ski-and-stay packages offered by Jackson Hole Central Reservations (☎1-888/838-6606, ⓦwww.jacksonholewy.com). Jackson Hole's respected **ski school**, founded by Olympic gold medallist Pepi Stiegler, offers a wider range of programmes than most resorts, and though the mountain isn't at all suited to beginners, the school does offer first-timer courses ($113) and a comprehensive kids' programme, with discounted lift tickets available through each. Beyond the basics, the school also runs plenty of intermediate/advanced **clinics** for those looking to ratchet their skills up a notch.

Grand Targhee

Dominated by the bulky, jagged peak of Grand Teton towering in the background, **Grand Targhee** (☎307/353-2300 or 1-800/827-4433, ⓦwww.grandtarghee .com), 45 miles from Jackson near the Wyoming/Idaho border, is far less daunting than its rugged counterpart Jackson Hole. A quick peek at the trail map reveals an abundance of wide-open intermediate runs spilling down the mountain's two thousand acres, along with a substantial web of beginner routes by the base. Some terrain is suitable for advanced riders only, but this is not a mountain for adrenaline-crazed kamikazes looking to break the sound barrier. Rather, the thrills here are all about blasting through powder, an arcing spray of snow behind you and large swathes of untouched terrain ahead.

Indeed, snow is Grand Targhee's strongest attribute. In an average year, over forty feet of **fresh powder** falls, while in an amazing season, sixty feet will come down. Even with these unreal figures, the resort's slopes remain secluded, as the only other group besides locals and the powder-hound contingency that seems to have already caught on are families, here to take advantage of the relatively affordable prices (an all-day **lift ticket** costs $69), quality ski school and kids-ski-free programmes. It's not all good news at Grand Targhee, however: when storms hang on the surrounding peaks, they tend to wreak havoc on visibility, making it possible to vacation in "Grand Foghee", as locals sometimes call it, for several days and never even spot the Tetons looming above. Off-slope activities are minimal, the nightlife scene is meagre, and nearby **Driggs**, the closest town (twelve miles across the border in Idaho), has few options.

All things considered, it's not surprising then that many visitors base themselves in Jackson 42 miles away and drive over Teton Pass to enjoy Grand Targhee's slopes just for the day. Should you not have a car – or would simply rather leave the perilous mountain driving to an expert – AllTrans operates the Targhee Express ($88 fare includes lift ticket; ☎307/733-1719, ⓦwww.jacksonholealltrans.com), a daily return **shuttle bus service** picking up at various points around Jackson and Teton Village between 7 and 8am, and leaving Grand Targhee at 4.15pm; advance reservations are necessary.

Snow King

Sloping above Jackson's compact downtown, **Snow King** (☎307/733-5200 or 1-800/522-5464, ⓦwww.snowking.com) would look like little more than a pocket-sized playground if placed next to nearby Jackson Hole Mountain Resort. There's a bit more to this three-hundred-acre ski area than meets the eye, however, and it has successfully carved its own happy niche since opening as Wyoming's first ski area in 1939. The mountain is a much more comfortable proving ground for beginners than its world-famous neighbour, and it runs the sole **night skiing** programme in the area, with a pair of lifts staying open until 7pm (Tues–Sat) – a terrific way for visitors to shoehorn as much skiing as possible into their vacation. A full-day **lift ticket** costs $42, while a night skiing ticket is only $20.

Cross-country skiing and snowmobiling

Teton Village's Jackson Hole Nordic Center (daily 8.30am–4.30pm; ☎307/739-2629, ⓦwww.jacksonhole.com) boasts several looping **cross–country ski** trails of variable ability totalling 10.5 miles; a trail pass is $14 and rental packages cost $30, with lessons also available. Far more impressive are the half- and full-day ski tours the Nordic Center leads into adjacent Grand Teton National Park – expect to spend $325 for a full-day tour (including lunch), but considering it's only $55 per additional person, it pays to bring along friends or family. Snowshoe and telemark tours are also available.

Legislation and environmental impact studies have curtailed **snowmobiling** opportunities in certain areas of the region, with the activity's future anybody's guess (see p.175 for details); still, for the time being anyway, you're unlikely to find a more exhilarating locale. Guided tours operated by Jackson Hole Mountain Tours (☎307/733-6850 or 1-800/633-1733, ⓦ www.jacksonholesnowmobile .com) include rides into Yellowstone ($399–419 for two) and over Togwotee Pass east of Grand Teton ($220/person), all featuring unforgettable views. Self-guided rentals ($130–200/day) and multi-day trips into Yellowstone and along the Continental Divide Snowmobile Trail are also available.

Listings

Banks Wells Fargo, 112 N Center St, Jackson. Bank of Jackson Hole, 990 W Broadway, Jackson, also operates a branch location in Teton Village.
Car rental Jackson Hole Airport: Alamo (☎307/733-0671), Avis (☎307/733-3422), Hertz (☎307/733-2272) and National (☎307/733-0671); Jackson: Dollar (☎307/733-9224) and Thrifty (☎307/734-8312).
Hospital St John's Medical Center, 625 E Broadway, Jackson (☎307/733-3636), has the area's only 24hr emergency care.
Internet Teton County Library (see below) has free wireless internet access, as well as a row of 15min-access terminals that are free of charge and in high demand; Albertsons supermarket (see below) and a number of Jackson cafés, including *Pearl Street Bagels* (see p.208), also offer free wireless.

Laundry Broadway Laundry, 850 W Broadway, Jackson (daily 6am–10pm; ☎307/734-7627).
Library Teton County Library, 125 Virginian Lane, Jackson (Mon–Thurs 10am–8pm, Fri 10am–5.30pm, Sat & Sun 1–5pm; ☎307/733-2164).
Pharmacy Inside Albertsons supermarket (see below).
Police 150 E Pearl Ave (☎307/733-1430).
Post office Jackson: 220 W Pearl Ave (Mon–Fri 7.30am–5pm; ☎307/739-1740); Teton Village: Mon–Fri 9.30am–4pm, Sat 9.30am–12.30pm; ☎307/733-3575.
Supermarket Albertsons, 105 Buffalo Way, Jackson (daily 6am–midnight; pharmacy Mon–Fri 9am–9pm, Sat 9am–7pm, Sun 10am–4pm; ☎307/733-5950).
Taxi Snake River Taxi ☎307/732-2221; Teton Taxi ☎307/733-1506.

12

West Yellowstone
and Big Sky

Snug up against Yellowstone's western border, **WEST YELLOWSTONE** is a busy, commercialized grid where family restaurants and motels, souvenir shops and outfitters elbow each other for your business. Unlike Gardiner and Cooke City, Montana's other gateway towns retaining a frontier atmosphere, West Yellowstone's main drags have a tourist-trap vibe and the town's overarching calling is plain: to provide park visitors with comfort and entertainment. In summer the town overflows with tourists, bikers on Harleys and even hot rod conventions, while in winter it becomes a haven for snowmobilers.

Tourism has been West Yellowstone's main economic engine from its founding, when the first stagecoaches made the arduous journey through the area from Monida, Montana, en route to the nascent national park in 1881. In 1907, the town (then called Riverside) became an official park entrance, and the following year, when the Union Pacific's Oregon Short Line Railroad arrived to shuttle tourists in on the Yellowstone Special, it was renamed Yellowstone; the "West" was added twelve years later to avoid confusion with the park. Tourists were provided for by *Murray's Yellowstone Hotel* (now *Madison Hotel*) and a general store operated by Sam and Ida Eagle that still trades under their surname today. With the development of the highway from Bozeman, more and more tourists began arriving by car, and the train service was discontinued in 1960. These days, the handsome former depot is a museum dedicated to regional history.

While the railroad spurred on West Yellowstone's rise, **BIG SKY**, an hour's drive north, can thank air travel for its widespread reputation among outdoor enthusiasts. The resort area has boasted world-class **downhill skiing** and **whitewater rafting** for decades, but the advent of regular flights into nearby Bozeman in the 2000s has seen Big Sky position itself from sleepy Rockies hideaway to Jackson Hole's potential rival, even if the recent recession has hit the area's retail villages particulary hard.

West Yellowstone

Although **"West"**, common shorthand in the region, is not a particularly peaceful place, it's an undeniably handy stopover to stock up on supplies, grab a quick meal and perhaps spend a few nights. There are few points of real interest around town,

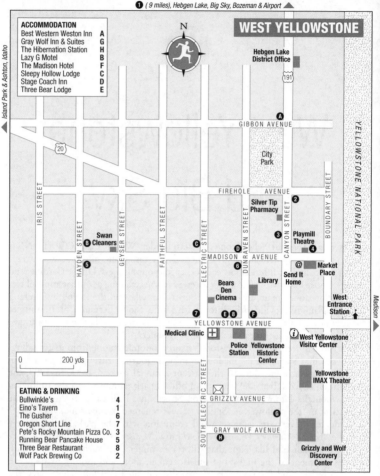

❶ (9 miles), Hebgen Lake, Big Sky, Bozeman & Airport ▲

WEST YELLOWSTONE

ACCOMMODATION
Best Western Weston Inn	A
Gray Wolf Inn & Suites	G
The Hibernation Station	H
Lazy G Motel	B
The Madison Hotel	F
Sleepy Hollow Lodge	C
Stage Coach Inn	D
Three Bear Lodge	E

Hebgen Lake
District Office

GIBBON AVENUE

City Park

FIREHOLE AVENUE

Silver Tip Pharmacy

Swan Cleaners

Playmill Theatre

MADISON AVENUE

Send It Home

@ Market Place

Bears Den Cinema

Library

West Entrance Station

YELLOWSTONE AVENUE

Medical Clinic

Police Station

Yellowstone Historic Center

ⓘ West Yellowstone Visitor Center

Yellowstone IMAX Theater

GRIZZLY AVENUE

GRAY WOLF AVENUE

Grizzly and Wolf Discovery Center

0   200 yds

EATING & DRINKING
Bullwinkle's	4
Eino's Tavern	1
The Gusher	6
Oregon Short Line	7
Pete's Rocky Mountain Pizza Co.	3
Running Bear Pancake House	5
Three Bear Restaurant	8
Wolf Pack Brewing Co	2

but the area's menu of outdoor activities in Yellowstone and the surrounding Gallatin National Forest is superb.

Arrival and information

West Yellowstone is about ninety picturesque miles south of **Bozeman** on Hwy-191, with the turn-off leading up Lone Mountain in **Big Sky** marking the halfway point. Cutting diagonally out of town, Hwy-20 heads west into Idaho over Targhee Pass (7072ft) before turning south through Island Park en route to Ashton fifty miles away. West Yellowstone's town grid is easy to negotiate: Hwy-191 forms the main north–south drag of Canyon Street, which intersects with Yellowstone Avenue leading a block east to Yellowstone's **West Entrance Station** (closed to automobile traffic Nov–April). From the entrance, it's a fourteen-mile drive to Madison, and a little more than twice that to Old Faithful.

It's possible to fly into the town's tiny **Yellowstone Airport** (☎406/646-7631, ⊛www.yellowstoneairport.org) via SkyWest Airlines from early June until late September, but considering connection times and the extra cost, it's wiser to use Bozeman's Gallatin Field Airport (☎406/388-8321, ⊛www.bozemanairport .com), which has more daily services. **Car rental** agencies have desks at both airports and in town (see "Listings" at end of chapter for details). There's no public transportation in town – everything is within walking distance in any case – but Karst Stage ($94 return; ☎406/556-3500 or 1-800/845-2778, ⊛www.karststage .com) runs **shuttle buses** from Bozeman's airport to West Yellowstone; reservations are essential.

The main source for **information** in town is the highly visible West Yellowstone Visitor Center at the corner of Canyon Street and Yellowstone Avenue (late May to early Sept daily 8am–8pm; rest of Sept daily 8am–6pm; Oct to late May Mon–Fri 8am–5pm; ☎406/646-7701, ⊛www.westyellowstonechamber.com), where a National Park Service employee is available to answer questions about Yellowstone during the months the adjacent park entrance is open. Just north of town on Hwy-191 is Gallatin National Forest's **Hebgen Lake District Office** (Mon–Fri 8am–noon & 1–4.30pm; ☎406/823-6961), good for obtaining information on everything from camping to off-road motorcycling on nearby public lands.

Accommodation

Located on the main drag, the *Ho-Hum Motel*'s name succinctly sums up the **accommodation** picture in West Yellowstone: there are plenty of places to stay, but nothing all that exciting. For anything remotely luxurious, you'll need to head north to Big Sky, and if you're planning a summer visit, reserve well in advance. A few places in town shut down in the winter, but most remain open and generally offer substantially reduced rates. There are several **campgrounds** in town, with nearly all geared toward RVs and lacking shade or any sense of privacy. Those pitching a tent should opt instead for Yellowstone's *Madison Campground* (see p.184) fourteen miles to the east, or one of the many campgrounds within Gallatin National Forest – *Baker's Hole* ($14), three miles north on Hwy-191 is closest, followed by several more attractive options around Hebgen and Earthquake Lakes further northwest. Prices listed below reflect the lowest available rate for a double-occupancy room.

Best Western Weston Inn 103 Gibbon Ave ☎406/646-7373 or 1-800/528-1234. The standard motel rooms here could use an update, but they're clean and quiet nonetheless, and reasonably priced at around $100 a night. Amenities include free continental breakfast, heated outdoor pool and hot tub. Open May–Sept.

Gray Wolf Inn & Suites 250 S Canyon St ☎406/646-0000 or 1-877/600-4308, ⊛www .visityellowstonepark.com. This large property is one of the newer inns in town, with spacious, comfortable standard suites, and even larger two-bedroom suites; there's a free continental breakfast, plus a laundry, sauna, small indoor pool and hot tub. Summer $189 (standard) and $369 (suite), winter $79 and $189.

The Hibernation Station 212 Gray Wolf Ave ☎406/646-4200 or 1-800/580-3557, ⊛www .hibernationstation.com. Located on the southern edge of town, this is by far the most eclectic accommodation option in West. Shoehorned onto a couple of sculpture-rich acres are nearly fifty cabins, each individually decorated with themes ranging from the Wild West to a suite known as "The Wizard" for its Gandalf-like carving in the bed frame. Summer prices range from $119 for a basic cabin with a king-size bed to $289 for a two-bedroom family unit with three king-size beds; choice is greatly reduced in winter, when a two-bed cabin goes for $259 and snowmobile rentals are available.

Lazy G Motel 123 Hayden St ☎406/646-7586. Basic and dated wood-panelled rooms that remain some of the best year-round deals in town ($68–79). For $15 more, you can get a simple kitchenette.

Madison Hotel 139 Yellowstone Ave ⓣ406/646-7745 or 1-800/838-7745, ⓦwww .madisonhotelmotel.com. Although it calls itself a hotel, the *Madison* also offers motel and hostel accommodation options to budget-minded visitors. The attractive log-hewn building dates back to 1912 and has four-bunk rooms for $32 each. Rates in the motel (in a separate building) range from $64 for the most basic room to $89 for one with two king-size beds. There's spotty internet access in rooms, with a more reliable signal in the lobby. Open May–Sept.

Sleepy Hollow Lodge 124 Electric St ⓣ406/646-7707, ⓦwww.sleepyhollowlodge .com. A dozen attractive log cabins with fully equipped kitchens; bonuses include a basic continental breakfast, plus a fly-tying bench and guide service for anglers. It's fair value at $119–149 per night (with

off-season discounts in May and Oct), but note that there are no in-room phones. Open May–Oct.

Stage Coach Inn 209 Madison Ave ⓣ406/646-7381 or 1-800/842-2882, ⓦwww.yellowstoneinn .com. One of the town's oldest buildings, this block-long inn features straightforward hotel rooms, a pleasant lobby and reading area, two indoor hot tubs, laundry facilities and the attached *Coachman Bar and Casino* (with nightly poker games). Discounts are available through website bookings, and there's a free continental breakfast each morning. Summer $134, winter $80.

Three Bear Lodge 217 Yellowstone Ave ⓣ406/646-7353 or 1-800/646-7353, ⓦwww .threebearlodge.com. A warm lodge featuring sizeable standard rooms (some with balconies) fitted with king-size beds and hand-carved wood furnishings, as well as two-room family units that sleep six. Summer $159 (standard) and $189 (suite), winter $89 and $119.

The town and around

West Yellowstone is small enough to wander around quite easily, although peak-season crowds can lead to a certain amount of ducking and weaving on pavements. Along with a flood of trinket and T-shirt shops, the town's biggest visitor draw is the **Grizzly and Wolf Discovery Center**, 201 S Canyon St (summer daily 8.30am–6pm, call for seasonal hours; $10.50; ⓣ406/646-7001, ⓦwww.grizzlydiscoveryctr .org) – the one place in the region you're guaranteed to see grizzly bears. The centre houses "problem" grizzlies and non-native Kodiak bears that had either become addicted to raiding garbage cans or were orphaned at a young age and, thus, could no longer live safely in the wild. Though it's rather sad seeing these animals hemmed in by fences, proponents of the centre rightfully argue that the only other option is to have them put down. You can get up to within a few feet of the bears, while inside there are some very good interpretive and taxidermy displays, as well as shocking photos of illegally obtained bear gallbladders, sold for upwards of $20,000 in Asia for their alleged medicinal wonders. Opposite the bears' pen is another smaller enclosure, home to a grey wolf pack born in captivity, though their inclusion feels rather tacked on. Next door, the **Yellowstone IMAX Theater** (daily May–Sept 8.30am–9pm, call for seasonal hours; $9; ⓣ1-888/854-5862, ⓦwww.yellow stoneimax.com) regularly projects *Yellowstone* – a visually appealing feature that nonetheless ineffectively attempts to squeeze the park's geological and human history into forty minutes – onto a six-storey screen.

Around the corner on Yellowstone Avenue, the **Yellowstone Historic Center** (daily: early May to early Oct 9am–9pm; $5; ⓣ406/646-7461, ⓦwww.yellow stonehistoriccenter.org), housed in the 1908 Union Pacific Depot, is much more worthwhile; the building itself – beautifully renovated all the way down to the original ticket window – is perhaps the main attraction. Exhibits focus on the early years of tourism in the park, including a day-by-day description of the Grand Tour visitors once took via stagecoach, while other exhibits spotlight the fires of 1988 (see p.77) and the catastrophic earthquake that struck north of here in 1959 (see "Earthquake Lake", below). Perhaps most popular is the stuffed bear known as Snaggletooth, a one-thousand-pound grizzly who famously roamed the town with a crooked grin in the 1960s before being illegally shot. Though not part of the museum, take a moment to admire the equally attractive buildings to the west – designed by eminent national park architect Gilbert Stanley Underwood – that were also part of the depot during its working heyday.

Hebgen and Earthquake Lakes

It's a delightful eight-mile drive north on Hwy-191 between thickly timbered hillsides to the Hwy-287 turn-off leading to **Hebgen Lake**. A hangout for fishermen, boaters and even windsurfers, the shores of the idyllic lake boast aspen groves, helping make it a lovely photo spot come late September and early October. To the west is four-mile-long **Earthquake Lake**, and a cursory glance at the dead trees poking above its surface indicates that it's no ordinary lake. Indeed, there wasn't even a lake here until August 17, 1959, when an **earthquake** measuring 7.5 on the Richter Scale released a vast slide of rock, damming the Madison River Canyon. Twenty-eight people camping in the area were killed, while back up the road, Hebgen Lake's north shore dropped by eighteen feet, causing a tidal wave to race down the lake and sweep over Hebgen Dam; incredibly, the dam held under the pressure. The tragic incident is remembered at the **Earthquake Lake Visitor Center** on Hwy-287 at the west end of Earthquake Lake, around 25 miles from West Yellowstone (daily: June–Aug 8.30am–6pm; $3; ☎406/682-7620), from where there's a good view of the scene and plenty of interpretive placards. As it stands, the lake is slowly receding and will be gone within two hundred years.

Eating and drinking

When it comes to **food** and **drink**, West Yellowstone doesn't offer much in the way of fanciness. However, if you're in the market for a heaped plate of huckleberry pancakes to start the day, or an affordable, filling dinner for the entire family come evening, you're in the right place. There are several bars dotted about, but the most popular evening entertainment in summer is a town stroll, rapidly melting ice-cream cone in hand; once winter arrives, sled-heads bar-crawl via snowmobile, buzzing from place to place before getting too buzzed to continue. Along with the IMAX theatre, the single-screen Bears Den Cinema, 15 N Electric St (☎406/646-7777), plays first-run Hollywood **movies**, while the Playmill Theatre, 29 Madison Ave (☎406/646-7757, @www.playmill.com), has been putting on stage performances nightly throughout summer for several decades. Phone numbers are listed for establishments where it's smart to reserve seating ahead of time.

Bullwinkle's 19 Madison Ave. Named after the huge bull-moose head hanging above the dining room, this relaxed restaurant and sports bar is one of West's most popular. The sprawling menu includes pub grub ($9 burgers), pastas ($13–21) and a selection of steaks and chops, although the best items might be the rainbow trout and baked walleye fish (both $20) and the welcome range of meal-sized salads ($10–15).

Eino's Tavern 8955 Gallatin Rd ☎406/646-9344. This rustic roadhouse is nine miles north of town, poorly signed just past the Hwy-287 turn-off to Hebgen Lake. It's a favourite of beer-drinking fishermen and snowmobilers, with decor consisting of hundreds of signed dollar notes taped virtually everywhere. As for food, you grill it yourself in a mottled open kitchen – burgers are about $5 per pound, steaks run $15 and up, and you know whom to blame if your meal is ill-cooked. Definitely one of a kind, all the way down to its hours of operation, so call ahead to make sure it's open.

The Gusher 40 Dunraven St. One of the top spots in town for quick, no-hassle eats. Friendly counter service pairs with a solid range of pizzas ($16–25), sandwiches (around $10) and even salads and vegetarian dishes (around $11), plus takeaway and free delivery.

Oregon Short Line 315 Yellowstone Ave ☎406/646-7365. West's most sophisticated dining alternative offers Rocky Mountain cuisine: Idaho trout ($22), elk medallions ($36) and the like. Before sitting down to eat, take a walk through the perfectly preserved 1903 railcar next to the entrance, or have a drink in the attached *Iron Horse Saloon*. Dinner only.

Pete's Rocky Mountain Pizza Co. 104 Canyon St. A busy family restaurant with a varied menu of pastas ($11.50–15) – order the spaghetti with either meatballs or hot Italian elk sausage – as well as build-your-own-combo pizzas for $14–23.

Running Bear Pancake House 538 Madison Ave. Open daily for breakfast and lunch, this is the first place to come for a filling, affordable breakfast; most items are under $10. The affable servers' most popular order is the plate-sized pancakes served with huckleberry syrup, though both the omelettes and biscuits and gravy are tasty as well. Lunch options are less remarkable and include sandwiches, fish and chips, and a few Mexican dishes best avoided.

Three Bear Restaurant 215 Yellowstone Ave ☎406/646-7811. A bustling restaurant boasting a cosy log interior, with old black-and-white photos and assorted artefacts on the walls. The food is good, if predictable for the region – sandwiches and burgers ($7–13) and pastas ($14–20), plus pricier steaks and chops ($20–30); be sure to save room for the Apple Brown Betty a la Mode dessert. Open for breakfast (from 6.30am) as well.

Wolf Pack Brewing Co 139 N Canyon St. West Yellowstone's own brewing company offers` a range of traditional beers heavy on hoppy flavours. There's a limited menu as well, but the beer is the main draw.

Outdoor activities

Despite the obvious attractions of the national parks, you may want to get out and play outside its boundaries, not least because there are **fewer restrictions** here on what you can do – snowmobilers can buzz along independently without a guide, mountain bikers find more trails open to them and anglers are faced with fewer fishing regulations. The following information includes only outdoor activities found *outside* Yellowstone and Grand Teton, though most of the outfitters listed have permits to run trips into the parks as well – see chapters 6 to 7 for details (including winter **snowcoach tours**). For information on the excellent **white-water-rafting** and **downhill skiing** options in Big Sky and Gallatin Valley to the north, see the sections further along in this chapter.

Fishing

The area around West Yellowstone is excellent **fishing** territory. The Madison River is within easy reach, with especially good fishing in autumn, when large brown trout and rainbows swim in from Hebgen Lake for spawning. Huge, trophy-sized brownies also lurk in several nearby beaver ponds, which you'll need a guide or willing local to find. A short drive west into Idaho on Hwy-20 is the community of **Island Lake**, a paradise for fly-fishermen strung along Henry's Fork of the Snake River, regarded as one of the finest dry-fly streams in the country. There are numerous fishing outfitters in West Yellowstone, with the three best for information, gear and guide services being Blue Ribbon Flies, 305 Canyon St (☎406/646-7642, ⊛www.blueribbonflies.com), Bud Lilly's Trout Shop, 39 Madison Ave (☎406/646-7801 or 1-800/854-9559, ⊛www.budlillys.com) and Jacklin's Fly Shop, 105 Yellowstone Ave (☎406/646-7336, ⊛www.jacklinsflyshop.com) – see p.160 for more details on each.

Horseriding

There are good **horseriding** routes about ten miles north of town at Whit's Lake Road Trailhead on US-287, and also two miles further on at Red Canyon Road, which opens up to great views of the Madison Range. Top local outfitters include Yellowstone Wilderness Outfitters (☎406/223-3300, ⓦwww.yellowstone .ws) and Diamond P Ranch (☎406/646-7246, ⓦwww.yellowstonehorses.com); expect to spend anywhere from $68–110 for a half-day trail ride to $165 per night for a full-day mount.

Mountain biking

Mountain bikers will find good rides on old logging roads and technical single-track trails close to West Yellowstone. The eighteen-mile **Rendezvous Trails** (ⓦwww.rendezvousskitrails.com) start from Geyser Street on the south side of town and are especially popular for their mix of rolling terrain and steeper ascents and descents. More details, including trail maps, are available from Freeheel and Wheel, 40 Yellowstone Ave (☎406/646-7744, ⓦwww.freeheelandwheel.com) and the somewhat grottier Yellowstone Bicycle, 132 Madison Ave (☎406/646-7815); both shops rent bikes at daily rates in the $20–25 range.

Snowmobiling

The clearest sign of West Yellowstone's dedication to **snowmobiles** is that once winter hits, the town's main streets are left unploughed, enabling sleds to zip around freely. The community's economy, which relies heavily on the snowmobiling trade, has taken a major hit in recent years due to restrictions within Yellowstone (for more information, see p.175), and fewer hotels, motels and restaurants are remaining open throughout winter to serve sledders. It's safe to say you won't win many sled-banning arguments hereabouts; in fact, you're best off not raising the topic, if that's your belief.

That said, there's no shortage of riding possibilities around town. Along with the necessary **guided tours** into Yellowstone, there are hundreds of miles of **trails** leading out of town in practically every direction, varying from steep expert trails such as the ten-mile Lionhead Loop to Two Top, the first designated snowmobile trail in the US. The latter route takes around three hours to complete, although additional loops can shorten or lengthen the ride; it begins just west of town and climbs up past several "play areas" to the Continental Divide, offering magnificent views.

There are almost as many snowmobile **rental outfits** around West Yellowstone as there are miles of trails; among the best are Back Country Adventures (☎406/646-9317 or 1-800/924-7669, ⓦwww.backcountry-adventures.com) and Two Top Snowmobile Rental (☎406/646-7802 or 1-800/522-7802, ⓦwww .twotopsnowmobile.com). Daily rates start at $109 for basic sleds and climb to $179 for the highest-horsepower monsters; keep in mind that the more environmentally friendly four-stroke engines are not required outside the parks, although conservation-minded visitors might consider foregoing a bit of speed and opting for one.

Cross-country skiing

Given that the US Ski and Biathlon teams have used the town as a training camp, it's no surprise that West Yellowstone boasts excellent **cross-country skiing** trails. The **Rendezvous Trails** (ⓦwww.rendezvousskitrails.com) are the big attraction, with a number of groomed trails that start on the south side of town on Geyser Street. Day passes cost $5 and can be purchased at Freeheel and Wheel (see "Mountain biking") or Bud Lilly's Trout Shop (see "Fishing"); both shops also rent skis and snowshoes starting at $20 per day. Along with West Yellowstone's main visitor centre, both shops stock a free handout detailing trails into Yellowstone: the **Riverside Trail**, accessed from along Boundary Street, ranges up to four miles in length and covers a series of loops along the lovely Madison River, while north along Hwy-191, over a half-dozen more trailheads access the park, including long trails along **Specimen Creek** and up **Bighorn Pass**.

Listings

Bank First Security Bank, 106 S Electric St.

Car rental Yellowstone Airport (May–Oct only): Avis (℡406/646-7635) and Budget (℡406/646-5156); West Yellowstone: Budget (℡406/646-7882). Bozeman Gallatin Field Airport: Alamo, Avis, Budget, Dollar, Enterprise, Hertz, National and Thrifty (see p.26 for contact details).

Hospital Yellowstone Family Medical Clinic, 11 S Electric St (Mon–Fri 8am–3pm, ℡406/646-0200).

Internet West Yellowstone Public Library (see below) has free wireless internet access – ask librarian for password; Send It Home, 27 Madison Ave, charges $3 to use its public computer for 30min.

Laundry Swan Cleaners, 510 Madison Ave (daily 8am–8pm; ℡406/646-7892).

Library 23 Dunraven St (Tues & Thurs 10am–6pm, Wed 10am–8pm, Fri 10am–5pm, Sat 10am–3pm; ℡406/646-9017).

Pharmacy Silver Tip Pharmacy, 120 N Canyon St (Mon–Fri 9am–5pm; ℡406/646-7056).

Police 124 Yellowstone Ave (℡406/646-7600).

Post office 209 Grizzly Ave (Mon–Fri 8.30am–5pm; ℡406/646-7704).

Supermarket Market Place, 22 Madison Ave (daily 8am–9pm; ℡406/646-9600).

Taxi Yellowstone Taxi (℡406/646-1118).

Big Sky and Gallatin Valley

North of West Yellowstone, less than an hour's drive on Hwy-191 leads to **BIG SKY**. Centred around towering **Lone Mountain** in winter and the rushing **Gallatin River** in summer, the resort area is blessed with an outstanding selection of outdoor activities, along with a few of Montana's top luxury lodges. Still, although Westfork Meadows tries, there's no real town centre to speak of, and the area's Achilles' heel remains a lack of things to see or do once you've had your fill of strenuous activities on the mountain or the river – something that's unlikely to change in the immediate future, as construction has come to a standstill over the last few years.

Fortunately, much of the area's development to date has been clustered around the bases of the two ski resorts or hidden off the main roads in small subdivisions, and the trip north from West Yellowstone remains defined by its scenic splendour. The first half of the drive along Hwy-191 weaves in and out of Yellowstone, passing deep-green forested hills, the occasional patch of burned woods and a small handful of cross-country skiing and hiking **trailheads** (see **H1** & **H2**, on p.44). Just before leaving Yellowstone for good, the highway passes the Gallatin River's source, from where the natural beauty is ever more apparent. Following the clear water as it flows out of the park, north past Big Sky and onwards to **Bozeman**, the roadway is framed on either side by steep rising and forested hillsides rising to the Gallatin Range to the east and the Madison Range to the west. The twisting highway was constructed in 1911 and has been a major artery for Yellowstone travellers ever since; it's not rare for visitors to get their first eyeful of the region's wildlife along this route, with moose frequently photographed munching on riverside willows and bighorn sheep spotted grazing roadside (though be alert for **animal crossings**, as several wolves have been hit and killed along this stretch over the past fifteen years). One sight you're certain not to miss on the western skyline is magnificent Lone Mountain, an 11,166ft pyramid of snow and rock that attracts adventure-minded skiers and snowboarders looking to test their mettle on the connected runs at **Big Sky Resort** and smaller **Moonlight Basin**.

Orientation and information

Bozeman is forty-five miles north of Big Sky, and you likely won't get lost travelling through scenic Gallatin Valley en route – its only major road is Hwy-191, with just the occasional turn-off up into the mountains branching off to either side. The one intersection you won't want to miss is Hwy-64 (Big Sky Spur Road) leading west up to Big Sky Resort, approximately fifty miles from both West Yellowstone and Bozeman. At the junction, look for the humble **Soldier's Chapel**, a small log building commemorating Montana soldiers who died in World War II; step inside to see the window behind the altar that perfectly frames Lone Mountain's peak. Karst Stage ($80 return; ☎406/556-3500 or 1-800/845-2778, ⒲www.karststage.com) operates **shuttle buses** from Bozeman's airport to Big Sky, with reservations essential.

On the eight-mile drive up to Big Sky Resort's **Mountain Village**, you'll pass the small settlements of **Meadow Village**, a couple of miles after the turn-off, and **Westfork Meadows**, about four miles further up the road. Both have been built to cater to the tourist trade and part-time residents, and have regular **shuttle services** to and from the ski slopes. For more information on the area, check in with the Big Sky Chamber of Commerce (☎406/995-3000 or 1-800/943-4111, ⒲www.bigskychamber.com) or look for the free *Big Sky Weekly* newspaper.

Accommodation

Where you choose to **stay** in the area depends largely on the season. If you're visiting in **winter**, try for something in Mountain Village, as it saves the drive up to the ski hill – a hassle after heavy snow. Slopeside accommodation, including a wide array of popular condominiums, is run by Big Sky Resort (☎1-800/548-4486, ⒲www.bigskyresort.com). In **summer**, options within Gallatin Valley are smarter for proximity to the river and nearby trailheads. If you're interested in roughing it, there are several **campgrounds** (most $10–12) in the surrounding Gallatin National Forest, as well as a smattering of Forest Service-managed **backcountry cabins** ($20–30) equipped with wood stoves and either fold-up beds or bunk beds. Some cabins are accessible by car, while others require a short hike; for more information, contact either the Bozeman District Office (☎406/522-2520) or the Hebgen Lake District Office (☎406/823-6961).

Mountain Village

The Huntley Lodge Operated by Big Sky Resort. The resort's original hotel received a facelift several years back, sprucing up the still-drab rooms a notch. The facilities, though, are excellent, and include a swimming pool, whirlpool tubs, workout room and the popular *Chet's Bar & Grill*. Rates include a generous buffet spread at breakfast, while ski-and-stay packages help defray costs. Winter rates start at $168.

Shoshone Operated by Big Sky Resort. A seven-storey condominium hotel comprising ski-in/ski-out suites with private bedrooms, full kitchens, two bathrooms, gas fireplaces and balconies with a view, plus access to *The Huntley Lodge*'s large health club and

⑫

pool. Suites are comfortable and can sleep up to six. Winter rates start at $285.

Summit at Big Sky Operated by Big Sky Resort. The most modern among Mountain Village lodges, the ten-storey *Summit* features large, elegant, standard rooms and condominium-style suites of varying sizes – most with sublime mountain views – along with minibars, small kitchens, fireplaces and large tubs. There's also a workout room and an on-site spa. Winter rates start at $199 (standard) and $297 (suites).

Off-mountain

Buck's T-4 Hwy-191, less than a mile south of Big Sky junction ☎406/995-4111 or 1-800/822-4484, ⊛ www.buckst4.com. While the very affordable rooms ($99 year-round) at this former hunting lodge are fine enough – comfortable king-size beds, TV, coffee-maker, free wireless internet – it's the common areas that are truly outstanding. The lobby with fireplace exudes no shortage of charm, and both the large country hall (which plays host to live music on occasion) and highly recommended restaurant (see p.227) also help set the place apart. Rates include a huge buffet breakfast.

The Corral Motel Hwy-191, five miles south of Big Sky junction ☎406/995-4249 or 1-800/995-4249, ⊛ www.corralbar.com. Attached to the valley's most popular roadhouse

(see p.227), this small motel fills with snowmobile enthusiasts in winter; come summer, it's well located for rafting and horseriding. Clean (if plain) rooms all include king-size beds, cable TV and access to a large hot tub, and a shuttle is available for the long trip to Big Sky's slopes. A double room costs $80 year-round, while the "Quad Room" is a bargain at $100; if you stay six nights, the seventh is free.

Rainbow Ranch Lodge Hwy-191, five miles south of Big Sky junction ☎406/995-4132 or 1-800/937-4132, ⊛ www.rainbowranchbigsky .com. Only a few steps from the Gallatin River, *Rainbow Ranch's* luxury accommodations are mixed between deluxe cabins and individually decorated rooms, including larger suites with fireplace overlooking a stocked trout pond. There's an outdoor hot tub, Western lounge featuring its own roaring fireplace and overstuffed leather couches, and a very fine restaurant (see p.227) and wine cellar. Rates in summer start at $295 per night.

Whitewater Inn Hwy-191, less than a mile south of Big Sky junction; operated by Big Sky Resort. One of the area's lowest-priced and most family-friendly offerings, with over sixty rooms, an indoor pool (with lengthy water slide) and laundry facilities. Double rooms and family suites available starting at $109, including continental breakfast.

Big Sky Resort

Rugged and crowd-free, the best single word to describe **Big Sky Resort** (☎1-800/548-4487, ⊛www.bigskyresort.com) is massive. Indeed, now that it has teamed up with neighbour – and one-time bitter rival – Moonlight Basin (see opposite) to share trail networks, the combined 5300 acres of terrain makes this the largest ski area in the country. The resort was originally the brainchild of American newscaster Chet Huntley, who, with other major investors, bought a huge chunk of Lone Mountain in 1969. These days, current owners Boyne Resorts have massive designs of their own: a decade-long plan to build a pedestrian village similar to those at Whistler in British Columbia and Keystone in Colorado is in full swing, though for now, nature still holds the upper hand at this wild ski hill where wildlife sightings are not unheard of.

The resort's terrain spreads across three mountains – Lone Mountain (11,166ft), Andesite Mountain (8800ft) and Flat Iron Mountain (8092ft) – with 3800 acres and 85 trail miles open to **skiing and snowboarding**; Big Sky also boasts the third longest **vertical drop**, 4350ft, on the continent (only those at Whistler and Snowmass, Colorado, are longer). Lines at Big Sky's 21 lifts are rare, and the only place you'll have to wait is for a ride up the thrilling fifteen-passenger Lone Peak Tram, topping out at the summit of Lone Mountain and coming within an arm's breadth of the mountain's vertiginous crags. The **annual snowfall** is a mighty 400 inches – more in heavy winters – and the resort can open as early as October (weekends only), though its official season lasts from late November to late April.

Beginners may feel a little left out here, as beginner green runs make up only about fifteen percent of the mountain; nearly twice that percentage are rated intermediate blues, with the rest designated advanced and expert blacks. Intermediates will love cruisers such as Bighorn on Andesite Mountain for its reasonably challenging pitch and wide-open curves. Advanced skiers have a huge range of options, from the bumps of Snake Pit and Mad Wolf on Andesite, to the big bowl beneath Turkey Traverse or the double-blacks beneath the aptly named Challenger lift on Lone Peak. Experts, meanwhile, will want to take on the fantastically steep double-black runs high up Lone Peak – including **Big Couloir** and even nastier **Little Couloir**, 45-degree slopes that require you to have a partner and avalanche rescue gear in tow. Freestylers will want to head over to Andesite Mountain, where there's a **terrain park** and **half-pipe**, though the natural gully on the front face of Lone Peak is a blast as well.

Cross-country skiers and **snowshoers** will find fifty miles of exceptional trails at Lone Mountain Ranch (full-day passes: cross-country ski $20, snowshoe; $15 ⓣ406/995-4644 or 1-800/514-4644, ⓦwww.lmranch.com), a couple of miles down the spur road from Mountain Village; gear rental is available for $20 a day. Summer and autumn around the resort are laidback to the point of boredom, with most visitor numbers made up by corporate conventions. There's decent **hiking** around Lone Mountain, a **zip-line course** (two hours for $59) and lift-accessed **mountain biking** (daily 10.30am–3.30pm; $30), but there's much more to do and see down in Gallatin Valley.

With so much terrain, it takes several days to cover everything at Big Sky. It makes little sense, therefore, to splurge on the combined Big Sky/Moonlight Basin **Lone Peak Pass** ($95), an option better suited to expert locals and their season passes. **Lift tickets** for just Big Sky start at $81 per day, with slight discounts on multi-day purchases. Facilities include *The Dugout* on Andesite Mountain, which does good bbq, and several restaurants and ski and board rental shops in Mountain Village – expect to pay $35 a day for skis or board rental. If you're staying down below, a free **shuttle** bus runs from Westfork Meadows and Meadow Village to Mountain Village from 7am–11pm.

Moonlight Basin Resort

Sharing Lone Mountain to the north of Big Sky Resort, **Moonlight Basin Resort** (ⓣ406/993-6000 or 1-888-893-7698, ⓦwww.moonlightbasin.com) opened its ski area in 2003, the final piece to a real-estate development over a decade in the making. Already at odds with its larger neighbour, within a year the two ski areas were battling in court, allegations of trespassing and even errant avalanche explosions being lobbed back and forth. The fight wasn't helping either side win positive publicity or, more importantly, real-estate sales, and the resorts reconciled and announced a partnership in 2005. While great for media hype, for most non-local skiers the interconnected trails mean nothing more than a pricier combined pass (see above), and the average visitor should only head to Moonlight's 1900 acres of skiable terrain after they've tested Big Sky's offerings. A full-day **lift ticket** at the smaller resort runs to $58, and allows access to a quirky network of trails that are flat at the bottom and scarily steep at the top, with not a great deal in between. The one group who has gained most from the resorts' partnership are adrenaline-junkie skiers and boarders, who can now ride up Big Sky's Challenger lift to quickly access the double-black diamonds of Moonlight's **Headwater Chutes**; likewise,

Moonlight's daring **North Summit Snowfield** can only be accessed via Big Sky. Both zones are seriously experts-only, and should only be attempted with a knowledgeable local in tow.

Gallatin Valley

Despite the fact that Hwy-191 follows nearly every twist and turn of **GALLATIN VALLEY** and its eponymous river, this detracts very little from the beauty of one of Montana's finest fly-fishing regions (and the filming location for much of 1992's *A River Runs Through It*). Just keep your eyes glued to the road when driving, as this is one of Montana's most accident-prone stretches of highway.

In summer, **whitewater rafting** is the biggest draw, and enthusiasts will find plenty of challenges on the Gallatin – stretches such as the "Mad Mile" along its upper reaches have plenty of Class IV–V rapids sloshing about. Be prepared to get soaked and freeze a bit; outfitters supply wetsuits, but the water is still frigid year-round. The top local guide is Geyser Whitewater Expeditions, located due south of the Big Sky junction (☎406/995-4989 or 1-800/914-9031, Ⓦwww.raftmontana .com), with half-day trips ($56) ranging from a scenic and relaxing raft ride to a thrilling run through the rapids, along with a strenuous full-day voyage that combines both ($93), traversing Class I–IV rapids along the way.

Anglers can pretty much pull off the road anywhere to access quality fishing, and while boat fishing is prohibited on the Gallatin, there's no closed fishing season; indeed, drive past in winter and you'll spot super-dedicated fishermen clearing ice from their lines as they stand waist-deep in the bone-chilling river. Some of the best access points include *Greek Creek* and *Red Cliff Campgrounds* (both off Hwy-191 in Gallatin Canyon), but first-timers should definitely consider a guide, as the river is fast and lined with deep holes. Try Gallatin Riverguides (☎406/995-2290, Ⓦwww.montanaflyfishing.com), a respected outfitter with a well-stocked shop on Hwy-191 one half-mile south of the Big Sky junction.

With spectacular mountains on either side of the valley and 25 peaks over 10,000ft in the Gallatin Range alone, this is an area long on great **hiking** and **climbing** opportunities. One of the most popular areas to trek is **Lee Metcalf Wilderness**, which runs west of the valley along much of the Madison Range. Within this wilderness – from which all motorized vehicles and bicycles are barred – the **Spanish Peaks** are laced with several prime hiking trails, although their altitude keeps their upper reaches covered in snow until July; contact Gallatin National Forest's Bozeman District Office (☎406/522-2520) for trail recommendations and maps. If you'd rather ride a horse than walk into the wilds, several ranches in the area offer one-hour ($30–35) to week-long trips on **horseback**; one of the longest established is the *320 Guest Ranch* (☎406/995-4283 or 1-800/243-0320, Ⓦwww.320ranch.com), about a dozen miles south of the Big Sky junction.

Eating and drinking

There's a wide selection of memorable dining spots both on the mountain and in Gallatin Valley, encompassing sophisticated fine-dining **restaurants** and true-grit Western **bars** and roadhouses. Only a few of the slopeside bars and restaurants stay open year-round, and be warned that in summer, things at Big Sky Resort can become rather comatose; given the ski area's lack of huge crowds, the place is a mellow scene at times even in winter, so visitors requiring livelier nightspots should consider Jackson or Teton Village instead.

Mountain Village

Cabin Bar & Grill Arrowhead Mall
☎406/995-4244. With exposed beams,
high ceilings and a menu studded with
$25–30 meat and seafood options galore,
this restaurant is one of Big Sky Resort's
most ambitious offerings. Lunch available
only in winter.

The Carabiner Lounge Summit at Big Sky
☎406/995-8078. The *Carabiner* wears a
number of hats at the Summit: breakfast
café, lunch hideaway, après-ski lounge and
dinner destination. Mornings see skiers
filling up on pancakes, omelettes and even
steak and eggs ($7–17), while the level of
sophistication is taken up a notch or two
by evening, when saffron-crusted halibut
($31) and petit filet mignon ($29) anchor
the menu.

Chet's Bar & Grill The Huntley Lodge. This
convivial destination is busiest immediately
after the lifts close thanks to a great happy
hour that includes nightly entertainment. If
you stick around beyond that, try the
smoked pheasant quesadilla starter or, for a
main course, the chargrilled buffalo strip
steak. Starters average $10, while mains
come in at $15 and up.

Mountain Top Pizza Pies Mountain Mall.
Serviceable pizzas and salads served from
lunchtime onwards. Expect to pay around
$14 for a large pizza with a few toppings;
free delivery.

M.R. Hummers Mountain Mall. A dimly lit,
popular après-ski spot with good baby back
ribs and filling sandwiches (around $10) to
accompany a wide selection of beers.

Off-mountain

Allgoods Westfork Meadows. A welcoming
place specializing in bbq ribs and chicken
($15 and under) and, in the morning, burly
omelettes ($8–10). The bar comes alive

later in the evening with a pool table, darts
and poker.

Blue Moon Bakery Westfork Meadows. Good
coffee and freshly baked bagels and
pastries make this a great morning pit stop
on the way to the ski areas. At lunch and
dinner, the menu is based around pizza,
pastas, salads and sandwiches – most
under $10.

**Buck's T-4 Hwy-191, less than a mile
south of Big Sky junction** ☎406/995-4111.
Featured in *Gourmet* and *Wine Spectator*,
Buck's T-4 specializes in imaginatively
prepared exotic and local game. Standout
mains include New Zealand red deer
tenderloin ($34) and pheasant breast ($34),
with an extensive wine list – and even a
couple of meatless options – to match.
Reservations essential.

**The Corral Steakhouse Hwy-191, five
miles south of Big Sky junction.** *The
Corral* does breakfast every morning, but
it's the half-pound buffalo burgers ($11)
and standout prime rib platters ($24–28) in
the afternoon and evening that make it
worth a visit. It's also *the* place to come in
Gallatin Valley for a beer amid genuine
Western roadhouse atmosphere; the
attached motel is convenient if you've had
one too many.

**Rainbow Ranch Lodge Dining Room Hwy-191,
five miles south of Big Sky junction** ☎406/995-
4132. Inventive starters like beet-cured
salmon and a wild game tamale lead into a
host of mesquite-grilled delights (buffalo
ribeye and lamb rack among them); just
make sure you've packed your credit card,
as mains here *start* at $31 and stretch well
into the $40-plus category. While you're
living it up, ask to see the Bacchus Room,
an extraordinary 10,000-bottle wine cellar
complete with private dining table.

Gardiner and Paradise Valley

he dusty Montana town of **GARDINER,** only five miles north of Yellowstone's headquarters at Mammoth Hot Springs, is the only park access point open to cars year-round. Strung above the Yellowstone River in desert-like surroundings, the small town is more often than not the hottest and driest spot in and around the park, averaging a paltry ten inches of rain a year. What Gardiner lacks in precipitation, however, it makes up for in hospitality; compared to the other gateway towns, it's not as isolated as Cooke City, as far off as Cody, or as over-commercialized as West Yellowstone. And as for comparing easy-going Gardiner to the region's most famous town to the south, a popular local T-shirt states the case best – "Gardiner: It Ain't No Jackson Hole".

Though named after fur trapper Johnson Gardner (see box below), the town, like so many in the West, owes its existence to both miners and the railroad. The Northern Pacific's spur line from Livingston, fifty miles north, didn't actually terminate in Gardiner until 1902; prior to that, the first major wave of Yellowstone tourists were shuttled here on stagecoaches from the Cinnabar terminus in **Paradise Valley**, twenty miles north. Gardiner still retains a faint frontier whiff,

There's no "I" in Gardner: Gardner vs Gardiner

After tumbling down Osprey Falls, the **Gardner River** flows north alongside Yellowstone's North Entrance Road before spilling into the Yellowstone River just east of the town of **Gardiner**. Along this route, many first-time visitors understandably think they've uncovered a misspelled sign or map – and in a way they have, although the typo dates back to the nineteenth century. A tough character who allegedly scalped his fair share of natives (and met his own doom in a similarly grim manner), fur trapper **Johnson Gardner** trudged through the area's dry valleys in the 1830s, and in the same way fellow trapper Davey Jackson earned lasting fame with Jackson's Hole to the south, the headwaters of the local river soon became known as Gardner's Hole. The name stuck until the Washburn Expedition rolled through in 1870; famed teller of tales **Jim Bridger** (see box, p.61) was working in the area at the time, and when asked for the name of the river, it's believed his thick Virginia accent added an "i" sound between the two syllables. "Gard-i-ner" was thus born on the Expedition's maps, and the name stuck until new map projects in the 1940s changed the river's name back to its proper spelling. By that time, the town had long been settled, however, and its name remained unchanged.

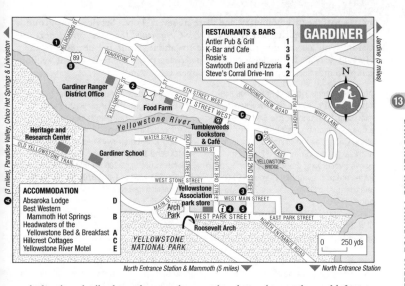

RESTAURANTS & BARS

Antler Pub & Grill	1
K-Bar and Cafe	3
Rosie's	5
Sawtooth Deli and Pizzeria	4
Steve's Corral Drive-Inn	2

ACCOMMODATION

Absaroka Lodge	D
Best Western Mammoth Hot Springs	B
Headwaters of the Yellowstone Bed & Breakfast	A
Hillcrest Cottages	C
Yellowstone River Motel	E

North Entrance Station & Mammoth (5 miles)

North Entrance Station

and there's a laidback quality to the town's relationship with world-famous Yellowstone – and the loads of tourists it brings in. Many of the region's biologists and naturalists live here, and Yellowstone's **Heritage and Research Center** opened next door to the town's school in 2005.

North of Gardiner, scenic Paradise Valley also merits a visit, even if only to enjoy the lovely roadside views. Activities in the valley revolve mainly around the Yellowstone River, with the firm favourite being a **whitewater-rafting** trip through narrow Yankee Jim Canyon. Kayakers and fly-fishers also flock to the river, but for the most relaxing of all the area's water-based recreation, head for the mineral baths at eminently enjoyable **Chico Hot Springs**, about a 45-minute drive north of Gardiner.

Arrival and information

The closest major **airport** to Gardiner is in Bozeman, 75 miles away. Karst Stage's fleet of buses ($159 return; ☏406/556-3500 or 1-800/845-2778, ⓦwww.karst stage.com) runs expensive **shuttles** from the airport to Gardiner, as well as to Chico Hot Springs ($116) and Mammoth ($311) – reservations are essential. You'll find tourist **information** at the Gardiner Chamber of Commerce on West Park Street near the corner of South Third Street (late May to early Sept Mon–Fri 8am–8pm, Sat & Sun 10am–6pm; rest of year Mon–Thurs 9am–5pm; ☏406/848-7971, ⓦwww.gardinerchamber.com); for outdoor recreation information outside of Yellowstone, contact Gallatin National Forest's Gardiner Ranger District Office, 805 Scott St W (Mon–Fri 8am–5pm; ☏406/848-7375). Gardiner's **post office** is at 707 Scott St W, and wireless **internet access** is available year-round at *Tumbleweeds Bookstore and Cafe* at 501 Scott St W.

Accommodation

Gardiner has a fair selection of mid-range **accommodation**, but places can book solid well ahead of time for summer, so try to reserve rooms in advance. If you'll be **camping**, Yellowstone's *Mammoth Campground* (see p.185) is only four miles away across the park boundary, and there are several Forest Service **campgrounds** in the area as well: closest is *Eagle Creek Campground* ($8), two miles north of Gardiner on a steep dirt road en route to Jardine, while the nearest site along Hwy-89 via Paradise Valley is *Canyon Campground* ($7), seventeen miles away. Both campgrounds are very basic and remain open year-round.

Absaroka Lodge 310 Scott St E ☎406/848-7414 or 1-800/755-7414, ⓦwww.yellowstonemotel.com. With unbeatable winter rates and a great location on the north side of Yellowstone Bridge, all the pleasant, if plain rooms at this year-round motel are fitted with decks overlooking the rushing river. Kitchen suites are also available. Summer $110 (standard) and $125 (suite), winter $45–55 and $60–70.

Best Western Mammoth Hot Springs 905 Scott St W ☎406/848-7311 or 1-800/828-9080, ⓦwww.bestwestern.com/mammothhotsprings. One of Gardiner's more sophisticated options, this hotel on the western edge of town offers both spacious rooms and three-bed suites equipped with kitchenette; other amenities include heated indoor pool, whirlpool tub, two saunas and internet access, plus a restaurant, lounge and casino. Summer $175 (standard) and $250 (suite), winter $95 and $160.

🏃 **Headwaters of the Yellowstone Bed & Breakfast** Hwy-89, 3 miles north of Gardiner ☎406/848-7073, ⓦwww.headwatersbandb.com. Managed by longtime locals, this friendly inn is a fantastic place to spend a few days on the banks of the Yellowstone River not far north of town. The main house's lower level contains a fair-sized common area filled with books and local art, as well as four guest rooms ($140 per night, including full breakfast), each with private bath. The property's pair of cabins – one sleeping up to four, the other up to six

– are great deals, with the smaller going for $165 per night, the larger $195 (breakfast not included). The main house shuts in winter, but the cabins remain open throughout the snowy season and go for $100 and $125 nightly.

Hillcrest Cottages 200 Scott St W ☎406/848-7353 or 1-800/970-7353, ⓦwww.hillcrestcottages.com. Within walking distance of Park St, *Hillcrest*'s collection of fifteen affordable cottages ranges from one-bed units for two guests ($60–80) to two-bedroom cottages ($80–100) that sleep up to six, with one duplex that can host up to eight ($150) also available. As long as you don't get your hopes up for luxury – this is lodging at its most basic (and dated) – you'll have little reason to be disappointed. Closed in winter.

Yellowstone River Motel 14 Park St ☎406/848-7303 or 1-888/797-4837, ⓦwww.yellowstonerivermotel.com. Though the rooms in this motel's older wing are a bit on the musty side, its nearly forty units are nevertheless clean and come equipped with phones, cable TV and wireless internet; a few family suites are also available. An attractive picnic area (complete with bbq) overlooks the adjacent river, and the motel's setting near the far east end of Park St makes it one of Gardiner's quietest lodging options. Rates are in the range $75–105 through the heart of summer and $59–76 in shoulder months (May and Oct). Closed in winter.

The Town

With a population of less than nine hundred, Gardiner is split in two by the **Yellowstone River**. The town's north bank is dominated by a strip of motels, restaurants and tourist facilities along Hwy-89 – known as **Scott Street** as it runs through town parallel to the river, then Second Street once it turns south and crosses Yellowstone Bridge. Gardiner's southern side is older and more attractive, with elk and deer often seen grazing in local gardens bordering Yellowstone parklands. The main thoroughfare here, **Park Street**, is lined with ice-cream shops, saloons and a new Yellowstone Association park store and exhibit gallery (daily 8am–8pm) at the corner of Third Street, and makes for a short but enjoyable stroll. At its west end looms the **Roosevelt Arch**, which marks the park's North Entrance; it was dedicated in 1903 by President Theodore Roosevelt in front of several thousand people at the end of his two-week trip into Yellowstone. Bearing the inscription, "For the benefit and enjoyment of the people", the iconic stone structure was designed by Yellowstone's head engineer, Hiram Chittenden, to offset what he had deemed visitors' "very unfavorable" first impressions of Gardiner's arid area, and it remains a popular photo stop today.

Beyond (but not through) the Roosevelt Arch – and built over a century later – is Yellowstone's **Heritage and Research Center** (T 307/344-2662), where a remarkable collection of several million historical park items is, sadly, available only to scientists, writers and other accredited researchers. Its **library** (Tues–Fri 9am–4pm) is open to anyone, however, and limited looks at the centre's seemingly bottomless archives are available via free, hour-long public **tours** (early June to early Sept Tues & Thurs 10am; reserve well ahead by phone). Though not held in the library, artefacts inside the attractive facility – many of which were rescued from the leaky basement of Mammoth's Albright Visitor Center – include several of painter Thomas Moran's original field sketches from the Hayden Survey of 1872, journals and notes from early explorers and army officials up to last year's ranger logbooks, thousands of pieces of antique furniture and souvenirs, and even the skulls of Yellowstone's original fourteen re-introduced wolves (see *The wolves of Yellowstone* colour section).

Eating and drinking

In keeping with the town's stripped-down take on tourism, there's not a whole lot of variety to Gardiner's small line-up of **restaurants** and **bars**, which offer little else aside from burgers, pizza, and for those willing to spend a bit more, pastas, steaks, chops and seafood. Bar-goers will have no trouble finding a place to down a drink, as several saloons line both Park and Main Streets; as for **groceries**, head to Food Farm at 701 Scott St W (Mon–Sat 7am–7pm, Sun 8am–7pm; T 406/848-7524). Finally, take extra caution if you'll be driving back to Yellowstone after dark, as elk crossings along the winding road to Mammoth are frequent.

Antler Pub & Grill 107 Hellroaring St
T 406/848-7536. Located inside the local *Comfort Inn*, this green-carpeted restaurant (with upstairs bar) certainly won't be winning any design awards. The menu, however, includes some of the best mid-priced food in Gardiner: pepper steak, filet mignon, bbq ribs and the "Crazy Pasta", a blend of penne, Italian sausage, chicken and red bell pepper. Call for winter hours.

K-Bar and Cafe 202 Main St. A basic watering hole with a bar, pool table, slot machines and plenty of good ol' boys in the front, and austere table seating in the back. Pizzas are unspectacular and cost around $15 (slices also available), while a filling calzone goes for about half that. Burgers and salads are also on offer, but the place is best for drinking.

Rosie's 204 West Park St T 406/848-9950. With an open, airy environment and blonde wood furnishings that help make it one of the most pleasant places to eat in Gardiner, *Rosie*'s menu includes a few tempting pasta mains ($14–21), dry-rubbed ribeye steak

($26) and, perhaps heartiest of all, chicken breast stuffed with Italian sausage and *fontina* cheese ($18).

Sawtooth Deli and Pizzeria 220 West Park St. A friendly place featuring generously sized hot and cold sandwiches and salads (under $10), plus vegetarian specials and six types of pizza ($14–17) that are better than any others in town. Breakfast, lunch and dinner are served, and there's a covered outdoor dining patio on the side. Open daily June–Sept, with a nightly barbecue pit in summer and limited hours in shoulder seasons; closed in winter.

Steve's Corral Drive-Inn 711 Scott St West. Grilling burgers in Gardiner since 1960, this unassuming shack makes a just reward after a long hike or overnight stay in the backcountry. The legendary burgers ($7–10; choose from beef, bison or elk) are huge and delicious, while the thick milkshakes are equally impossible to pass up. Eat inside or, if the weather's cooperative, grab a spot at one of the covered picnic tables outside.

Outdoor activities

As float trips on the Yellowstone River are banned within the park, Gardiner has become a popular base for **whitewater-rafting** trips north of the park boundary. While the rapids here are not as ferocious as those on the Gallatin River in Big Sky (see p.226) or the Snake River south of Jackson (see p.210), there are still some rollicking Class III rapids to negotiate, and leaving from Gardiner to float north through Paradise Valley on the wide river, past clusters of speedy pronghorn and grazing elk, is a wonderful way to spend a summer day. The longest-established outfitter in town is Yellowstone Raft Company (☎406/848-7777 or 1-800/858-7781, ⓦwww.yellowstoneraft.com), 111 Second St, where half-day trips cost $37 and full-day excursions $80; also recommended is Montana Whitewater (☎406/848-7398 or 1-800/799-4465, ⓦwww.montanawhitewater.com), 603 Scott St West, which offers similar rates, several rafting trips (including overnighters), and **kayak** rentals. **Anglers** should call in at Parks' Fly Shop, 202 South Second St (☎406/848-7314, ⓦwww.parksflyshop.com), for fly tackle and spinning gear, information on guided trips and free fishing maps; see p.160 for further details. Come winter, the store is also the best place in town for **cross-country ski** and **snowshoe** rentals ($15 and $10/day; third day free), as well as information on trails in Yellowstone. Reasonably priced **horseriding** trips into both Yellowstone and Absaroka-Beartooth Wilderness are offered by North Fork Creek Outfitters (☎406/848-7859) in Jardine, six miles from Gardiner.

Paradise Valley

North of Gardiner, Hwy-89 leads into **Paradise Valley**, weaving between the **Absaroka Mountains** and **Gallatin Range** on its way to Livingston just over fifty miles away. This was the first access route to Yellowstone, and is still one of the most popular, with activities in the valley increasingly encouraging folks to stick around for a day or two instead of zipping straight through. The Yellowstone River flowing along the valley floor is the longest undammed river in the 48 contiguous states, running some 680 miles east to eventually join the Missouri in North Dakota. Its route here is paralleled by Hwy-89 and, in the valley's northern half, the less travelled **East River Road** (Hwy-540), a narrower route that offers a better feel for the valley and landscape.

Between Gardiner and Livingston, there are few settlements of any real size, and much of the land is taken up by large ranches – one of which is the headquarters of the **Church Universal and Triumphant**, whose leaders unsuccessfully predicted Armageddon several times throughout the 1980s and 1990s, leading members to build massive bomb shelters within the complex; the once-icy relationship between Yellowstone and the organization has thawed in recent years due to large land donations on the latter's part. One can only guess, however, what these New Age visionaries think of **Devil's Slide**, the first sight of note heading north out of Gardiner. A road viewpoint five miles from town offers the best look at this geological oddity: a long red gash cutting down the face of Cinnabar Mountain, caused by the oxidation of iron in the rock face. Also nearby, look for the steam rising from **LaDuke Hot Springs** spilling into the river. If you haven't spotted a bighorn sheep yet, take your time here as well – a series of viewpoints access some of the best viewing areas in the entire region.

Continuing north, Hwy-89 passes several access points for fishing and floating on the Yellowstone before diving into **Yankee Jim Canyon**, named for Jim George, who dynamited a toll road to Yellowstone through here in the 1870s; the railroads soon followed, buying out his right-of-way and laying down tracks to

Gardiner. Near *Canyon Campground* (see p.230), there's an easy interpretive trail on the river's west bank that explores the history of transportation through the narrow canyon.

Cruising into the scenic heart of Paradise Valley, the highway passes the last turn-off of note before Livingston, a side road some thirty miles from Gardiner that leads to ⚡ **Chico Hot Springs** (☎406/333-4933 or 1-800/468-9232, ⓦwww .chicohotsprings.com). It's a turn worth making, as the relaxed place makes for one of the most enjoyable getaways in the entire region. Family-owned since opening in 1900, this country resort has been pulling in travellers and local families alike to soak in its spring-fed pools (daily 8am–11pm; $7 non-overnight guests) ever since. **Accommodation** is wide-ranging, beginning with the three-storey main lodge – suitably decked out in antiques and full of small, but wonderfully atmospheric rooms – and on through a more modern lodge, as well as a host of hilltop log cabins, cottages, chalets and even a restored train car; rates start at $49 for an en-suite room in the main lodge, but the majority of options cost $89–179. A plethora of other amenities and activities are available, including the *Chico Saloon*, a rollicking poolside honky-tonk **bar** (with live music every Friday and Saturday night); there's also a day spa, and the resort operates horseback rides, rafting excursions and even winter dogsled trips. Chico's one somewhat formal turn is its dimly lit **dining room**, featuring a renowned beef Wellington for two ($55) along with a bevy of creative mains in the $25–27 range; an excellent breakfast buffet ($9) is available come morning.

Outdoor activities

Heading the area's list of **outdoor activities**, the Yellowstone River cutting through Paradise Valley makes for yet another prime regional **fly-fishing** destination, and it's usually at its best from July to September. As for **hiking**, one of the best overnight options leads up to the foothills of forbidding **Mount Cowen**, at 11,206ft the highest point in the Absaroka Mountains. It's a tough, eighteen-mile round-trip that starts easily enough before turning north onto Upper Sage Creek Trail, on which it relentlessly ascends over 3000ft up to Elbow Lake; there are backcountry campsites at the lake. To get to the trailhead, turn east onto Mill Creek Road (Forest Road 486) off Hwy-89 about thirty miles north of Gardiner; after eleven miles, turn northeast onto Forest Road 3280 and drive a final mile to the trailhead. To explore the Gallatin Range on the valley's west side, head up Hwy-89 about twenty miles north of Gardiner and turn up Big Creek Road to **Big Creek Trailhead**, which offers access to several trails leading to gorgeous alpine lakes and high mountain country.

Though no trails are specifically marked as such, any route outside Absaroka-Beartooth Wilderness is open to **mountain biking**, and there's a good network of logging and service roads in both the Gallatin Range and the Absarokas. For bike rentals ($20 for a full day) and advice on the best rides in the area, stop in at Big Sky Whitewater Rafting (☎406/848-2112 or 1-866/848-2112, ⓦwww .bigskywhitewater.com), about nine miles north of Gardiner along Hwy-89.

Whether hiking or biking, be aware that you're in prime **rattlesnake** country. When it's hot, these slitherers lurk under bushes and wood debris; in cooler moments, they sun themselves on paths and on top of rocks. Watch where you step and, even more crucially, where you place your hands, and you should be able to avoid any painful encounters.

Cooke City and around

ugging the northeast corner of Yellowstone, **COOKE CITY** (7600ft) is the park's least visited gateway community, a one-street town that can almost entirely be taken in with a single glance. Hemmed in tightly by two separate wilderness areas, the town is accessible year-round from the west, as the road through Yellowstone from Gardiner is ploughed all through winter. However, the spectacular **Beartooth Highway** (Hwy-212) to the east is impassable from mid-October to late May, meaning that for well over half the year, this already isolated outpost – home to 350 residents, about a hundred of whom tough out the winter – literally becomes the end of the road. Between Cooke City and the park entrance four miles away sits even tinier **Silver Gate**, where come winter, the full-time population dips, along with the temperature, into single digits.

Cooke City got its start around 1870, when a group of trappers found gold in the gravel of **Soda Butte Creek**. They were quickly chased away by Crow people, but as news of the discovery spread, the natives were inevitably pushed out in exchange for smelters and saloons. In 1882, the settlement, known at the time as Shoofly, was renamed for Jay Cooke (see p.255), a Pacific Railroad contractor feverishly promoting railroad development; alas, the tracks never arrived, leaving the hamlet's fortunes to fluctuate with the luck of the local **New World Mining District**. The area was mined extensively for gold, silver, lead, zinc and copper until the 1950s, when brutal winters and the costs of isolation finally brought about their demise; mining ruins now dot the surrounding area, visited by hikers and off-road vehicles in summer, and cross-country skiers and snowmobilers in winter.

With its minimal civic services – there's no police station in sight, and the smattering of local kids are educated in a one-room schoolhouse – Cooke City's **naturally insulated environs** dictate far more than just its complete lack of mobile phone reception. The town's rough edges are the stuff of Montana legend, from its rough beginnings as a mining outpost to its long-held romantic image as an end-of-the-highway enclave. In recent years, it's seen a changing of the guard in terms of business ownership, with a number of "newer" arrivals who showed up in the 1990s having taken over bars and cafés from true Cooke City old-timers; it's a testament to the town's identity, then, how despite these changes, things here haven't changed all that much through the decades. Indeed, spend a short time poking into the few shops and eating (and drinking) around town, and you're bound to sense before long that everyone here really does know everyone else.

Arrival and information

Located 55 miles from Gardiner, Montana, to the west and eighty miles from Cody, Wyoming, to the southeast, Cooke City is set just inside Montana; all routes to it, however, pass through Wyoming. Its sole paved road, Hwy-212, is known as **Main Street** as it cuts through town, ending just to the east once snowfall closes the road. After the highway shuts, dedicated **winter visitors** coming from the east can park near the junction of Hwy-212 and Hwy-296 (Chief Joseph Scenic Byway; see p.246) thirteen miles east and snowmobile in; those driving hereabouts in spring or autumn should check Montana's road report (☎1-800/226-7623) for current conditions. Housed near the far west end of town in a sharp new building, Cooke City's **visitor centre** (summer daily, winter Mon–Fri, call for hours; ☎406/838-2495, ⓦwww.cookecitychamber.org), is best visited for exhibits on local mining history and information on the nearby Beartooth Mountains.

Accommodation

Since there are a mere handful of **accommodation** options to choose from in and around Cooke City – mostly split between motel rooms on Main Street and cabin rentals in the outlying areas – reservations are essential during busy periods. There are no luxury options to speak of, but prices are very reasonable across the board, with little fluctuation between summer and winter. If you'll be pitching a tent, several Forest Service **campgrounds** ($8–9) are located east of town along Hwy-212, although due to frequent bear activity, it's not uncommon for these to be reserved for RVs and vehicles with camper shells, especially in September. If this is the case, try Yellowstone's *Pebble Creek Campground* (see p.185), nine miles past the Northeast Entrance Station.

Alpine Motel 105 Main St ☎406/838-2262 or 1-888/838-1190, ⓦwww.cookecityalpine.com. With wireless internet, on-site laundry facilities and a range of about two dozen tidy rooms (around $80 for a double with two king-size beds), this is a solid, if basic lodging choice. A pair of two-bedroom suites, sleeping up to five each and with tiny kitchen areas, are also available.
Big Moose Resort 3 miles east of town along Hwy-212 ☎406/838-2393, ⓦwww.bigmoose resort.com. The four modern cabins at this highway-side "resort" are a good deal at $100–110 per night, with multi-night

discounts available. Two boast full eat-in kitchens, and all are remarkably clean and spacious with satellite television and wireless internet; there's also a hot tub on site. Since Hwy-212 goes unploughed, winter access is restricted to snowmobiles.
Elk Horn Lodge 103 Main St ☎406/838-2332, ⓦwww.elkhornlodgemt.com. This small lodge features two cabins ($120) with kitchenettes and six clean, plainly decorated motel rooms ($99). All come with television, mini-fridges, microwaves and common hot tub access.

Eating and drinking

Cooke City's **restaurant** scene is easily explored, with choices limited to places strung along Main Street, plus one notable seasonal café down the road in Silver Gate. As for **nightlife**, there are a few bars along the main drag that fill with hard-riding bikers in summer, hard-partying snowmobilers come winter and hard-bitten locals year-round; the most welcoming of the bunch is the *Miner's*

Saloon, 108 Main St. Limited **supplies** can be found at the atmospheric Cooke City General Store (daily 8am–7pm), open on Main Street since 1866, but it's best to stock up on groceries before arriving.

Beartooth Café 209 Main St ☎406/838-2475. Inviting and distinctive – all the way down to the looped belt that opens its front door – the continually buzzing *Beartooth Café*, a Cooke City mainstay since the 1970s, offers nightly pasta specials, fine salads and excellent takes on regional fare such as mountain trout ($18). Lunchtime sees a rush for the garlic-heavy Funk Burger ($10), while attentive service, outdoor seating and 130-plus beers on draught and in bottles all help make this the best dining option in town.

Buns "N" Beds Deli, BBQ & Cabins 201 Main St ☎406/838-2030. A good choice for a casual lunch, this local favourite makes terrific hot and cold sandwiches (well under $10) on unusual breads such as sun-dried tomato, with burgers and periodic bbq specials available as well. As for the "beds", three very basic cabins behind the restaurant go for $45–65 a night, depending on season.

Log Cabin Cafe Hwy-212, Silver Gate. A summer (and early autumn) fixture in wee Silver Gate now in its eighth decade of business, the charming and comfortable *Log Cabin Cafe* does all three meals, though its kitchen specializes in trout (about $19) at dinner.

Loving Cup Cafe Main St. One of Cooke City's main morning and afternoon gathering spots, with front patio seating and vintage jazz LP artwork lining its interior walls. The limited food menu consists of soups and bagel sandwiches (all under $7), and this may well be the only place in town that serves a mocha. There's no formal address, but it's right across the road from *Hoosier's Bar*.

Outdoor activities

Not all Cooke City visitors are here to see Yellowstone; a fair percentage come to take advantage of less stringent **snowmobiling** regulations in the surrounding Gallatin and Shoshone National Forests. A mecca for so-called slednecks, the village becomes snowmobile central throughout the snowy months, when the loudly whirring machines easily outnumber cars along Main Street. If you'd like to join the fun and explore the sixty-plus miles of groomed trails nearby, rentals and information are available at Cooke City Exxon (☎406/838-2244, Ⓦwww.cookecityexxon.com); expect to pay $125–225 per day, depending on the quality of the sled. **Cross-country skiers** and **climbers**, meanwhile, should head straight for Silvertip Mountain Center (☎406/838-2125, Ⓦwww.silvertipmountaincenter.com) in Silver Gate, a treasure-trove of local information that also rents snowshoe, ski and ice climbing gear.

Beartooth Highway

Constructed in the 1930s and only open from May until October due to extreme alpine conditions, the snaking 69-mile **Beartooth Highway** (Hwy-212), connecting Cooke City to the one-time mining town of Red Lodge, is one of the most unforgettable drives in the country. Other roads in the Rockies may be higher, but none offer the same top-of-the-world feeling as this succession of tight switchbacks, steep grades and overwhelming vistas. Even in summer, the springy tundra turf around 10,947ft Beartooth Pass can be covered with snow that, due to algae content, turns pink when crushed. All around are gem-like tarns, deeply gouged granite walls, tumbled piles of scree and huge blocks of roadside ice. Viewpoints along the way allow you to admire the sights without the risk of driving off the road, and a number of trailheads invite exploration on foot (see box opposite).

The brooding mass of the Absaroka Mountains, and to the east the even more rugged alpine landscape of the Beartooth Mountains, together make up the nearly 100,000-acre **Absaroka-Beartooth Wilderness**, widely acknowledged as some of the most remote terrain in the Yellowstone region – or to put a finer point on it, "As close to Alaska as you're gonna get in the lower 48", in the words of one knowledgeable Cooke City local. Straddling the Wyoming/Montana border, the area has several access points along the spectacular **Beartooth Highway** east of Cooke City, with a solid network of **trails** leading through timbered mountainsides and alpine meadows that erupt with bright wildflowers during the brief (as short as six weeks) summer growing season. Above treeline, it's a harsh but beautiful high-alpine landscape that can see snow any time of year. These factors alone are reason enough to visit the region, but mountaineers will also be drawn to Montana's highest point, remote **Granite Peak** (12,799ft), which rises above a series of wind-scoured tundra plateaus and alpine meadows incised by steep canyons. The wilderness also features a true geologic oddity: **Grasshopper Glacier**, an isolated, slowly moving icefield embedded with millions of frozen – you guessed it – grasshoppers.

If you only have the time or capacity for a day hike, try the fairly flat six-mile round-trip amble to **Rock Island Lake** – at 8200ft, it makes a fine introduction to one of the area's most accessible corners. The hike begins at Clarks Fork Trailhead about three miles east of Cooke City along the north side of Hwy-212. From here, follow Trail 3 along the southern shore of Kersey Lake, then bear to the far right at the double-fork; Rock Island Lake, set beneath craggy mountaintops, is less than a mile ahead.

For maps and more **information** on trails within Absaroka-Beartooth Wilderness, drop into the Beartooth Ranger District office, three miles south of Red Lodge on US-212 (Mon–Fri 8am–4.30pm; ☏406/446-2103).

One longer turn-off that shouldn't be missed, especially on a clear day, is the one leading up toward **Clay Butte Lookout** (9811ft), eight miles east of the junction with Chief Joseph Scenic Byway (Hwy-296). Here, a good dirt road winds a few miles to a trailhead accessing Granite Lake; park here and walk the final mile or so up to the hilltop area, which affords stunning panoramic views.

Forest Service **campgrounds** are plentiful along the route, while the only **lodging** option is the four-room motel ($55–79) at 9400ft *Top of the World Resort* (☏307/587-5368, ⊛www.topoftheworldresort.com), located about twelve miles east of the junction with Chief Joseph Scenic Byway; if you're camping in the area, stop by the resort's handy store for a bundle of firewood.

Cody and around

The eastern gateway to Yellowstone, **CODY** sits alongside the North Fork of the Shoshone River some 52 miles east of the park in Wyoming. Mountain man John Colter stumbled through the Shoshone Canyon here in the early 1800s, dubbing the area – and not Yellowstone itself, as many histories inaccurately claim – **Colter's Hell** for its now-inactive geysers and sulphur-rich airs. While the sickly smell of sulphur still occasionally wafts through town, Cody owes its existence not to Colter, but to the sponsorship of an even more famed Western hero. The town was the brainchild of investors, who in 1896 persuaded **William "Buffalo Bill" Cody** to become involved in their development company knowing his approval would attract homesteaders and visitors alike. Being at the western end of the dry Bighorn Basin, it was always clear that Cody would need a significant irrigation source if the town was to grow into a centre of agriculture and a gateway for Yellowstone tourism. Bill Cody was probably the only person who could have drawn the support and funding for the dam and reservoir that today bear his name, so this town of about nine thousand really does owe its existence to the man; it's fitting, then, that the vast majority of today's visitors come to see the phenomenal **Buffalo Bill Historical Center**, although the summer-long **Cody Nite Rodeo** is another prime draw.

Arrival, orientation and information

Cody sits at the junction of several highways, including Hwy-20 leading west to Yellowstone. **Yellowstone Regional Airport** (T 307/587-5096, W www.flyyra .com), which receives daily year-round flights from Denver and Salt Lake City, is located 1.5 miles east of downtown, just off Hwy-20. Town **orientation** is easy enough, with most places of interest strung along two main sections of Hwy-20: Sheridan Avenue takes in the nine blocks that make up the downtown precinct, while Yellowstone Avenue, stretching west towards the national park, has a handful of motels and campgrounds, as well as the rodeo arena and the town's secondary attractions. Stop by Cody's helpful **visitor centre**, 836 Sheridan Ave (June–Sept Mon–Fri 8am–6pm, Sat 9am–5pm, Sun 10am–3pm; rest of year Mon–Fri 8am–5pm; T 307/587-2777, W www.codychamber.org) for town information. Cody Trolley Tours ($24; T 307/527-7043, W www.codytrolleytours .com) offers corny hour-long **tours** of town, complete with running commentary, daily throughout summer. If you're heading to the rodeo arena, hop aboard the Cody Nite Rodeo Bus ($4 return), which picks up passengers at 7.30pm nightly during summer at the *Irma Hotel*.

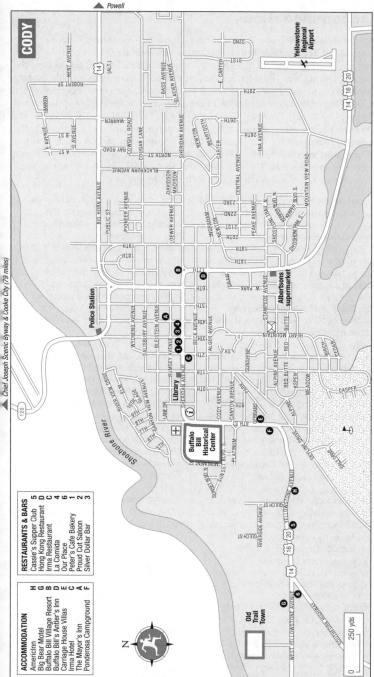

▲ Powell

◀ Chief Joseph Scenic Byway & Cooke City (79 miles)

Yellowstone
Regional
Airport

15

239

ACCOMMODATION

AmericInn	H
Big Bear Motel	G
Buffalo Bill Village Resort	B
Buffalo Bill's Antler's Inn	D
Carriage House Villas	E
Irma Hotel	C
The Mayor's Inn	A
Ponderosa Campground	F

RESTAURANTS & BARS

Cassie's Supper Club	5
Hong Kong Restaurant	D
Irma Restaurant	C
La Comida	4
Our Place	6
Peter's Cafe Bakery	1
Proud Cut Saloon	2
Silver Dollar Bar	3

Police Station

Library

Buffalo
Bill
Historical
Center

Albertsons
supermarket

Old
Trail
Town

N

0   250 yds

▲ Rodeo arena, Buffalo Bill State Park & Yellowstone National Park, East Entrance (52 miles)

Shoshone River

Accommodation

As the main eastern gateway for driving vacations to Yellowstone, Cody boasts no shortage of **accommodation** choices, and while there aren't a lot of flashy places to stay, many of them fill quickly in summer, so the earlier you can reserve, the better. During the shoulder seasons, you should have little trouble finding somewhere to stay even if you arrive unannounced, but come winter many of Cody's inns shut down. If you don't have any luck with the lodging options listed below, try Cody Lodging Company (☎307/587-6000 or 1-800/587-6560, ⓦwww.codylodgingcompany.com), which operates a number of properties in the area, including B&Bs, cabins and cottages. Apart from the excellent *Ponderosa Campground* detailed below, a handful of more rustic, slightly cheaper Forest Service **campgrounds** ($10–15) are located along nearby highways running west into Wapiti Valley and north into the Beartooth Mountains.

AmericInn 508 Yellowstone Ave ☎307/587-7716 or 1-800/634-3444, ⓦwww.americinn.com. One of Cody's newest inns, this chain property is a cut above most other places in town. Rooms have king-size beds and large televisions, while on-site facilities include heated indoor pool and hot tub; breakfast and internet access are included in rates, which start at $189. Open year-round.

Big Bear Motel 139 W Yellowstone Ave ☎307/587-3117 or 1-800/325-7163, ⓦwww.bigbearmotel.com. Set close to the rodeo arena on the west end of town, this year-round motel features a range of mid-priced accommodation, from standard rooms with one king-size bed ($105 in summer) to cramped family suites that theoretically sleep up to eight ($144); a pair of townhouses ($199–229) are also available.

Buffalo Bill Village Resort 1701 Sheridan Ave ☎307/587-5544 or 1-800/527-5544, ⓦwww.blairhotels.com. Located at the eastern end of Cody's main drag and fronted by a gift shop sporting a false Western facade, this summer-only resort consists of 83 individual cabins ($104) varying in size, all en suite and sporting charmingly tacky rodeo decor. Next door, and operated by the same management, is both a *Holiday Inn* and *Comfort Inn* with standard chain hotel-style rooms (around $140) and wireless internet; each is open year-round. All three inns share access to the *Holiday Inn*'s heated outdoor pool.

Buffalo Bill's Antler's Inn 1213 17th St ☎307/587-2084 or 1-800/388-2084, ⓦwww.antlersinncody.com. Although hardly memorable, this two-storey property on the main drag east of downtown fits the bill if you're looking for cleanliness and simple motel-style comfort. Rooms are affordable even at the height of the summer tourist season – generally about $100. Closed in winter.

Carriage House Villas 1816 8th St ☎307/527-5779, ⓦwww.carriagehousevillas.com. This trio of delightful c.1920 two- and four-bedroom homes ($135–195) constitutes one of Cody's more unique lodging options. Each unit comes complete with laundry and televisions, while the larger pair boast a bbq grill and yard.

Irma Hotel 1192 Sheridan Ave ☎307/587-4221 or 1-800/745-4762, ⓦwww.irmahotel.com. The hotel built and named for Buffalo Bill's daughter remains a downtown landmark. Although a little less expensive, avoid booking a room in the 1980s annex and opt instead for one in the 1902 building's "historic section", where classic corner sinks, chunky antique wardrobes and stylish light fixtures are the norm. Non-smokers should beware that the *Irma*'s public areas are typically smoky. Rates start at $112 in summer.

The Mayor's Inn 1413 Rumsey Ave ☎307/587-0887 or 1-888/217-3001, ⓦwww.mayorsinn.com. This early 1900s home was moved to its present location piecemeal from its original spot on Sheridan Ave in 1997, then lovingly restored as a B&B. Furnishings include antiques salvaged from local houses and even the *Irma Hotel*, and the five rooms ($125–215) have luxury touches such as fluffy robes and jetted tubs.

Ponderosa Campground 1815 8th St ☎307/587-9203, ⓦwww.codyponderosa.com. A friendly and well-managed campground with clean shower and toilet facilities, the *Ponderosa* also offers laundry facilities, a general store and a games room. Overnight options include tepees ($25), cabins ($42; no linens provided) and grassy tent sites ($22); if you tent-camp, try to snag a site below the main campground beside Sulphur Creek. Open April–Oct.

The town and around

Despite Cody's main thoroughfare, **Sheridan Avenue**, being wide enough for a couple of wagon teams at least, there's little else here that evokes the feel of the Old West. Native American arts, crafts and jewellery feature heavily among the stores along the main drag, and there are a few shops selling every conceivable variation of the cowboy hat – although in presentation and price, these places are clearly aimed at would-be cowboys from LA and London rather than real ones from northwest Wyoming.

Cody's corny street **gunfight** is quite a production, with up to twelve participants shooting off their mouths and guns to entertain crowds; it kicks off in front of the *Irma Hotel* at 6pm from Monday to Saturday throughout summer. The town's biggest annual festival is the **Cody Stampede**, held on the weekend of July 4 (℡307/587-5155 or 1-800/207-0744, ⓦwww.codystampederodeo .com), which features parades, street performances, fireworks and, naturally, a huge rodeo ($16–24). Smaller but still popular, the lively **Cody Nite Rodeo** (June–Aug nightly 8pm; same contact info; $8–18) pulls in participants from all over the West.

Buffalo Bill Historical Center

The nation's most comprehensive collection of Western Americana, Cody's **Buffalo Bill Historical Center**, 720 Sheridan Ave, comprises five distinct museums (May to mid-Sept daily 6am–6pm, check website for seasonal hours; $15; ℡307/587-4771, ⓦwww.bbhc.org); keep your ticket for a free return visit the following day, as there's a lot to get through. First up is the excellent **Buffalo Bill Museum**, which chronicles William Cody's involvement in the Pony Express, Civil War, Indian Wars and Wild West Shows through an endless stream of artefacts. Among the highlights are the nine-passenger Deadwood stagecoach used in Cody's Wild West Show, and the remains of Cody's celebrated Springfield rifle used to hunt down countless buffalo. Likewise intriguing are certain photos of the man on display – contrast one in which he resembles an overdressed (and overweight) dandy with another that finds him in classic mounted pose, cutting a dash with a leather gauntlet in hand, experience and gravitas etched into his weathered face.

The lives of western Native Americans are celebrated in the **Plains Indian Museum**, the centre's most affecting museum. Many ceremonial garments are displayed in stunning condition; one prize exhibit is a shirt – made from deer hide and brightly decorated with both horse and human hair, glass beads, porcupine quills and more – that belonged to Red Cloud, a Lakota Sioux chief who visited Washington several times during the 1870s to petition for peace on behalf of his people. Just as marvellous is the circle of six buffalo-horn bonnets, worn to capture the sacred power of the buffalo before big hunts. Lending a tragic note to the collection is the display of Ghost Dance shirts: in the late 1880s, western tribes were swept by the religious revelation of Paiute prophet Wovoka, who declared that ritual purification through song and dance would hasten the day when all whites would be buried by a heaven-sent fall of soil, allowing dead native warriors and huge herds of buffalo to return to the Plains. The US army condemned Ghost Dances as unacceptable shows of resistance and mobilized troops to disrupt ceremonies.

One of the most famous Americans of his era, **William Frederick Cody** was born on February 26, 1846. Within fifty years of his modest start in a small Iowa farmhouse, upwards of five hundred pulp novels starring "**Buffalo Bill**" had been published, and his legendary Wild West Show had circled the globe. Cody's much-mythologized exploits began at an early age, soon after his father – an anti-slavery advocate who had recently moved his family to Kansas – was stabbed to death after making his views known to an angry, pro-slavery mob. After his father's death, Cody, the eldest living son at only 11 years old, took work on a wagon train to support the family. To escape from an ambush on one early outing, Cody reputedly shot a man for the first time, earning him fame as the "Boy Indian Slayer"; four years later, he became the youngest rider on the **Pony Express**, averaging a blazing 15mph on his leg of the storied mail route.

The day after his mother's funeral, Cody, still underage at 17, signed on to fight for the Union army in the **Civil War**. His wartime heroics (whether real or trumped-up) are relatively under-reported, but after his stint fighting for the North, Cody found work – and a lifelong nickname – supplying buffalo meat to workers laying down tracks for the Kansas Pacific railroad. Under contract to kill a dozen buffalo per day for $500 a month, Cody claimed to have killed over 4200 in just eighteen months. In 1868, at 22, he rejoined the US army as its chief scout; over the next decade, when the **Plains Indian Wars** were at their peak, he earned a Congressional Medal of Honor and a remarkable record of never losing any troops in ambushes. Among the battles in which he participated was an 1877 encounter with Sioux forces, when he killed – and some legends claim, scalped – Chief Yellow Hand. During this time, Cody also was introduced to author **Ned Buntline**, who cemented Cody's fame back East with a series of exaggerated accounts of Cody's adventures in scores of "dime novels", starting with *Buffalo Bill, King of the Border Men*.

As the Indian Wars calmed, Cody took to guiding Yankee and European gentry – grand dukes and famed US generals Sherman and Custer, for example – on buffalo hunts, and the theatrical productions he laid on for his rich guests developed into Cody's long-running **Wild West Show**. First staged in 1883, these spectacular carnivals usually consisted of a re-enactment of an Indian battle such as Custer's Last Stand, featuring Sioux warriors (including, for a short time, **Sitting Bull**) who had been present at Little Bighorn; shows also featured stagecoach attacks, trick riders, buffalo, clowns, and shooting and riding exhibitions by the man himself. Later shows expanded to include a "Congress of Rough Riders of the World", complete with Arab horsemen, Russian Cossacks, Cuban rebels and sharpshooting **Annie Oakley**. The show spent ten of its thirty years in Europe, where, dressed in the finest silks and sporting a well-groomed goatee, Cody stayed in the grandest hotels and dined with heads of state. Ever the showman, Cody hoped to hold his show in Rome's crumbling Colosseum, but found it too dilapidated to suit his purposes. And in England, Queen Victoria was so enthusiastic in her admiration that rumours circulated of an affair between the two.

In his later years, a mellowed Cody played down his past exploits, to the point of urging the US government to respect all Native American treaties and put an end to the wanton slaughter of buffalo and game. Cody also spent significant time living on a ranch not far from his adopted hometown of Cody, describing the nearby Bighorn Basin to the east as "one of nature's masterpieces". Although his Wild West Show was believed to have brought in as much as $1 million annually, too many of his investments failed badly, and on January 10, 1915, not long before his 70th birthday, a penniless Buffalo Bill died at his sister's home in Colorado. His grave can be found atop Lookout Mountain, just west of Denver.

Next door, in the **Whitney Gallery of Western Art**, the contrasting styles of Frederic Remington and Charles M. Russell command the most attention. The propagandist Remington, whose studio is also on display, dwells on conflict, depicting natives as savages blocking the path of progress; Russell's work, on the other hand, demonstrates a consistent respect for native life. Among scores of paintings with titles such as *Last of Their Race* and *Last of the Buffalo* by other painters, look out for Edgar Paxson's *Custer's Last Stand* (1899), an epic work displayed alongside a diagram pointing out all the major players within the battle scene; Custer stands, gut-shot and near death, in the middle of the melee.

For something altogether different, head to the centre's newest addition, the **Draper Museum of Natural History**. The circular gallery is lined with interactive exhibits and beautifully laid-out taxidermy displays, all of which help detail the geology and wildlife of the Greater Yellowstone region, as well as the role humans have played in the area's history. As part of the museum's "participatory experience" approach, classes are frequently offered, and visitors are invited to share their own views. One notable display on whether wolves should remain around Yellowstone featured handwritten responses such as "Wolves: government-sponsored terrorists" and "Save the elk, moose and buffalo babies – shoot the wolves" – common opinions in this rancher-rich area.

Finally, a quick tour of the centre's final gallery, the **Cody Firearms Museum**, is worthwhile for a look at a number of superbly crafted rifles, pistols and revolvers dating back to the 1500s – particularly those made through the course of the nineteenth century, when manufacturers strove to outdo one another with elaborate designs.

Old Trail Town

A random collection of log cabins, firearms, wagons and other relics salvaged from all over the region, **Old Trail Town**, 1831 DeMaris Drive (mid May to mid Sept daily 8am–8pm; $8), nevertheless makes for a handy one-stop viewing of frontier culture on the far west edge of Cody. The 25 buildings date between 1879 and 1901 and include a re-created general store, schoolhouse, trapper's cabin and blacksmith's shop. Photographs in the buffalo hunter's cabin give some idea of the scale of the 1800s buffalo slaughter, depicting piles of hides and some of the hapless beasts being skinned. On display inside Curley's Cabin are photos of the structure's namesake, a Crow Indian scout who survived the Battle of Little Bighorn; nearby, in the cabin hideout of the infamous Hole in the Wall Gang, where the Sundance Kid and other outlaws bedded down, more photos await, including a grisly shot of three unnamed outlaws being hanged near Laramie in the late 1800s. At the western end of the area, you'll find a memorial to the mountain men of the fur-trapping era, including a number of gravesites of various trappers and buffalo hunters. Among them is one for infamous John (Jeremiah) "Liver Eating" Johnston, who some claim earned his nickname by killing and scalping – and then eating the livers of – the Crow Indians who killed his wife.

Buffalo Bill State Park

Nine miles west of Cody along Hwy-20, **Buffalo Bill State Park** (May–Sept; $6; ☏307/587-9223) sits prettily in the midst of the Absaroka Mountains, but most of its action takes place on the boomerang-shaped, man-made lake at its centre. The obvious first stop – and the only one necessary for those not fishing or camping – is the Buffalo Bill Dam Visitor Center (Mon–Sat 8am–6pm). Exhibits detail the narrow structure's 1905–1910 construction and how, upon completion, it was the highest in the world at 325ft; a 1993 addition raised it another 25 feet, and it's worth a quick stop to absorb the stomach-churning view straight down its front into Shoshone Canyon. Besides providing water for the residents of Cody and other towns in the Bighorn Basin, the reservoir is popular for fishing, boating, windsurfing and kitesurfing. Bare and gusty sites at two highway-adjacent **campgrounds**, *North Shore Bay* and *North Fork*, cost $17 per night.

Eating and drinking

For a town that sees over one million visitors pass through each summer, Cody is hardly over-endowed with an interesting **restaurant** scene. A good steak is easy enough to find, but options beyond that are fairly limited; at least most of the best establishments are located on or just off Sheridan Avenue, meaning you can browse a number of menus on a lazy stroll. Those heading west to Yellowstone should definitely stock up at the large Albertsons **supermarket** (see "Listings", opposite). Cody's **bars** are fairly basic watering holes, although the pair of places listed below offer a fair representation of the town's party scene. During summer a variety of regional country and rock bands pass through town, but night-time entertainment is otherwise limited to a little "boot-scootin'" or a game of pool.

Cassie's Supper Club 214 Yellowstone Ave ☎307/527-5500. You may need a cowboy hat to feel comfortable at *Cassie's*, but for a true Wyoming cultural experience, this is your best bet in Cody. Along with pool tables, entertainment at this 1920s roadhouse – and rumour has it, former brothel – ranges from line-dancing classes to country and country-rock bands. You can even settle in with a steak ($15–30) in the dining room and make it a full evening.

Hong Kong Restaurant 1201 17th St. While not exactly made from authentic old-country recipes, the Americanized Chinese selections ($8–13) here are a welcome change of pace in this meat-and-potatoes region. The $9.25 lunch buffet is a good deal.

Irma Restaurant Irma Hotel ☎307/587-4221. A good spot for a slab of prime rib – billed as the house specialty – for dinner, this evocative hotel dining room also lays out extensive breakfast and lunch buffets (both $9.50; Sun lunch $13). The striking cherry-wood bar, constructed in France for the hotel's 1902 opening, was a gift to Buffalo Bill from none other than Queen Victoria.

La Comida 1385 Sheridan Ave. Open daily for lunch and dinner and boasting an invitingly attractive patio, *La Comida*'s Mexican standards ($8–14) are augmented by light selections such as *pechuga* salad (chopped chicken over leafy greens, doused in sour cream and green chilli). Service may require extra patience at particularly busy times.

Our Place 148 Yellowstone Ave. Tiny and very popular (particularly with locals), this is the sort of classic, small-town American diner where a cup of coffee is only 25 cents and efficient servers bring hot, heaped breakfasts and lunches (starting at $6) to your table in short order. Mon–Sat 6am–2pm; cash only.

Peter's Cafe Bakery 1219 Sheridan Ave. A bright, cheerful place with a simple selection of bagels and muffins, a nice range of coffee and terrific full breakfasts (most well under $8). Come lunchtime, deli sandwiches of titanic proportions ($5–9) crowd the menu, with $8 picnic boxes also available.

Proud Cut Saloon 1227 Sheridan Ave ☎307/527-6905. Despite a waiting staff prone to slothfulness and disorganization, the *Proud Cut*'s self-described "Cowboy Cuisine" remains a local favourite. Bring your best appetite for the big garlic burger ($9) at lunch and even more humungous steaks ($15–26) at dinner.

Silver Dollar Bar 1313 Sheridan Ave ☎307/587-3554. This should be the first place you check for live music – more often rock than country. The scene of lively drinking on the large street-side patio and pool-playing inside, the *Silver Dollar* also makes tasty burgers, gloriously greasy slabs served in a basket (with onion rings) for under $8.

Outdoor activities

Along with fishing and watersports at Buffalo Bill Reservoir, many outdoor pursuits near Cody are found en route to Yellowstone, either in Wapiti Valley to the east or north off the Chief Joseph Scenic Byway (both covered later in this chapter). There's **whitewater rafting** (Class II–IV; half-day trip around $70) throughout summer on the North Fork of the Shoshone River well west of town, as well as gentler two-hour **float trips** (around $30) along the same waterway that are ideal for spotting elk and bighorn sheep; among Cody's river outfitters, try Wyoming River Trips, 233 Yellowstone Ave (☎307/587-6661 or 1-800/586-6661, ⓦwww.wyomingrivertrips.com). **Fishing** enthusiasts can get licenses and expect top advice from North Fork Anglers, 1107 Sheridan Ave (☎307/527-7274, ⓦwww.northforkanglers.com), which boasts a superbly stocked fly shop and also runs guided trips on the North and South Forks of the Shoshone, as well as on the Clark's Fork of the Yellowstone to the north and into the national park itself; rates for these trips range from $350–550 per day. **Hikers** can drop by the Shoshone National Forest office at 203A Yellowstone Ave (Mon–Fri 8am–4.30pm; ☎307/527-6921) for maps and trail recommendations in the Shoshone, designated as the country's first national forest in 1891; those looking for tips on local **mountain-biking** trails should check with Absaroka Bicycles (☎307/527-5566), located in the Kmart-anchored shopping plaza on 17th Street south of downtown.

Listings

Wapiti Valley and Buffalo Bill Cody Scenic Byway

The hour-long drive west from Cody to Yellowstone on Hwy-20 provides superb preparation for the splendours of the park itself, with the scenery along the way worthy of a half-day – or more – of exploration should time permit. The first half of the drive begins by skirting along the north shore of Buffalo Bill Reservoir before running alongside the Shoshone River into wide-open **Wapiti Valley**, the heart of Wyoming's "beef country" and home to a handful of dude ranches and horse-packing outfitters. About halfway to Yellowstone, the highway enters Shoshone National Forest and becomes the **Buffalo Bill Cody Scenic Byway**. A busy two-lane route that runs into the park alongside the North Fork of the Shoshone, the byway is lined by fantastical rock formations, known as "hoodoos", that'll have you thinking you've stumbled upon the set of a psychedelic Spaghetti Western. The crenellated-buttes and sandcastle bluffs here are made from breccia, a mixture of rock and ash deposited by volcanic eruptions some fifty million years ago that's been continually eroded ever since; it's safe to say they're unlike any other rock formations you'll see in either nearby national park. Be sure to stop at the viewpoint 28 miles west of Cody to marvel at **Holy City**, perhaps the most extraordinary of the formations, so named for the way early explorers believed its silhouette mirrored that of the city of Jerusalem.

There's more to appreciate beyond geological formations, and passengers should scan the landscape to spot the likes of bighorn sheep, pronghorn and mule deer; there's also a fair amount of grizzly activity on the south side of the highway. With a wealth of access spots, the North Fork of the Shoshone here is prime **fly-fishing** territory; as well, a half-dozen **trailheads** for both hiking and cross-country skiing (biking not permitted) lead into the volcanic landscapes of North Absaroka and Washakie Wildernesses, located north and south of the byway, respectively. For trail maps and other useful information in summer, pull over and visit the historic **Wapiti Ranger Station** (late May to early Sept daily 9am–4pm; ☏307/578-1200), two miles west of Holy City along the Byway.

Practicalities

Other than during the busy July and August period, few visitors stop overnight at the numerous pleasant **campgrounds** and **lodges** strung between Cody and Yellowstone; several are located within a few miles of the park's East Entrance (early May to early Nov), and are worth considering as a base if you're particularly interested in fly-fishing or horseriding. Only two miles east of the park boundary is *Pahaska Tepee* (☏307/527-7701 or 1-800/628-7791, ⓦwww.pahaska .com), Buffalo Bill's one-time hunting lodge – Pahaska, meaning "long hair", was Cody's Indian name. Along with a gift shop, restaurant and trail rides into the surrounding Shoshone National Forest, the c.1904 lodge offers an array of distinctive A-frame cabins; nightly rates start at $120 in summer and drop as low as $70 in shoulder seasons. Similar accommodation and activities are available at *Shoshone Lodge and Guest Ranch*, one mile further east (☏307/587-4044, ⓦwww .shoshonelodge.com), and *Elephant Head Lodge*, another seven miles towards Cody (☏307/587-3980, ⓦwww.elephantheadlodge.com). A string of appealing Forest Service campgrounds ($10–15) are scattered along the Buffalo Bill Cody Scenic Byway, and most have piped water, chemical toilets, fire rings and bear-proof metal bins for food storage; several operate between May and October, but *Elk Fork* and *Newton Creek Campgrounds* remain open year-round, with piped water turned off for the winter in September.

Chief Joseph Scenic Byway

If you arrive in Cody from Yellowstone on the Buffalo Bill Cody Scenic Byway, consider looping back into the park via Cooke City and the quiet Northeast Entrance along the **Chief Joseph Scenic Byway**. Though not as immediately impressive as the drive through Wapiti Valley, the 90-minute journey through Sunlight Basin and Clark's Fork Valley boasts dramatic vistas and plenty of opportunities for wildlife spotting and outdoor activities.

Start by heading north out of Cody on Hwy-120 as it cuts through lonely ranchlands. Local landmark **Heart Mountain** dominates the view to the northeast, and the peak has long presented a geological puzzle: it's topped by a three-hundred-million-year-old limestone cap that's not only loaded with the fossils of invertebrate sea creatures, but is markedly older than the rock *beneath* it. After seventeen miles, Hwy-120 meets Hwy-296, the latter known as the Chief Joseph Scenic Byway – so named for the chief of the Nez Percé tribe, as the road follows the route of their historic flight (see box below). The first eight miles of the 47-mile-long Byway weave past herds of grazing cattle on the private Two Dot Ranch before entering Shoshone National Forest; the road climbs ever higher over the next five miles, eventually cresting at **Dead Indian Summit** (8060ft). A lay-by here provides spectacular views of the Absaroka and Beartooth mountain ranges ahead, lined with a combined two dozen peaks that soar beyond 12,000ft.

Flight of the Nez Percé

By the time the first white settlers moved into the United States' northwest reaches in the nineteenth century, the **Nez Percé** (pronounced NAY-pur-SAY) people had been living in what is now northeast Oregon, north Idaho and southeast Washington for thousands of years. Their first contact with whites was when Lewis and Clark passed through the area in 1805; relations between the natives and expedition members were friendly, but the situation began to sour over the next half-century. An 1855 treaty moved the peaceable tribe to the **Nez Percé Reservation**, a five-thousand-square-mile area that reserved much of their traditional lands for exclusive use. However, after gold was discovered on the plot and settlers came pouring in, a new treaty was drawn up in 1863 that reduced the reservation to a mere ten percent of its previous size. The majority of the Nez Percé, including one large band under the leadership of **Chief Joseph**, refused to recognize the agreement.

In 1877, after much vacillation, the US government decided to enact its terms and gave the people only thirty days to leave. This led to skirmishes that resulted in the deaths of a handful of settlers – the first whites ever to be attacked by Nez Percé – and soon the government gathered a large (if poorly trained) army to round up the increasingly hostile bands. That June, the group embarked upon what is known today as the **Flight of the Nez Percé**, a miserable trek that followed a circuitous route through the northern Rockies, the Yellowstone region and, ultimately, to northern Montana. Several chiefs led eight hundred tribal members (including many elderly, women and children) and four times that many horses, outmanoeuvring multiple army columns in a series of daring escapes along the way. Still, the march was horribly arduous and saw multiple changes in chief leadership, and the unspeakable tragedy of having to leave unfit elders and other sick and wounded to die along the way inevitably took a heavy emotional and physical toll. Once the Nez Percé were ambushed and cornered amid freezing October weather in the Bear's Paw Mountains – a mere forty miles from refuge beyond the Canadian border – Chief Joseph made his much-quoted speech of **surrender**:

"I am tired of fighting. Our chiefs are killed. It is cold, and we have no blankets. The little children are freezing to death. My people, some of them, have run away to the hills and have no blankets, no food. Hear me, my chiefs! My heart is sick and sad. From where the sun now stands, I will fight no more forever".

Despite promises of being allowed to soon return to reservations in the Northwest, the Nez Percé were taken to Fort Leavenworth, Kansas, before being shuttled again to squalid living conditions in Oklahoma. Chief Joseph laboured tirelessly for his people's **return to their ancestral homes**, and by 1885, the 268 Nez Percé still alive were shunted homeward by train, a pitiful remnant of the group's pre-flight numbers, geographically splintered into Christian and non-Christian groups upon their return north.

The Byway then swirls steeply downward past *Dead Indian Campground* ($10) and into **Sunlight Basin**, named as such by nineteenth-century trappers because sunlight was the only thing that could get into this remote area come winter. Here the road crosses the **Sunlight Creek Bridge**, Wyoming's tallest at over 300ft, spanning the deep and narrow Sunlight Creek Gorge. Around fifteen miles on, the highway passes over the Clark's Fork of the Yellowstone – widely recognized as one of the finest fly-fishing and kayaking rivers in North America – and through the tiny hamlet of **Crandall**. Here you'll find Painter Outpost (T307/527-5510), a collection of services consisting of a gas station, tiny market, RV park and riverside campground ($11), as well as *Clark's Fork and Spoon*, a café best known in the region for its terrific pies. Past Crandall, dramatic Index and Pilot Peaks come into view, after which the Byway soon meets Hwy-212: to the east is the epic Beartooth Highway, while a turn to the west leads to Cooke City, thirteen miles away: both are covered in detail in Chapter 14.

Contexts

Contexts

History 251

Geology, flora, and fauna 263

Books 271

History

W hat follows is a condensed **history** of America's most hallowed national park, one that has faced several precarious junctures throughout its story. Were it not for the efforts of many judicious and preservation-minded individuals – several of whom are spotlighted on the following pages – the mighty Yellowstone River would probably be dammed today and Old Faithful would be little more than a hydrothermal facility converting steam into electricity. This account also touches on the greater Yellowstone region, but for a detailed look at the creation of **Grand Teton National Park**, see the box on p.89. Certainly the area's story starts well before recorded history, and we've covered the Yellowstone region's early **geology** under "Geology, flora, and fauna", beginning on p.263.

Native history: hunter-gatherers to the Sheepeaters

For a whole host of reasons, whites in the nineteenth and early twentieth centuries loudly claimed that **Native Americans** refused to inhabit or often even visit the Yellowstone region, frightened off like superstitious children by its gurgling mudpots and bellowing geysers. In fact, humans have been living in, and travelling through, the area for more than eleven thousand years, arriving soon after the last wave of glaciers and ice sheets receded to the north. The first people to inhabit the region were **hunter-gatherers** subsisting on seeds, roots and game, including Ice Age mammals such as the **giant bison** and **mammoth**. As these creatures gradually disappeared, the attention of hunters shifted to the smaller game familiar to park visitors today. Obsidian projectile points, grinding stones and tools have all been excavated by archeologists throughout the area, helping paint a picture of the lives of these early inhabitants. Moving seasonally, groups would arrive from the neighbouring plains in spring, camping by lakes and streams to pick wild onion and balsamroot and hunt plentiful game. As summer arrived, these groups would split into smaller family parties to follow both the game and blooming plants such as biscuit-root and whitebark pine, moving up to the high-altitude tundra for several weeks; large stone circles thought to hold religious significance have been found at these sites high upon mountaintops. As the cold autumn winds blew in, the seasonal circle was completed, with the groups returning to lower ground.

For thousands of years, this system evolved only gradually, with technological advances including the introduction of the **bow and arrow** along with the development of bison **corrals** and bighorn sheep **traps**. Native use and exploration of the area seems to have continually increased into the 1400s, the point at which more recent historians begin ascribing names to the area's tribes. Ancestors of the **Shoshone**, **Bannock**, **Blackfeet**, **Nez Percé**, **Bannock** and several other tribes all crisscrossed Yellowstone on numerous trails, with the Fishing Bridge area often used as a rendezvous site. Another major stopping point was **Obsidian Cliff** (see p.61), a vital source for obtaining the material used for spear and arrow tips.

The arrival of **horses** in the Rockies around 1700 helped create the last major shift before the coming of whites. One group who didn't take to the horse, however, were the **Sheepeaters** (also known as **Tukaduka**), a branch of the Shoshone who were the primary occupiers of Yellowstone when the first whites arrived in the early 1800s. Moving seasonally, the Sheepeaters spent summers hunting bighorn sheep high in the mountains (hence their name), though they also fished and tracked smaller mammals such as squirrel and porcupine. Come winter, they huddled in **wikiups**, tepee-like shelters made by balancing hundreds of long branches. In the spirit of the era, the Sheepeaters were typically disparaged as dirty and poor by whites encountering them, but trapper Osborne Russell (see p.52) writes positively about meeting a family in his journals, noting they were "neatly clothed in dressed deer and sheepskins of the best quality and seemed to be perfectly happy", and he gladly traded for top-quality elk, deer and sheep skins. Along with being expert tanners, Sheepeaters were skilled bow-makers, using material from a ram's horn to construct bows powerful enough to send an arrow completely through a bison.

Early exploration

The first non-native to explore Yellowstone was probably **John Colter**, who entered the region as a private with the **Lewis and Clark** expedition. The famed two-year, eight-thousand-mile expedition left from St Louis in 1804, passing north of Yellowstone country on the Missouri River en route to the Pacific Ocean. In no rush to return to civilization, Colter was given permission to leave the group on the expedition's return journey, joining with two other fur trappers – Forest Hancock and Joseph Dixson – to hunt for riches along the Missouri River in August 1806. Colter soon had a falling out with his temporary partners, and left to trap on his own. This launched the Kentucky native into years of adventure, including one of the West's great stories in which Colter, captured by a band of Blackfoot, was stripped naked and given a head-start before a band of braves set off in deadly pursuit. Running for his life, Colter eluded his attackers by hiding out in a freezing river before escaping on a three-hundred-mile march back to the nearest trading post, eating roots for survival.

Colter's other marathon journey into the Yellowstone region took place in 1807, while working under the employment of **Manuel Lisa**, a Spaniard from New Orleans. Lisa ran the first organized crew of trappers in the area from a fort by the confluence of the Yellowstone and Big Horn Rivers, east of where Billings is today. Colter left the fort at the start of winter on what ended up becoming an epic five-hundred-mile circuit through portions of modern-day Yellowstone and Grand Teton National Parks. Specifics are hazy, including even which direction, clockwise or counterclockwise, Colter followed on the loop; it has been established, however, that Colter passed both Yellowstone and Jackson Lakes, and stumbled across many of the area's bizarre thermal features. One steamy, sulphurous area – barely active today on the outskirts of Cody – became known as **Colter's Hell**, a designation later mistakenly applied to thermal basins within Yellowstone.

The **War of 1812** between the United States and Great Britain halted most US-led trapping in the region for years, giving Canadian and French fur trappers a near monopoly on the trade. In 1818, a group of trappers led by Canadian **Donald McKenzie** recorded the sight of "boiling fountains", though not enough detail was given to locate exactly which geysers they may have come across. Both the war's end and published reports from the Lewis and Clark expedition helped to spark excitement about what the West had in store for courageous explorers. In the East, newspaper ads were placed to recruit trappers to fulfil, in part, the booming demand for beaver pelts used to make hats that were all the rage on both sides of the Atlantic. By 1825, famous **Mountain Men** like tall-tale teller **Jim Bridger** (see box, p.61), journal-keeping **Osborne Russell** (see review, p.272) and **Davey Jackson**, namesake of Jackson Hole, began heeding the call, becoming part of the first wave of trappers to flock to the region.

The life of a fur trapper in the Rockies was far from easy, filled with cold nights, tyrannical deals with their companies and many a tough slog through swamps in search of beaver. Most trappers worked alone or with a partner, disappearing into the mountains for the winter and spring months, when the beaver fur was at its most thick and lush. They would emerge in summer with as many as 150 pelts, bushy beards and stories of survival against the odds. Some of these tales included details of the natural wonders within Yellowstone and helped confirm Colter's stories, which many had believed to be great exaggerations at best and mirage-like delusions at worst.

By 1840, due to **over-trapping** and the **decline in fashion** for hats made with beaver pelts, the heyday of fur trapping had run its course in the Northern Rockies. Those Mountain Men who stayed behind tried their luck at homesteading, became guides to rich tourists and the US army, and organized businesses such as trading posts and ferry crossings. Still, for the next two decades, whites rarely visited the Yellowstone plateau, and a collection of Native American tribes continued to maintain the strongest grip on the land.

Official exploration

As with so many other areas in the rugged and unforgiving Rockies, it took the discovery of **gold** to motivate whites into moving in to scratch out a living in semi-permanent settlements. Gold strikes in Idaho in the early 1860s are what drew fortune-seekers into this portion of the Northern Rockies, and mining activity and exploration saw small parties of whites re-entering Yellowstone. Quite a few parties marched through the territory of today's Yellowstone National Park in the mid 1860s, looking for riches rather than the fame of exploration, and while they found only traces of gold, they did return with fantastic tales describing the areas's wonders, adding more credence to the ever-expanding series of Mountain Man "myths" collected over the previous sixty years. These stories, passed around in the bars, meeting halls and streets of Montana's burgeoning mining towns, helped kick-start a series of planned outings in the area that were to confirm, finally, Yellowstone's singular sights to the rest of the world.

The Cook-Folsom Expedition

First out of the gate was the **Cook–Folsom Expedition** in 1869, a three-person party consisting of Charles Cook and David Folsom, two Quakers, and William Peterson, a former sailor, all of whom had spent several years mining in the Northern Rockies. Leaving in early September from Helena, Montana, the trio entered Yellowstone from the north, via Bozeman, with five horses and limited supplies. Encountering small parties of Sheepeaters along the way, they followed the Yellowstone River south, passing Tower Fall and camping at the Grand Canyon in view of its falls. They got as far south as Yellowstone Lake's northern shores, where they gorged on trout and waterfowl, before turning west to wander past Great Fountain Geyser, where it's claimed they all took off their hats and hollered with astonishment. Upon returning home on October 11, just over a month after leaving Helena, their stories quickly spread through town and eventually out to the East Coast, where both the *New York Tribune* and *Harper's* found the information too far-fetched to publish.

The Washburn Expedition

Big-city papers may not have trusted the Cook-Folsom stories, but Helena's citizens certainly began to, and in the following year a larger, better-organized and fully funded expedition set off. Known as the **Washburn Expedition**, the nineteen-man party was led by **Henry Dana Washburn**, Surveyor General of Montana and formerly a Civil War officer and Congressman. Known for his fairness, Washburn died soon after returning from the explorations due to frail health stemming in part from his practice of taking on extra guard and scout duties. Along with an escort of soldiers led by crack shot **Gustavus Doane** and a handful of helpers, the expedition included the likes of bank president (and later Governor of Montana Territory) **Samuel Hauser**, Yale lawyer (and later state Senator) **Cornelius Hedges**, and **Nathaniel Pitt Langford**, soon to become the first Superintendent of Yellowstone and the expedition's most successful diarist; see p.272 for a review of his journal.

The forty-day adventure left Helena on August 22, 1870, following a similar route as the Cook-Folsom Party. The group spent the first few days feasting on venison, elk and trout before tackling, in order, Tower Fall, which they named, the Grand Canyon and Yellowstone Falls, and Yellowstone Lake. Instead of heading west at the northern edge of the lake, however, they continued south along its eastern edge and circled the massive body of water, mapping it clearly for the first time. After that, they marched through exceedingly difficult country to reach Upper Geyser Basin, marvelling at the accuracy of Old Faithful, a name bestowed by Washburn himself. In regards to naming, the group agreed before setting out to not identify any features after themselves, but the promise of immortality must have been too great, as evidenced by other names left behind including Mounts Washburn, Langford and Doane.

The group returned to Helena hungry and emaciated, but nonetheless under their own power on September 22. There were no battles with natives or grizzly attacks to spice up their tales, and along with nearly starving to death towards the end of their trip, the worst incident befell **Truman C. Everts**, who wandered lost for 37 days in the Yellowstone wilds before being found (see p.50). Along with leaving behind a string of names still used today, the group's most lasting contribution was helping boost the idea of creating a national park for the area, a notion Langford first put into words in his journal on their way home on September 20, 1870:

"I do not know of any portion of our country where a national park can be established furnishing to visitors more wonderful attractions than here. These wonders are so different from anything we have ever seen – they are so various, so extensive – that the feeling in my mind from the moment they began to appear until we left them has been one of intense surprise and of incredulity. Every day spent in surveying them has revealed to me some new beauty, and now that I have left them, I begin to feel a skepticism which clothes them in a memory clouded by doubt."

The Hayden Survey

During the winter after their return, **Langford** gave a series of lectures on his experiences in the Yellowstone region. **Dr. Ferdinand V. Hayden**, head of the US Geological Survey of the Territories, was at one such lecture in Washington DC, and soon afterwards Hayden asked Congress to fund a larger expedition. Incidentally, Hayden had already come close to surveying Yellowstone's natural wonders years earlier in 1859 while working on a two-year exploration of the upper Missouri River. With Jim Bridger as his guide, Hayden's party had begun heading south towards Yellowstone when a blizzard blocked their path and forced them to turn back. The Civil War soon put on hold any further explorations by Hayden at that time, though he did rise to become the Union army's chief medical officer.

Congress approved $40,000 for the new expedition, and by July 1871 an even larger group than the Washburn Expedition was ready to set off for additional mapping, surveying and adventure. Close to three dozen men signed on to take part in the **Hayden Survey** – the first government-sponsored survey of Yellowstone – including Hayden's right-hand man **James Stevenson**, topographer **Anton Schoenborn** and photographer **William Jackson**. Painter **Thomas Moran** was also added to the group at the request of the Northern Pacific Railroad, whose head **Jay Cooke** had already begun hatching plans for monopolizing railroad routes to a region Americans would undoubtedly want to flock to. Jackson's black-and-white photographs and Moran's elegant landscapes both ended up being instrumental in convincing Congress to create the national park.

The large group departed from Fort Ellis in Gallatin Valley in July 1871, and quickly crossed paths with the **Barlow-Heap Expedition**, a smaller military team also visiting Yellowstone, and with whom the Hayden Survey often ended up exploring. The two groups followed a similar route to the two previous expeditions, including a stop at the Grand Canyon, where Moran created the pencil and watercolour field sketches used to paint his famed **oil painting** of the canyon and falls upon returning home to his studio; look closely at the painting and you'll notice members of the survey team, including Hayden and the artist himself, in the foreground. The group created the finest maps of their time, while also launching *Anna*, a 12ft canvas-side boat, onto Yellowstone Lake, making it the first such craft to cross its waters.

A park is born

Hayden's subsequent reports on his forays in the summer and autumn of 1871 put to rest once and for all any doubts about the wonders of Yellowstone, and by December of the same year a draft bill for the creation of a national park was introduced into Congress. This wasn't the first time such an idea had been voted on; eight years earlier, President Abraham Lincoln signed into law the **Yosemite Grant**, setting aside California's Yosemite Valley and the great sequoias within the nearby Mariposa Grove as an area reserved for public use and recreation. Responsibility for the new park, however, was given to California, making it a state park. While the congressional draft for the creation of Yellowstone National Park used much the same language as the Yosemite Grant, a major difference was the notion of federal control over Yellowstone, needed in part to avoid a battle between Montana and Wyoming, both of whom had a stake in the region.

Several interested parties helped push along the national park idea, none more fervently than Northern Pacific Railroad chief Jay Cooke, whose influence in Congress can hardly be understated. Thanks to his persistence, along with Moran's grand paintings and Jackson's awe-inspiring photos, the bill was signed into law on March 1, 1872 by President **Ulysses S. Grant**, creating the country's – and the world's – **first national park**. While capitalistic desires were the engine for the park's creation, high ideals still prevailed, as noted by the bill's eloquent notion that Yellowstone was "dedicated and set apart as a public park or pleasuring-ground for the benefit and enjoyment of the people…", the last eight words of which would later be inscribed into the Roosevelt Arch at the park's North Entrance.

Not all "the people", however, were pleased with the region's new designation. Editorials in Montana and Wyoming newspapers warned that keeping the area protected would shut out businesses and keep away the roads and railways needed to haul visitors; for the first few years, these sceptics were proved correct, as little was done to improve access to the park. Penny-pinching Congress had no plans to fund Yellowstone, instead figuring that tourists would begin arriving once the Northern Pacific Railroad was extended into Montana, thus launching dozens of concessionaires from whom the government could charge rent and other fees; in short, the park would receive money when it started earning money. However, the financial **Panic of 1873** threw these plans into disarray. The countrywide economic crisis was started by none other than Jay Cooke, who, upon finding his banking and railroad interests far over-extended, was forced to declare bankruptcy. It would take nearly another ten years before the railroad reached Yellowstone.

The early years

As the man put in charge of the newly formed national park department, Secretary of the Interior **Columbus Delano** was responsible for picking the **first Superintendent** to manage the nascent park. On May 10, 1872, he appointed **Nathaniel Langford** to the post, a position carrying few actual powers and no salary. Known thereafter as "National Park" Langford, the diarist's first order of business was to tag along on the Hayden Survey's second trip into the region in the summer of 1872, this one even better funded than the expedition one summer earlier.

The **Hayden Survey of 1872** split into northern and southern divisions, and both headed into Yellowstone in early July, sticking it out through September and mapping some nine thousand square miles of terrain. Langford joined the southern division, led by Hayden's right-hand man James Stevenson, which hiked south through the park, past Shoshone and Lewis Lakes, and close by today's Southern Entrance. Continuing onwards, the party reached the Tetons, where Langford and Stevenson claim to have crested **Grand Teton** on July 24 (for more on this controversial claim, see p.102). The southern division continued to map the Teton Range until early August, after which they marched back to Yellowstone to reunite with the northern division at Lower Geyser Basin.

Langford soon left the survey behind to check on an unauthorized toll road being built to **Mammoth Hot Springs**, an area starting to attract invalids to bathe in its supposedly therapeutic waters. These bathers were among the first Yellowstone **tourists**, though they hardly constituted a flood. It's estimated that less than three hundred visitors came in 1872, and, by 1877, no more than five hundred annually. Those few who did visit, however, brought back stories of the park's **mismanagement and neglect**, including the wanton slaughter of game by professional hunters. Langford was relieved of his duties in 1877 after a new Secretary of the Interior, **Carl Schurz**, received one too many letters detailing Langford's lack of action. To be fair, Langford had no funds and little power, but he was also far from proactive, visiting the park only twice as Superintendent and refusing virtually all requests from concessionaires to build or operate services in the park. Even more damning, it appears that Langford's loyalties weren't with "the people", but the Northern Pacific Railroad; he was waiting for the company to rise back up so he could assign it plum concessions.

Superintendent Norris

With Langford let go, **Philetus W. Norris** was appointed the second Superintendent of Yellowstone on April 19, 1877. Quite the opposite from Langford, Norris, as described by Yellowstone historian Aubrey L. Haines, was a natural leader – a kind and sincere man whose "sense of stewardship had a biblical purity as evident to the mountaineer as it was to the savant". One of his first orders of business was to help lead the first of many military tours through the park, this one led by Civil War leader **General William Tecumseh Sherman**, who brought along a small band of soldiers on a sightseeing expedition. Ironically, as the famed military leader left the park to the north, some six hundred natives entered Yellowstone from the west via Madison River Valley on the infamous **Flight of the Nez Percé** (see box, p.247). Having been cheated out of their land yet again, several bands of the people were on the run, hoping to reach safety on the Great Plains or in Canada. Within Yellowstone, scouting parties of Nez Percé braves ran into two separate groups of tourists, taking a few individuals temporarily hostage and stealing critical supplies. The rushed procession of hundreds of natives passed through the park in under two weeks, eventually following a path that traces today's Chief Joseph Highway, near the Beartooth Mountains northeast of the park.

In 1878, Congress finally approved minimal funding and a salary for the Superintendent position, meaning Norris, who often patrolled in full buckskin regalia, could start on much-needed **road-building projects**. Soon after receiving the $10,000 annual stipend, only a fraction of which went to his own salary, Norris commenced in building a rough road from Mammoth to Firehole Basin, through the intersection that now bears his name. Road building and trail blazing are perhaps Norris' finest legacies, and during his four-year reign, park roads increased from 32 miles to 150, while trails increased from 108 miles to over 200. Norris was also the first to officially record the park's weather and geyser eruptions – noting correctly the link between earthquakes and eruption schedules – and also supplied a great deal of archeological and historical research, much of which was sent straight to the Smithsonian Museum. He also hired **Harry Yount** to live in Lamar Valley in an attempt to stop **poachers** from slaughtering game, one of the park's most pressing problems; Yount lasted less than a year in his lonely position, but is considered by many to be the first national park ranger.

Norris, however, liked to designate park features after himself – look no further than Mount Norris, Norris Fork, Norris Geyser Basin and Norris Pass – a habit for which he was ridiculed in the area's press. His allegedly egocentric naming system wasn't the only thing that landed him in hot water; he also found himself alienated from the powerful railroad companies that once again began plotting routes into the Yellowstone region. Embroiled in a political fight in which he was powerless, and facing character assassination from pro-railroad interests in the press, Norris was pushed out in 1882.

Monopolies take hold

Throughout the remainder of the 1880s, three Superintendents shuttled in and out of Yellowstone. The most important event during this time had little to do with any of these ineffective leaders, but instead foreshadowed the eventual influence of the Army within Yellowstone. In 1882, General Sherman again toured the park on a large junket, including some 150 men and 300 horses. Soon after blazing the Sheridan Trail from Jackson Hole to the thumb of Yellowstone Lake, his party encountered a construction crew from the reformed Northern Pacific Railroad working beyond the park's northern boundary. From speaking to employees of the railroad, the general began to work out a better understanding of the so-called **Yellowstone Park Improvement Company**, which had recently worked out a deal with the Secretary of the Interior that ensured them a **monopoly** on future facilities and services, including accommodations, park guides and even horses within the park. Among other rights, the group of influential investors was also given permission to cut as much lumber as needed for fuel, and allowed to raise both crops and cattle – all for a rock-bottom rental fee.

Sherman quickly made his views on the situation known, and his warnings helped create new legislation curtailing the power of the Yellowstone Park Improvement Company, limiting their monopoly to a ten-year lease and forbidding any further exclusive privileges from being granted by the Secretary of the Interior. While all the political wrangling was occurring, the company was furiously at work to make eviction impossible, and by 1883 they had opened a portion of the **National Hotel** at Mammoth. Torn down in 1935, the hastily erected building had room for upwards of five hundred guests, who were often, much to their surprise, forced to share a room – and even beds – with unknown fellow guests. Also in 1883, the Yellowstone Park Improvement Company opened three expensive, poorly run tent-hotels at the Grand Canyon of the Yellowstone, Norris Geyser Basin and Upper Geyser Basin.

Capping the busiest year yet for Yellowstone, in 1883 the Northern Pacific Railroad also completed its **branch line** connecting Livingston – a town whose population had exploded from less than a hundred to more than three thousand over the previous twelve months – to **Cinnabar** in Paradise Valley, twenty miles north of Gardiner. With a railroad connection finally completed, both the Northern Pacific Railroad and Yellowstone Improvement Company hosted **lavish tours** of the park and its new facilities in late summer 1883, bringing along such guests as former President Ulysses Grant and numerous Senators – so expensive, in fact, that the heads of both companies ended up getting sacked, in part, for overspending. As if there weren't enough dignitaries stuffed into the park, **President Chester Arthur** visited with his own party for a tour during the same period. Yellowstone was now open for business, though the question of who would ultimately control the park's trade was still being fiercely debated.

The army arrives

Business may have been booming in Yellowstone by the mid 1880s, but so was poaching and squatting, and many of the park's finest features were in danger of being chipped away to nothing by souvenir-stealing vendors and visitors. Congress, justifiably weary of inactive and ineffectual stewardship, refused to allocate any more money to park administrators, forcing the Secretary of the Interior to call on the War Department for assistance. The **US army** was given control of the park, and on August 13, 1886, **Captain Moses Harris** marched fifty men from Fort Custer's Company M in the Montana Territories to Mammoth. Upon arriving, Harris assumed the title of Park Superintendent, the first of twelve army officers to run the park, and run it well, for the next thirty years.

Still, the army had marched into a volatile situation: frontiersmen in the region had no regard for the park's toothless rules, and some citizens, upset with park administrators, had taken to setting fires to woods and grasslands within Yellowstone in fits of petty revenge. Led by Harris, troops immediately set about enforcing a long list of new park regulations – some far ahead of their time – including the prevention of cutting green timber, banning the molestation of natural curiosities (particularly throwing items into springs and "soaping" geysers to force eruption), stopping the sale of liquor, forbidding all hunting and allowing fishing with line and hook only. Preparing for the winter, Harris also set about beginning the construction of **Camp Sheridan** in Mammoth, erecting five buildings, including a large barracks.

Almost immediately, the army reversed the park's steady decline into chaos, taking the lead on everything from firefighting to road-building. Soldiers, stationed at various tourist destinations such as Old Faithful throughout the summer, also kept an eye on visitors and ensured they obeyed the rules. Indeed, the soldiers were so dedicated to the laws that they even arrested and expelled executives from the Northern Pacific Railroad in 1888 after their guide, **E.C. Waters**, soaped Beehive Geyser to make it erupt. Waters, manager of the *National Hotel* at the time, took serious umbrage and would become a thorn in the side of park administrators for years to come.

Ed Howell and the Lacey Act

The army's status as absolute administrator and law enforcer of Yellowstone continued to grow, with **Fort Yellowstone** replacing Camp Sheridan in 1891. What started off as a dozen buildings – including a barracks for sixty men and a prison – would continue to expand to a complex of 37 structures by 1917. Over the same period, sixteen **soldier stations** were built throughout the park, allowing troops to patrol Yellowstone year-round from locations as isolated as Sylvan Pass in the east and Bechler in the southwest. However, as demonstrated by the eviction of E.C. Waters, the army remained hamstrung during its formative years in the park by one major issue: its inability to prosecute lawbreakers. While army personnel had taken to confiscating the hunting gear and traps of poachers along with the compulsory punishment of expulsion, it took only days for illegal hunters to stock back up and return to their trade.

All this changed, however, with the watershed arrest of Ed Howell in 1894. In the words of Yellowstone historian Aubrey L. Haines, "a scoundrel seldom accomplishes so much". A known poacher, Howell was tracked down and arrested in a daring capture by two soldiers on snowshoes in Pelican Valley on March 13. Caught literally red-handed – the poacher was removing the heads of five slaughtered buffalo to sell to a taxidermist – Howell was later being marched back to Fort Yellowstone when the soldiers happened to bump into a group of writers exploring the park for *Field and Stream* magazine. Writer **Emerson Hough** dashed off a story relating Howell's crime and capture, and quickly sent it to his East Coast publisher. Upon learning of the weak punishment Howell was to receive, public anger boiled over, spurring conservationist Representative **John F. Lacey** of Iowa – himself a victim of a stagecoach robbery in Yellowstone seven years prior – to introduce a congressional bill that would finally dole out the appropriate powers to punish park lawbreakers. Known as the **Lacey Act**, the bill was quickly pushed through and signed into law less than two months after Howell's arrest, giving the army the power to fine, imprison and permanently banish lawbreakers, while also helping kick-start a wave of **wildlife preservation and protection** that continues today. The story came full-circle when Ed Howell himself, upon returning to Yellowstone against the orders of the army later that summer, was the first person arrested under the act.

Trains, reigns and automobiles

Right through the army's time in power, Yellowstone tourism numbers climbed at a steady clip, rising from an estimated 5000 visitors in 1886 to more than 35,000 by 1916. The catalyst for this steady increase were the **railroad companies**, which, along with building lines closer and closer to park entrances, continued to funnel money to park concessionaires, themselves employing dubious bookkeeping practices to downplay any monopolistic appearances. To obtain an even stronger grip on the park's economy, the railroad companies lobbied fiercely throughout the late 1800s and early 1900s for the rights to lay tracks into and through Yellowstone. Government officials in the debt of railroad executives attempted to push numerous pro-railroad bills through Congress – one proposal even called for an electric railway, to be powered by the waterfalls on the Yellowstone River – though all were thankfully blocked by more forward-looking politicians.

Since the era's numerous railroad routes skirting park boundaries were prevented from actually snaking into and through Yellowstone itself, visitors needed to be shuttled around the park – a job for the **stagecoach**. Such tours that departed from train stations in the gateway towns of Gardiner and West Yellowstone were far from cheap (most were run by the railroad companies themselves), making them the domain of middle- and upper- class visitors. Indeed, "sage brushers" – visitors who rolled through under their own steam, unable to afford the all-inclusive tours – were looked down upon and made to feel unwelcome. The dusty, bone-rattling, horse-drawn stagecoach tours were mostly taken in eleven-passenger "**Yellowstone Wagons**" that required five days to complete the park's Grand Loop. Beginning in Mammoth or West Yellowstone, the tours worked their way counterclockwise, passing sights such as Obsidian Cliff and Roaring Mountain, past Lower, Midway and Upper Geyser Basins, and on to Old Faithful. From there, the tours would usually head east to Yellowstone Lake before turning north to the Grand Canyon of the Yellowstone and eventually back to Mammoth. Overnight stops included accommodation that still stands today – **Lake Yellowstone Hotel** and **Old Faithful Inn** – and some that doesn't, such as the **Canyon Hotel** (which featured a chained-up bear outside) and a collection of candy-striped tent camps run by **William Wylie**, a former Bozeman school teacher turned successful Yellowstone entrepreneur.

Inevitably, the stagecoach era came to an abrupt end with the introduction of the **automobile**. While cars had made the occasional foray into Yellowstone as early as 1902, they were banned for more than a decade due in part to their startling, potentially dangerous effect on horses. In the summer of 1915, however, they were officially permitted to enter, provided they followed a series of regulations that included a speed limit of 20mph (lowered to 12mph for uphill travel and 10mph downhill). Within a year, it was obvious that stagecoaches and cars could not coexist, and autos won out; buses and other motorized transport were brought in, while stagecoaches disappeared virtually overnight.

A new Park Service – and a new park

Along with killing off the stagecoach, the automobile played a role in ending the army's reign in Yellowstone as well. Among other car-related tasks, the army refused to take on the responsibility of checking in cars at all entrances, necessitating the hiring of four park rangers to patrol the gates. At the same time, the federal government was realizing that something needed to be done to better manage the growing number of independently run national parks and monuments across the country. On August 25, 1916, President Woodrow Wilson signed the **National Park Service Act**, creating an agency that would "conserve the scenery and the natural and historic objects and the wildlife therein" of more than a dozen national parks.

By 1918, **National Park Service rangers** – including some soldiers formerly stationed at Mammoth – were officially put in charge of Yellowstone and the park's new Superintendent became **Horace M. Albright**, who successfully ran Yellowstone before eventually taking over as head of the National Park Service. Along with expanding interpretive facilities, Albright's main mission was to make Yellowstone more accommodating to automobiles, both for the benefit of tourists and the park itself. He set out at once to improve the roads from one-lane stagecoach paths to two-lane highways, and also ordered the building of general stores, service stations, campgrounds and cabins. In the ten years that Albright led Yellowstone, annual visitor numbers more than quadrupled from 62,000 to 260,000. His most lasting legacy, however, is found due south of Yellowstone at **Grand Teton National Park**, created in 1929 thanks in large part to Albright's crucial behind-the-scenes work (see the box on p.89 for details).

World War II to the new millennium

During **World War II**, budget cuts and the loss of employees to the war effort caused park facilities to slide into disrepair. This problem was compounded by a lack of incoming money due to limited tourist numbers, a direct effect of gasoline rationing and the fact that many families were reticent to take a holiday while the country was at war. As soon as the war ended, however, annual visitor numbers spiked, cresting the one-million mark in Yellowstone by 1948. Many facilities nevertheless remained in desperate need of improvement, and, in 1955, the Park Service kicked off a programme known as **Mission 66**, an intensive plan to modernize national park amenities by the National Park Service's fiftieth anniversary in 1966. Among projects completed was Canyon Village, built around a large car park and a clear indication that the car was indeed king for tourism.

Throughout the 1960s and 1970s, attitudes on how to manage and experience Yellowstone continued to evolve, switching from a concept of the park as a tourist's playground to an awareness of its unique ecological habitats requiring special protection. The complete suppression of wildfire was lifted in light of the discovery of fire's regenerative powers, while the active "management" – i.e. slaughter – of wildlife such as elk and bison was halted after the publication of the **Leopold Report**, a watershed document greatly influenced by **Aldo Starker Leopold** (1887–1948), a biologist who advocated for allowing ecosystems within national parks to find their natural balance. Other critical environmental laws enacted during this era include the Clean Air and Clean Water Acts and the Endangered Species Act, all passed between 1970 and 1973 under the watch of President Richard Nixon.

The most dramatic and newsworthy event in the Yellowstone region during the second half of the twentieth century was the **wildfires of 1988**. Described in detail in the box on p.77, these summer-long conflagrations affected 36 percent (nearly 800,000 acres) of Yellowstone's land. Over the following few years, the park awoke from its fire-induced hangover to find that, contrary to some expert opinions, visitor numbers were not dropping precipitously; the landscape itself began to attract life again, becoming a visible living example of the positive effects of fire on forest systems. Just before the dawn of the new millennium, another major event occurred with the 1995 **reintroduction of wolves** to Yellowstone. Though the decision remains a controversial flashpoint to this day, the successful addition of these fierce predators back into the landscape – along with the 1996 halting of divisive plans to open the **New World Mine** near Yellowstone's northeast border – saw Yellowstone enter the 21st century with an optimistic step.

Yellowstone and Grand Teton today

With two or more sides to seemingly every heatedly debated issue, it's easy to create a laundry list of **problems** currently facing Yellowstone and Grand Teton: severe budget cuts to the National Park Service under the Bush administration have damaged both the morale and effectiveness of park rangers; diseases and invasive species are destroying native populations, from cutthroat trout to the whitebark pines that grizzlies rely on for much of their autumn diet; issues over management of bison and wolves, as well as the use of snowmobiles within Yellowstone, continue to cause deep divides both locally and nationally; and the overdevelopment of suburban tracts and large second-home mansions throughout the Greater Yellowstone Ecosystem is adversely affecting the hunting and migratory land of the region's fauna. And that, as any ranger or local expert will tell you, is only scratching the surface.

Still, with Yellowstone on the verge of its 140th birthday and Grand Teton having recently celebrated its 80th, it's impossible to deny that the region's grand national park experiment has been an amazing success. Visitor numbers continue to balloon on practically an annual basis, and, given that a total of four new visitor centres have debuted in the two parks since 2006, the Park Service is clearly attempting to keep pace with demand. All but the most cynical believe the parks will continue to find compromises – alternately brilliant and brittle – to their problems, for what began with the creation of Yellowstone National Park in 1872 has morphed into a global movement, leading citizens around the world to realize the preciousness of the land and the importance of preserving it.

Geology, flora and fauna

One of the major thrills of travelling through the Yellowstone region is the chance to see some of North America's most distinctive wildlife in its natural habitat – vast meadows and sagebrush flats, hydrothermal wonderlands and surrounding mountain ranges among the most dramatic on the continent. The determining factors for the kinds of animals and birds you might encounter while exploring are altitude, terrain and vegetation. All three are inextricably linked, with altitude and terrain determining what kinds of vegetation can grow in a given area; the region is thus made up of a number of distinct ecosystems, each one supporting particular types of animals and birds.

Geology

While nowadays bison, grizzly bears, wolves, cutthroat trout and the rest of the region's incredible array of wildlife share the spotlight, both Yellowstone and Grand Teton were originally set aside as national parks for one reason: they're home to some of the most incredible **geological wonders** on the continent. What follows is an overview of how these wonders came about; for more in-depth explanations, look for some of the books reviewed on pp.271–274. For a specific look at how the **Teton Range** came into existence, see the box on p.98.

At a glacial pace

The region's various mountain ranges – including (but not limited to) the **Absaroka**, **Beartooth**, **Teton**, **Snake River** and **Wind River** mountains – are all part of the **Rocky Mountains**, which extend some two thousand miles from central New Mexico to northeastern British Columbia, effectively dividing North America in a manner not unlike that of the Mississippi River to the east. Indeed, this iconic range delineates what is known as the **Continental Divide**, which dictates North America's water flow pattern. Rivers on the west of the divide drain into the Pacific Ocean, while those on the east eventually drift into the Atlantic or Arctic Oceans.

The Rockies are relatively young mountains, formed mainly by the **Laramide Revolution**, a period of tectonic uplifts that took place in the late Cretaceous Period around 65 million years ago, which itself was followed by volcanic activity, folding and faulting that continued into the early Tertiary Period. By contrast, the Blue Ridge Mountains in the eastern United States are thought to have formed some two hundred million years ago with the first great tectonic collision.

Much of the landscape on view today was sculpted, geologically speaking, a short time ago. As with the rest of the continent, the Yellowstone plateau has experienced several periods of intense **glaciation** over the last couple of million years. During these ice ages, most of the region was buried beneath massive migrating glaciers, which formed when more snow fell throughout the year than melted. Once snow depths reached a certain level, their overall size and weight forced gravity into action, moving them as they crushed and picked up rocks along their routes. During the two most recent glacier eras, giant rivers of ice inched their way across the land, grinding down mountains, carving out massive U-shape canyons and leaving behind **terminal moraines** that turned into natural dams – which eventually formed the likes of Jenny Lake. The size of these ice sheets is mind-numbing: a mere 25,000 years ago, Yellowstone Lake was covered in a 4000ft-thick sea of ice, with only the tallest peaks of the Beartooths and Tetons poking above – which explains why they remain jagged today, not worn smooth like their neighbouring, lower peaks. As temperatures warmed, the glaciers melted and retreated, dropping random rocks in their wake – known as **erratics** – along with large chunks of ice that melted to form **kettle lakes**. Glacial activity continues to affect the landscape of the area's higher mountain ranges even today, as evidenced by several glaciers, including **Teton Glacier** (the largest), located just below the summit of Grand Teton itself.

A hydrothermal wonderland

Along with ice, fire has played a vital role in Yellowstone's geological story. Beneath much of the park lies what is termed a **hot spot**, where **magma** (molten rock from the Earth's mantle) rises to within three miles of the surface. Originally located as far west as present-day Nevada, this hot spot now sits directly beneath Yellowstone, as the continental plate on which the park rests has been drifting to the southwest over the past several million years. The volcanic activity of this hot spot across this same period has been epic, with several cataclysmic **ash-flow volcanic eruptions** occurring; these eruptions dwarf any in recorded history, with the greatest being 2500 times more powerful than Mount St Helens' significant 1980 eruption.

The largest of these events, the **Huckleberry Ridge** eruption, occurred some two million years ago, spreading thick layers of ash as far as California and the Gulf of Mexico. A smaller, though still earth-shattering explosion, known as the **Island Park** eruption, occurred 1.3 million years ago, followed by the larger **Lava Creek** eruption some 640,000 years ago. During this most recent event, a huge underground chamber disgorged 250 cubic miles of molten rock before collapsing upon itself, creating the **Yellowstone Caldera**; its rim measures about 47 miles by 28 miles at its broadest. With these **supervolcano** eruptions occurring on average every 650,000 years, Yellowstone could be due for another major eruption anytime – geologically speaking.

Also playing an important role in Yellowstone's ever-changing geology are **earthquakes**. An average of two thousand are recorded annually in the region, though they're only occasionally felt and are rarely disastrous; see **Earthquake Lake** (p.219) northwest of West Yellowstone for an example of one that was. Even quakes that aren't felt, however, play an important role: their shakes and rattles ensure that the region's hydrothermal features remain active by breaking any clogs formed by mineral deposits that would otherwise seal off and eventually shut down geysers and hot springs.

Hydrothermal features

Into the **Yellowstone Caldera** are crammed more than half the world's geysers, plus thousands of fumaroles jetting plumes of steam, mudpots gurgling with acid-dissolved muds and clays, and hot springs. Most of the park's hydrothermal features sit within the caldera – as does much of Yellowstone Lake – but there is plenty of peripheral volcanic activity as well, including that at Norris Geyser Basin and Mammoth Hot Springs, both of which are outside the caldera boundary. For an in-depth look at the park's geysers, hot springs and other assorted hydrothermal features, see the *Hydrothermal Yellowstone* colour insert.

Fauna

Yellowstone is home to no less than sixty different **mammals**, a line-up that includes the most fascinating megafauna on the continent: grizzly bear, American bison, moose, mountain lion and grey wolf, to name but a charismatic few. Given that they don't show up on demand, there's inevitably a mix of excitement and frustration that comes with spotting animals; in fact, the more intelligent and secretive of them make a point of avoiding human contact altogether. You can, however, reliably expect to see certain animals, especially bison and elk, and even to have quite close encounters with some of them.

If wildlife **viewing and photographing** is a priority for your visit, definitely bring along binoculars or a spotting scope, as well as a powerful zoom lens (200–300mm) for your camera.

Large mammals: bison and the deer family

The title of Yellowstone mascot goes to the **American bison**, the largest land mammal in North America. Known alternately (though incorrectly) as buffalo, these magnificent creatures once roamed the Rockies and Great Plains in vast herds as many as five million strong. Their rapid destruction is a well-known story, and Yellowstone is the sole place in the lower 48 states that has hosted a continuous population since the eve of their decimation. Though poaching saw their population dip as low as two dozen by the early 1900s, the creation of the Buffalo Ranch in Lamar Valley (see p.54) helped them survive. Thanks to such foresight, their presence in the parks is now strong, with bison easily spotted everywhere from the Gardiner area in northern Yellowstone to the southern reaches of Grand Teton; nearly four thousand of the giants currently live in two major herds in Yellowstone alone. Feeding on grasses and sedges, male bulls can weigh as much as two thousand pounds but still gallop up to 30mph and jump heights taller than themselves. Save for the summer mating season, bulls spend most of the year living alone, while cows and their reddish brown calves cluster in herds year-round. Both sexes sport horns, with those on males being wider at the base and slightly less curved.

Another of the larger animals you're virtually guaranteed to encounter is the **elk** – known by local Shoshone tribes as "wapiti", or "white-rumped deer". Approximately thirty thousand elk spend the summer in Yellowstone (half that come winter), and the larger bulls – weighing up to nine hundred pounds and sporting huge antlers that alone can weigh as much as fifty pounds – are quite a sight. Other than during autumn's mating season, bulls generally live a solitary existence, while cows and calves herd together in groups; all spend most of their time grazing on grasses and woodland vegetation. The most dramatic time to observe elk is during the autumn rut, which generally begins in September and may continue into early November. The bulls strut and display their necks and antlers to the cows, but the most extraordinary part of their display is an unearthly call to a potential mate called "bugling" – a bizarre, ear-piercing squeal.

Another beautifully antlered ungulate is the **mule deer**. Roughly one-third the size of an elk – and only a quarter of the weight – the mule deer is further distinguished by the much lighter, almost tan colouring of its coat, an overly generous set of mule-like ears, and a short, black-tipped tail attached to its cream-coloured rump; males display a delicate set of antlers. Around two thousand mule deer call Yellowstone home in summer, though nearly all migrate out of the park come winter. Similar in size, but much scarcer, are **white-tailed deer**. The few who spend summer in Yellowstone are most often spotted by the side of streams in the park's northern reaches. Somewhat smaller than the mule deer is the **pronghorn**, a particularly prominent animal in Wyoming, occupying grassy flatlands and often seen grazing on sagebrush by roadsides and on ranches. Sometimes spotted in Lamar Valley and the sagebrush flats of Jackson Hole, pronghorn have a pale reddish hide, large white rump and short horns that jut inwards; males are easily identified by their pronged horns and patch of black on the cheek. Capable of sprinting in quick spurts up to 70mph, they are North America's fastest land animal.

The largest member of the deer family is the **moose**. With the largest bulls reaching seven feet at the shoulder and weighing a thousand pounds, their bulbous heads topped by a broad spread of antlers, and with a pendulous dewlap slung beneath the chin, this marvellous animal, once encountered, is not easily forgotten. More so then their deer cousins, however, moose can be irritable, and you should always keep your distance. Their long gangly legs are built for wading, and moose generally browse wetland grasses and aquatic plants found along rivers and in riparian meadows; amazingly, moose have been spotted diving as deep as twenty feet to munch on aquatic foliage. It's estimated that fewer than five hundred moose live in Yellowstone, with the 1988 fires playing a major role in their decreasing population due to the loss of winter habitat; these days, they're more commonly spotted in Grand Teton, especially in the Willow Flats area behind *Jackson Lake Lodge*.

Equally photogenic are **bighorn sheep** – there are few more indelible Rocky Mountain images than a lone bighorn perched on a rocky ledge. Both rams and ewes grow horns, although the two are easily distinguished: the ram has the classic "C"-shaped horns, while ewe's grow as near-vertical spikes up to eight inches long. Rams, which can weigh as much as three hundred pounds, put on an extraordinary display during the rutting season – roughly mid November until December – when they square off and crack horns with sickening impact to assert their authority and establish mating rights. Built to negotiate rocky ledges and deal with cool temperatures, bighorn sheep are archetypal high-country dwellers and mostly stick to Yellowstone's alpine reaches, including Mount Washburn and Gardner Canyon.

Predators: bears, wolves and mountain lions

Many visitors hope, above all, to spot predators such as grizzly bear, mountain lion and grey wolf – invariably from a distance. Of course, there are special rules of engagement that go with encountering these animals, particularly the fearsome **grizzly bear**. It's worth noting some of the differences in appearance between the grizzly and its slightly smaller cousin, the **black bear** – also a resident of the area – in order to be able to distinguish between the two. Both come in similar shades of colour, with the misleadingly named black bear ranging from blond to cinnamon to brown to black, while grizzlies range from cinnamon to a deep reddish brown. More useful are distinctions related to the animals' body shape: grizzlies have a fairly pronounced hump behind their necks (a feature the black bear lacks) and its hindquarters slope downward, while a black bear's tailbone sits level with or just above the height of its shoulders. For advice on what to do if you encounter a bear, see the box on p.110.

Park officials estimate that some six hundred grizzly bears live within Yellowstone, most commonly spotted early in the morning or at dusk in Hayden and Lamar Valleys. Males can weigh up to seven hundred pounds and sprint as fast as 45mph; a similar number of black bears call the area home, with males weighing upwards of three hundred pounds. Both mate from mid May to mid July, though remarkably, embryos don't begin to develop for four months, allowing females to store energy until entering hibernation in December; cubs are born during hibernation in January or February, and males take no part in raising them afterwards.

Voracious eaters, grizzly and black bears treat the Yellowstone ecosystem like a vast, all-you-can-eat buffet, feasting on virtually anything. They hunt elk calves and spawning trout; dig out rodents from their underground homes; slurp down insects such as ants and moths; chow on plant life, ranging from roots and bulbs to berries and whitebark pinenuts, the latter of which they often steal from hoarding squirrels; and, lastly, they are talented scavengers, taking food from both humans and fellow predators such as wolves, often stealing kills to quickly feast on twenty pounds of fresh meat. Their hunger reaches epic levels in autumn before denning, when bears enter a state known as hyperphagia and eat furiously to pack on enough calories to sleep through winter.

The **grey wolf** is one of Yellowstone's greatest success stories, and simply hearing a howl is an unforgettable highlight for many visitors. Wolves were once the most abundant predator in North America, with at least five subspecies in existence and a population of up to two million spread coast to coast. They were hunted to extinction in the region by the 1920s, but in 1995 and 1996, a group from western Canada was relocated here. Population totals in the region tend to swoop up and down due to disease and natural selection, but at the time of writing approximately one hundred wolves roamed the region in fourteen packs. See *The wolves of Yellowstone* colour section for more details on the park's successful wolf programme, along with information on wolf behaviour and wolf-watching.

Far more secretive – yet equally dangerous – is the **mountain lion**; also known as puma or cougar, this sleek, muscular animal has perhaps the most accurate Latin name of all – *felis concolor*, or the "one-coloured cat". Mountain lion sightings are exceedingly rare in the region, and it's estimated that fewer than twenty live full-time within Yellowstone, mainly in the park's northern expanses. These solitary hunters, which weigh between 100 and 165 pounds, mainly prey upon elk and mule deer, though they have been known to kill bighorn sheep, pronghorn, coyotes and even porcupine. After killing their prey with a quick bite to the neck or base of the skull, they cache their kill to eat later – provided a bear doesn't find it first.

Smaller mammals

Affectionately known to some Native American peoples as the "singing trickster", the **coyote** is a highly adaptable and opportunistic predator fairly common in the region. Coyotes hunt small animals such as rodents and ground squirrels, but also prey upon elk calves in spring and scavenge the carcasses of bigger animals such as elk, deer and even bison when the opportunity arises. Sometimes confused with wolves from afar, coyotes are much smaller (weighing around thirty pounds, in comparison with 110–130 pounds for a grey wolf); also, unlike wolves, they'll often appear by roadsides and in populated areas where a free meal might present itself. Along with ranchers, coyotes are probably the least enthusiastic local group when it comes to wolf restoration. Before wolves returned, their sole major predator was the mountain lion; now the coyotes find themselves several rungs lower on the food chain, and some biologists claim the local coyote population has decreased by as much as half thanks to marauding wolf packs. Other experts, however, believe coyote numbers haven't gone down nearly as much, positing instead that the flexible scavenger has adapted and is now simply better at hiding.

Sadly, the **beaver** has failed to be so malleable in the face of danger, and their story is one of the sorrier tales of human impact on wildlife: the pelt of nature's most energetic engineer was at one time so desired for hat-making that the animal was very nearly wiped from the face of the earth. Weighing up to sixty pounds, the beaver – North America's largest rodent – is entrusted with designing and building wetland habitat for countless plants and animals. Its dam-building creates ponds and marshy meadows that support wetland grasses and trees such as willow and cottonwood, as well as waterfowl and grazing animals such as moose, elk and deer. It's thought that somewhere around seven hundred beavers live in Yellowstone, scattered in upwards of a hundred colonies. For visible evidence of their handiwork, visitors are best off looking for lodges in the park's isolated Cascade Corner; in Grand Teton, the ponds in the Colter Bay area are active beaver grounds.

Among the long list of other smaller mammals within the region are **red fox**, **squirrels** (Uinta ground, red and golden-mantled), **chipmunks**, **weasels**, **martens** and **snowshoe hares**. You'll need a fair bit of luck to spot a **lynx**, **bobcat**, **wolverine** or **river otter**; more common are **pika**, small but rotund rodents which announce their presence by squeaking loudly as they pop out from a rocky hideaway, and **yellow-bellied marmot**, an inveterate sunbather that closely resembles a groundhog.

Birds

Well over three hundred species of birds have been spotted in Yellowstone, and close to 150 of them are known to nest in the area. The leading lights for casual birdwatchers are the predators, including **bald eagle**, **peregrine falcon** and **osprey**, all three of which are typically spotted near water. Osprey feed almost exclusively on fish, while bald eagles also swoop down on unsuspecting water-fowl; peregrine falcons feast on waterfowl as well, along with songbirds, which they snatch out of mid air on high-speed dives that can exceed 200mph. Osprey and falcons migrate south come autumn, while bald eagles remain in the region year-round – look for them perched on riverside cottonwood snags. Other preda-tors to watch out for include the **golden eagle**, **red-tailed hawk**, **Cooper's Hawk** and **turkey vulture**.

Easier to spot and just as remarkable are the region's herons and waterfowl, including the **American white pelican**, which spends its summers on Yellow-stone Lake; author Gary Ferguson describes these surprisingly graceful birds in *Hawks Rest* (see p.271) as "startling in their ability to seem both heavy and full of grace – size 16 ballerinas, on a planet with half the gravity of Earth". Also large and white is the equally balletic **trumpeter swan**, a species that came perilously close to extinction in the early 1900s. Today several thousand trumpeters spend winter in the area, though they're often confused with the **tundra swan** that only passes through the Yellowstone region; a trumpeter is distinguished by a pink streak along its black bill. Other notable water birds include the long-legged **great blue heron**, the greenish-black **double-crested cormorant**, the black-and-white **Barrow's Goldeneye** and the rare, beautiful **harlequin duck**. Also found by the waterside is the playful **American dipper**, a small grey bird that dives in and out of rivers in search of water bugs, and the **sandhill crane**, which nests in the region in summer.

Nearly a dozen species of owls are known to call the Yellowstone ecosystem home, including the **great horned owl** and the **great grey owl**, the latter featuring a distinctive dish-shaped face. An equal variety of woodpeckers can be spotted, such as the **three-toed woodpecker** and **black-backed woodpecker**, most often seen pecking for bugs on the remains of charred trees. Other popular terrestrial birds include the **Steller's Jay** and **Clark's Nutcracker** (both commonly found harassing picnickers for crumbs of food), and the oft-spotted **raven**, the air version of a coyote which deserves special mention for its trickster personality. Invariably spotted at kills made by wolves – and believed by some to point wolves toward injured or sick prey – ravens themselves are practised thieves, having learnt to unzip the backpacks of careless, unwitting snowmobile riders in winter for a cleverly plied snack.

Fish, amphibians and reptiles

Fish are abundant in the region's numerous mountain lakes and rivers, and even if you've no interest in casting for them, you can't fail to miss seeing folks throwing a line into any available stream. It's hardly necessary to be an angler to enjoy watching fish, however, so when hiking, take time to sit still by a riverbank, watching trout face upstream in search of incoming snacks. Most celebrated is the native **cutthroat trout**, sporting a telltale red slash along its jaw, and divided into three subspecies – Yellowstone, Snake River and Westslope. All three are facing an uphill battle nowadays, with both whirling disease and **lake trout** having cut a major swathe through their overall population (see box, p.81). The Yellowstone region's two other native sport fish are the **Arctic grayling** and **mountain whitefish**, though most anglers are just as happy to reel in non-native **rainbow trout**, **brown trout** and **brook trout**.

Sharing the water with these fish are four species of amphibians, namely **boreal spotted** and **Columbia chorus frogs**, **boreal toad** and yellow-spotted **tiger salamander**. Found in many Yellowstone ponds and lakes, the wide-headed tiger salamander grows up to ten inches in length and emerges from hibernation in May or June. As for reptiles, there are a half-dozen species in Yellowstone, including the harmless **valley** and **wandering gartner snakes**, as well as the **bullsnake**, which grows up to six feet in length and is the region's largest reptile. Bullsnakes are often confused with the **prairie rattlesnake**, as both coil up and produce a rattling noise when disturbed. Found sunning themselves on rocks and paths only in the drier, northern reaches of Yellowstone and not at all in Grand Teton, the prairie rattlesnake is the only dangerously venomous snake in the region; however, according to park sources, only two bites have been documented in Yellowstone's history, proving that these snakes are far more frightened of humans than we should be of them.

Ecosystems and flora

Stretching across portions of Idaho, Montana and especially Wyoming, the Greater Yellowstone Ecosystem covers close to thirty thousand square miles of terrain. Along with the rich variety of wildlife detailed above, some 1100 species of plants grow here, and the types of forests, plants and flowers you'll encounter depends mainly on the altitude you explore. As with the rest of the Rockies, the mountain environment here consists of three essential ecosystems: the **montane** (6000–9000 feet), **subalpine** (9000–11,500 feet) and **alpine** (above 11,500 feet).

Most prevalent is the **montane**, where you'll find immense forests of tall and straight **lodgepole pine**, by far the most common tree in the region; upwards of eighty percent of Yellowstone's forested area is composed of these hardy specimens (see p.76). Also found in this zone are forests of **Douglas fir** – easily picked out for its reddish-brown bark, as well as its cones that have prominent, three-pointed bracts sticking out – and stands of **aspen**, whose leaves quiver romantically in the wind. Part of the willow family, aspens grow in large colonies derived from a single seedling, which is why entire patches turn gold together in autumn seemingly overnight. **Engelmann spruce** (sporting greyish, scaly bark and slender, cylindrical cones), **subalpine fir** (grey, smooth bark with larger, purplish cones) and **whitebark pine** (yellow-green needles in bundles of five with small, purple cones) take over above 9000ft, where temperatures are cooler and greater open spaces begin to appear. The seeds and nuts from whitebark pine are a particularly important food source for everything from Clark's Nutcrackers to squirrels to grizzly bears, an alarming fact considering that a disease known as **white pine blister rust** has been devastating large forests of these trees across the Rockies for several years.

Above the montane zone, the **alpine tundra** supports only slow-growing plants such as mosses, lichens and a variety of delicate wildflowers, all of which can survive on the thinnest soil and air, and with a minimal supply of water. Because they grow so slowly – the tiniest wildflower may take many years to reach maturity – any damage done to these plants impacts the alpine ecosystem dramatically, so hikers have a special duty of care whenever exploring these areas.

Another important zone in the region is the **sagebrush valley**, which composes much of Grand Teton's flatlands and is dominated by **big sagebrush**. Though the dry and dusty sagebrush flats seem devoid of life, in reality they hold a wide variety of plant and animal life, ranging from a variety of tough grasses to prong-horn and sage grouse.

Wildflowers

Of all the different forms of flora in the region, **wildflowers** draw the most attention. While few hikers walk with checklists to mark off the different varieties of lichens or bushes they've encountered, many floral enthusiasts do just that, stooping low to photograph their favourite types. As soon as snow begins to melt in spring, wildflowers bloom, beginning at lower altitudes and working their way up mountainsides as summer progresses. On the sagebrush plains, the yellow **arrowleaf balsamroot**, purple **low larkspur** and **scarlet gilia** begin sprouting in late spring. By late June, the wildflower show is in full production, with the montane and subalpine zones staging the likes of yellow **monkeyflowers**, red **bitterroots**, pink **elephant's heads** and purple **harebells**; **larkspurs**, **fringed gentian**, **blue camas**, and white **yarrow** and **phlox** also pepper area hillsides. Later in the season, high in the alpine zones, skunk-scented purple **sky pilots** and blue **alpine forget-me-nots** show themselves off.

Books

M any of the following **books** can be found in the visitor centres in and around Yellowstone and Grand Teton. If you're hoping to do some background reading before heading out, most can also be purchased through the "Park Store" on the Yellowstone Association's website (Ⓦwww.yellowstoneassociation.org), or via major online booksellers such Ⓦwww.amazon.com and Ⓦwww.alibris.com. Particularly recommended books are marked with the 🏃 symbol.

Travel and impressions

🏃 **Tim Cahill** *Lost in My Own Backyard*. This brief but highly entertaining book finds longtime Montana resident Cahill using a number of short walks around landmark Yellowstone features as a springboard for sharing historical and scientific tidbits on the park. Writing wittily in his characteristic conversational style, he makes a number of trenchant observations along the way, noting everything from flatulent mudpots to visitors' imprudent interactions with wildlife.

Gary Ferguson *Hawks Rest*. Montana writer Ferguson's 2003 book relates his tale of a summer spent at the isolated Hawks Rest patrol cabin, just outside Yellowstone's southeastern corner within the Thorofare passage. Wolves and bears abound, but so does a not-so-peaceful mix of hippy hikers, trail crews and renegade outfitters, the latter group drawing Ferguson's ire for their rough camping and illegal use of salt to bait elk for hunting.

Gary Ferguson *Walking Down the Wild*. Another backcountry account by Ferguson, this one spent completing a five-hundred-mile loop hike through the Greater Yellowstone Ecosystem during 1990–91. Spending only around a fraction of his trail miles within Yellowstone and Grand Teton, Ferguson, an accomplished naturalist, highlights the region's most critical ecological aspects, and is most interesting for his take on landscapes

regenerating in the wake of the great wildfires of 1988.

🏃 **Norman Maclean** *A River Runs Through It*. While the movie adaptation of the book was filmed on the Gallatin River north of Yellowstone, the action within the novel takes place mainly around the Blackfoot River in western Montana, far to the north. That said, Maclean's lyrical masterwork is still essential reading for anyone with an interest in fly-fishing or, broader yet, Rocky Mountain literature.

Paul Schullery *Mountain Time*. A fine hiking companion, this memoir contains a series of essays on life in Yellowstone by a longtime park employee, from wry observations on tourists to insights gained from days spent fishing and wildlife-spotting alone in the park's secret corners.

Paul Schullery (ed) *Old Yellowstone Days*. A collection of journal entries, stories and essays on Yellowstone's early days by the likes of John Muir, Theodore Roosevelt, Owen Wister and, most engagingly, Rudyard Kipling. Well worth searching out.

Mark Spragg *Where Rivers Change Direction*. A raw memoir by novelist Spragg, who grew up tending to both horses and dudes on the Crossed Sabers Ranch just east of Yellowstone en route to Cody. There's little about Yellowstone, but plenty of illuminating essays on everything from bear hunting with tourists to spending an isolated winter caretaking for a rich couple's Wyoming home. One of the finest, most candid looks at the tough life of a cowboy.

History and biography

Gary Ferguson *The Great Divide*. An elegant cultural history of the Rocky Mountains, covering the rise of the mountain men and tourism to the arrival of 1960s counterculture and modern times. While there's little specific information on the greater Yellowstone region, it's a concise study of America's evolving relationship with this grand range.

Aubrey L. Haines *The Yellowstone Story*. Acknowledged as the definitive Yellowstone history, Haines' incredibly detailed chronicle is broken into two large volumes. The first details the park's history up to the arrival of the army, while the second volume – notable for an entertaining chapter on stagecoach tourism – stretches into the 1970s. Whether you'll want to wade through both volumes is debatable, but as a reference tool it's unassailably worthy.

Burton Harris *John Colter: His Years in the Rockies*. While it contains more information than most readers probably need, this is nonetheless the best biography on the famed trapper and explorer. Much of the book is dedicated to piecing together Colter's winter circuit of Yellowstone in 1807.

Nathaniel Pitt Langford *The Discovery of Yellowstone Park*. A journal chronicling the 1870 Washburn Expedition, by Nathaniel Pitt "National Park" Langford, who later became the first Superintendent of Yellowstone. Though immodest at times, Langford manages to capture well the expedition's awe and disbelief upon crossing paths with the Grand Canyon, Yellowstone Lake and Old Faithful.

Karen Wildung Reinhart *Yellowstone's Rebirth by Fire*. Published to coincide with the twentieth anniversary of the park's 1988 wildfires, the author – a former ranger – expertly combines striking colour photography with first-hand accounts of those who fought the blazes, in the process weaving an engrossing tale of a region both devastated and born anew by Yellowstone's legendary "Summer of Fire".

Osborne Russell *Journal of a Trapper*. A superb first-person account chronicling the final years of the mountain man lifestyle. Russell spent years trapping beaver and hunting grizzly, buffalo and elk in and around the Yellowstone region, and his prosaic day-to-day travel accounts are enlivened by tales of hardship, fascinating run-ins with native tribes and the author's own inspired reflections on the landscape around him.

Helen Cody Wetmore *Buffalo Bill: Last of the Great Scouts*. A loving biography of William Cody, written by his younger sister, in which the heroic Buffalo Bill never loses a race nor misses a shot. Historically suspect as it may be, it's still a rollicking read of the multi-tasking showman's life. Includes an equally effusive short forward and epilogue by Western author Zane Grey.

Lee H. Whittlesey *Death in Yellowstone: Accidents and Foolhardiness in the First National Park*. An offbeat, gloomy inventory of deaths within Yellowstone, ranging from the expected – drowning, the number one cause of death in the park outside of car crashes – to more startling demises, including poisonous fumes, boiling hot springs and, yes, the odd grizzly attack. A potent reminder that wilderness demands attention and respect, or else.

Landscapes: geology, flora and fauna

Peter Alden (ed) *National Audubon Society Field Guide to the Rocky Mountain States*. A lavishly illustrated and extremely informative guide to the flora and fauna of the Rockies, covering everything from lichens and wildflowers, spiders and beetles, to feral horses and mule deer. There's also an appendix detailing parks and preserves, images of constellations visible from Yellowstone, and sections on the region's topography, geology, ecology and weather patterns.

T. Scott Bryan *The Geysers of Yellowstone*. The quintessential guide for geyser gazers, now in its fourth edition. Along with descriptions of the most popular geysers in Upper Geyser Basin and around, the guide covers backcountry basins around Heart Lake, Shoshone Geyser Basin, Seven Mile Hole, etc. Also includes an appendix listing all the world's known geyser basins.

Mary Ann Franke *To Save the Wild Bison*. A historic account of the bison's struggle in and around Yellowstone, from the early days of poaching and the Lacey Act up to today's pressing brucellosis and migration issues. Often weighed down by an overabundance of facts and figures, Franke still does an admirable job critiquing current policies and suggesting possible compromises.

James Halfpenny *Yellowstone Wolves In the Wild*. A short but first-rate overview of wolves in Yellowstone, both for the chapters on subjects ranging from hunting and reproduction to tips on wolf-spotting, as well as for the dozens of striking colour photos throughout. The author has led wolf tours in Yellowstone for years and is also recognized as one of the top animal trackers in the US (see p.197).

Bernd Heinrich *Mind of the Raven*. An eye-opening, eminently readable book that'll have you looking at ravens in a whole new light. From Yellowstone to the Arctic to his home in Maine, universally respected biologist Heinrich offers plenty of insight into his study of ravens, detailing everything from their relationship with wolves to how they care for their young.

Scott McMillion *Mark of the Grizzly*. While grizzly attacks are fairly uncommon in the mountains, this book documents eighteen that took place between 1977 and 1997, several of them in and around Yellowstone. Quite well written and more intriguing than you'd expect.

John McPhee *Rising from the Plains*. Those who can't tell their Pleistocene Age from their Miocene Age will still enjoy this landmark work. Following renowned Rocky Mountain geologist and lifelong Wyoming resident David Love (1913–2002) across the state, McPhee weaves their discussions on the region's incredible array of geology together with the difficult yet fascinating history of Love's frontier family.

Paul Rubinstein, Lee H. Whittlesey and Mike Stevens *The Guide to Yellowstone Waterfalls and Their Discovery*. The name says it all. This volume covers nearly three hundred waterfalls, including photos, details of their "discovery" and tips on how to reach them by either car or foot.

Jean L. Seavey *Wildflowers of the Yellowstone Area*. Available at park bookstores, this inexpensive and handy set of identification cards offers details on nearly one hundred different wildflowers known to bloom in Yellowstone.

Douglas W. Smith and Gary Ferguson *Decade of the Wolf.* Told from the point of view of Douglas W. Smith, a leader of Yellowstone's wolf re-introduction programme from the start, this book provides an insider's account of the successful return of wolves to the park. Light on the bureaucratic battles that have tried to hamstring the plan, the book instead focuses on the responsibilities of local biologists and volunteers, along with the animals themselves – including several outstanding "portrait" chapters on specific wolves.

Robert Smith and Lee Siegel *Windows into the Earth: The Geologic Story of Yellowstone and Grand Teton National Parks.* As advertised by the title, this is an exposition on the weird and wonderful geology of the greater Yellowstone region. Lucid and filled with incredible facts, the book includes wonderful colour photos and ends with a handy tour of both parks.

Outdoor activities

Mark C. Marschall and Joy Marschall *Yellowstone Trails: A Hiking Guide.* Once you've checked off all the hikes within the book you're holding, pick up this excellent work by a pair of former Yellowstone rangers. Now in its ninth edition, the guide details over one hundred hikes in clear and concise terms; it's also valuable for its wealth of first-hand knowledge on how to best handle bear encounters.

Craig Mathews and Clayton Molinero *The Yellowstone Fly-Fishing Guide.* A comprehensive rundown of the park's many fishable streams, giving as much insight to small creeks as it does the mighty Yellowstone River.

Leigh Ortenburger and Reynold Jackson *A Climber's Guide to the Teton Range.* With well over a hundred routes detailed, including some ice-climbing routes, this is the definitive Teton climber's bible.

Rebecca Woods *Jackson Hole Hikes.* Chronicling day ambles and extended expeditions alike, Woods details well over a hundred hikes, from well-travelled paths in the Tetons to more obscure routes in the nearby Gros Ventre Mountains. The latest fifth edition also includes hikes leading from Jackson up into its neighbouring ski area, Snow King.

Small print and
Index

A Rough Guide to Rough Guides

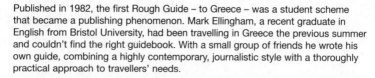
Published in 1982, the first Rough Guide – to Greece – was a student scheme that became a publishing phenomenon. Mark Ellingham, a recent graduate in English from Bristol University, had been travelling in Greece the previous summer and couldn't find the right guidebook. With a small group of friends he wrote his own guide, combining a highly contemporary, journalistic style with a thoroughly practical approach to travellers' needs.

The immediate success of the book spawned a series that rapidly covered dozens of destinations. And, in addition to impecunious backpackers, Rough Guides soon acquired a much broader and older readership that relished the guides' wit and inquisitiveness as much as their enthusiastic, critical approach and value-for-money ethos.

These days, Rough Guides include recommendations from shoestring to luxury and cover more than 200 destinations around the globe, including almost every country in the Americas and Europe, more than half of Africa and most of Asia and Australasia. Our ever-growing team of authors and photographers is spread all over the world, particularly in Europe, the US and Australia.

In the early 1990s, Rough Guides branched out of travel, with the publication of Rough Guides to World Music, Classical Music and the Internet. All three have become benchmark titles in their fields, spearheading the publication of a wide range of books under the Rough Guide name.

Including the travel series, Rough Guides now number more than 350 titles, covering: phrasebooks, waterproof maps, music guides from Opera to Heavy Metal, reference works as diverse as Conspiracy Theories and Shakespeare, and popular culture books from iPods to Poker. Rough Guides also produce a series of more than 120 World Music CDs in partnership with World Music Network.

Visit www.roughguides.com to see our latest publications.

Rough Guide credits

Text editor: Brendon Griffin
Layout: Ajay Verma
Cartography: Ashutosh Bharti
Picture editor: Emily Taylor
Production: Louise Minihane
Proofreader: Karen Parker
Cover design: Nicole Newman, Dan May, Mark Thomas
Editorial: **London** Andy Turner, Keith Drew, Edward Aves, Alice Park, Lucy White, Jo Kirby, James Smart, Natasha Foges, James Rice, Emma Beatson, Emma Gibbs, Kathryn Lane, Monica Woods, Mani Ramaswamy, Harry Wilson, Lucy Cowie, Alison Roberts, Lara Kavanagh, Eleanor Aldridge, Ian Blenkinsop, Charlotte Melville, Joe Staines, Matthew Milton, Tracy Hopkins; **Delhi** Madhavi Singh, Jalpreen Kaur Chhatwal, Jubbi Francis
Design & Pictures: **London** Scott Stickland, Dan May, Diana Jarvis, Mark Thomas,

Nicole Newman, Sarah Cummins; **Delhi** Umesh Aggarwal, Jessica Subramanian, Ankur Guha, Pradeep Thapliyal, Sachin Tanwar, Anita Singh, Nikhil Agarwal, Sachin Gupta
Production: Rebecca Short, Liz Cherry, Erika Pepe
Cartography: **London** Ed Wright, Katie Lloyd-Jones; **Delhi** Rajesh Chhibber, Rajesh Mishra, Animesh Pathak, Jasbir Sandhu, Swati Handoo, Deshpal Dabas, Lokamata Sahu
Marketing, Publicity & roughguides.com: Liz Statham
Digital Travel Publisher: Peter Buckley
Reference Director: Andrew Lockett
Operations Coordinator: Becky Doyle
Operations Assistant: Johanna Wurm
Publishing Director (Travel): Clare Currie
Commercial Manager: Gino Magnotta
Managing Director: John Duhigg

Publishing information

This second edition published July 2011 by
Rough Guides Ltd,
80 Strand, London WC2R 0RL
11, Community Centre, Panchsheel Park, New Delhi 110017, India

Distributed by the Penguin Group

Penguin Books Ltd,
80 Strand, London WC2R 0RL

Penguin Group (USA)
375 Hudson Street, NY 10014, USA

Penguin Group (Australia)
250 Camberwell Road, Camberwell, Victoria 3124, Australia

Penguin Group (NZ)
67 Apollo Drive, Mairangi Bay, Auckland 1310, New Zealand

Rough Guides is represented in Canada by Tourmaline Editions Inc. 662 King Street West, Suite 304, Toronto, Ontario M5V 1M7

Cover concept by Peter Dyer.

Typeset in Bembo and Helvetica to an original design by Henry Iles.

Printed in Singapore
© Stephen Timblin, 2011
Maps © Rough Guides
No part of this book may be reproduced in any form without permission from the publisher except for the quotation of brief passages in reviews.
288pp includes index
A catalogue record for this book is available from the British Library
ISBN: 978-1-84836-771-5
The publishers and authors have done their best to ensure the accuracy and currency of all the information in **The Rough Guide to Yellowstone and Grand Teton**, however, they can accept no responsibility for any loss, injury, or inconvenience sustained by any traveller as a result of information or advice contained in the guide.

1   3   5   7   9   8   6   4   2

MIX
Paper from responsible sources
FSC   www.fsc.org   FSC™ C018179

Help us update

We've gone to a lot of effort to ensure that the second edition of **The Rough Guide to Yellowstone and Grand Teton** is accurate and up-to-date. However, things change – places get "discovered", opening hours are notoriously fickle, restaurants and rooms raise prices or lower standards. If you feel we've got it wrong or left something out, we'd like to know, and if you can remember the address, the price, the hours, the phone number, so much the better.

Please send your comments with the subject line "**Rough Guide Yellowstone and Grand Teton Update**" to ⓔ mail@uk.roughguides.com. We'll credit all contributions and send a copy of the next edition (or any other Rough Guide if you prefer) for the very best emails.

Find more travel information, connect with fellow travellers and book your trip on ⓦwww.roughguides.com

Acknowledgements

Charles Hodgkins would like to thank: Mani Ramaswamy and Keith Drew at Rough Guides HQ for the opportunity to visit and immerse myself in this singular region; my frequent co-author Nick Edwards for the good word; Brendon Griffin, Scottish Borders' finest editor and homesteader, for improving the text at every turn and being a complete pleasure to work with; Stephen Timblin, whose prodigious work on this book's first edition, along with his steady counsel and good humour throughout its second, can't be overstated; Rough Guides' editorial, production and cartograpy staff for their invaluable contributions; Chad Repinski, Nathan Dragoo, Hans and Nancy Johnstone, Steve Koning, Luca Diana, Adena Chernosky and that guy John in Jackson; Levi Thorn, Darla Cook and our friends the Rockefellers in Grand Teton; Mona Mesereau, Rick Hoeninghausen, Al Nash, Rick Wallen, Doug Smith, Todd Koel and the fellow who fished our snowcat out of the ditch in the snowstorm in Yellowstone; Chris Warren and Scott Denniston in Cooke City; Colin Kurth Davis and Sharon Nardin at Chico Hot Springs; Mike Harrelson and Molly Brewer in Bozeman; Chad Jones, Greer Schott and David O'Connor in Big Sky; Marysue Costello in West Yellowstone; Jim Promo in Salt Lake City; Japandroids for the punk rock jolt at the Urban Lounge; Thrifty for the rad Nissan Versa sedan; Gregory Dicum, Jeff Cranmer and Andrew Rosenberg for helping me get into this mess in the first place; Linda for all the understanding and co-operation; Todd, Emily, Tyler and Aaron for being pals among pals; Mom for the memories and Dad for the support; and Sonja, for the love, affection, laughs…and patience.

Photo credits

All photos © Rough Guides except the following:

Index

Map entries are in colour.

A

Absaroka Mountains 167
Absaroka-Beartooth
    Wilderness 237
Abyss Pool 76,
    Hydrothermal Yellowstone
    colour section
accommodation
    Big Sky............................ 223
    Cody................................. 240
    Cooke City 235
    Gardiner 229
    Grand Teton 186–188
    Jackson.....................203–205
    West Yellowstone............ 217
    Yellowstone...............182–186
Aerial Tram....................155
airlines 23
airports 19
Albright, Horace M.
    ....89, 260
Albright View Turnout 88
Albright Visitor Center 46
altitude sickness.............30
amphibians 269
Amphitheater Lake 138
Amtrak 21
Anderson, Ole................48
Antelope Flats Road.......93
Artemisia Geyser 74
Artist Point.............58, 122
Artists' Paint Pots...........60
Ashton 108
Aspen Ridge Trail 143
ATMs.............................35
Avalanche Peak......83, 128

B

Bannock Trail..................55
Bearpaw Lake 137
Beartooth Highway.......236
beaver..........................268
Beaver Ponds...............116
Bechler Falls................130
Bechler Meadows
    ....83, 130
Beehive Geyser 73
Big Sky................ 222–227
Big Sky Resort 224
bighorn sheep 172, 266

biking 27
    Cody 245
    Gardiner 233
    Grand Teton 165
    Jackson........................... 210
    West Yellowstone............. 221
    Yellowstone...................... 165
birds.............................268
Biscuit Basin...........74, 126
bison..............54, 172, 265
black bears............172, 266
Black Canyon of the
    Yellowstone 148
Black Growler Steam Vent
   61
Black Pool 76
Black Sand Basin 74
Blacktail Butte 92, 141
Blacktail Deer Plateau...117
Blacktail Plateau Drive ...51
Blacktail Ponds 51
Blacktail Ponds Overlook
   94
boating
    Big Sky............................ 226
    Cody................................. 245
    Gardiner 232
    Grand Teton 163
    Jackson........................... 210
    Yellowstone...................... 163
Boiling River 50, 169
books 271–274
Boulder Ridge Trail 143
Bradley Lake 103, 140
Bridge Bay 79
Bridge Bay Marina........163
Bridge Creek 127
Bridger, Jim 61, 78
Bridger Lake 151
Bridger-Teton National
    Forest.........................133
Briggs, Bill 103
Brothers Bathhouse and
    Plunge.........................70
brucellosis 54
buffalo............................54
Buffalo Bill 242
Buffalo Bill Cody Scenic
    Byway..........................245
Buffalo Bill Historical
    Center..........................241
Buffalo Bill State Park... 243
Buffalo Ranch..........52, 54
Bunsen Peak 117
bus travel.......................21

C

Cache Creek.................120
Calcite Springs 118
Calcite Springs Overlook
   55
Caldera, Yellowstone......63
Camp Sheridan 47
campgrounds
    backcountry camping
       144–148
    Big Sky............................ 223
    Cody................................. 240
    Cooke City 235
    Gardiner 229
    Grand Teton 188
    West Yellowstone............. 217
    Yellowstone...................... 184
Canary Spring 50
canoeing..........see boating
Canyon (Yellowstone)
   56–59
Canyon (Yellowstone)
   57
Canyon Hotel.................56
Canyon Lodge................56
Canyon Village...............56
Canyon Visitor Center
   56
car rentals......................26
Cascade Corner 83
Cascade Lake 121
Cascade Lake Picnic Area
   55
Castle Geyser................74
Cave Falls...............83, 130
Cave Falls Road 108
Celestine Pool 69
Chapel of the Sacred Heart
   99
Chapel of Transfiguration
   91
Chico Hot Springs........233
Chief Joseph Scenic Byway
   246
children, travelling with
   31
Chinese Spring...............70
Chittenden Road 55
Cistern Spring 60
Cleft Falls.....................139
Cleopatra Terrace..........49
Cliff Geyser....................74
climate 11

climate change 20
Climber's Ranch ...103, 171
climbing
  courses 167
  Grand Teton 167
  guides 168
  West Yellowstone 226
  Yellowstone 167
clinics 28
Cody 238–248
Cody 239
Cody, William 242
Colter, John 252
Colter Bay Nature Trail
.................................134
Colter Bay Village 105
Colter Bay Village 104
Colter Bay Visitor Center
.................................106
Cooke City 234–237
Cook-Folsom Expedition
.................................253
costs 32
coyote 267
Crackling Lake 61
Craig Thomas Discovery
  and Visitor Center 90
Crandall 248
credit cards 35
cross-country skiing
  around Jackson 213
  Big Sky 225
  Cooke City 236
  Gardiner 232
  Grand Teton 177
  tours 178
  West Yellowstone 221
  Yellowstone 176
Cunningham Homestead
.................................97
cutthroat trout
.......................80, 81, 269
cycling 27

D

Daisy Geyser 74
Davis, Eleanor 103
Deadmans Bar 96
Death Canyon 154
Devil's Thumb 49
disabilities, travellers with
.................................40
Dornan's 91
driving 21, 24–27
Dunraven Pass 55

E

Eagle Peak 167
Earthquake Lake 219
eating and drinking
  Big Sky 226
  Cody 244
  Cooke City 235
  Gardiner 231
  Grand Teton 193
  Jackson 207
  recommendations 192
  West Yellowstone 219
  Yellowstone 189–193
Echinus Geyser 60
ecosystems 269
electricity 32
Elephant Back Mountain
.................................127
elk 172, 265
Emerald Pool 74
Emerald Spring 60
Emma Matilda Lake
.........................98, 135
entrance fees 32
entry requirements 32
Everts, Truman C. 50
Excelsior Geyser 70
Exum Guides 103

F

Fairy Falls 125
Falls River 83, 131
Firehole Canyon Drive 67
Firehole Cascades 67
Firehole Falls 67
Firehole Lake Drive 69
Firehole River 67, 159
Firehole Swimming Area
.................................67
fires of 1988 ....77, 261
fish 269
fishing 81
  Big Sky 226
  Cody 245
  Grand Teton 162
  guides 160
  Jackson 210
  West Yellowstone 220
  Yellowstone 159
Fishing Bridge 80
Fishing Cone 70, 76
Flagg Canyon 132
Flagg Ranch 107
Flagg Ranch Information
  Station 108
Flagg Ranch Resort 133

Flat Creek 162
Flight of the Nez Percé ...247
flights
  from Australia and New
    Zealand 20
  from UK and Ireland 19
  from US and Canada 19
flora and fauna 265–270
Forces of the Northern
  Range Trail 52
Fort Yellowstone 47
Fountain Flat Drive ...69, 124
Fountain Geyser 69
Fountain Paint Pot 69
frostbite 30

G

Gallatin Field Airport
  (Bozeman) 19
Gallatin Petrified forest
.................................115
Gallatin Valley 226
Gardiner 228–232
Gardiner 229
Gardner Bridge 51
Gardner River
.................117, 160, 228
Garnet Canyon 139
gas 24
Gem Pool 74
geology 98, 263–265,
  Hydrothermal Yellowstone
  colour section
Geysers ... see box overleaf
Geyser Hill 73
Giant Geyser 74
Gibbon Falls 67
Gibbon Meadows ...60, 123
Gibbon River 159
Glacial Boulder 58
Glacier View Turnout 95
Golden Gate 63, 64
Golden Gate Canyon 62
Grand Canyon of the
  Yellowstone 57
Grand Canyon of the
  Yellowstone 57
Grand Geyser 74
Grand Prismatic Spring
.................................70,
  Hydrothermal Yellowstone
  colour section
Grand Targhee 213
**Grand Teton National
  Park** 85–108
Grand Teton National Park
.................................86

Geysers

Artemisia Geyser 74
Beehive Geyser 73
Castle Geyser 74
Cliff Geyser 74
Daisy Geyser 74
Echinus Geyser 60
Excelsior Geyser 70
Fishing Cone 70
Fountain Geyser 69
Gem Pool 74
Giant Geyser 74
Grand Geyser 74
Great Fountain Geyser
.... 70, 72
Grotto Geyser 74,
Hydrothermal Yellowstone
colour section
Imperial Geyser 125
Ledge Geyser 61
Lone Star Geyser 75,
152, *Hydrothermal Yellowstone*
colour section
Old Faithful 72
Pearl Geyser 60
Pinwheel Geyser 61
Porkchop Geyser 60
Riverside Geyser 73, 74,
Hydrothermal Yellowstone
colour section
Sapphire Pool 74,
Hydrothermal Yellowstone
colour section
Solitary Geyser 73
Steamboat Geyser 60
Sunset Lake 74
Thermos Bottle Geyser 123
Whirligig Geyser 61,
Hydrothermal Yellowstone
colour section
White Dome Geyser 70

Grand Teton National Park,
central 95
Grand Teton National Park,
northern 104
Grand Teton National Park,
southern 88
Grand Teton National Park
history 89
Grand View 58
Grand View Point 136
Grand Village Visitor Center
.... 76
Granite Canyon Entrance
Station 88
Granite Hot Springs 169
Grant Village 76
Grassy Lake Road 108
Great Fountain Geyser
.... 70, 72
Grebe Lake 121, 161

grey wolf ... 267, *The wolves
of Yellowstone* colour
section
Greyhound 21
grizzly bears 172, 266
Gros Ventre Junction 92
Gros Ventre River 88, 92,
162
Gros Ventre Slide 92, 94
Grotto Geyser 74,
Hydrothermal Yellowstone
colour section

H

Handkerchief Pool 70
Harris, Captain Moses ... 47,
258
Hayden Survey 254–256
Hayden Valley 82
health 28–30
Heart Lake 153, 161
Hebgen Lake 219
Hellroaring Creek Trail ... 149
Henderson, George 48
Hermitage Point 135
Hidden Falls 102, 138
hiking 109–157
hiking 114
  backcountry permits 145
  bear awareness 110
  bear spray 111
  camping 145
  campfires 146
  clothing 147
  Continental Divide Trail 149
  day hikes 109–143
  equipment 147, 148
  gear 147, 148
  maps 112
  overnight hikes 147–159
  ratings 113
  river crossings 113
  safety 112
  shuttles 157
  taxis 157
  water safety 113
hiking trails, Grand Teton
  Amphitheater Lake and
    Overlook 138
  Aspen Ridge/Boulder Ridge
    loop 143
  Blacktail Butte traverse 141
  Cascade Canyon to
    Paintbrush Canyon 153
  Colter Bay Nature Trail 134
  Death Canyon loop 154
  Flagg Canyon 132
  Garnet Canyon 139
  Glade Creek Trail 133
  Hermitage Point 135
  Hidden Falls and Inspiration

Point 138
  Marion Lake and Granite
    Canyon via Aerial Tram ... 155
  Phelps Lake loop 142
  Schawbacher's Landing ... 140
  Sheffield Creek Trail 133
  Signal Mountain loop 136
  String Lake to Bearpaw Lake
    137
  Taggart and Bradley lakes
    139
  Teton Crest Trail 156
  Two Ocean and Emma
    Matilda lakes 135
hiking trails, Yellowstone
  Avalanche Peak 128
  Beaver Ponds 116
  Bechler Meadows 130
  Bighorn Peak 115
  Black Canyon of the
    Yellowstone 148
  Cascade Lake and
    Observation Peak 121
  Elephant Back Mountain ... 127
  Fairy Falls and Imperial
    Geyser 125
  Heart Lake and Mount
    Sheridan 153
  Lamar River Trail to Cache
    Creek 119
  LeHardy's Rapids 127
  Lewis Channel and Dogshead
    Trails 129
  Monument Geyser Basin ... 123
  Mount Washburn 120
  Mystic Falls 126
  Natural Bridge Road 126
  Osprey Falls 117
  Pelican Valley to Wapiti Lake
    loop 150
  Purple Mountain 124
  Riddle Lake 129
  Sentinel Meadows 124
  Seven-Mile Hole 121
  Shelf Lake 115
  Shoshone Geyser Basin ... 152
  Slough Creek 118
  South Rim, Point Sublime and
    Lily Pad Lake 122
  Thorofare Trail to Bridger Lake
    151
  Union Falls 131
  Wraith Falls 117
  Yellowstone River Picnic Area
    Loop 118
history 251–262
holidays 35
Holly Lake 154
Hoodoos 62, 167
horseriding
  dude ranches 185
  Grand Teton 167
  Jackson 211
  West Yellowstone 226
  Yellowstone 166
hospitals 28

Hot springs

Abyss Pool ... 76, *Hydrothermal Yellowstone* colour section
Black Pool........................76
Calcite Springs 55, 118
Canary Spring...................50
Celestine Pool..................69
Chico Hot Springs 233
Chinese Spring 70
Cistern Spring...................60
Crackling Lake..................61
Emerald Pool 74
Emerald Spring.................60
Gem Pool..........................74
Grand Prismatic Spring .....70, *Hydrothermal Yellowstone* colour section
Granite Hot Springs..........169
Handkerchief Pool 70
Huckleberry Springs 108
Kelly Warm Spring..............93
Morning Glory Pool 74
Orange Spring Mound.......50, *Hydrothermal Yellowstone* colour section
Palette Spring 49
Polecat Springs 108
Queen's Laundry Spring...125
Sapphire Pool ....74, *Hydrothermal Yellowstone* colour section
Silex Pool.........................69
Steamboat Springs............83
Sulphur Cauldron..............82

hot springs .... see box above and *Hydrothermal Yellowstone* colour section
Howard Eaton Trail.......127
Howell, Ed 259
Huckleberry Springs.....108
hypothermia 30

I

Imperial Geyser 125
Indian Arts Museum 104
Indian Pond 82
information..............38–40
Inspiration Point 58, 102, 138
insurance.......................33
internet 33

J

Jackson 201–214
Jackson.........................202

Jackson, William 47
Jackson Hole Airport
........................19, 88, 203
Jackson Hole Mountain
Resort 212
Jackson Lake
....................134, 162, 164
Jackson Lake Dam
............................99, 100
Jackson Lake Lodge.... 105
Jenny Lake 101, 164
Jenny Lake Ranger Station
......................................103
Jenny Lake Visitor Center
......................................102
jobs in the parks..... 33–35
John D. Rockefeller, Jr.
Memorial Parkway.....107
Junior Ranger Program ...31

K

kayaking .... see boating
Kelly...........................92, 94
Kelly Warm Spring..........93
Kepler Cascades............75
Kipling, Rudyard.............73
Knowles Falls 149

L

Lake Butte Road 83
Lake Lodge....................80
Lake Ranger Station.......80
Lake Solitude................154
Lake Village 79
Lake Village and around
......................................78
Lake Yellowstone Hotel...79
Lamar Canyon................52
Lamar River 52, 160
Lamar Valley.... 119, 52–54
Lamar Valley 53
Langford, Nathaniel
.............................47, 102
Laurance S. Rockefeller
Preserve......................89
Ledge Geyser 61
Lee Metcalf Wilderness
......................................226
Leek, Stephen 107
Leeks Marina................106
LeHardys Rapids.....80, 81, 127
Leigh Lake............101, 137

Lewis Canyon.................77
Lewis Channel..............129
Lewis Falls.....................77
Lewis Lake 77, 130, 161, 163
Lewis River 77
Liberty Cap.....................49
lightning.........................30
Lily Pad Lake................123
lodgepole pine................76
Lone Star Geyser ...75, 152, *Hydrothermal Yellowstone* colour section
Lone Star Geyser Group
......................................152
Lookout Point.................58
Lower Falls 57
Lower Geyser Basin 69
Lower Hamilton's Store ...72
Lower Slide Lake.............94
Lunch Tree Hill.............105

M

Madison Canyon 66
Madison Information
Station 66
Madison Junction...........66
Madison River 66, 159
mail.................................35
Mammoth Hot Springs
...............................44–46, *Hydrothermal Yellowstone* colour section
Mammoth and around... 46
Mammoth Hot Springs
Terraces......................48, *Hydrothermal Yellowstone* colour section
maps...............................35
Marion Lake..................155
Mary Bay 83
Maude Noble Cabin 91
Menor's Ferry Historic
District 91
Midway Geyser Basin 70
Minerva Terrace..............49
mobile phones................37
money.............................35
Monument Geyser Basin
......................................123
Moonlight Basin Resort
......................................225
moose..................172, 266
Moose.............................90
Moose Falls 78
Moose Visitor Center......90

Moran, Thomas 47
Moran Entrance Station ... 98
Moran Junction 98
Mormon Row.................. 93
Morning Falls................ 132
Morning Glory Pool 74
Moulton Barns............... 93
Mount Everts 50, 117
Mount Moran................. 99
Mount Moran Turnout ... 101
Mount Sheridan............ 153
Mount Washburn.... 55, 120
mountain lions 173, 267
Mud Volcano 81
Muir, John...................... 57
mule deer 266
Museum of the National
  Park Ranger................ 59
Mushpots, The 150
Mystic Falls 126

N

National Elk Refuge...... 206
National Fish Hatchery... 207
National Museum of Wildlife
  Art, Jackson 206
National Park Mountain ...66
National Park passes...... 36
Natural Bridge 79, 133
Nez Percé..................... 247
Nordic skiing .... see
  cross-country skiing
Norris 59–61
Norris................................ 59
Norris, Philetus W.... 60, 256
Norris Geyser Basin 60
North Rim Drive.............. 57
North Rim Trail................ 58
Northern Range............. 51

O

Observation Peak......... 121
Observation Point........... 73
Obsidian Cliff............ 61, 64
Ojo Caliente Spring 124
Old Faithful (geyser) 72
Old Faithful and around... 68
Old Faithful Inn.............. 72
Old Faithful Lodge.......... 72
Old Faithful Visitor Center
  72
opening hours 35
Orange Spring Mound... 50,
  Hydrothermal Yellowstone
  colour section

Osprey Falls.................. 117
Ouzel Falls................... 131
Owen, William............... 103
Oxbow Bend 87
Oxbow Bend Turnout 99

P

Pacific Creek Road......... 98
Paintbrush Divide 154
Palette Spring................ 49
Paradise Valley 232
Pearl Geyser.................. 60
pelican 268
Pelican Creek 150
Pelican Valley 82, 150
Petrified Tree 51
pets................................ 36
Phelps Lake.................. 142
Phelps Lake Overlook 90
phones........................... 36
Pinwheel Geyser............ 61
Point Sublime 122
Polecat Springs 108
Porcelain Basin.............. 61
Porkchop Geyser 60
post offices..................... 35
prairie rattlesnake......... 269
prices............................ 32
pronghorn..................... 266
Purple Mountain 67, 124

Q

Queen's Laundry Spring
  125

R

rafting .... see boating
ranger programmes...... 195
raven.........269, The wolves
  of Yellowstone colour
  section
Reamer, Robert C..... 72, 80
Reclamation Road........ 108
Red Rock Point 58
Red Spouter 69
reptiles......................... 269
Riddle Lake 129
Riverside Geyser 73, 74,
  Hydrothermal Yellowstone
  colour section
RKO Road 101
road conditions 24

Roaring Mountain.......... 61,
  Hydrothermal Yellowstone
  colour section
rock-climbing ...see climbing
Rockefeller, John D. Jr. 89
Rockefeller, Laurence S.
  89
Roosevelt Arch 230
Roosevelt Lodge 55
Russell, Osborne............ 52
RV rentals 27

S

safety 28–30
Salt Lake City Airport 19
Sapphire Pool................ 74,
  Hydrothermal Yellowstone
  colour section
Sawmill Ponds................ 90
Schoolroom Glacier...... 157
Schwabacher's Landing
  .... 96, 140
scrambling......see climbing
senior travellers 37
Sentinel Meadows........ 124
Sepulcher Mountain Trail
  116
Seven-Mile Hole........... 121
Sheep Mountain 92, 94
Sheepeater Canyon...... 117
Shoshone Geyser Basin
  152
Shoshone Lake...... 75, 136,
  152, 161, 163
Shoshone Lake Ranger
  Station 130
Signal Mountain 136
Signal Mountain Lodge...99
Signal Mountain Road... 100
Signal Mountain Summit
  Road 87
Silex Pool 69
Silver Cord Cascade 58,
  122
Silvertip Ranch 119
skiing and snowboarding
  backcountry, around Jackson
  211
  Big Sky Resort 224
  Grand Targhee 213
  Jackson Hole Mountain
    Resort 212
  Moonlight Basin Resort
  225
  Snow King........................ 213
Sleeping Indian............... 92
Slough Creek........ 118, 160
Snake River 162, 163

Snake River Overlook
.................................87, 96
Snow King 213
snowcoach tours..........173
snowmobiling..... 174–176,
213, 221, 236
snowshoeing .... see
cross-country skiing
Soda Butte Creek
...................52, 119, 160
Solfatara Plateau 58
Solitary Geyser 73
Sour Lake 82
Spalding, Franklin.........103
Spalding Falls 139
Static Peak 155
Steamboat Geyser 60
Steamboat Springs 83
Stevenson, James........102
Stevenson Island............79
String Lake 101, 137
Sulphur Cauldron 82
Sulphur Creek...............122
Sunset Lake....................74
Surprise Lake 138
swimming 168

T

Taggart Lake.........103, 140
temperature 11
Teton Crest Trail............156
Teton Glacier 95
Teton Park Road
...........................99–103
Teton Point Turnout 96
Thermos Bottle Geyser
......................................123
Thorofare Trail...............151
time zones 38
tipping 38
Tonnar, John 96
Top Notch Peak............128
tour operators.................23
tours.....................195–198
Tower Fall 55
Tower-Roosevelt Junction
......................................51
trains..............................21
Trapper Lake 137
travel agents...................23
trees.............................270
Triangle X Ranch 97
Trout Lake.....................161
trumpeter swan 268
Twin Falls......................122
Two Ocean Lake.....98, 135

U

Uncle Tom's Trail 59
Underwood, Gilbert Stanley
............................72, 105
Undine Falls....................51
Union Falls..............83, 131
Upper Falls 57
Upper Geyser Basin
................................71–75
Upper Geyser Basin 71

V

Virginia Cascade.............59
Visa Waiver Program 32

W

Wapiti Lake...................150
Wapiti Valley 245
Washburn Expedition
...........................50, 253
waterfalls .... see box below
weather......................11, 30
websites 39
West Thumb Geyser Basin
......................................75
West Thumb and around
......................................75

Waterfalls

Bechler Falls 130
Cave Falls 83, 130
Fairy Falls.....................125
Firehole Falls.................67
Gibbon Falls..................67
Hidden Falls.............102, 138
Kepler Cascades 75
Knowles Falls 149
Lewis Falls 77
Lower Falls 57
Moose Falls 78
Morning Falls.................132
Mystic Falls 126
Osprey Falls...................117
Ouzel Falls 131
Silver Cord Cascade
.............................58, 122
Tower Fall.......................55
Twin Falls 122
Undine Falls...................51
Union Falls...............83, 131
Upper Falls 57
Virginia Cascade............59
Wraith Falls 51, 117

West Yellowstone
..........................215–222
West Yellowstone 216
Whirligig Geyser 61,
Hydrothermal Yellowstone
colour section
White Dome Geyser 70
white-tailed deer...........266
wildflowers...................270
Willow Flats Overlook.....87
Winegar Hole Wilderness
......................................108
winter...................170–178
winter camping.............177
winter driving.................25
winter road closures.....171
wiring money 35
Wister, Owen 100
Wolf Lake.....................161
wolves ......173, *The wolves
of Yellowstone* colour
section
wolves, re-introduction of
..............261, *The wolves
of Yellowstone* colour
section
work in the parks
.................................33–35
Wraith Falls.............51, 117

Y

Yellowstone, Northern
.................................43–62
Yellowstone, Northern
.................................44–45
Yellowstone, Southern
.................................63–84
Yellowstone, Southern
.................................64–65
Yellowstone Association
......................................196
Yellowstone Caldera........63
Yellowstone Heritage and
Research Center........231
Yellowstone Institute 196
Yellowstone Lake
...............78–80, 161, 163
Yellowstone Regional
Airport (Cody) 19, 217
Yellowstone River 159
Yount, Harry............52, 257

Map symbols

maps are listed in the full index using coloured text

— · ·	State boundary	✕	Regional airport
——	National Park boundary	⅏	Viewpoint
——	Other park boundary	🕮	Waterfall
	Caldera boundary	⚶	Hydrothermal feature
·········	Continental divide	◉	Accommodation
=⑤=	US highway	▣	Restaurant
=⑤=	State highway	⚐	Campground
··········	Limited-access road	ⓘ	Information office
=====	Other road	⊠	Post office
H22	Recommended hiking trail	⛽	Gas station
··········	Other trail	⛳	Golf course
——	River	⊞	Hospital
▲	Peak	⛱	Picnic area
♦	Point of interest	▬	Building
⛬	Park entrance	▨	Glacier
⬚	Ranger station	░	Park
⚱	Church	░	Geyser Basin
⛷	Skiing		

So now we've told you about the things not to miss, the best places to stay, the top restaurants, the liveliest bars and the most spectacular sights, it only seems fair to tell you about the best travel insurance around